CN00921477

THE INVENTION OF CHINA

THE INVENTION OF CHINA

BILL HAYTON

YALE UNIVERSITY PRESS
NEW HAVEN AND LONDON

For information about this and other Yale University Press publications, please contact:
U.S. Office: sales.press@yale.edu yalebooks.com
Europe Office: sales@yaleup.co.uk yalebooks.co.uk

Set in Adobe Garamond Pro by IDSUK (DataConnection) Ltd
Printed in Great Britain by Gomer Press Ltd, Llandysul, Ceredigion, Wales

Library of Congress Control Number: 2020937932

ISBN 978-0-300-23482-4

A catalogue record for this book is available from the British Library.

10 9 8 7 6 5 4 3 2 1

For my parents – givers and doers. Thank you for everything.

CONTENTS

ILLUSTRATIONS

PLATES

MAPS

ACKNOWLEDGEMENTS
Xiexie – Thank you

This book began in the bar of the Omni New Haven Hotel and a conversation with Bradley Camp Davis of Eastern Connecticut State University. Over a couple of bottles of Newcastle Brown Ale we discussed the vexed history of the Vietnamese borderlands. At one point, Bradley replied to one of my naive questions about nineteenth-century frontiers with the line, 'It depends what you mean by China'. It was a head-spinning moment. After several years of thinking, dithering, researching and writing, this book is the result of that conversation. I hope you will find my attempt to understand 'what you mean by China' as fascinating as I did.

None of what follows would have been possible without the library of the School of Oriental and African Studies in London: for me a portal to a new plane of consciousness. My thanks to all who labour there. As I took my first nervous steps into this intellectual world I was greatly encouraged by my discussions with participants at a conference organised by Kreddha at the University of California, Davis in September 2016. There I met Michael van Walt van Praag, Miek Boltjes, the late Arif Dirlik of the University of Oregon and Timothy Brook of the University of British Columbia who were all generously supportive of my ambitions.

They were only the first in a long line of academics who answered further naive questions. In particular I would like to thank: Tim Barrett of SOAS; Chad Berry of the University of Alabama; May Bo Ching of the City University of Hong Kong; Chris P.C. Chung of the University of Toronto; Pamela Kyle Crossley of Dartmouth College; Stephen Davies of the University of Hong Kong; Frank Dikötter of the University of Hong Kong; Josh Fogel of York University; Ge Zhaoguang of Fudan University; Michael Gibbs Hill of the

College of William and Mary; Tze-ki Hon of the City University of Hong Kong; Chris Hughes of the London School of Economics; Bruce Jacobs of Monash University; Thomas Jansen of the University of Wales Trinity Saint David; Elisabeth Kaske of Leipzig University; Cheng-Chwee Kuik of the National University of Malaysia; Jane Leung Larson of the Baohuanghui Scholarship forum; James Leibold of La Trobe University; Victor Mair of the University of Pennsylvania; Melissa Mouat of the University of Cambridge; Peter Perdue of Yale University; Edward Rhoads of the University of Texas at Austin; Julia Schneider of University College Cork; Rich Smith of Rice University; Rachel Wallner of Northwestern University; Jeff Wasserstrom of the University of California, Irvine; and Peter Zarrow of the University of Connecticut.

George Yin of Swarthmore College was a great source of advice on my many questions of translation and etymology. Geoff Wade put me right on things Ming. Evan Fowler and Trey Menefee advised me on the Hong Kong section; Erik Slavin walked me around Yokohama and Jeremiah Jenne was a huge help in Beijing. Paul Evans, Brian Job and Yves Tiberghien of the University of British Columbia hosted and helped in Vancouver. Timothy Richard's great-granddaughter Jennifer Peles and his biographer, the late Eunice Johnson, helped with my research into the missionary-educator's life and work.

My thanks to all at Yale University Press, especially Heather McCallum for taking a risk with this book; Marika Lysandrou who shepherded me through the writing; Clarissa Sutherland and Percie Edgeler who managed the production process; and Charlotte Chapman for her rigorous copy-editing. Three anonymous referees provided extremely helpful comments on the manuscript, thank you.

My BBC colleagues tolerated my late-night research and my family granted me permission to travel. My wife, Pamela Cox, is a proper historian and showed me how to be one. My love to her. Our children, Tess and Patrick, provided encouragement and happiness. Thank you; you can have the kitchen table back now.

Colchester, March 2020

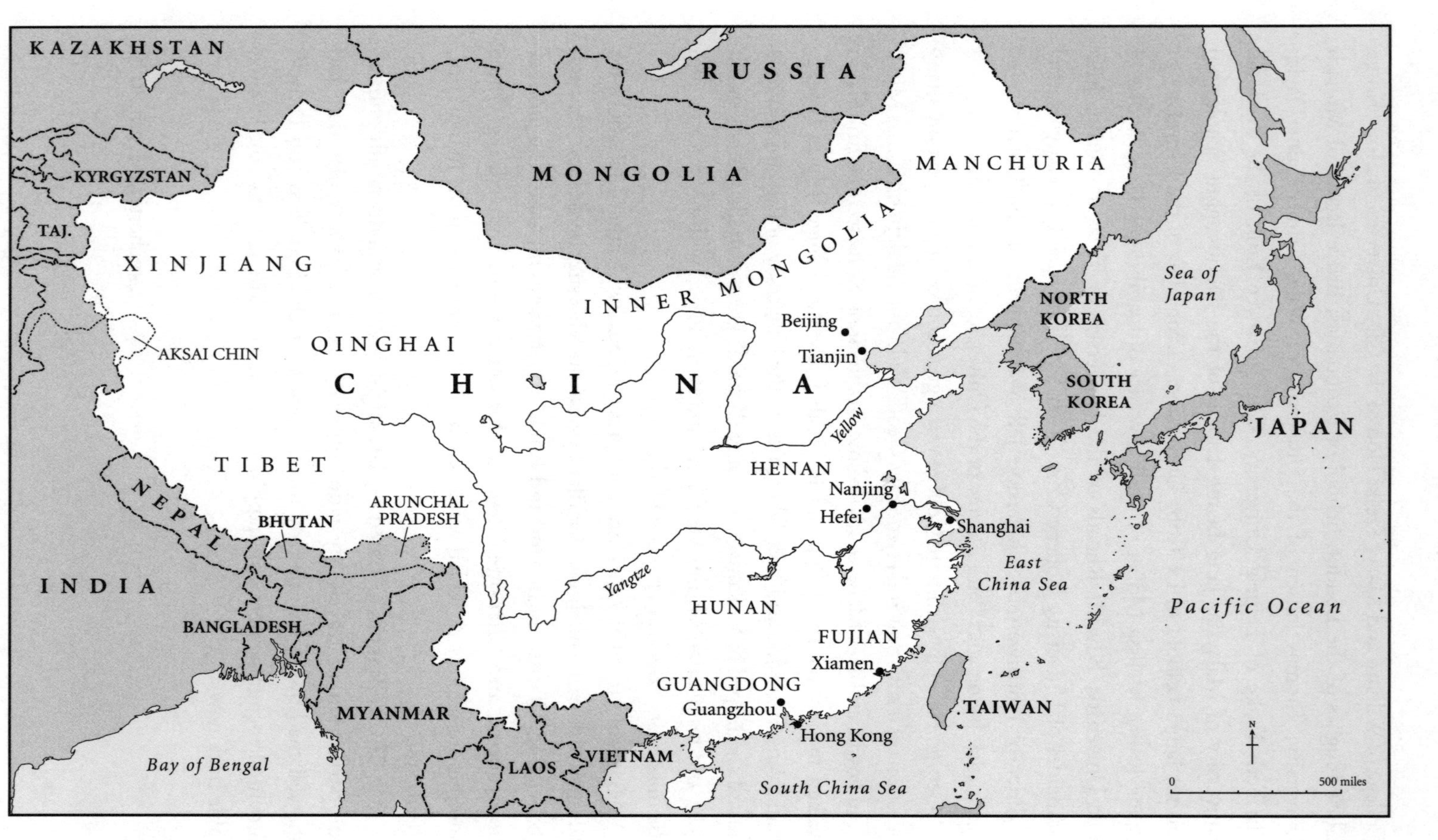

1. The Contemporary People's Republic of China

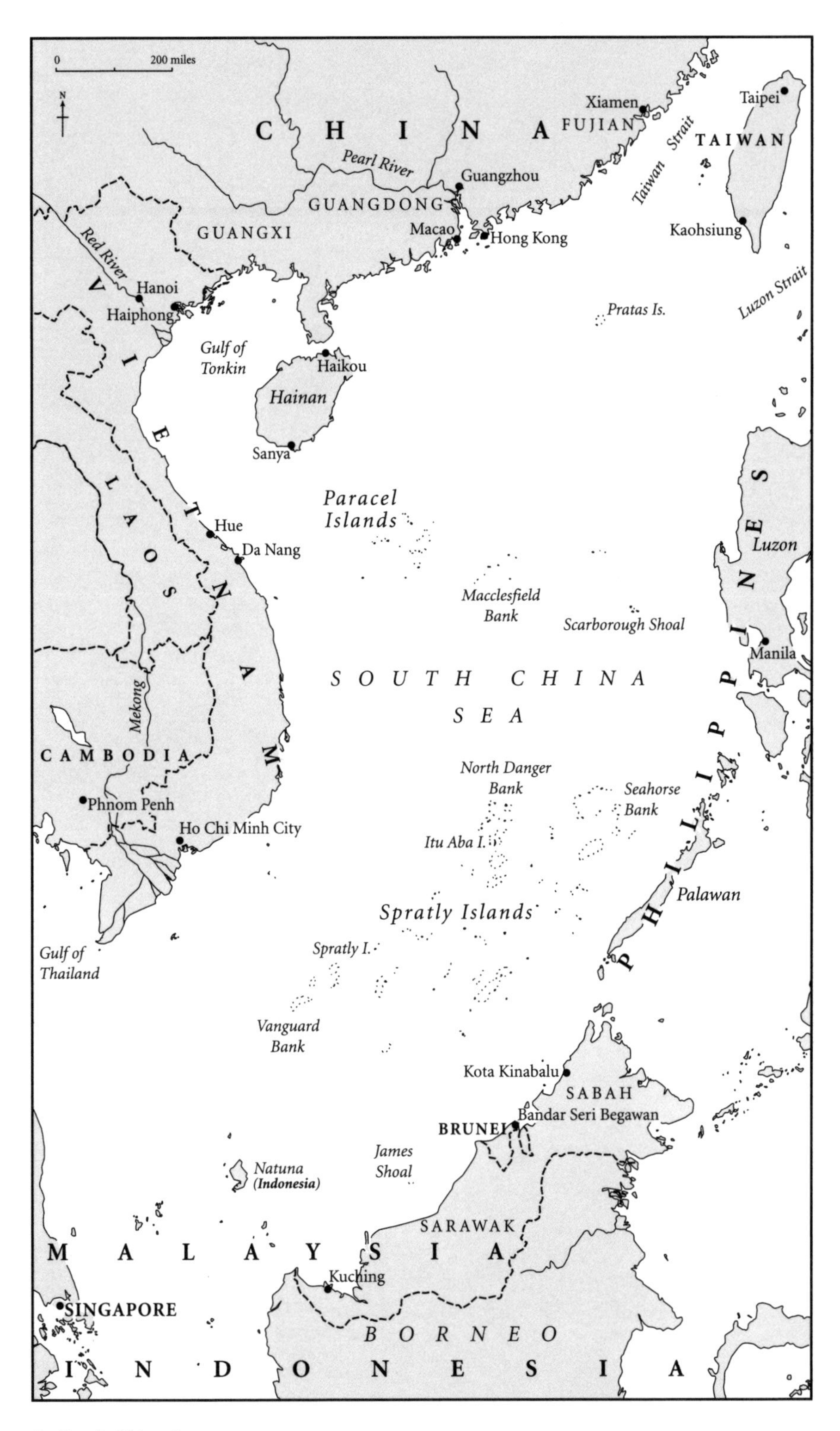

2. South China Sea

INTRODUCTION

What kind of country is China going to become? We know it will be huge in population and, if present trends continue, economically strong and militarily powerful. But how will this superpower behave? How will it treat its own people, its neighbours and the rest of the world? China is one of two countries with populations greater than a billion, massive armed forces, nuclear weapons and volatile border disputes. But whereas few see India as a threat to international stability, China dominates the thoughts of policy-makers, analysts and commentators. There is something different about China. While plenty regard its rise as an opportunity – for trade, investment, profit and development – few do so without reservations. What kind of country is China? What kind of world will it make?

There is a lazy answer to this question, one that has become catechism for the Communist Party of China and many commentators. It is to simply invoke the 'century of national humiliation'. On 18 October 2017, Xi Jinping stood before a giant hammer and sickle at the nineteenth Congress of the Communist Party of China and summarised this catechism in a paragraph. 'With a history of more than 5,000 years, our nation created a splendid civilisation, made remarkable contributions to mankind, and became one of the world's great nations,' he told his audience.

> But with the Opium War of 1840, China was plunged into the darkness of domestic turmoil and foreign aggression; its people, ravaged by war, saw their homeland torn apart and lived in poverty and despair. With tenacity and heroism, countless dedicated patriots fought, pressed ahead against the odds, and tried every possible means to seek the nation's salvation. But

> despite their efforts, they were powerless to change the nature of society in old China and the plight of the Chinese people.[1]

This is a curious vision of the past. It is founded upon the idea that, for a century, 'the Chinese people' were hapless victims of foreign aggression, and played little part in their own destiny. It is easy to see why an authoritarian political party would find it useful. By robbing 'the Chinese people' of their agency, it avoids having to ask or answer difficult questions about how change came about. As a result, Xi's version of history is the one taught in Chinese schools, and also one that many people outside China have come to accept. Yet almost every aspect of it has been challenged by recent research. Unfortunately, the insights unlocked by this research are not part of the mainstream conversation about China: they languish in libraries and specialist academic seminars. In this book I will try to bring them out into the open. I will show how Xi Jinping's view of China is not some timeless expression of 'Chineseness' dating back to 'ancient times' but a modern invention. Modern China's ethnic identity, its boundaries and even the idea of a 'nation-state' are all innovations from the late nineteenth and early twentieth centuries.

In this book I will try to show how China came to think of itself as 'China'. I will look at the ways that the Chinese elite adopted unfamiliar ideas, starting with the concept of 'China' itself, before going on to examine how Western notions about sovereignty, race, nation, history and territory became part of Chinese collective thinking. I will show how key concepts were adopted from abroad by Chinese intellectuals, and adapted to create and bolster a myth of a 5,000-year-old unified country and people. This is not merely an academic exercise. We cannot understand the present-day problems of the South China Sea, Taiwan, Tibet, Xinjiang, Hong Kong, and ultimately China itself, without understanding how this modernising vision came to be adopted by the country's elite and how future problems were embedded within it. China today behaves the way that it does largely because of choices made a century ago by intellectuals and activists and because the ideas they adopted and propagated were sufficiently well received by enough of the population to change an entire country. The ways that these ideas were argued over between rival political interests and the ways they were resolved still live with us today.

China is far from unique in this. Every modern 'nation-state' – Germany, Turkey, Italy and Britain, to name just a few – has gone through this process. For the historian Arif Dirlik, a Turkish-born Marxist, the issue was familiar. The process through which the old Qing Empire evolved into modern China was paralleled only few years later by the Ottoman Empire's transition into Turkey. An ostensibly simple process – a violent change of government – actually required fundamental changes in society's understanding of the world, of the relationships between rulers and the ruled and in the meanings of the words that described what was going on. It was an article of Dirlik's, on the name of China, that inspired me to open this book by writing about that subject. His article demonstrated that the change from old empire to modern nation-state really ran in the opposite direction. Change began with words. As intellectuals struggled to explain and address the problems created by rapid modernisation, they created new words – or modified the meanings of old ones – to describe the new situation. Those new words crystallised new ways of looking at society and changed the relationships between rulers and ruled. The result was government overthrow.

I met Dirlik only once: he died just as I was starting to write this book. Some found Dirlik difficult but I liked him and he opened my eyes to this issue. Dirlik believed the emergence of the ideas that underpin modern China was not an obscure historical story but a live issue that continues to animate the actions of an emerging superpower. When we look at China now we see, in effect, the victory of a small group of people who, around a century ago, created new ideas about the nature of society and politics and persuaded the rest of the country – and the wider world – to believe them. These ideas were a chaotic fusion of modern, Western conceptions of states, nations, territories and boundaries and ostensibly traditional notions about history, geography and the rightful order of societies.

While this book is about 'the invention of China', I am not trying to single out China for special criticism. All modern states have gone through this process of 'invention': selectively remembering and forgetting aspects of their pasts in order to present an ostensibly coherent and unifying vision for the future. I write this in a United Kingdom consumed by arguments over Brexit. Every day we see politicians and commentators selectively remembering or forgetting aspects of Britain's relationship with continental Europe or with the island of Ireland, or of

England's union with Scotland in order to create 'authentic' foundations for their political programme. Long-suppressed questions of sovereignty, identity and unity have burst into the open and become new sources of emotion and confrontation. Thousands of miles away, Hong Kong is in flames and at least a million Turkic Muslims are incarcerated in 're-education camps'. The contexts and consequences are vastly different but they share similar roots: the contradictions between sovereignty, identity and unity that are generated by the nation-state.

Most visitors to the Forbidden City in Beijing enter through the gates once used by tributaries, envoys and junior officials. Passing through the giant red walls, they encounter layer after layer of real and symbolic defences. The first comes in the form of a moat laid out in the shape of a recurve bow, facing southwards as a warning to the emperor's enemies. Beyond the moat lies the huge courtyard that once hosted imperial ceremonies; then the Hall of Supreme Harmony, where emperors were enthroned; and after that, the Hall of Preserving Harmony, where the emperor dined with the heads of tributary missions. Continuing north along the city's central axis takes the visitor into progressively more intimate areas: the Palace of Heavenly Purity, which housed the emperor's chambers, the Hall of Union where the solstices and New Year were celebrated, and then, finally, the Palace of Earthly Tranquillity. This building was originally constructed to house the empress's chambers but in 1645, after their capture of Beijing, the Qing Dynasty gave it a new purpose.

The Qing were Manchu: invaders from the northeast. They spoke their own language, which had its own script, and followed their own religion: a form of shamanism. These would remain the official language and religion of the court right up until the fall of the dynasty in 1912. Just like the British in India or the Ottomans in Arabia, the imperial elite sought to preserve their sense of separateness. The inhabitants of the Forbidden City, in particular, maintained many of the rituals that their ancestors had observed in the mountains of the northeast. They practised archery with their recurve bows, they danced in Manchu style and, in the repurposed Palace of Earthly Tranquillity, they practised animal sacrifice.

Every day, after morning worship in the shamanic tradition, the imperial household would gather in the Palace's central hall while a pig was despatched. The animal was then butchered and its meat partially cooked. The greasy, semi-raw flesh was passed around the assembled members of the Manchu nobility who competed with one another to receive the best cuts. The Palace became filthy, its floor spattered with animal fat and its rafters infused with the odours of boiled pork.[2] This did not matter to the royal family. It was an intimate, sacred place closed to outsiders. It was so intimate that the building was also used as the emperor's honeymoon suite – presumably after it had been cleaned up. What happened in the Palace stayed in the Palace.

These traditions continued right up until the revolution of 1911/12, yet the modern guardians of the Forbidden City gloss over this side of imperial life. It does not fit with the conventional image of a Chinese emperor. The son of heaven is traditionally pictured sitting serene on a mighty throne, not squatting on a greasy floor. But by denying or minimising the Palace's Manchu history, these tourist guides are performing a vital role in defending the legitimacy of the People's Republic of China. The People's Republic regards itself as the latest ruler of a Chinese state with a continuous history stretching back millennia. This history, in its view, makes it the rightful authority across a vast territory stretching from the Pacific to central Asia: it underpins the PRC's right to rule Tibet, Xinjiang, Mongolia, Manchuria and Taiwan. It also gives it the authority to define who is Chinese and how they should behave.

Yet, as the history of the Palace of Earthly Tranquillity demonstrates, for 268 years 'China' was a conquered province of a Manchu empire. It was the Manchus who extended the rule of their state as far as the Himalayas and the Xinjiang mountains. The transition of 1912 turned this empire inside out. Chinese nationalists assumed the right to rule the entirety of what was a largely non-Chinese empire. They also assumed the right to decide who was Chinese, how their Chinese-ness should be expressed, what language they should speak and so on. The current Chinese leadership are their successors. The Communist Party has a monolithic view of what it means to be China and to be Chinese and appears determined to impose it, whatever the consequences. Time and again, it justifies its actions by reference to a particular, politicised vision of the past. If we are to understand China's future actions we need to understand the origins of this vision. This book traces the answers back to the period around a century ago when the old imperial order collapsed and the modern 'nation-state' emerged from the wreckage.

* * *

A few words about terminology. Some may object to the word 'invention' in my title. Professional historians would use the word 'construction', but a book on the 'construction of China' runs the risk of being filed under civil engineering. My meaning is the same. I am not claiming that China was invented out of nothing but that the idea of China as a coherent territory with a seamless history was actively constructed/invented from a jumble of contradictory evidence by individuals acting in the particular circumstances of their times. The ideas, arguments and narratives that they borrowed, adapted and asserted were products of those times but they continue to guide the actions of the Chinese leadership to this day.

I have also tried to avoid using the term 'China' except where it is appropriate – generally from the period after the declaration of the Republic of China in 1912. To use it before this date is to fall into the nationalist trap of projecting terms (and their meanings) back into a past where they don't belong. This opens the question of exactly how we should refer to this piece of the earth's surface through time. Dirlik used the term 'East Asian Heartland', which is useful but unwieldy. For the period between 1644 and 1912, I have generally used the term 'Qing Great-State', borrowing from Timothy Brook. Brook argues that 'Great-State', or *Da Guo*, was a uniquely Inner Asian form of rule and was the term that states, from the Mongols onwards, used to describe themselves. For this reason it is more appropriate than the western term 'empire'.[3] I have transliterated many compound Chinese words as individual syllables on first usage. While this may annoy readers who already know Chinese, it may help others who do not.

Finally, I need to clearly state that this is a work of synthesis. It rests on the pioneering research of a new generation of academics over the past couple of decades. The schools of 'New Qing History' and 'Critical Han Studies' and others have allowed us to look at old questions with new eyes. I have credited many of these scholars in the main text and more in the Acknowledgements but for those who seek greater detail there is a full list in the Further Reading section. I am indebted to their expertise. This re-examination of the Chinese past has only been possible because of the academic freedom provided by universities in North America, Australia, Europe and Japan. These issues cannot be addressed with candour inside the People's Republic of China itself: questions of sovereignty, identity and unity are still far too sensitive. This book tries to explain why.

1
THE INVENTION OF CHINA
Zhongguo – China

Eight lucky steps took Xi Jinping to the stage in the Great Hall of the People; three military trumpeters heralded his ascension to the podium of regional power. From its heights Xi could gaze down, with his habitual look of practised boredom, upon the thirty-six heads of government, several chiefs of international organisations and a few of their spouses waiting expectantly at the top table. Behind them, a further 126 smaller tables stretched into the far corners of the room, around which sat over 1,000 members of foreign delegations. Xi stood alone at the apex of the arrangement. It was hardly necessary to further emphasise China's centrality but the set designers did so anyway. The stage was flanked by a pair of giant montages: compilations of landmarks and monuments from the ancient Silk Road, their arid landscapes contrasting with the ornate flower arrangements on the top table. Between the diners, swans courted on floral lily ponds, peacocks strutted through miniature gardens and doves took wing from delicate forests.

It was 26 April 2019, the opening banquet of the Second Belt and Road Forum in Beijing. As well as offering fine words about regional cooperation, Xi wanted to talk about history. 'For millennia, the Silk Road had witnessed how countries achieved development and prosperity through commerce and enriched their cultures through exchanges,' he told the delegations. 'Facing the myriad challenges of today, we can draw wisdom from the history of the Silk Road, find strength in win-win cooperation in the present day and build partnerships across the globe to jointly usher in a brighter future where development is shared by all.'[1]

History, or rather a particular version of history, underpins events such as this. Through staging and rhetoric, Xi Jinping presents China as the natural leader of East Asia and perhaps beyond. The metaphor of the Silk Road is deployed as a diplomatic tool: ultimately, all its roads lead to Beijing. The tool, ironically, is a European invention. The name 'Silk Road' was probably first coined by an early German geographer, Carl Ritter, in 1838, adopted by another geographer, Ferdinand von Richthofen, in 1877 and popularised by a Swedish explorer, Sven Hedin, in the 1930s.[2] None of this seems to concern Xi. In the official Beijing version of history, the Silk Road is proof of the enduring centrality of China. Its rightful position has always been at the apex of regional politics. This is the natural historical order and this is how things will be in the future.

But the view of China that Xi projects at events such as these is a political concoction. In this chapter I will try to show that it too owes as much to European images of China as it does to China's ideas about itself. Just as the term 'Silk Road' was originally a European one, imposing an imagined order on a far more complex and chaotic history, so the very name 'China' was adopted by Westerners and given new meanings which were then transmitted back to East Asia. Over centuries, Europeans had developed a vision of a place they called 'China' based upon scraps of information sent home by explorers and priests and subsequently amplified by storytellers and orientalists. In European minds, 'China' became an ancient, independent, continuous state occupying a defined portion of continental East Asia.

In reality there was no state called 'China' during this period. From 1644 until 1912, 'China' was, in effect, a colony of an Inner Asian empire: the Qing Great-State. The Qing had created a multi-ethnic realm, of which 'China proper' – the fifteen provinces of the defeated Ming Dynasty – was just one part. The previous Ming state lasted for almost 300 years but it had not used the name China, either. Before the Ming, those territories had been part of a Mongol Great-State that had stretched as far as the Mediterranean: East Asia was just one part of its domain. Before the Mongols, they were controlled by the rival Song, Xia and Liao states. These had occupied various parts of the territory we now call China and they, in turn, were different from the fragmented states that existed before them.

Each state was different in its territorial extent and its ethnic composition but each one needed to present itself as the legitimate successor to its predecessor. To retain the loyalty of officials and the wider population, therefore, each new governing elite needed to claim continuity with tradition. To receive the necessary 'mandate of heaven', it had to speak in certain ways and perform the rituals expected of a ruling class. In certain eras this may have been genuine belief, in others it became political theatre but in some it became outright deception. The Mongols and Qing elites inwardly retained their Inner Asian cultures while externally presenting themselves – at least to a portion of their subjects – as heirs to Sinitic traditions of rule. Where, then, was 'China'? In short, it only existed as a unified and defined country in the foreign imagination. Until the very end of the nineteenth century, rulers in Beijing would not even have recognised the name 'China'. More significantly, they would not have understood the meaning that was represented by foreigners' use of the word.

Western thinkers privileged their 'China' over other political formations in the region and promoted it, conceptually, above its hinterland. In their minds 'China' was the region's dynamic engine while Inner Asia only mattered when its horse-borne hordes streamed into China to rape and pillage. In European eyes, 'China' was a constant presence on the historical stage while Inner Asians were reduced to playing repeated 'ride-on' parts before retreating to the dustbin of history. Hence the 'Silk Road'. China was regarded as the driver of trade and Inner Asian states merely as the corridors through which it passed. In the late nineteenth and early twentieth centuries, this idea of a pre-eminent 'China' travelled from Europe to East and Southeast Asia and found a new home in the private discussions and public journals of Qing intellectuals. These were mainly people who had travelled abroad and were able to look back on their homeland from afar. From their place of exile or sojourn, they too began to imagine a place called 'China', just like the Westerners. In time they returned home and spread this new vision of a state – a defined piece of territory with a continuous history – among a population eager for new ideas to resolve a profound political crisis. Key to this evolution in thinking was a debate about the name of the country.

These days, Xi and his fellow Chinese leaders use two names for their country in general speech: *Zhongguo* and *Zhonghua*. Within their etymology both names make claims to regional supremacy. Both are translated into English as 'China' but they carry particular meanings in Chinese. *Zhong guo* is literally the 'central state' of an idealised political hierarchy. *Zhong hua* is literally the 'central efflorescence', but its more figurative meaning is the 'centre of civilisation', an assertion of cultural superiority over the barbarians in the hinterland. These terms have deep historical roots but they were not used as formal names for the country until the very end of the nineteenth century. They only became its names because of the transformation of ideas about the country, under the influence of Western ideas of nations and states. During this process, the meaning of those names changed profoundly. This is the story of those names.

Along the coasts of Guangdong and Fujian the local merchants and literati welcomed Galeote Pereira. He sold them sandalwood and spices from the Indies at cheap prices and then paid twice the market rates for the food and supplies he took on board. A gentleman soldier from a noble family, with contacts at the highest levels of Portuguese society, Pereira was a good man to do business with. He personified the first wave of European exploration of East Asia: combining imperial interests with self-advancement and a bit of Catholic proselytising. In the decade since leaving home, Pereira had been a merchant in India, a mercenary in Siam and by 1548 was sailing between Malacca and points east trading the luxury goods of East and Southeast Asia.

The provincial governors and the Ming court in faraway Beijing hated Galeote Pereira. To them, he was a foreign smuggler, importing contraband in defiance of an edict specifically banning the *fo-lang-ji* – the 'Frankish' (a term borrowed from Arab merchants) Europeans – from trading. Two decades earlier, Portuguese ignorance of Ming diplomatic protocol, and their arrogance in the face of officialdom, had caused them to be banned from the country altogether. Now Pereira and the others were playing a cat-and-mouse game: trading with local merchants while hiding from central government among the thousands of islands that fringe the coast between the cities that they called Amoy and Liampo (modern-day Xiamen and Ningbo).

On 19 March 1549, the cat caught the mouse. The viceroy of Fujian and Zhejiang, an apparently honest man called Zhu Wan, had ordered his provincial coastguard to destroy the smuggling trade. They caught Pereira, and the two ships under his command, hiding in the quiet anchorage of Zoumaxi – 'Running Horse Creek', somewhere near Xiamen. They hauled the crews off to jail in the provincial capital, Fuzhou. There, on Zhu Wan's orders, ninety-six of them, mainly local vagabonds, were executed.

But Zhu Wan's diligent enforcement of the law had alienated all those local worthies – the 'robe and cap class' – who enjoyed the fruits of the smuggling trade. To safeguard their supplies of contraband, they conspired with their associates at the imperial court to impeach Zhu for overstepping his authority: the executions should not have been carried out without formal approval from Beijing. As a result, the charges against the Portuguese were dropped and Zhu was convicted of embezzlement. Pereira and his surviving shipmates were given lenient sentences while Zhu took his own life.

Pereira probably spent two or three years in various forms of custody but in conditions that became increasingly relaxed and comfortable. Eventually he was able to bribe his way to liberty. We know that he was free by 27 February 1553 because he attended the exhumation of Francis Xavier – one of the founders of the Society of Jesus – on the island of Shangchuan, just down the coast from modern Hong Kong. This was a tiny Portuguese settlement – a toehold for both proselytising and smuggling – that the local elite tolerated and tried to keep secret from the court in Beijing. Xavier believed there was great potential for his Jesuit order in the East and he doesn't appear to have had any qualms about working with those whose motives were more financial than spiritual as both wings of Portuguese imperialism strived to increase their market share.

Once Pereira was back with his countrymen he wrote what became one of the first accounts of life under the Ming Dynasty to reach European audiences. His descriptions, unsurprisingly, focused on prison and punishment and included criticism of idolatry and sodomy ('the greatest fault we find among them'). Nonetheless, he had high praise for the quality of the roads and bridges he had travelled over, for the hygienic chopsticks and for the large and sophisticated estates of the rich. However, he puzzled over one detail that appeared curious to Europeans who had set sail in search of the mysterious country that they called 'China'.

> We are wont to call this country China, and the people Chins; but as long as we were prisoners, not hearing amongst them at any time that name, I

> determined to learn how they were called . . . I answered them that all the inhabitants of India called them Chins . . . Then I did ask them what name the whole country beareth . . . It was told me that of ancient time in this country had been many kings, and though presently it were all under one [king], each kingdom nevertheless enjoyed that name it first had: these kingdoms are the provinces . . . In conclusion they said, that the whole country is called *Tamen* and the inhabitants Tamenjins so that their name China or Chins is not heard of in that country.[3]

In other words, the Chinese didn't call themselves Chinese, nor their country 'China'. Instead they referred to it as *Tamen* – or, as we might write it today, *Da Ming*, which translates as 'Great Ming'. They called themselves *Tamenjins* – or *Da Ming Ren*, 'people of the Great Ming'. The people Pereira encountered do not appear to have identified themselves as belonging to an ethnic group nor to a piece of territory but only as subjects of a ruling dynasty. The only place names they referred to were the towns and provinces in which they lived, not the country to which Pereira assumed they all belonged.

Within a few decades, by the end of the sixteenth century, Portuguese traders and preachers were faring better than Pereira had done. They had swapped the toehold of Shangchuan for a slightly larger one on Macao and Francis Xavier's missionary hopes had borne fruit. Jesuits were now welcomed in the imperial court. Rather than being imprisoned, the priest-scientist Matteo Ricci became the first European to enter the Forbidden City in Beijing. Officials were fascinated by his ability to predict eclipses and the movement of planets and, although the emperor declined to meet him, Ricci was treated as an honoured guest, awarded land upon which to build a church and became an unofficial adviser to the court.

Ricci too was initially intrigued by the same issue as Pereira – the lack of a national name, but after several years living in the country, he noted in his journal that, 'It does not appear strange to us that the Chinese should never have heard of the variety of names given to their country by outsiders and that they should be entirely unaware of their existence. . . . It is a custom of immemorial age in this country, that as often as the right to govern passes from one family to another, the country must be given a new name by the sovereign whose rule is about to begin.' Compared to their own Europe of emerging nation-states, Pereira and Ricci had discovered a very different way of describing political allegiances. 'The people of the Great Ming' were subjects of a ruling dynasty. There was no sense of living in 'China' or being part of a 'Chinese' nation.

But Ricci also noted that 'among the Chinese themselves . . . besides the name assumed with the coming of the new sovereign, the country also has a title which has come down through the ages and sometimes other names are joined to this title. Today we usually call this country *Ciumquo* or *Ciumhoa*, the first word signifying kingdom, and the second, garden. When put together, the words are translated, "To be at the centre".' In the modern era we transliterate *Ciumquo* as *zhong guo* and *Ciumhoa* as *zhong hua*. But Ricci understood that *zhong guo* was not really the name of the country but a statement of political hierarchy. 'The Chinese . . . imagine that the world is flat and that China is situated in the middle. . . . The few kingdoms contiguous to their state . . . were, in their estimation, hardly worthy of consideration.'[4] These terms are still with us. *Zhonghua* and *Zhongguo* are almost interchangeable in the same way that the terms 'United Kingdom' and 'Britain' or 'United States' and 'America' are official and unofficial ways of referring to the same place.

The phrase '*zhong guo*' has a long lineage: it has been found inscribed on 'oracle bones' discovered in modern-day Henan province and dating back to the Shang Dynasty (1600–1000 BCE). A few centuries later, during what is known as the 'Eastern Zhou' period – approximately 2,500 years ago (770–221 BCE) – *zhong guo* referred to the feudal states in the '*zhongyuan*', the central plains in the Yellow River basin, west and south of Beijing. They were, collectively, the 'central states' – the *zhong guo*. But Richard J. Smith, among the foremost experts on Chinese map-making, notes that in this period the phrase actually had three interconnected meanings: as a place, as a culture and as a political system.[5] The fifth-century BCE text 'Strategies of the Warring States' (*Zhang Guo Ce*) notes that:

> *Zhong guo* is where the intelligent and discerning people dwell, where the myriad creatures and useful implements are gathered together, where the sages and worthies instruct, where benevolence and right behaviour are expressed, where the books of Poetry, History, Ritual and Music are used,

> where different ideas and techniques are tried, where distant people come to observe, and where even the [non-Chinese] Man and Yi people exhibit appropriate conduct.

In other words, *zhong guo* was a place with a particular culture that these days we might call 'Chinese' or, more precisely, 'Sinitic'.

Seventeen centuries later, twelfth-century writers under the Song Dynasty used *zhong guo* to assert an identity in the face of threats from invaders from Inner Asia. It was both a physical place, the old heartland, and a cultural memory. The Song saw themselves as keepers of the *zhong guo* even after they had lost control of the actual territory of the central plains to the Mongols. Importantly, however, they didn't call their state *Zhong Guo*. They called it *Da Song Guo* – the Song Great-State – after themselves. Two centuries later, when Zhu Yuanzhang, founder of the Ming Dynasty, announced himself as the ruler who defeated the Mongols, he declared, 'I am now ruler of the *zhong guo* and all under heaven are at peace.' But he didn't call his country '*Zhong Guo*', either. Again, he named it after his dynasty: '*Da Ming Guo*' – the Ming Great-State.

The fact that '*zhong guo*' was used in the distant past and is a name for China today has led nationalistic historians to claim that '*Zhongguo*' has been a continuous state across three, or even five, millennia. A wiser look at the evidence shows that this is not the case. The words took long journeys over space and through time before coming to mean what they do today. Peter Bol, professor of Chinese language at Harvard University, argues that the consistent element through the intermittent uses of the term spread over 3,000 years was not to name a particular state but to maintain a sense of cultural difference between those within the *zhong guo* and those outside it: the barbarians, or *Yi di*.[6] *Zhong guo* was not intended to be the name of a country but a claim to legitimacy. Some writers have translated the phrase as 'middle kingdom' but that makes it sound too much like a home for hobbits. A much better translation is 'central state' or even 'centre-of-the-world' since it is really a description of a political hierarchy between 'us' on the inside and 'them' on the outside.

As we shall see, the terms '*zhong guo*' and '*zhong hua*' were revived in the late nineteenth century by modern nationalists and given new meanings. These ideologues constructed a new vision of the past that linked together disparate episodes to construct a history in which *Zhongguo* appeared to be a permanent presence. The story is more complicated and interesting than that and it reveals much about why China is the way it is today.

Where then does the English name 'China' come from? The most common explanation for the name of 'China' is that it is derived from the ancient dynasty of Qin (pronounced 'chin'), which formed as a small fiefdom in what is now Gansu province in the northwest of modern China. The Qin Dynasty originally took its name from a small piece of land granted to it in 987 BCE.[7] For six centuries, the Qin led one among several 'warring states' located in the lands along the Yellow River and its tributaries. The dynasty gradually expanded the area under its rule but was never dominant until King Zheng finally managed to conquer the last of his rivals in 221 BCE.

As a new type of ruler, with a domain occupying (albeit briefly) the central plains and the lower reaches of both the Yellow River and the Yangtze, Zheng chose a new title: *Shihuangdi*, or 'first emperor'. In search of immortality he built a tomb near what is now the city of Xi'an and surrounded it with an army of terracotta warriors. But the Qin Dynasty lasted little longer than Zheng himself. Within four years of his death, his successors were overthrown by a former Qin official turned rebel leader, Liu Bang, who seized the throne, created his own dynasty and named it the *Han*. In retrospect, the Qin have been seen as the first rulers to unify the core territory of modern China. But while it might sound like an easy leap from 'Qin' to 'China', there's no evidence that the dynastic name Qin was ever actually used as the name of the territory. In fact there's significant evidence to the contrary.

The Indian professor of Chinese studies Haraprasad Ray has argued that there are mentions of a place called 'Cina' in Sanskrit manuscripts that date from before the time of the Qin state. The *Vayupurana*, thought to have been written in the fifth to the fourth century BCE, mentions people from 'Cina'. The *Matsyapurana*, composed from the fourth century BCE, asserts, for example, that these 'Cina' people are not suitable to perform the rituals associated with death and burial. 'Cina' also appears in the two great Hindu epics, the *Mahabharata* and *Ramayana*, composed during and after the fourth and third centuries BCE respectively. A fourth-century BCE political treatise, the

Arthasastra, mentions 'Cina' and the *Susruta*, a fourth-century BCE medical guide, describes 'China cloth' – *Cinapatta* – as useful for bandaging. In Sanskrit texts, therefore, 'Cina', referring to a place in or just over the Himalayas, seems to pre-date the Qin.

Ray was following the work of the Chinese scholar Su Zhongxiang, who assembled huge amounts of evidence to argue the same point. Su argues that, strange as it may seem to English speakers, the correct source of the name 'Cina' is the much earlier state of '*Jing*', also known as *Chu* in Chinese texts. Pronunciations have shifted over the centuries and the phonetic connection between '*Jing*' and 'Cina' that now appears somewhat distant would once have been much closer. The *Jing/Chu* heartland lay in what is now Hubei province and was associated with the Miao people, an ethnic group that would be described as 'barbarian' outsiders (*Yi*) by historians writing in the later Han period.[8]

The Australian scholar Geoff Wade has argued that a slightly different linguistic switch might source 'Cina' to another ethnic group. A mountain people in the southwestern Chinese province of Yunnan are known today in Chinese as the '*Yelang*'. However, they have a collection of epic poems dating back to the fifth century BCE in which they describe themselves as the '*Zhina*'. Wade notes that this is an almost perfect phonetic match for the Sanskrit 'Cina'. This group's traditional domain in what is now Yunnan province gave them control of the overland trading routes between what are now China and India. Goods that arrived in India from over the eastern mountains through this region would have been naturally described as coming from 'Cina'.

There is evidence for both of these theories but no firm conclusion has yet been reached. If either is true, the irony would be that the word most Westerners now use for China is ultimately derived from places that were outside what is commonly regarded as the traditional 'Chinese' heartland – outside the '*zhong guo*'. Going a step further, the majority cultures in these places at the time were not ethnically 'Chinese' as that word is currently defined. The *Jing/Chu* state was linked to the Miao minority and the *Yelang/Zhina* state with the Li people. 'Cina' may not even have been within the '*zhong guo*' at all! But whichever explanation we prefer, what is clear is that no 'Chinese' state used the word 'China' to describe its territory before the twentieth century. It was only ever a name used by outsiders.

But, however it emerged, the name 'China' travelled far: by the second century CE, the Greco-Roman geographer Ptolemy was mentioning Sinae and Thinae in his writings, even if he was unsure of their exact locations. In what is, in effect, a metaphor for this entire book, the name China acquired a meaning outside China that it had never had within it. In Europe, it became the name of a mythical place: a source of silk and wonder. Europeans imagined a place called 'China' without ever knowing what it was. They also heard about another place in the east – Cathay, also a source of silk and wonder but apparently further to the north. 'Cathay' is derived from the name '*Khitan*', the Inner Asian people who established the tenth- to twelfth-century Liao state in what is now northern China, Mongolia and eastern Russia. 'Cathay' was reached by land, whereas 'China' was reached by sea, but they were, in effect, rival names for the same 'East Asian Heartland'.

From the 1500s onwards, China/Cathay became the objective of Portuguese, Spanish and then Dutch and English expeditions to the East. But when adventurers like Galeote Pereira reached their objective they found that 'China' did not exist in the form they had imagined. Three centuries later, however, their idea of a country, a continuous state with its origins rooted in antiquity, was adopted by a small, elite fraction of 'Chinese' society. They chose to become China.

In the summer of 1689, an envoy of the double tsars of Russia, Peter I and Ivan V, sat down with representatives of the Kangxi Emperor, the fourth ruler of the Qing Dynasty, by the side of the Nercha River in Siberia. The Russians sat on chairs while the Qing representatives preferred cushions. In the specially pitched tent, 5,000 kilometres east of Moscow and 1,300 kilometres north of Beijing, they argued over who had the right to exploit the frontier lands stretching all around them. This event has sometimes been used to justify the claim that, as early as the seventeenth century, the Qing state formally called itself '*Zhongguo*'. However, a closer look at what happened demonstrates that this is mistaken. Instead, it is more evidence for the foreigners' invention of China.

For several decades, Russian pioneers had been exploring and settling further and further along the Amur River and its tributaries, reaching areas the Qing elite regarded as rightfully theirs. The Qing had resisted and the result, during the 1680s, was a series of conflicts. By the end of the decade, Qing forces had turned back the encroachments and both empires were ready to negotiate peace. After exchanges of messages between the two governments, a meeting was agreed outside the newly established Russian settlement of Nerchinsk.

Who were the people who founded the Qing state? They were a people from what is now northeastern China and they spoke a Siberian language: Manchu. In 1644 they had ridden out of their chilly homeland and taken over the moribund Ming state. They were people from outside the *zhong guo* but they quickly realised that if they were to rule the former Ming domain successfully they would have to adopt some of the techniques of their predecessors. Yet even while they did so, they remained Manchu. They continued to rule in an Inner Asian style, which the American historian Pamela Crossley has called 'simultaneous ruling'.[9] Each part of their 'great-state' was ruled differently, according to what was thought culturally appropriate. Yet at its centre, Manchu language and script remained the official language and script of the state and the new elite sought to preserve their traditions: riding, archery and hunting; rites, prayers and sacrifices to ancestors. More importantly they maintained Manchu regiments – known as banners – to control the society they had conquered. In effect, from the mid-seventeenth century, the *zhong guo* became a province of a Manchu 'great-state'.

The Kangxi Emperor sent two relatives, Songgotu and Tong Guogang, to lead the talks in Nerchinsk. Neither spoke Russian. The Russian tsars had sent Count Feodor Alekseyevich Golovin as their representative but he could not speak Manchu. The fact that the negotiations even took place, and that they were successful, was largely due to the roles played by two European Jesuit priests. They were a Frenchman, Jean-François Gerbillon, and a Portuguese, another Pereira: Thomas. The Jesuits' privileged access to the imperial court had survived its takeover by the Manchus. By 1689 Thomas Pereira had been attached to the Qing court for sixteen years. We know he spoke good Manchu since he also wrote textbooks in the language explaining Western mathematics.[10]

Thomas Pereira was a remarkable man. As the second son of an aristocratic family he could not inherit his father's title and instead devoted himself to the Church. He joined the Jesuits at the age of seventeen and then studied at the University of Coimbra where he excelled in both mathematics and music. Among his fellow students there was the first Macao-born Jesuit, Zheng Weixin. Perhaps inspired by Zheng, Pereira sailed east at the age of twenty, the youngest of a consignment of missionaries headed to Asia. After more studies in Goa and Macao he was summoned to Beijing, arriving in early 1673 at the age of twenty-six. He would spend the rest of his life there.[11]

The Jesuits needed to impress the young emperor and Pereira was set to work making clocks, scientific instruments and pipe organs. One of his most extravagant creations involved a caged bird and a set of ten bells. Whenever the bird drank water or opened its food box, it would trigger the playing of a melody. The attraction probably paled after a while. Nonetheless, through his scientific skills, Pereira seems to have got to know Kangxi well. In 1680 he wrote to his superiors that he had had long conversations with the emperor in his own chambers. In 1688 he told them, 'From me (if I want) nothing can be hidden at the Court.'[12] It was this confidence, together with respect for the Jesuits' knowledge of the wider world, that led to Kangxi sending Pereira and Galeote out to meet the Russians at Nerchinsk.

When the Qing delegates wanted to say something in the negotiations they spoke to the Jesuits in Manchu, the Jesuits translated the Manchu into Latin for a Polish translator, Andrei Belobotski. Belobotski then translated the Latin into Russian for Golovin. Both priests left detailed accounts of how the talks unfolded and it is clear that they interpreted more than just language. They were also responsible for translating concepts of law, government and the nature of political authority between the worlds of western Europe and eastern Asia.

In his memoir, Thomas Pereira describes how he had to convince the Qing that the Russians were not savages but civilised people with whom they could make an agreement. But he expresses some exasperation with the Qing's perception of their status: 'From the beginning of the world, China had never received foreigners in its empire except as tribute-bearers,' he wrote in his diary. 'In their crass ignorance of the world, the Tartars [i.e. the Qing], with the same pride as the Chinese, considered other nations shepherds like their neighbours. They thought everything was part of the China which they proudly called *Tian Xia* – i.e. "all under heaven" as if nothing else existed.'[13] By his own account, Pereira introduced the Qing to what Europeans were starting to call the 'Law of Nations' – a view of states as territorial entities with boundaries and sovereignty that other states were obliged to accept. This was a relatively novel view of international society, one that had been embodied in the Treaty of Westphalia, which ended the Thirty Years War in 1648, just four decades before the talks on the banks of the Nercha River.

The Russian leadership had a reasonable understanding of this 'Westphalian' view of the world. It was a view that the Jesuits understood (even if the Pope disapproved of it) and it was up to them to persuade the Qing to accept enough of it to sign a formal boundary agreement with the tsars' delegates. The discussions, including the three-stage translations in each direction, were protracted and nearly broke down at several points. But finally, on 6 September 1689, the negotiations were complete and an agreement, the Treaty of Nerchinsk, was signed. Significantly, it was not written in Chinese. The Jesuits and Belobotski agreed the final text in Latin and each side subsequently made their own translations into Russian and into Manchu – the language of the Qing court. No Chinese translation was made until much later; indeed, it seems likely that the treaty text was actually kept secret from Chinese-reading audiences.

The Latin text of the treaty uses the name 'Imperii Sinici' to refer to the Qing realm. The Manchu text uses the term 'Dulimbai Gurun', which can be translated as 'central state', apparently the Manchu equivalent of *zhong guo*. But it is vital to remember that these are European Jesuit interpretations of the Qing world-view. Pereira himself says the court used a different term, *Tian Xia*, but he knew that the idea of a Qing state claiming to rule 'all under heaven' would not fit with a Russian state claiming to follow the 'Law of Nations'. This is almost certainly the reason why the treaty text was kept secret from Chinese audiences. If they had discovered that the emperor had signed a boundary agreement, they might have concluded that he was not, after all, the ruler of 'all under heaven' – *tianxia*. The implication for the political philosophy behind *zhong guo* could have been catastrophic.

The Treaty of Nerchinsk has subsequently become famous as the first document in which China represented itself as 'China' to a foreign power. However, this version of events misunderstands what took place. The accounts of those present at the talks make clear that Chinese was not used in the official negotiations. No Chinese secretaries were attached to the negotiating mission (so no Chinese-language records were made) and Pereira makes clear that the Qing emissaries spoke Manchu or Mongolian. Rather than seeing the Treaty of

Nerchinsk as a 'coming of age' document for a nascent 'China', therefore, it is more accurate to see it as the Jesuits' attempt to present an Asian state in terms that Europeans would understand. In this sense, Gerbillon and Pereira weren't just translating between languages, they were interpreting entirely different conceptions of political order and the nature of states. To some extent they were misrepresenting the nature of the Qing Great-State in order to make it fit into the European diplomatic order in the wider interests of peace between the two. The Treaty of Nerchinsk was not the first moment that a 'Chinese' state used *Zhongguo* as its name, no matter what later nationalist historians have written. It was the moment at which the Jesuits used their knowledge of East and West to accommodate within the 'Law of Nations' a quite different regional order in which states were not defined by their territory but by their allegiance to a ruler.

While the Kangxi Emperor may have been grateful for the peace on his northern frontier, he was not sufficiently enthusiastic about his government's implicit endorsement of the Law of Nations to publicise the Treaty of Nerchinsk within his own realm. Joseph Sebes, himself a Jesuit and a twentieth-century Sinologist at Georgetown University, noted that there was no trace of the text of the treaty in any of the Chinese sources of the time. However, Peter C. Perdue, professor of Chinese history at Yale University, has found a copy in the *Kangxi Shilu*, a collection of documents of the emperor's daily activities published at the end of his reign. It does not seem to have been made public until around 200 years after the original Treaty of Nerchinsk was signed. This was a time, in the late nineteenth century, when the Qing state was again being forced to deal with Russia at the point of a gun and it had an interest in making use of the original treaty.

The Jesuits were a small but highly influential presence at the Qing court during the seventeenth and eighteenth centuries. Priests sometimes spent decades living in Beijing (Thomas Pereira spent thirty-two years in the city) speaking directly with officials and even the emperors themselves. They sent back detailed reports to the Jesuit and Catholic hierarchies and through them Europe came to know more about the mysterious land of the east. It is they, primarily, who give the name 'China' to this land and presented it to European audiences through maps and books. After Galeote and Thomas, one might say that 'China' really begins with the writings of a pair of Pereiras.

When the Jesuits chose '*Zhongguo*' to represent the Qing Great-State in its dealings with Russia they did far more than translate a name. They started a process through which the state began to present itself and then think of itself in a new way. Although the phrase had been used for millennia, it was only towards the end of the Qing era that *Zhongguo* became commonly used in its international relations. Research by the Japanese historian Kawashima Shin found that in the first half of the nineteenth century just twenty-eight diplomatic documents used the terms *Qing* and *Zhongguo* in the same text. But *Zhongguo* became more common in the second half of the century, appearing in treaties with Russia in 1861 and the United States in 1880, for example. Yet, the wording of the 1861 Chinese-Peruvian Trade Agreement only refers to *Da Qing Guo* (Qing Great-State). Arif Dirlik surmised that where an agreement referred to actions by the government, Qing diplomats used the term '*Da Qing Guo*' but where it was a reference to a piece of territory they used '*Zhongguo*'.[14]

However, the American geographer Richard Smith notes that, historically, *Zhong guo* was not a consistently used name. It was only one of many terms used in old texts to describe this amorphous piece of territory. He lists several others, including: *Zhong hua* – 'Central florescence'; *Shen zhou* – 'Spiritual region'; *Jiu zhou* – 'the Nine regions'; *Zhong ru* – 'Central land'; and *Tian xia* – 'All under heaven'. He argues that the relationship between these terms, and the differences between their exact meanings in ancient documents, is far from clear. The twentieth-century Chinese historian Chen Liankai argued that *zhong hua* was first used during the third or fourth century and combined *zhong guo* with *hua xia* – two ways of describing the 'civilised' regions under the rule of the Jin Dynasty. Chen argued that both *zhongguo* and *zhonghua* were used interchangeably from then on. Lydia H. Liu, professor of Chinese language at Columbia University, notes that the words *hua* and *xia* were both used to draw a distinction between the 'illustrious' or 'civilised' people within the '*zhong guo*', and the 'barbarians' living outside it: the *yi* or *yi-di*. Liu says the words *hua* and *xia* encompass the 'essence' of an identity but she agrees that their actual meaning and connotations have shifted over millennia.[15]

When we see modern China's self-image being put on display at events such as the Belt and Road Forum, we see the results of ideas that were consciously imagined, debated and imposed by intellectuals and activists in the late nineteenth and early twentieth centuries. As we shall see, it was discussions between thinkers in colonial cities such as Shanghai, and others in exile overseas that created an idea of a nation-state that appeared to be indigenous but was actually constructed in the image of the Western notion of 'China'. These discussions were inseparable from two other arguments: about whether the new state would be a reformed monarchy or a revolutionary republic and about whether it needed to be ethnically homogenous.

Zhang Deyi was a poster boy for the Qing Great-State in the second half of the nineteenth century. He would become well known as one of the very first of its subjects to travel and live in Europe and America. He came of age just in time to participate in the first phase of cooperation between reformers inside the Manchu court and the newly arrived envoys pressed upon them by foreign powers after the Second Opium War. In 1862 the fifteen-year-old Zhang was chosen to be one of the first ten students admitted to the *Tongwen Guan* – the Translators' College – in Beijing. The college was founded by the reformers and funded by the new 'Imperial Maritime Customs Service', which was itself run jointly by the court and foreign powers.

The Customs Service was another consequence of the Opium Wars. It emerged, as a curious hybrid organisation, from the chaos of the immensely bloody Taiping Rebellion, the simultaneous attacks by the European powers and from internal palace coups. The Cambridge historian Hans van de Ven traces its origin to an informal arrangement reached in 1854 between British and Qing officials in the international 'concession' of Shanghai. In 1861, shortly after British and French troops had destroyed the emperor's Summer Palace outside Beijing, it became a formally established body. While it nominally answered to the emperor, it was actually run by British officials.[16] It needed translators for its work, hence the establishment of the Translators' College. The college would do more than just translate documents, however. It became a crucial portal for Western ideas to enter elite Qing society.

Zhang spent three years learning English and French at the Translators' College and in 1866 he was an obvious candidate to join the Qing court's first official fact-finding mission to Europe. Then, in 1868, he joined a longer mission to the United States and Europe and in 1871 went to France immediately after the Franco-Prussian War. He kept diaries of his travels – just like Galeote and Thomas Pereira 300 years before – in which he recorded his impressions of the 'divergent sartorial and degustory predilections' of the people he encountered.[17] While he was impressed by most of those he met, he was frustrated by Europeans and Americans who insisted on calling his country by the wrong name. 'After decades of East-West diplomatic and commercial interactions, [they] know very well that my country is called the *Da Qing Guo* [Qing Great-State] or the *Zhong Hua* [Central Efflorescence] but insist on calling it "China", Zhaina, Qina, Shiyin, Zhina, Qita, etc.,' he complained. '*Zhong Guo* has not been called by such a name over four thousand years of history. I do not know on what basis Westerners call it by these names!'[18] For Zhang, the proper way to refer to his country was to invoke its ruling dynasty, not describe a piece of territory.

Zhang wrote this in May 1871 but he failed to convince his Western interlocutors of his case. Instead, over the following few decades, opinion, even among his own colleagues, would shift in the opposite direction. By 1887 another Qing diplomat, Huang Zunxian, would complain that his country lacked a 'proper name'. Huang had been sent to Japan in 1877 as an assistant to the newly appointed Qing ambassador there and spent five years watching the country open up to the outside world and begin to modernise.[19] He was impressed by the rapid improvements in Japanese living standards and wrote a long account of what he had seen in order to educate his fellow diplomats back home. They weren't particularly interested. Huang's manuscript was ignored until after Japan had defeated China in the 1894/5 Sino-Japanese War. Only then did it become the most important Chinese-language source of information about Japan.

Huang didn't begin his book with praise for Japanese modernisation. Instead, he opted for criticism of his home country and his priority was to address the naming problem, writing:

> Research indicates that the diverse countries of the globe, such as England or France, all boast their own state names, the only exception being *Zhong Guo*. . . . But 'China', as variously transliterated in these languages, is not a name that we have used ourselves. Recently, when addressing foreigners, we have come to use the term *Zhong Hua* [Central Illustriousness]. But our

neighbours have denounced us for this, pointing out that all countries on earth see themselves as situated in the centre, and, moreover, that treating ourselves as 'illustrious' and others as 'barbaric' constitutes no more than glorifying oneself in order to demean others.[20]

In 1897, having served as a diplomat in Japan, San Francisco, London and Singapore, Huang was appointed the 'surveillance commissioner' (*ancha shi*) of Hunan province. He used his position – officially intended to oversee local officials – to advocate reform of the Qing state. He created a new school, the 'Hall of Current Affairs', in the provincial capital Changsha and invited one of the most famous reformers of this period, Liang Qichao, to be its chief lecturer. The previous year, the two had co-founded (along with another reformer, Tan Sitong) a journal, *Qiangxue Bao* – 'Strength Through Education Journal' – that would become particularly influential in what would follow.[21]

While Huang and Liang agreed on the need for constitutional reform and on the need for the country to have a 'proper' name, they disagreed about what that name should be. Huang didn't like *Zhong*, with its meaning of 'centrality'. In his 1887 essay he had argued instead for the more grandiose *Huaxia*, a name that literally translates as 'flourishing greatness' but also incorporates '*Hua*' and '*Xia*': ancient names for the peoples he considered to be the essence of his nation. Others argued, however, that *Huaxia* was properly the name of a people rather than a state. Huang's idea was generally ignored.

From their new positions the two men continued to press for modernisation. Together with Liang's mentor, the radical scholar Kang Youwei, they petitioned and then met the young ruler, the Guangxu Emperor, to argue for constitutional reform. In 1898, as a result of this lobbying, the emperor announced forty edicts heralding modest changes in education, the military and the civil service. They were far from dramatic but they so worried conservatives at the court that, 103 days later, the emperor's aunt, Empress Dowager Cixi (the real power behind the throne) organised a coup and forced her nephew to abandon them all. Guangxu continued to sit on the throne for another decade but was stripped of real power and Cixi, in effect, ruled through him. Six supporters of the Hundred Days Reform were executed while others, including Kang, Liang and Huang, fled. Huang found sanctuary in his hometown in the south and retired to write poetry. Kang and Liang faced execution and fled further: to Japan, where they continued to agitate.

These days Chinatown in Yokohama is a neon-lit tourist magnet but at the turn of the twentieth century it was a cauldron of subversion. From his base there, Liang wrote essays and published newspapers to circulate the ideas that he thought would propel his homeland along a road that Japan had already travelled: into modernity. But creating a modern nation-state required having a state with a name. In his much-read 1900 essay 'On the source of China's weakness', Liang echoed Zhang Deyi, thirty years before, by telling his readers, 'Foreigners call our country "Cina" or "China" but that is not how we view ourselves.' But, unlike Zhang, Liang was particularly unhappy with the traditional way of referring to the country by its ruling dynasty: 'the Ming Great-State' or 'the Qing Great-State'. This, he feared, implied there was no Chinese nation at all. According to the Australian Sinologist John Fitzgerald, the lack of a name was, for Liang, proof of the Chinese people's cultural and intellectual immaturity: Liang called it a conceptual error 'lodged in every person's brain'.[22]

The name that Liang chose, indeed the word he used for 'China' in the title of his essay, was *Zhongguo*. He took the historic idea of *zhong guo* as the 'central state', with the implied meaning of 'centre of the world' in the old hierarchical cosmology, and gave it a new purpose. *Zhongguo* would cease to represent a regional political system and become merely a name but a 'name' that he could argue had been used for centuries. *Zhong guo* the concept would be displaced by *Zhongguo* as a direct equivalent for the foreigners' word 'China'. This process of retaining a word while utterly changing its meaning was key to the entire process of constructing – inventing – modern China. Liang chose *Zhongguo* for entirely pragmatic reasons: it was a name that was already starting to be used by the Qing state in its relations with other countries. But as we have already seen, even this process was not as simple as it sounds. By choosing *Zhongguo* to represent the native home of the Chinese nation, Liang was unknowingly adopting something that was originally a foreign idea.

Zhongguo is now the name commonly used as the Chinese word for 'China', but in the first decade of the twentieth century it was only one of several candidates for that honour. It was challenged, in particular, by revolutionaries who had no interest in reforming the Qing state but wanted to tear it down. One of them was a young man called Zhang Binglin. Zhang had started his adult life training to be a classical scholar-official. However, after the Qing Great-State's defeat in the Sino-Japanese War of 1894/5 he had resigned and joined the Shanghai branch of Kang and Liang's reform movement. He started to write for reformist newspapers and in 1896 became editor of Liang's *Shi Wu Bao* – 'Current Affairs Paper'. A difficult figure, Zhang repeatedly fell out with bosses, editors and officials and in late 1898, to escape the suppression of the 'Hundred Days' reformers, he fled to Taiwan (which had been under Japanese occupation since the end of the war in 1895). From there he wrote articles for Liang Qichao's next newspaper, *Qing Yi Bao* – 'The Pure Opinion Paper'. The paper was the mouthpiece of the *Bao Huang Hui* – 'The Protect the Emperor Society' – created by Kang Youwei and Liang to push for reform and, in particular, the restoration of the power of the Guangxu Emperor. In 1899, facing yet more troubles, Zhang moved to Japan at Liang's invitation and lived there for several months. Towards the end of the year, though, he moved to the International Settlement in Shanghai, to write for a newspaper with a more radical attitude, the *Su Bao*.

Shanghai was the intellectual hub of the Qing realm: a bubble of Western capitalism and culture forced into a declining empire. The International Settlement, nine square miles of colonial territory, was a place where there was some basic freedom of speech. Connected to the world by shipping lines and to the rest of the country through networks of newspaper and book publishing, it was a city where ideas could be exchanged and sedition could survive.

Zhang was living there when the anti-foreigner uprising known in the West as the 'Boxer Rebellion' broke out. Foreigners were besieged in Beijing in June 1900 and an eight-nation army was despatched to rescue them. A summer of atrocities on both sides ended with defeat for the Boxers and the flight of the Qing court. Zhang remained aloof from the turmoil but his views about the Qing underwent radical change. As the foreign armies marched on Beijing, he abandoned his previous belief in reform and began to argue for the downfall of the Qing instead.[23] He became a revolutionary and would eventually split with Liang and Kang.

An important part of the change in Zhang's views was his growing belief in racialism. Having seen the failure of the Hundred Days Reform and the response to the Boxer Rebellion, he came to see the Qing rulers not simply as corrupt and incompetent but as alien. They were Manchus, outsiders from the northeast, who had seized the Ming realm in 1644 and therefore had no right to rule. By August 1901 he was arguing, in the country's first revolutionary student magazine *Guominbao*, that Liang's arguments for national unity were wrong because Manchus were fundamentally different, pointing out that 'Manchus have their own writing system', slept on felt mats and ate milk products.[24]

While Zhang fulminated, the foreign armies remained in occupation in Beijing. They only departed in 1901 once the Qing court signed a peace agreement, the 'Boxer Protocol', in which it agreed to pay reparations to the imperial powers. Zhang was disgusted by the capitulation of people he had looked up to as reformers and became more committed to the need for revolution to rid his country of the Manchus who had so clearly failed it. To demonstrate the split he changed his name from Zhang Binglin to Zhang Taiyan. It was a public commitment to his new anti-Qing beliefs. 'Taiyan' honoured two scholars who had resisted the Qing takeover 250 years before: 'Tai' came from Taichong, the pen name of Huang Zongxi, and 'Yan' from Gu Yanwu.[25] Zhang saw these two 'Ming loyalists' as guardians of the true spirit of the country: heroes in the resistance to invaders from Inner Asia. By 1903 he was ready to criticise the emperor openly and directly – as well as those who still thought the Manchu/Qing regime could be reformed. This would lead him into new thinking about his country's future and its proper name.

Into this fevered setting stepped a young wannabe, Liu Shipei. In early 1903 Liu tried to become a bureaucrat for the Qing state but by the end of the year he would be trying to bring it down. One catalyst for his change in views would be a meeting with the freshly renamed Zhang Taiyan. Descended from a family of classical scholars on one side and government officials on the other, Liu was expected to proceed into the elite of the Qing state. In 1903, at the age of nineteen, the family despatched him to Beijing to take the *jinshi* imperial examination. He failed. Perhaps unwilling to face his disappointed parents, Liu did not return to his hometown of Yangzhou but travelled a further 200 kilometres downstream along the Yangtze River to Shanghai. There he met the thirty-three-year-old Zhang Taiyan, already a veteran of the struggle for political reform and disappointed with its failure. Zhang had broken with the Qing and was ready to take the revolutionary road. He took Liu with him. Almost overnight Liu changed from a potential servant of the Qing state into an agitator seeking its destruction.[26]

In mid-1903 Zhang made use of the relative freedom within the International Settlement to challenge the Qing directly. In an article in the *Su Bao* newspaper entitled 'In rebuttal of Kang Youwei's writings on revolution', he accused the emperor of, among other things, being a 'dim-witted buffoon'.[27] As a result, the Qing court issued a warrant for his arrest and on 30 June 1903 Zhang allowed himself to be captured by the International Settlement police – partly to demonstrate his commitment to the revolutionary cause,[28] but partly to avoid being captured by the Qing who would probably have sentenced him to death. Instead, he was convicted of seditious libel and sentenced to three years in a British-run prison where, ironically, conditions were so harsh that he contemplated suicide. He found succour in Buddhism and his increasingly anti-Manchu feelings.

Meanwhile, his young friend Liu Shipei was about to embark on his own anti-Manchu writing career. In 1904, at the age of just twenty, Liu published his first work, *Rangshu* – 'The Book of Expulsion'. As the German Sinologist Julia Schneider has pointed out, the phrase '*Rang Yi*' – 'expel the barbarians' – would have been well known to Liu's contemporaries. Rulers had uttered it in various historical tales handed down through the preceding millennia. Liu's book was intended to 'expel' the barbarians from Chinese history, as a prelude to expelling them from the country itself. This led him to consider what the most appropriate name for his liberated country should be.

In the *Rangshu*, Liu listed several possibilities based upon traditional documents. They included: *Xia*, *Da Xia* (great *Xia*), *Zhu Xia* (various *Xia*), *Zhu Hua* (various *Hua*) and the combination word: *Huaxia*. In the book, Liu stated that he wanted a name that would provide a border to his nation: one that made clear the difference between his people on the inside and aliens on the outside. He wanted a name that was truly authentic, dating back to a time before the Qin Dynasty, whom he saw as usurpers. He chose a name from the *Shan hai jing*, a classical text of this period. 'If [we want] to distinguish ourselves from the *Yi* (barbarians) of the four [directions],' he argued, 'we can only use *Da Xia* as a country name.'[29] Liu felt that *Da Xia* referred to an ancient civilisation, a pure people free from outside rulers – a fitting name for a future country free of the Qing.

On 24 November 1894, two months after Japanese forces had destroyed the Qing navy, three days after they had captured the Liaodong Peninsula and two weeks after his own twenty-eighth birthday, Sun Wen, his elder brother and a few of their friends met on a Pacific island to swear a revolutionary oath. They would, they pledged, 'expel the Tartars, revive China and establish a unified government'. This was the manifesto agreed at the first meeting of the *Xing Zhong Hui* – literally 'Revive the Centre Society', a group that would evolve from these tiny beginnings into the organisation that, seventeen years later, overthrew the Qing Great-State. By then Sun Wen would be better known as Sun Zhongshan or Sun Yat-sen.

Sun's family had sent him to Hawaii at the age of thirteen, after which he studied in Hong Kong. Almost all his teachers had been British or American[30] and, like the other members of the *Xingzhonghui* meeting that day in Hawaii, he spoke English and was well used to people asking him where he came from. When he answered the question in English, he had an answer – 'China'. That must have given him reason to think about the answer he would give in Chinese.

While a medical student in Hong Kong, Sun had developed a fierce hostility towards the Qing authorities. He watched them lose the 1884/5 conflict with France over the status of Vietnam while being simultaneously impressed by militant shipyard workers in Kowloon who refused to work on a French warship that had been damaged in the fighting. Sun was certainly not going to call his country *Da Qing Guo*. But the name that he and his revolutionary comrades chose for their country was not *Zhongguo* but *Zhonghua*. In this he was making a direct reference to history – and one with clear racial meaning to those who understood it.

The oath that the *Xingzhonghui* swore was borrowed from Zhu Yuanzhang, the founder of the Ming Dynasty. During his struggle against the Mongols in the fourteenth century, Zhu had used the slogan 'Expel the Tartars and revive *Zhonghua*'.[31] By adopting this pledge, Sun and his fellow revolutionaries were declaring that the Qing rulers, with their roots in the Manchu-speaking northeast, were 'Tartars' too. In their eyes, the Manchus were the same as the Mongols: outsiders from Inner Asia who had no right to rule the *zhong guo*.

The historian Peter Zarrow notes that *Zhonghua* – with its linguistic roots in *Huaxia* – has a more ethnic meaning than *Zhongguo*. As Lydia Liu has observed, it appears to describe a land for the *Hua* people – and thereby implicitly excludes the 'Tartars'. This would have been appealing to the revolutionaries who saw the 'foreign' Qing as the cause of *Zhonghua*'s modern troubles. The revolutionaries may also have become prejudiced against the name *Zhongguo* by the simple fact that the Qing themselves were starting to use it in their diplomatic dealings.

Over the following decade, the *Xingzhonghui* would try, and fail, several times to overthrow the Qing by force. After the defeat of its uprisings, it merged, in 1905, with other revolutionary groups to create the *Tongmeng Hui* – the 'Alliance Society'. The actual formation took place in Tokyo and the united leadership decided to keep two of the *Xingzhonghui*'s original demands and add two more. Its slogan became, 'Expel the Tartars, revive *Zhonghua*, establish a Republic, and distribute land equally among the people'.

The *Tongmenghui* adopted this position during the years that Zhang Taiyan was in prison in Shanghai. They recognised that Zhang would be a powerful advocate for their group and sent a delegation of activists to greet him when he was released in late June 1906. They offered him the job of editor-in-chief of the *Tongmenghui*'s magazine *Min Bao* – 'People's Journal'[32] – and took him immediately to the Shanghai docks and then to Japan where he was given a hero's welcome. On 15 July 1906, around 2,000 people, mainly Chinese students, turned out in the Tokyo rain to attend a meeting in his honour.[33] Almost exactly a year later he would announce his own candidate for the future name of the country and his would be the one that stuck. Zhang filled the pages of *Minbao* with the fruit of his incarcerated thinking: making the case for the anti-Manchu revolution. In a long essay published in 1907 he addressed the question of what the country should be called once the revolution had been successful. Since the Qing were to be deposed and expelled, it was clear that it could not be called *Da Qing Guo*. Nor did Zhang support Liang's *Zhongguo*. '*Zhongguo* is meaningful only insofar as it refers to the four outlying boundaries,' he wrote, and he argued that since Indians and Japanese also used terms similar to 'central state' for their own countries, 'it is not unique to the land of the Han'.[34] (See Chapter 3 for more on the development of the term 'Han'.)

By this time, Liu Shipei had also arrived in Japan. Once there, he declared himself to be an anarchist and also contributed to the pages of *Minbao*. But he failed to persuade the movement to adopt *Da Xia* as the name for the yet-to-be-created country. Zhang argued for an ethnically based name, just like Liu, but he wanted to make a distinction between the name of the state and the name of the race that inhabited the state. Zhang felt *Xia* was the correct term for the race, based upon its origins along the Xia River. But in that 1907 article he wrote that it was 'originally the name of a tribe, not a state', which is why, disagreeing with both Liu and Huang Zunxian, he didn't want *Xia* as the name for the modern country.

Instead, Zhang Taiyan argued that *Hua* – literally meaning 'efflorescence' but carrying the connotation of 'civilised' – was a better choice. According to Julia Schneider, it had an implicitly ethnic meaning among the exiled revolutionaries during this period, since they argued that Manchus could not be part of the *Hua* population. Zhang then offered a pseudo-historical explanation for his choice: 'The name *Hua* came from the place which our people first occupied. . . . Mount Hua [*Hua Shan* in Shaanxi province] formed the boundary, giving our country the name *Hua*. . . . *Hua* was originally the name of a country and not the name of a race but today it has become a general term for both.'[35] According to Schneider, Zhang preferred *Hua* because it referred to what he regarded as the nucleus of the new state while also being sufficiently flexible. 'It could be stretched over the territory of all Chinese people, including those Zhang assumed to have been assimilated' in the northwestern provinces of Yong and Liang as well as parts of modern-day Korea and Vietnam – places where, in Zhang's words, 'the *Hua* people tilled the soil' in Han Dynasty times, 2,000 years earlier.

Zhang then added *Zhong* to the name, calling it *Zhonghua*, or 'central Hua'. This was, he declared, intended 'to distinguish between the *Hua* high culture and the *Yi* [barbarian] low culture'.[36] A final piece of the name was needed to satisfy the part of the *Tongmenghui*'s slogan about 'establish a republic' so the word *Min-Guo* was coined – literally 'people's state'. By the end of the article, the post-Qing country had a name – *Zhonghua Minguo*, literally the 'Central Efflorescence People's State'.

As Peter Zarrow has observed, Zhang, having endured prison, had enormous prestige in revolutionary circles and his arguments carried particular weight. In the wake of his 1907 article, the debate over the future name of the future country was finished, certainly within the revolutionary camp. While Liang Qichao might stick to his reformist agenda and to *Zhongguo*, the *Tongmenghui* had opted for *Zhonghua Minguo*, with its roots in the anti-Mongol, Ming Dynasty declaration of Zhu Yuanzhang 500 years earlier. Liang continued to regard Sun and the revolutionaries as Western-educated upstarts who didn't understand history or culture, but that didn't matter. They were going to seize power – and he wasn't.

Liu, meanwhile, abandoned his anarchistic pretensions, returned to his homeland and pledged allegiance to the Qing. In 1908 he began working as private secretary to the viceroy of Zhejiang and Anhui provinces where, by some accounts, he informed on his former comrades in the revolutionary movement. While Zhang Bingling/Taiyan eventually changed his views on race, deciding that non-*Xia* peoples needed to be included in the *Zhonghua Minguo*, Liu remained firm. He continued to believe that including the non-*Xia* would pollute the *Xia*. But he would play no further part in the naming debate.

These were arguments taking place among a tiny group of people living in exile in Japan, across the sea from the country they were discussing in such vehement terms. But within five years China had had a revolution and, on 1 January 1912, Sun Yat-sen was declared provisional president of the Republic of China – the *Zhonghua Minguo*. Liang Qichao's choice – *Zhongguo* – may not have become the name of the new state, but it won a better prize. It may not be the official name of the country, but it is the name all Chinese use informally to refer to it. But then again, perhaps that honour really belongs to the Jesuits.

That Friday evening in Beijing, as the assembled heads of government raised their glasses to toast Xi Jinping's version of history, they were unknowingly performing an act of circularity. They were there to validate an image of China as the natural leader of East Asia, an image which was constructed by foreigners in the first place, belatedly adopted by Chinese nationalists and now, through their presence, projected back to the world by the Communist Party leadership. The idea of Beijing as the central city of a regional order is not new. Most of those orders were, however, Inner Asian great-states that used Beijing as an administrative centre. The idea of a regional order led by a state called 'China' or *Zhongguo* or *Zhonghua* existing in a defined East Asian territory is a distinctly modern invention.

Westerners probably first heard of China through the translations of peoples living along the frontier with India, and of Cathay through their interactions with Inner Asia. 'China' became shorthand for an East Asian kingdom about which little was known. When the first traders reached the mysterious country they were bemused by its different political outlook. As Galeote Pereira and Matteo Ricci discovered, there was no conception of 'China' within the country in the mid-sixteenth century, and the phrase '*zhong guo*' was an elite assertion of political superiority over surrounding, tributary, rulers rather than the name of a state. The inhabitants assumed their state ruled 'all under heaven' – *tianxia*.

The idea of the '*zhong hua*' continues to drive China's internal policies. It encapsulates the notion of a homeland that can expand as its culture encounters new peoples, and transforms and assimilates them. As we shall see in subsequent chapters, what Arif Dirlik called 'proprietary perceptions' – a sense of ownership – still drive Beijing's policies towards minority regions under its control.[37] As a result, the former regions of the Miao, the Manchu and the Mongols are now regarded as lands of the *Hua*. On the other hand, cultural struggles continue in Tibet and Xinjiang. The troubles with Taiwan and Hong Kong can also be traced back to a sense of the 'natural' cultural boundary of the *zhong hua*.

It took until the end of the nineteenth century for the European vision of China to become implanted in the minds of the Qing political elite. A crucial role was played by those in exile – whether in Japan, the West or Southeast Asia – looking back on their homeland with sensibilities acquired outside of it. They were the ones who translated international ideas about a place called 'China' into a place called *Zhongguo*. They came to see their state as outsiders see it – as a bounded state with a defined territory. In order to do so they had to come to terms with the Western notions of nation, history, geography and, above all, sovereignty – to which we turn next.

2
THE INVENTION OF SOVEREIGNTY
zhuquan – sovereignty

Friday 18 December 2009. The leaders of most of the world's countries are gathered in Scandinavia's largest conference venue, the Bella Center, on the southern outskirts of Copenhagen. They have come to seal an international agreement on combating the world's climate crisis. The British prime minister is calling it, with some hyperbole, 'the most important conference since the Second World War', but talks are not going well. His Chinese counterpart, Wen Jiabao, is refusing to leave his hotel, claiming some diplomatic slight. Instead, he has sent a deputy foreign minister, He Yafei, to the top table to negotiate with Gordon Brown, Barack Obama, Angela Merkel, Nicolas Sarkozy, Manmohan Singh and the rest. It is a calculated insult.

Developed countries have already pledged to cut their carbon emissions by 80 per cent and to fund efforts by developing countries to reduce theirs. The USA has offered $100 billion. The EU is offering a 30 per cent cut in emissions by 2020. What are the developing countries willing to give in exchange? Negotiations have been going on for a year but even on this, the final day of the summit, they are deadlocked. Officials and deputies spent the previous ten days discussing details. The heads of government, plus Mr He, have now been talking for ten hours. An audio recording, made in the translators' booths, reveals what happened next. Barack Obama addressed He Yafei directly: 'If there is no sense of mutuality,' he warned, 'it is going to be difficult for us to ever move forward in a significant way.'

Obama knew that whatever deal he struck at Copenhagen would have to survive extreme scrutiny back home. Any treaty would have to be ratified by a two-thirds majority in the Senate, a test that the Kyoto Treaty had failed back in 1997. Why should American taxpayers' money be sent overseas to help countries that weren't prepared to make sacrifices themselves? And how could those taxpayers know that other governments were living up to their sides of the bargain? As a result, the Obama administration had belatedly decided to include a clause in the agreement to ensure that countries' climate pledges were, in the jargon, 'measurable, reportable, and verifiable'. This, however, was too much for China. He Yafei gave the leaders a lecture on the history of the Industrial Revolution, blaming the rich countries for the climate problem. An exasperated Angela Merkel pointed out that even if all the rich countries cut their emissions to zero, China would still have to make cuts in order to prevent global temperatures from rising. It got even worse. He Yafei then insisted that even the rich countries' targets be removed from the agreement. The other leaders were mystified. The only concession China would make was a vague commitment to start cutting emissions 'as soon as possible'. He Yafei then demanded a recess to consult with Wen Jiabao. The meeting never reconvened. The other leaders assumed that that had been the plan all along.

In the words of Lars-Erik Liljelund, director-general of the Swedish Environmental Protection agency, 'China doesn't like numbers'.[1] But it would be more accurate to say the Chinese government was vehemently opposed to internationally agreed numbers, together with a regime of inspection to verify those numbers. The only outcome the Chinese delegation was prepared to accept involved voluntary 'international exchanges' of information.[2] But even that compromise was blocked and all the assembled leaders could do was 'note' the document. In the words of Mark Lynas, who was in the room advising the small island states most at risk from rising sea levels, 'China wrecked the Copenhagen deal'.[3] As a result, the world's chimneys kept on belching out carbon and its ice sheets continued melting.

12 December 2015: six years later, almost to the day, and in another European capital everything is different. 195 countries, plus the European Union, have agreed what United Nations Secretary-General Ban Ki-moon calls, 'a monumental triumph for people and our planet'. What made the difference? In short, the world's climate change policies were watered down to take account of China's concerns about sovereignty. At Copenhagen, most of the world wanted

internationally agreed and legally binding targets to reduce carbon emissions. They failed to comprehend China's objections. In the years that followed, they came to understand and changed their approach.

The key to the success of the Paris conference was 'Nationally Determined Contributions'. Each country would set its own target for reducing carbon emissions, the process would be voluntary and there would be no enforcement agency to compel any government to act. China had delayed international agreement on climate change for six critical years in order to make sure that it could not be forced by an outside power to do something that it said it wanted to do anyway.[4] It was the principle of 'sovereignty' that was non-negotiable.[5]

Sovereignty is a concept that emerged in Europe in the fourteenth century and became a cornerstone of Western international law. It is far from being an indigenous Chinese idea and yet it has become the foundation of China's international relations. On 17 October 2017, Xi Jinping gave a three-and-a-half-hour speech to the quinquennial congress of the Communist Party of China (CPC). About halfway through he unveiled the fourteen new fundamental principles that 'underpin the endeavours to uphold and develop socialism with Chinese characteristics in the new era'. The thirteenth principle was declared to be 'Promoting the building of a community with a shared future for mankind'.[6] This phrase, and its alternative translation, 'common destiny for mankind', seem empty and vague to foreigners but they have a specific meaning for Xi and the CPC. They describe a future in which sovereign countries are placed at the centre of international relations, free from interventions into their internal affairs. It is, in effect, an attack on the multilateral order of international organisations, alliances and shared sovereignty that has attempted to manage the world since 1945. Beijing is chafing at some of the interventions and restrictions mandated by currently prevailing concepts of international law and seeks to redefine them. And as China becomes more influential, its vision of how the world should be reordered will become more influential, too.

The CPC's vision of this 'shared future' is a legacy of the past and the progeny of a collision between European ideas of international law and the Qing Dynasty's ideas about its place as the *zhong guo*, the centre of the world. This traumatic encounter, forced upon a declining empire at gunpoint, gave birth to a curious hybrid, China's sovereignty-fundamentalism, that Beijing sees as a template for a new world order.

The first American to be received by a Chinese ruler arrived in Beijing on 9 January 1795. He was Andreas Everardus van Braam Houckgeest and he was born Dutch as his name suggests. For fourteen years he worked for the Dutch East India Company (VOC) in Canton (Guangzhou) and Macao but in 1783 he settled in Charleston, South Carolina and became a citizen of the newly independent country. With his knowledge of rice cultivation he established a plantation but it was not a success. By 1790 he was back in Asia working for the company again.

In 1794 the Dutch learned about the failure of a high-profile British 'embassy' to the Qing court the previous year and began to plot a way to turn the situation to their own commercial advantage. The British aristocrat George Macartney had been deputed by the government in London to request 'fair and equitable' trading rights from the Qianlong Emperor and invite him to establish diplomatic relations on an equal basis. It was a costly venture. To impress the emperor, Earl Macartney took with him three ships full of modern wonders, among them a mechanical planetarium, a new imperial carriage and a hot air balloon. Much has been written about Macartney's failure. The emperor was not impressed with the earl's refusal to kowtow before him and Macartney was sent away with a message for King George III. It said that the Celestial Empire 'possesses all things in prolific abundance' and 'has no need to import the manufactures of foreigners'. The request for trading rights was not granted and the idea of equal diplomatic relations not even understood.[7]

Van Braam saw an opportunity and set about planning his own mission. He knew that 1795 was the sixtieth anniversary of Emperor Qianlong's accession to the Qing throne and he worked his Canton contacts to engineer an invitation to the ceremonies. It took his delegation forty-seven wintry days to make the 2,000-kilometre journey by cart and sedan chair to Beijing. They arrived just in time for the lunar new year celebrations.[8] Unlike the British, they hadn't packed their gifts properly and, in van Braam's account, 'Not a single article escaped undamaged'.[9] But also unlike the British, they had arrived prepared to comply with every request for imperial kowtowing. In fact they went even further: they pulled off an international fraud.

The episode has been examined by the historian Richard J. Smith. He has shown how van Braam presented the Qianlong Emperor with a superbly obsequious message from the Dutch king, '[we foreigners] have all been transformed by China's civilising influence', it oozed. 'Throughout history there has never been a monarch with such a peerless reputation as you possess, my exalted emperor.' In reply, Qianlong offered gifts with the hope that they 'strengthen your bonds of loyalty and integrity, preserving good government in your kingdom and making you forever worthy of my esteem'. The only problem with this diplomatic exchange was that the Dutch king didn't actually exist: 1795 was the time of the Dutch Republic. However, van Braam thought modern governance was unlikely to impress the emperor, so he invented a monarch who could send the necessary tribute.

The details of these early encounters between European governments and the Qing court have been much argued over but one thing is clear: the Qing rulers did not present themselves as equal members of an international community of separate, sovereign states. Their court rituals positioned them at the pinnacle of a hierarchy. Their choice of maps made this clear. As Smith notes, the Qing had put away the maps the Jesuit priests had drawn for the Ming rulers in the sixteenth and seventeenth centuries and commissioned new ones. These depicted neighbouring states and even faraway Europe and Africa as appendages sitting on the western margins of their realm. In 1795 the Qianlong Emperor could really believe that the Netherlands considered itself a tributary of his great-state.

Having fooled the emperor and his court, van Braam and his colleagues may have laughed to themselves as they made their uncomfortable journey home. From the emperor's point of view, however, that did not matter: courtly protocol had been followed. The foreigners had submitted themselves to the emperor's presence, thus confirming that Qianlong was indeed the ruler of 'all under heaven' or, in Chinese, *tianxia*. His status as the emperor of the central state, the *zhong guo*, had been reinforced by the kowtow of the visitors from abroad. The primary audience of the rituals of tribute was not foreign but domestic. They confirmed the legitimacy of the emperor, his empire, his officials and their Confucian ideology. As the Sinologist John Fairbank once wrote, 'The ruler of China claimed the mandate of Heaven to rule all mankind. If the rest of mankind did not acknowledge his rule, how long could he expect China to do so?'[10] *Tianxia* had no formal boundaries: it was potentially universal. The only difference under *tianxia* was between cultured *hua*, those who accepted the emperor's wise rule, and those who didn't – the barbarian *yi*. In the Sinitic world, *yi* could elevate themselves to become *hua* if they accepted the rules of defined 'Confucian' culture and order.[11]

There was little economic benefit for the Qing Great-State in the rituals of tribute. The court hosted the delegations, some of which could be large, for several weeks and then showered them with gifts. Delegations would bring relatively small amounts of tributary goods for consumption by the elite: usually rare commodities such as ivory, sandalwood and gems. In exchange they would receive much larger quantities of commercial goods which they could sell back home. The whole process was expensive and burdensome and yet the court found it worthwhile, in fact necessary. The benefits were both symbolic and political. For the 'tributaries' the benefits were more direct and pecuniary. In addition to the valuable gifts delegates received from the court, traders might accompany the embassy to sell their domestic goods and produce along the way. But tributaries also received an intangible reward. Just as their acknowledgement of the emperor of *zhong guo* affirmed him in his role, so his recognition of them confirmed their political position as well.

By contrast, Western elites perceived no benefit from this form of relationship. The emperor's recognition of their tributary status meant nothing. Rather, it was perceived as a threat, as an attempt to impose subordinate status upon proudly independent states, some of whom had recently fought wars to be free of foreign domination back home. The consequences of those wars were still rippling around the globe and would ultimately destroy the emperor's unworldly delusions of *tianxia*.

In 1808 Napoleon's France invaded Spain, deposed the king and took the Spanish crown prince captive. Within months, Spain's colonies in the Americas were ablaze. Groups of nobles and military officers took over cities and declared independence in Venezuela, Colombia and Mexico. Fighting continued for a decade until, by 1825, all the continental colonies had thrown off Spanish rule. Among the many casualties of the fighting was the integrity of the Spanish

American currency, the peso. Before the independence wars, the peso had an unsurpassed reputation for quality: it was known to be 90 per cent pure silver and highly prized around the world.

Chinese traders loved it, particularly the coins marked with the 'foreign face' of King Charles III or his son Charles IV. The bookkeepers of the English East India Company noted in the 1790s that Chinese merchants were prepared to pay more for the 'Carolus' coins than for actual silver bullion by almost 9 per cent. It was portable, recognisable and there was no need to check the quality of the metal: the Carolus was trusted. Other coins were available, including French and Dutch ones, but they traded at an average 15 per cent discount to the Carolus. Spanish cash was king. North American traders made good profits selling silver coin to China: 2,247 tons of it were shipped across the Pacific between 1808 and 1833.

However, as the economic historian Alejandra Irigoin has shown, the wars for Spanish American independence severely damaged the reputation of the peso. To fund their fighting, the opposing elites adulterated their coinage. Worse, the Latin revolutionaries minted coins without featuring the Spanish king's head. The size and quality of these pesos varied widely, depending on where they were made. This wasn't just a problem for Spain and Spanish America. It had a major impact in China too.

The value of the peso began to wobble. By the 1820s the old 'Carolus' marked with the king's head was worth up to 30 per cent more than its equivalent weight in silver bullion. However, the price of the post-revolutionary coins went in the opposite direction: Chinese traders valued them at as much as 15 per cent less than bullion.[12] Trust in the money weakened, making it harder for traders to do deals, lend or borrow. Merchants hoarded the older coins and boycotted the new ones. Demand for new silver coins from the Americas collapsed. By 1828 imports were just 15 per cent of what they had been only a couple of years before. And as supplies of reliable pesos fell, the price of silver bullion in China rose. Wars thousands of miles away in Europe and Latin America were having a major impact on the economy in China.

At this time, the Qing court demanded payment of taxes in silver bullion, not in coins. It minted copper coins and set an official exchange rate between them and its own standard measurement of silver: officially, 1,000 copper coins bought one *kuping tael* of silver. However, as the supply of Carolus coins dried up in the late 1820s, the price of a *kuping tael* of silver climbed towards 1,400 copper coins. Peasants who were paid in copper found it increasingly difficult to afford silver and fell behind with their taxes. Government income fell accordingly. Since there was no longer a standard silver coin for long-distance trade, the costs of doing business also jumped and lending became more difficult. Demand fell and unemployment rose. As the price of silver increased, so the prices of commodities measured in silver fell: a classic case of deflation.

This shock compounded existing economic difficulties. The population of the Qing realm had doubled (at least) over the previous century while the area of land under cultivation had risen only by half. Although new crops, such as maize, peanuts and sweet potatoes, had been introduced from the Spanish Americas, the great-state began to experience food shortages. Over-intensive use of the land caused declines in soil fertility, increased erosion and downstream flooding. Food became more expensive, work became scarce, and corruption and mismanagement made things worse. Serious rebellions broke out in several provinces. The apparent stability at the court of the Qianlong Emperor masked increasing instability outside it. The emperor may have had 'no need to import the manufactures of foreigners' but millions of peasants were already going hungry. The problems were made worse by the consequences of those foreign manufactures, which were reducing global demand for Chinese exports of silk and cotton. In short, by the time that Qianlong's grandson, the Daoguang Emperor, took the throne in 1820, the great-state was facing an economic crisis.

There was another problem, too. Foreign traders had previously made fine profits from the silver trade. Because Chinese traders preferred silver pesos while people outside China preferred silver bullion, there was money to be made in arbitrage: exchanging one for the other. This worked well, argues Irigoin, until the supply of reliable coins dried up in 1828. It was only then that the arbitragers turned to a different commodity. In 1828, 18,000 chests of opium were exported to China, but by 1839 that had more than doubled to 40,000 chests.[13] 'Fast crab' boats with both sails and oars for speedily navigating shallow coastal waters transferred the illicit cargo to customers onshore and to cities far inland. Opium had been a part of elite life, from the emperor down, for many years but large-scale importation during the 1830s came to be seen as a threat to society.

In 1839 troubles with the government budget forced Daoguang to issue an ostensibly modest decree that, in retrospect, was an early nail in the coffin of *tianxia*. Tribute missions had become too expensive: regular traders were taking advantage of them to make profits at the expense of the Qing court. The states of Annam (modern-day Vietnam), Siam (modern-day Thailand) and the Ryukyu islands (now the southern part of Japan) would henceforth only be allowed to send tribute to the court every four years instead of annually or bi-annually.[14] According to the Japanese historian Takeshi Hamashita, this had two purposes: to save money by reducing the amount of 'tribute goods' given to the visiting delegations and to increase tax revenue by turning tribute into trade. Merchants would have to pay more taxes, and that revenue would have to be remitted to the central government rather than creamed off by officials in the ports. Economic necessity had weakened the bonds that held the regional hierarchy together.

This was an unusual moment of clear-sightedness by the imperial court: a recognition of reality. Chinese, Southeast Asian and European merchants were already making large profits by ignoring the tribute formalities and dealing directly with local officials and traders. Perhaps the most famous were William Jardine and James Matheson, 'country traders' outside the control of any government, who used floating warehouses to smuggle millions of pounds worth of contraband, including opium, into China to meet the demands that official channels were not satisfying.

In 1834 the British government had ended the (English) East India Company's monopoly on trade with China, allowing the country traders a freer hand. Daoguang's move was intended to bring them and their co-conspirators around the coast back under Beijing's control. The problem for the Qing court was that there were plenty of people in the coastal provinces who were more interested in their own prosperity than the court's tax receipts, and resisted. The battle between the centre and the coast resulted in what the American Sinologist James Polachek has called an oscillation 'from harsh, xenophobic rigidity to a collaborationist opportunism and back'.[15] This struggle oscillated throughout subsequent decades even as the international order shifted ever more against Beijing's interests. Resistance led to 'opium war' in 1840, defeat led to conciliation, further resistance led to another 'opium war' in 1860 and defeat led to further conciliation and so on. By the end of the century, the Qing court would have been forced to formally recognise its diminished position: it would no longer be the 'central state', the *zhong guo*. The emperor would no longer rule 'all under heaven' – *tianxia* – but simply one sovereign state among many.

In 1844 a twenty-one-year-old student from Hefei, a city in the prosperous Yangtze valley, joined an examination school run by his father's old classmate. It was typical of the privileged upbringing that Li Hongzhang had already enjoyed. His father was senior secretary of the Board of Punishments, a government official, and Li had enjoyed a reasonably comfortable upbringing. The family's privilege was obvious from its choice of teacher for Li. He was Zeng Guofan, a rising star in the Qing administration. Zeng had passed the *jinshi*, the highest-level imperial examination, at the strikingly young age of twenty-seven and then been assigned as one of the thirty-three secretaries for the Council of State: the emperor's closest advisers. As a secretary, Zeng helped to draft the imperial decrees and other documents that directed the great-state. A successful stint as a secretary generally opened the doors to higher office. However, before they could advance up the hierarchy, former secretaries usually had to spend time overseeing candidates for the provincial examinations – which is how Zeng came to be Li's teacher.

It was a wise choice by Li's family. Just three years later, Li came third in the *jinshi* exam, at the even younger age of twenty-four, and was admitted to the Hanlin Academy, an honour reserved for the brightest candidates. The Academy was a secretariat for the imperial court but also the keeper of the official Confucian ideology of the Sinitic part of the great-state. Its scholars were expected to provide interpretations of old texts to guide the emperor and the court in their deliberations. Success in the *jinshi* required a deep knowledge of the classics but little else. Those texts were thought sufficient to guide an official in his work and an emperor in his rule. There was no place for innovation and no appetite for new knowledge: only those who had laboured through the system of examinations had the right to interpret the old texts and offer advice. These 'scholar-officials' formed the core of the Qing state and saw themselves as guardians of a morally superior belief system. Their position in society depended upon their monopoly over this knowledge and they strove to maintain it. They were suspicious of change, hostile to foreigners and profoundly uninterested in the outside world.

Li Hongzhang was of similar outlook but was different in one key attribute. He was ambitious in a very un-Confucian way. At six feet four inches tall, he towered over his colleagues and made an impression on everyone he met. He would go on to a remarkable career. Two years after he died, one of his Western admirers would declare that, 'Writing the biography of Li Hung-chang [Li Hongzhang] is writing the history of the nineteenth century in China.' The author, Alicia Little, a social campaigner and missionary's wife, declared him to be 'the one man in China with whom foreign envoys found it possible to engage in reasonable discussion', but she also noted that 'many of his contemporaries . . . saw in him only the destroyer of his country's honour'.[16] It was Li's role as an intermediary between the highest levels of the Qing court and the wider world that would make him the key figure in the transition from the world of *tianxia* to the world of sovereignty. And key to this transition was Li's relationships with several leading Americans, including a former president and an ex-secretary of state.

Li began his studies under Zeng just a few years after the Qing realm's first bloody encounter with British naval firepower. Defeat in the 'First Opium War' had led to the signing of the Treaty of Nanjing in August 1842. The Qing agreed to open four more ports for British trade in addition to Guangzhou (Canton). They were also forced to cede the island of Hong Kong to Britain in perpetuity and to pay 21 million 'dollars' (actually Carolus pesos) in compensation for opium destroyed by the Guangzhou authorities and the costs of the fighting. (The British, of course, provided no compensation for the approximately 20,000 people killed during the war or the thousands of others wounded or brutalised.) Most importantly for China's future relations with the world, the Qing agreed that trade would be 'free' – on commercial lines rather than as tribute; that British officials would have the right to reside in the treaty ports and communicate directly with local officials; and that British citizens would not be subject to what they regarded as the Qing's barbarous laws. Later that year, in its first act of 'jackal diplomacy', the United States demanded for free the same rights that the British had just fought for. After initial refusal, in 1843 the emperor granted that the concessions would apply to all foreigners equally.[17] Neither Zeng nor Li played any role in the First Opium War but its legacy would define the rest of their lives. New, foreign ideas would provoke sedition at home and secession abroad. Repeated crises would force Qing officials to turn to foreigners for help. Zeng would rise to hero status and Li would rise on his coat-tails, only to be denounced in his dotage as a traitor.

In early 1851 a far more serious threat to Qing rule than the Royal Navy appeared in southwestern China, prompted by the worsening economic situation and increasing food shortages. A rebel group espousing a mixture of Christian theology, socialistic utopianism and hatred of the ethnic-Manchu elite declared itself to be the 'Heavenly Kingdom of Great Peace', the *Taiping Tianguo* – better known as the Taipings. By March 1853 the Taipings had captured the city of Nanjing just down the Yangtze valley from Li's home in Hefei: its 40,000 Manchu inhabitants were massacred. Nanjing became the Taipings' capital for the next eleven years. In January 1854 they captured Hefei itself.[18] Zeng Guofan's brother was killed in an unsuccessful attempt to recapture the city in 1858. By 1860 all or part of five provinces along the Yangtze and its tributaries were under Taiping control.

At the same time as fighting for its life against the Taipings, the Qing court was also being pressed by the British and French governments, with the tacit support of the United States, to grant more concessions to free trade. Violations of the Treaty of Nanjing led to renewed confrontations and the shelling of the port cities of Guangzhou and then Tianjin, the gateway to Beijing. In June 1858, under pressure from Western weapons, officials in Tianjin signed new treaties with their attackers granting them access to more ports, the right to navigate along the Yangtze River and the right to travel, trade and to preach Christianity throughout the country. Just as significantly, the treaties also allowed foreign governments to establish legations in Beijing. The foreigners wanted to be treated as sovereign equals, not tributaries.

Critically, however, the officials in Tianjin did not regard the treaties as solemn and permanent commitments. One of the signatories, an ethnic Manchu known as Guiliang, wrote a memorial to the emperor in which he stated, baldly, 'The treaties of peace with Britain and France cannot be taken as real. These few sheets of paper are simply a means to get troops and warships to leave the coast.'[19] That clearly was not how the British and French saw them. Two years later, the treaties had still not been ratified by the Qing court so, in 1860, an Anglo-French expeditionary force set sail from Hong Kong to compel it to do so. It would be the final act of the 'Second Opium War'.

The invaders pushed past the Qing defences on the Hai River and sailed on towards Beijing. They blocked rice shipments to the capital and appeared ready to sack the city. The Xianfeng Emperor (the son of Daoguang, who had died in 1850) fled Beijing, leaving his half-brother Yixin to deal with the British and French. Faced with the twin threat of Taipings and Europeans, the Qing agreed to a deal offered by a Russian envoy, Nikolay Pavlovich Ignatiev. He promised to mediate with the British and French, provided the Qing agreed to Russia's demands. In fact, Ignatiev had no leverage with London or Paris at all, but the Qing signed away the rights to 130,000 square miles of the most fertile part of Siberia regardless.[20] Just as significantly for the great-state's future foreign relations, on 24 October 1860 Yixin signed the Convention of Beijing with the British and the following day a similar document with the French.

Under the Convention, the Qing conceded to Britain approximately twenty square miles of territory on Kowloon Peninsula, opposite Hong Kong island. It also opened the port of Tianjin to foreign trade. More importantly the court conceded the right of foreigners to permanent diplomatic residence in Beijing: they would no longer need to endure lengthy journeys by cart from Guangzhou to Beijing. The Europeans did not see themselves as representatives of tributary states but as equals in an international system, but the Qing could still neither understand nor accept this arrangement. Their outlook was still that of *tianxia*, with the emperor standing as the rightful ruler of 'all under heaven'. The struggle between these two world-views would define the final half-century of Qing rule and Li Hongzhang would be the key player in the story.

The street rings with misery. A middle-aged woman sits on the kerb, howling. Her cries cut through the bustle of modern Beijing, but no one comes to her aid. There are plenty of people around who could help but none who wish to. A little further along the alley, a young woman sits on a camping stool holding up a long text on a large piece of paper for all to see. She is surrounded by tough-looking men, all haranguing her and jabbing their fingers in condemnation. Her sole defender is a peasant woman in a wheelchair, shouting back at the toughs. It is hard to tell if they are gangsters or plain-clothes security. Perhaps they are both.

The cause of all this woe lies further down Dongtangzi Hutong: a low building almost hidden behind a tall grey wall. An old tiled roof is all that can be seen from the street. Number 49 is the official complaints office for China's Ministry of Public Security. This is where contemporary Chinese citizens come to seek redress for abuses committed by the police. The chances of success must be minimal and yet there is a small queue outside the office on this September afternoon, lining up beneath a stone plaque set into the wall, the text of which reveals the history of this palace of unhappiness.

It seems hard to believe now but this building was once the focus of international life in Beijing. In the second half of the nineteenth century it was home to the *Zongli Yamen*, the very first 'foreign ministry' created to manage relations with the barbarians who came from the sea. These days it is dwarfed by its surroundings: overshadowed by the 'Legendale Hotel', built in the style of a fascist's birthday cake, and a Qing-era-styled shopping mall called Jinbao Place. Around the corner is another faux-Qing palace: the Beijing clubhouse of the Hong Kong Jockey Club. While the nouveau riche are ferried to and from these palaces of luxury, a tableau of grief plays out in the alleyway behind. History does not repeat itself but it surely rhymes.

The *Zongli Yamen* was established on 13 January 1861, an act forced upon the Qing court as a consequence of the Second Opium War.[21] The European powers had demanded payment of 8 million *taels* of silver to be paid in installments from the customs revenue at the treaty ports.[22] (The British and French had no qualms about demanding that the Qing pay for the invasion of their own country.) The three court officials who had negotiated and signed the Convention of Beijing suggested the emperor establish a new arm of the court to oversee its implementation. They did not see it as a permanent arrangement, however. In their memorial to the court, they wrote, 'As soon as the military campaigns [against the Taipings and other rebels] and the affairs of the various countries are simplified, the new office will be abolished and its functions will again revert to the Grand Council for management so as to accord with the old system.'

All three officials were senior Manchus: Yixin, who is better known by his Chinese name Gong; Hada Guwalgiya (known in Chinese as Guiliang) – Yixin's ageing father-in-law and the official who had been so dismissive of the Treaty of Tianjin in 1858; and Suwan Guwalgiya (known in Chinese as Wenxiang).[23] Yixin/Gong called for the new body to be named the 'office to manage affairs of the various countries' but he faced continuing resistance from conservative scholar-officials in the court who refused to acknowledge the new reality. They wanted to downgrade the importance of the new body and decreed it should be called the 'office to manage the *commercial* affairs of the various countries' – in effect denying its diplomatic role. Prince Gong lobbied to get this changed but only half-succeeded. As a result the office became generally known by the bland-sounding title of the 'Office of General Management', or, in Chinese, the *Zongli Yamen*. The mismatch of expectations was clear, since the British diplomats who had contact with the Yamen immediately referred to it as the 'Foreign Office'. The Qing were determined to make them feel subordinate by adding injury to insult. The office was located in a backstreet far from the imperial court – in the former office of the 'Department of Iron Coinage' in the Dongtangzi Hutong. The Yamen's first foreign visitors would describe it as 'small and inconvenient' and 'dirty, cheerless and barren'.[24] Modern visitors to the woe-filled site might still agree.

Gong, Wenxiang and Guiliang hoped to contain the European threat by making the *Zongli Yamen* the only channel through which foreign governments could communicate with the court. However, it wasn't just diplomatic requests that were channelled through the *Zongli Yamen*. The office also became a portal through which the late Qing elite encountered the wider world. In one of its earliest acts, the *Zongli Yamen* opened the college for translators, the *Tongwen Guan*, in 1862. The college hired foreign teachers and then began to translate books and ideas into Chinese. Among them were treatises on what Westerners called 'international law'. The concept was utterly alien to the three Manchus who had encountered it at the wrong end of Anglo-French canons in 1860, but they swiftly realised its importance to their attackers. They wished to know more about it.

When the Xianfeng Emperor died in August 1861, Prince Gong helped organise a coup that, in effect, handed power to Xianfeng's consort, the Empress Cixi. Her son, then just five years old, officially became the Tongzhi Emperor but there was no doubt who was really in charge. Cixi ruled from behind the scenes, as she would for the next half-century. Gong's success put his reforming clique in a powerful position at court but the conservatives had strength in depth. There were armies of scholar-officials in positions of authority across the country, all dependent on their continuing monopoly over classical teaching for their income and influence.

While all this was going on in Beijing, a far bloodier struggle was reaching its denouement around Shanghai. No one has been able to count the number of people who died as a result of the Taiping civil war but the best guesses are at least 20 million – something like a thousand times more than died in the Opium Wars. Unable to provide sufficient military support themselves, the Qing court in Beijing had authorised provincial leaders like Zeng Guofan to create their own armies to fight the rebels. Zeng and his colleagues used their official positions and unofficial networks to gather the money to raise and equip military units. These new provincial armies did win some victories but they failed to stop the Taipings. As the rebels advanced towards the treaty port of Shanghai, the city's panicked elite turned to foreigners for help. In addition to the 3,000 British, Indian and French troops already garrisoned in the city under the treaty port system, they recruited a further 3,000 Chinese under the command of foreign mercenaries to form what became known as the 'Ever Victorious Army'. Then, in late 1861, Zeng ordered Li Hongzhang to recruit a new army from his home province of Anhwei (now known as Anhui) and head to Shanghai.[25]

In April 1862 Li's world changed. He and his 'Anhwei Army' boarded a small flotilla of British steamships hired by the merchants of Shanghai and headed to the city. There he encountered Western modernisation for the first time. Li watched European weaponry and military discipline shatter the rebels. We know from his diaries and letters that he almost immediately resolved to bring the same kind of strength to his own society. But he was still a 'scholar-official' at heart: he was not interested in becoming 'Western'. On 23 April 1862 he wrote to tell Zeng that he would keep his troops separate from the Europeans and 'strive for self-strengthening and not mix with foreigners'.

Li had probably learned the phrase 'self-strengthening' from Zeng himself. The previous year Zeng had been lobbied by a reform-minded scholar-official turned military commander called Feng Guifen. Feng was distressed by his country's humiliation at the hands of foreigners and wrote a collection of essays, in which he argued, 'We have only one thing to learn from the barbarians: solid ships and effective guns.'[26] These were the ideas that would guide what became known as the 'self-strengthening movement' pioneered by Feng, Zeng and Li – learning the foreigners' techniques while remaining aloof from their ideas.

Two days after writing that letter to Zeng, Li was made acting governor of Jiangsu province, which included Shanghai. By August of 1862 he had become alarmed by the discovery that Chinese merchants in the treaty port area of the city preferred being ruled by foreigners than by their own government. In a letter to another leading self-strengthener, Zuo Zongtang (better known as General Tso, of chicken fame), he wrote, 'The hearts of the officials and the people have long since gone over to the foreigners'.[27] Li's resentment of the foreigners' power, and his desire to master the tools of that power, only grew during the two further years it took to crush the Taipings.

In March 1863 Li was appointed as acting trade commissioner for the southern ports. This was a job that the imperial court had created at the same time as *Zongli Yamen*, and its function was similar: to manage the foreigners. The two trade commissioners, one for the southern treaty ports and the other for the northern, were expected to be the court's 'barbarian handlers', policing the privileges grudgingly conceded under force of Western weaponry. Li became convinced that, despite their claims to be only interested in commerce, the foreigners were determined to grab more territory. Later that year he warned a friend, 'the long-range trouble is the Western people. Great as *Huaxia* is, she has been so weakened and has come to this pass.'[28]

But Li was also frustrated by the attitudes of his peers. In spring 1864 he wrote directly to the *Zongli Yamen*, complaining that his fellow scholar-officials were 'immersed in the time-honoured practice of essay-writing and of doing calligraphy in small and regular characters' rather than addressing the real issues of the day. The court needed to take the lead in ordering them to study new technology. Following the ideas of Feng Guifen, he told them the priority was to 'learn the Westerners' methods without having always to use their men'. Prince Gong was sympathetic and passed the letter to the throne but no action was taken.

A few months later, on 19 July 1864, the Taipings' rebel capital, Nanjing, finally fell to Zeng's provincial army. It was an extraordinarily brutal fight. Zeng's poorly paid army was let off the leash. As many as 100,000 people may have been killed, most of them after the surrender. Children and the elderly were slaughtered, women taken as booty, the city looted and whole districts razed to the ground.[29] In Zeng's world-view, there need be little sympathy for those who had up-ended centuries of correct Confucian behaviour.

With the Taiping threat gone, the central government could at last turn to the problem of rehabilitating a shattered society and addressing the challenge posed by the Westerners. The three decades, from 1864 until the war with Japan in 1894, would be the era of self-strengthening. A modernising elite, comprising people like Zeng, Li, Feng and their supporters in the capital, would work with the foreigners to create machine shops, a modern navy and a professional military into which much hope and prestige was invested. All of it would be dashed.

The self-strengtheners had seized the initiative after the Second Opium War, the 1861 coup and their success against the Taipings but in Beijing they faced entrenched opposition. The formation of the *Zongli Yamen* and its college, the *Tongwen Guan*, had been grudgingly approved but the institutions were barely functioning. The college was intended to teach a generation of interpreters who could interact with the British and French. Its Qing sponsors had originally wanted to keep the Westerners at arm's length but, after a few months, came to the conclusion that, 'since there are no Chinese possessing a thorough knowledge of foreign languages . . . we could not avoid seeking suitable persons among foreigners'.[30] (It's worth noting that 'foreign' here means 'European', since the Qing did have translators for the various languages spoken within their great-state.)

The first two language teachers hired by the college were British missionaries who were more interested in setting up a mission school to preach Christianity in Beijing than in training official interpreters. Both had learned Chinese in other parts of the country, neither spoke the Mandarin dialect and both resigned after a year. The quality of the students made things worse. By and large they were the least promising candidates, since the more ambitious ones wanted to concentrate on learning the traditional classics in order to advance through the Qing bureaucracy.[31]

Things began to change when the new inspector-general of the Imperial Chinese Maritime Customs Service, Robert Hart, began to take an interest.

He was in charge of the organisation that delivered the money from import tariffs to the *Zongli Yamen* – in part to pay the British and French 'compensation' for the recent war, in part to pay for the court's expenses. Although it was part of the Qing bureaucracy, the Customs Service was actually managed by foreigners – Britons, Frenchmen, Americans and Prussians – and produced considerable income. Hart, therefore, had a budget as well as an incentive to improve the quality of the officials he was dealing with. His personal manner seems to have been extraordinarily well suited to the job and the Northern Irishman built an easy rapport with his counterparts in the *Zongli Yamen*.

Early on, Hart had decided that Qing officials needed to know more about Western international law. According to his diary, on 15 July 1863 he began to translate the first English-language treatise on the subject: 'Elements of International Law' by the American lawyer and diplomat Henry Wheaton. At the end of that month he presented a few sections to the *Zongli Yamen*. They concerned the rights of diplomatic legations in foreign capitals – perhaps the most pressing issue of the moment for the Western powers. The historian Richard J. Smith has examined Hart's diaries and discovered that throughout the summer of 1863 he continued to translate sections of Wheaton and hand them over to the *Yamen*.[32] At this time, Prince Gong, by his own account, was under the impression that the foreigners might want to keep their precious text secret. Hart, however, was extremely keen to share it.

He wasn't the only one. That year France had begun to force its way into what Beijing regarded as one of its tributary states: Annam (modern-day Vietnam). On 14 April 1863 French forces coerced the Vietnamese emperor into signing the first Treaty of Hue, which ceded part of his country to France. This prompted an enquiry from the *Zongli Yamen* to Anson Burlingame, the American minister in Beijing, about a guide to this kind of treaty. According to the American linguistic historian Lydia Liu, Burlingame recommended Wheaton. He discovered that an American missionary, William A. P. Martin, had also been working on a translation with the assistance of four Chinese Christians.[33] Martin was already well known to American diplomats: he had been the translator for the US delegation at the negotiations for the Treaty of Tianjin in 1858. In fact, Martin's copy of Wheaton's book had been given to him by the American delegate there: William B. Reed. By his own account, Martin saw the translation of international law as an extension of his missionary vocation, 'a work that might bring this atheistic government to the recognition of God and his eternal justice', as he later put it.[34]

Martin faced more than the usual difficulties of linguistic translation. He was, in effect, trying to make one world-view intelligible to people from an entirely different one. He had to create new words to bridge the gap. 'These words and expressions may seem odd and unwieldy,' he wrote in the preface to a later book, '. . . [but] you will come to realize that the translators have really made the best of necessity.'[35] It was Martin who introduced the idea of 'sovereignty' to Qing officials but he had to do so by repurposing an old word with a different meaning. Through Martin's translation, the Chinese word for 'sovereignty' became *zhuquan*. The word does have ancient roots – it appears in a seventh-century BCE text, the *Guanzi* – but it had a different meaning there. As William Callahan has noted, back then *zhu* did not mean state but 'ruler', 'master' or even 'owner'. Martin chose the character *quan* to mean 'rights' but historically it meant 'power', with the implication that this power might be arbitrary or opportunistic. The literal meaning of *zhuquan*, therefore, can be both 'the legitimate power of the state' and also 'the arbitrary power of the ruler'. In the *Guanzi*, the word was used in the context of a warning: 'If you exercise too much *zhuquan*, you will fail.'[36] This manufactured equivalence between the Western concepts of 'sovereignty' and the different meanings embodied in the Chinese *zhuquan* helps to explain some of China's contemporary 'sovereignty fundamentalism'. If modern Chinese use the term with the implicit meaning of 'the authority of the ruler', then sovereignty can only be absolute, not relative. What ruler would want their authority diminished? From that difference emerges a different framework of international relations: the 'community of common destiny'.

In October 1863, after months of wrangling with the difficulties of translating one world-view into another, Martin finally went to present the finished result to the 'small and inconvenient' office of the *Zongli Yamen* in Dongtangzi Hutong. Martin was a friend of Hart and it was an easy matter to effect an introduction at the *Yamen*. There they handed over four volumes of translated Wheaton to Gong, Wenxiang and their colleagues.

Gong was certainly interested in Wheaton's work but conservatives in the court were not. The translation might never have been published at all were it not for the Schleswig-Holstein Question. In the spring of 1864 the conflict between Denmark and Prussia over the ownership of those two northern European provinces spread to the port of Tianjin. The new Prussian ambassador arrived there on a warship and promptly took captive three Danish merchant ships. Gong used his newly acquired knowledge of Wheaton's text to argue that such an act inside another country's territorial waters was illegal. He was impressed to see the Prussians acknowledge this, release the ships and even pay compensation to the Danes.[37] In the aftermath of that incident, on 30 August 1864, Gong wrote a memorial to the court, arguing that it showed the utility of this mysterious book and made the point that it contained 'laws which can, to a considerable extent, control the foreign consuls and this is certainly a useful thing'.

But even though Gong was interested in using Wheaton's book as a tool to manage the foreigners, he saw no reason why it should govern his own court's behaviour. In a letter, he assured the emperor that Wheaton's arguments would have no effect on the great-state. 'Your ministers forestalled [Martin's] attempt to get us to follow the book by telling him at once that China has her own laws and institutions and that it is inconvenient to follow foreign books,' he explained. Gong then concluded his note by informing the court that he had approved a budget of 500 silver *taels* to edit and publish Martin's work.[38] Martin had asked Gong to provide a preface to the translation but he declined. It would seem that Gong did not wish to be so publicly associated with foreign ideas. The *Zongli Yamen* didn't even publish the book. As the Swedish Sinologist Rune Svarverud has noted, that was done, in 1864, through a publishing house attached to a missionary school established in Beijing by Martin himself.[39]

The following year, Martin was appointed as an English teacher at the *Tongwen Guan* and in 1867 he was made professor of international law there. It was from this period onwards that the college became an engine of intellectual transformation among receptive sections of the Qing elite. They were, however, very much in the minority. There was determined resistance to Gong's efforts, and those of the other self-strengtheners, from within the ranks of the scholar-officials.

The chief conservative was the eminent figure of Wo Ren (sometimes written Wojen). Wo Ren was an ethnic Mongol who had risen through the examination system to simultaneously hold some of the most important offices of the great-state. Wo had cultivated a public image as an upright and abstemious man who urged strict conformity with the Confucian classics. One satirical story has him forming a 'Bran Eating Society' to avoid the pleasures of white flour. But high offices also brought high rewards and there were rumours that Wo Ren was a hypocrite who secretly enjoyed fine foods and even the smoking of opium. He was kept at arm's length by the Xianfeng Emperor – who even posted Wo to faraway Turkestan for a time. However, after the emperor's death in 1861 and Cixi's subsequent coup he rapidly acquired high positions. By 1866 he was not only a grand secretary, supervising the Board of Revenue, but also president of the Censorate, president of the Board of Works, chancellor of the Hanlin Academy and tutor to the child emperor.[40]

The clash between Gong and Wo Ren crystallised in March 1867 over whether junior officials and scholars at the Hanlin Academy should be encouraged to study the new subjects of mathematics and astronomy at the *Tongwen Guan*. Wo was opposed on the grounds that 'the basic need of the state is people's morals not technical skill'.[41] He also argued that the college should not be employing foreigners: Confucian integrity must remain supreme. The throne dismissed Wo's arguments and to drive home their displeasure, appointed Wo to the board of the *Zongli Yamen* so that he could learn more about foreign affairs. He begged to be excused, saying he was by nature a conservative and unprepared for the role. He claimed ill health and then, on the day he was due to take up his post, apparently fell from his horse, injuring his foot. Wo then resigned all of his official posts except tutor to the young emperor and disappeared from public life.

Nonetheless, Wo's sacrifice resulted in a significant victory for the 'neo-Confucianists'. As the Hong Kong-born historian David Pong has observed, Empress Cixi may have supported Gong against Wo and the *Zongli Yamen* against its conservative critics but she was not prepared to challenge the scholar-officials directly. The idea of requiring officials to study at the *Tongwen Guan* died a quiet death. The *Zongli Yamen* would later report that, 'ever since Wo Ren raised his objection, the scholar-officials have been gathering in groups and conspiring to obstruct [the *Tongwen Guan*]. . . . As a result no one came to the *Yamen* to take the entrance exam.' The court had made a choice in favour of Confucian orthodoxy and against learning about the wider world. Although these arguments had revolved around the study of 'Western affairs' – *yang wu* – they were also implicit rejections of any moves towards changing the underlying world-view of the court. The foreigners may have forced their way into the Qing realm and extracted concessions about trade but their way of looking at the world was still to be kept at arm's length: managed through the *Zongli Yamen*.

This is confirmed by the court's own correspondence. The treaties signed at Tianjin in 1858 contained clauses allowing either side to demand a revision after ten years. As that date approached in late 1867, Yixin/Gong authored an imperial edict to the most senior provincial officials in the country who had some experience of dealing with foreigners. He wanted their advice: what did they expect the foreigners to demand and how should the court respond? Seventeen officials replied, including Li Hongzhang, Zeng Guofan and Zuo Zongtang. This secret exchange tells us a great deal about the court's view of the world. What is most remarkable is how poorly these officials understood the changes taking place around them. The essential basis of the imperial world-view remained the same: the Qing state was *zhong guo*, centre-of-the-world, and remained culturally and morally superior to the barbarians. In the acid judgement of the American historian of China, Knight Biggerstaff, 'One is struck by their ignorance and blindness'. Only Li, Zeng and Zuo 'demonstrated any real understanding of the grave problems which their country faced in dealing with these aggressive Western powers'.[42] But how could they? In the words of the Canadian historian John Cranmer-Byng, 'China was being forced by circumstances and her own weakness into an international system in which the Chinese did not believe because, in their view, this system had no moral justification.'[43]

As it turned out, the aggressive Westerners did not demand any revisions of the 1858 treaties. In general, the 1860s were a period of cooperation between the Western powers and the Qing. The Europeans and Americans were enjoying their forcibly acquired trading rights and the self-strengtheners were trying to rebuild the great-state's war-shattered defences with the foreigners' technology. The treaty ports were little bridgeheads of modernity, but the 'neo-Confucianists' were holding the line everywhere else. The two world-views existed side by side.

The presence of foreign banks in the treaty ports (combined with the return of political stability in Latin America) had another impact. From about 1853 reliable Mexican silver coins began to flow into the Qing economy once again. The economic problems of converting between copper coins and silver began to ease. At the same time, people unearthed savings of silver that they had hoarded and buried during the Taiping Rebellion. As the peso supply resumed, the economy recovered. And as silver became more available, Western merchants moved away from trading opium. Instead, home-grown supplies of the drug rocketed. By the end of the 1860s more opium was grown domestically than imported.[44]

The years of grudging co-existence did not last beyond the decade. On 21 June 1870 rumours about Catholic orphanages kidnapping children, combined with the hasty overreaction of a French consul, resulted in the Tianjin Massacre in which around sixty Christians, both Chinese and foreign, were killed. The Europeans demanded recompense. As French warships approached the city, the court gave Li Hongzhang the job of managing the crisis. He was appointed governor-general of Zhili, the province that included Tianjin. Some alleged rioters were executed, a mission of apology was despatched to France and the hysteria abated. Within three months of taking on the Zhili role, Li was also made superintendent of the Northern Ports and promoted to 'imperial commissioner', or *qinchai*.[45]

This made Li one of the most powerful officials in the country. As well as Tianjin, Zhili included all the land surrounding Beijing, and as superintendent of the Northern Ports, Li was responsible for all dealings with foreigners in the treaty ports north of Shanghai. For the following quarter-century, if you were a Westerner and wanted to get to Beijing, whether geographically or politically, you had to go through Li's territory. And one Westerner who did get through would have a profound effect on both Li and, through Li, on China's relations with the wider world.

William N. Pethick had fought in the final stages of the American Civil War. At the same time as the Taipings were being vanquished in Nanjing in 1864, he joined the 25th New York Cavalry as a private. He fought through the Shenandoah Valley under General Sheridan until his regiment was mustered out in June 1865. He must have sought further adventure for, later that year, at the age of just nineteen, he departed for China. One account says he received a letter of introduction from President Lincoln to the American 'ambassador' in Beijing, Anson Burlingame.[46] Another says Pethick initially worked for a British trading house. Whichever is correct, Pethick then went travelling. He reputedly roamed for two years, covered thousands of miles, learned different dialects of Chinese and immersed himself in local cultures. On his return to Beijing, Li apparently requested a meeting with Pethick.[47]

The two men would remain friends until they died, within days of each other, in 1901. In 1872 Pethick was appointed the American consul in Tianjin and around the same time he also joined Li's personal staff.[48] By November 1874 Robert Hart of the Maritime Customs Service was describing him as 'one of Li's most useful and trusted employees'.[49] This double role made him the ideal intermediary between the United States and Li and, through Li, the Qing court. While most of his time was spent dealing with commercial opportunities and trade disputes, Pethick also found himself at the centre of China's foreign relations. Through Pethick, Li would involve the United States in four international crises over the following twenty years. Each American intervention would chip away at the Qing's position at the centre of *tianxia* and oblige it to accept, at least in external form, the rules of sovereignty and Western international law. This was not a deliberate strategy on the part of Pethick personally or Washington as a whole, it was simply a consequence of the way that Americans saw the world.

In the 1870s Li, as a Confucian scholar and Qing official, would have accepted as natural a world-view that pictured the emperor in Beijing at the centre of a regional order with power over officials, subjects and tributary states radiating away from him in all directions. In theory six states still paid regular tribute to him: Annam (Vietnam), Choson (Korea), Nanzhang (Laos), Liuquiu (the Ryukyu Islands), Xianluo (Siam/Thailand) and Miandian (Burma/Myanmar). A few others did so less regularly (the very last tribute mission came from Nepal as late as 1908). Ties, though, had been weakening for some time as a result of the Qing's economic and then political crises. Nonetheless, the 'tribute system', or rather the idea of *tianxia* upon which it was based, remained the official ideology of the state. It underpinned the emperor's right to rule. Even the disastrous Macartney embassy of 1793 had been recorded as 'tribute' from England by the court administrators, even though that contradicted the whole point of the expedition.[50] In the words of John Cranmer-Byng, 'The breakdown of China's traditional world-system took place faster than the erosion of the assumptions on which the order itself was based.'[51] The Qing elite simply could not comprehend what was happening.

Their world was slipping away nonetheless. During the Taiping Rebellion, Siam and Laos had simply stopped sending tribute: the last missions from each were received in 1853. Chinese and Southeast Asian merchants had found they could make more money by simply trading between Southeast Asia and the new treaty ports. In 1862, once the Taiping revolt had been crushed, the Qing authorities tried to restore the old relationship. The governor-general of Guangdong petitioned the Siamese government to resume tribute missions. The request was ignored.[52] Siam had left the tributary system.[53] Laos had gone too.

The next to fall was the Ryukyan kingdom. In March 1879 Japan annexed the Ryukyus, the chain of islands stretching between Japan and Taiwan. The Ryukyan elite was furious. For around 250 years, with direct trade between the Qing Great-State and Japan banned, they had played the middleman and enjoyed the profits. The Japanese had greater influence in the kingdom but they encouraged the Ryukyans to continue to offer tribute to Beijing to keep the commerce flowing. The Ryukyans had done so until the Guangxu Emperor ascended to the throne in April 1875.[54] The following month, the Japanese government ordered tribute missions to cease, much to the displeasure of the Ryukyans who repeatedly petitioned the Qing authorities for assistance. No help came. The islands' rulers were about to leave the world of *tianxia* and enter the world of 'sovereignty'.

William Martin's Chinese translation of Wheaton's law book had been translated into *kanbun* characters for Japanese readers within a year of its 1864 publication in Beijing. The Japanese saw its value immediately and around twenty different editions were published over the following twenty years, including a full Japanese translation in 1876.[55] In complete contrast to the suspicions it aroused among senior Qing officials, the text was wholeheartedly welcomed and adopted in Tokyo. Its fundamental message, that states were by right sovereign and independent, fitted the new ideas circulating in Japan about its proper regional status. These ideas had emerged following the country's forced opening by the US Navy in the 1850s. There was now an aggressive faction in Japanese politics looking to learn from the Europeans and, like them, acquire an empire. They began to covet the lands around them and their first move was into the Ryukyus. The expansionists had learned from Wheaton and turned his arguments to their advantage.

The Japanese annexation was a fait accompli; the Ryukyan king was spirited into exile and his kingdom absorbed into Japan. The Qing court had to decide how to respond. Having the Ryukyus as a tributary state brought no financial gain. In May 1878 Li had said as much in a letter to the Qing ambassador to Tokyo, He Ruzhang.[56] The relationship's importance lay in its symbolism. The annexation was a violation of the regional order and an insult to the emperor. Moreover, the deposed king of the Ryukyus had directly appealed for assistance. If the traditional order was going to be preserved, Beijing would be obliged to come to his aid. There were also now questions of realpolitik. After nearly four decades of Western interference, the top Qing officials believed that ceding the islands was likely to invite further aggression.

Li and Gong debated their reaction. Li felt the islands weren't worth fighting for, and opted for diplomacy and the deployment of international law. The first article of a treaty that Li had personally negotiated and signed with the Japanese government in 1871 stated, 'In all that regards the territorial possessions of either country, the two Governments shall treat each the other with proper courtesy, without the slightest infringement or encroachment on either side.'[57] In Li's view, Japan had violated the treaty and he instructed Ambassador He to write a letter of protest. Ambassador He's letter, however, was so imperious in its language, so imbued with the old order, that the Japanese refused to discuss the matter any further.

But then William Pethick had an idea. His former military commander, now the former president, Ulysses S. Grant, was making a grand tour of the globe after eight years in the White House. On 6 May 1879 Grant docked at Guangzhou (Canton) before heading on to Xiamen, Shanghai, Tianjin and Beijing. He wasn't impressed by what he saw. On 6 June he wrote from Beijing to his friend Adolph E. Borie, 'We have now been in this Capitol for three days and have seen all there is to see, and that precious little to interest. . . . Tientsin is a more populous city than Shanghai and more repulsively filthy.'[58]

Accompanying him on that trip was William Pethick. Pethick introduced him to Li and the two men discussed ways that Grant might mediate in the Ryukyu dispute. According to the American researcher Chad Berry, Li probably believed that Grant, as an anti-imperialist American who had fought a war to preserve his country's territorial integrity, would be sympathetic to the Chinese position.

In Beijing, Grant met Prince Gong, who told him he wanted the situation to return to the previous status quo, with Japan renouncing its claim of sovereignty over the Ryukyus. On his return to Tianjin, he had another meeting with Li. Li drew on his knowledge of international treaties to argue his case but Grant pointed out a contradiction. When relying on the 1871 Sino-Japanese Treaty, Li seemed to be saying that Ryukyu was a part of China. But when relying on the 1853 treaty between Ryukyu and the United States, he was arguing that Ryukyu was a separate country. Li tried to fudge the issue, describing Ryukyu as a 'semi-dependent power'. Grant agreed to help but he wanted something in return: an agreement to limit Chinese immigration into the United States. Well over 100,000 Chinese had arrived in the US during Grant's two terms and the backlash from whites had been immense. A pledge to halt Chinese immigration would be a huge help to Grant's ambitions for a third term in office. After their final meeting on 13 June, Li asked Pethick to tell Grant that he was willing to make a deal along those lines.

Grant then headed to Japan where he was much impressed by the country's rapid modernisation, calling it 'liberal and enlightened' in his personal diary. The contrast with China was clear and his sympathies seem to have shifted. Any desire that Grant might have had to press the Chinese arguments evaporated. According to the historian of China-US relations Michael H. Hunt, in his meetings with Japanese officials in July 1879, Grant proposed a partition of the Ryukyus. Grant lived within a world-view of sovereign states and agreed boundaries. The idea that a state could have two masters was incomprehensible. But perhaps he knew that this would be too controversial to express directly, since his letter to Prince Gong and the Japanese prime minister recommended only that the Chinese should withdraw the earlier offending letter from Ambassador He and that the two sides should meet for further discussions. He then left for home.[59]

It took a year for the meeting to actually take place. On 15 August 1880, Prince Gong met the Japanese ambassador at the *Zongli Yamen*. After two months of talks they reached a compromise along the lines that Grant had previously suggested to the Japanese: partition. China would receive the two southernmost islands of the Ryukyus but Japan would keep the rest. Japan would also get 'most favoured nation' status – the same rights to trade in China as the Western powers. But when Li heard about the deal he objected furiously. As he told Grant in a letter in February 1881, he 'thought it incompatible with the dignity of China to share in the spoliation of a tributary prince against whom she had no grievance whatsoever. Indeed, China, after protesting against the annexation of Ryukyu by Japan, could not without losing all self-respect and the esteem of the rest of the world suddenly turn around and participate in an act which at the outset she condemned as arbitrary.' Li still lived in an intellectual world of *tianxia*. What he needed was the preservation of the symbolic order of tribute. Without it, the political order of the great-state collapsed. How could it claim to be centre-of-the-world if it could not protect its tributaries? However, no further negotiations took place and Japan consolidated its control over the entire Ryukyus. China had refused to concur in the removal of its tributary but had lost it nonetheless. This, for Li, was an object lesson in how Western international law worked. It stood for nothing unless there was power behind it to enforce the rules.

In the summer of 1880, while discussions about the Ryukyus were still ongoing, Li came to hear of another American visitor to the region. Commodore Robert W. Shufeldt had been despatched aboard the USS *Ticonderoga* following a Senate resolution two years earlier calling for the United States to negotiate a treaty with Korea. Korea was still the 'hermit kingdom' and closed to Westerners, but Shufeldt visited Nagasaki to ask the Japanese for help. The Chinese consul in the city passed on the news to Tianjin and Li began to formulate a plan. Through Pethick's double role as personal employee and United States diplomatic representative, Li invited Shufeldt to pay a visit.

Li was concerned about Japan's expansionism and also Russia's ambitions in the East. Like Ryukyu, Korea was a traditional tributary state of the *zhong guo*, and also like Ryukyu, Japan had ambitions there. Taking a leaf out of the

Westerners' books, the Japanese government had despatched warships to the Korean coast in 1876 and coerced the court into signing its first international treaty. Korea reluctantly agreed to open two ports to Japanese traders and allow an ambassador to reside in Seoul.[60] Given what was happening in the Ryukyus, Li suspected that Japanese ambitions ran deeper. In his conversation with Shufeldt on 26 August 1880, presumably translated by Pethick, Li referred to these worries and offered to help American diplomatic efforts in Korea. It seems Li was attempting to 'use barbarians to control barbarians' by getting the United States, a country that seemed to have no hostile intent towards China, to neutralise the activities of the Japanese and Russians. In Shufeldt's account, Li was also seeking American assistance in building up his naval forces, and suggested Shufeldt could play a role as its commander.

The Qing court's formal relationship with its tributaries had always been handled by the 'Board of Rites', the highest-ranking of the government's six ministries. Strict procedures were followed to maintain the hierarchy of relations – as Andreas van Braam had discovered ninety years before. The board had managed relations between Beijing and Seoul for centuries but in the spring of 1881 this role was transferred to the *Zongli Yamen*. At the same time, the emperor wrote to the Korean king and encouraged him to sign a treaty with the USA. These moves, apparently at the behest of Prince Gong, might seem trivial but they represented a fundamental change in the court's foreign relations. It was no longer possible for the court to assume that the old ritualised relationship was sufficient. Beijing needed to play at foreign policy. However, the deeper aim of Gong and Li was to use the Westerners to keep the Japanese at bay and thereby preserve the traditional tribute relationship.

Shufeldt returned to Tianjin in July 1881. No reply had been received from Seoul so he was obliged to wait. It was only in December that he learned that Li had been able to persuade the Korean court to agree a treaty. In February Shufeldt travelled to Beijing to meet the American chargé d'affaires, Chester Holcombe, and prepare a draft. Their text contained no reference to Korea's tributary status: it was a document predicated upon Western concepts of sovereignty. But that was not how either Prince Gong nor Li Hongzhang saw the situation. Firstly, they insisted that the treaty would have to be agreed in

Beijing before it could be presented to the Koreans and, secondly, Li's version of the text stipulated that Korea would remain a tributary.

Li's wording was perplexing to the Americans. The first article of his version of the treaty stated that 'Choson [Korea], being a dependent state of the Chinese Empire, has nevertheless heretofore exercised her own sovereignty in all matters of internal administration and foreign relations.' This may have made sense to Li, but for the Americans the two halves of this sentence were incompatible. Sovereignty meant nothing without independence. Nonetheless, Li said its inclusion was non-negotiable. It is clear that what he really wanted was US recognition of Qing suzerainty over Korea. In reply, Shufeldt insisted that if Korea had sovereign powers, then the United States had the right to deal with it independently of China. This was the critical difference between the Qing and the Western world-views.

Finally, on 10 April 1882, Li Hongzhang made an expedient decision with enormous implications. He agreed to remove his wording from the text. In effect, he conceded the end of Korea's tributary status and a regional political arrangement in which Korea could independently make its own sovereign choices in its foreign relations. The consolation prize was that the Korean king would write a separate letter to the US president, after the treaty had been signed, which would state that the treaty had been made with the consent of the government of China. It was a fig-leaf to preserve Qing dignity. The critical threshold had been crossed. Li was so anxious to have the United States as a partner to minimise Japanese influence in Korea that he sacrificed the traditional tributary relationship and opened the door to Korean sovereignty. From other sources, and Li's subsequent behaviour, we know that he felt that he could continue to maintain the substance of the tributary relationship through personal contacts with the Korean court. Ultimately, however, this did not happen and the new form of sovereign relations displaced the old.

A month later, aboard the USS *Swatara*, moored in the mouth of the Seoul River, the treaty agreed between Li and Shufeldt was presented to a Korean delegation. Li had deputed a Chinese official to host the occasion but Shufeldt presented a letter to the Korean king directly from President Chester Arthur, as one sovereign to another, and requested an answer in the same terms. The Koreans did not object and the treaty was signed on the beach on 22 May.

A letter from the king arrived two days later but its text contradicted the treaty by saying, 'The Choson country [Korea] is a dependency of China, but the management of her governmental affairs, home and foreign, has always been vested in the sovereign.' Thus, the Korean court presented a version of its relationship with Beijing that matched Li's version and which, from an American perspective, was equally oxymoronic.

All the efforts expended by Shufeldt came to very little, however. The treaty was ratified by the US Senate at the end of July and ambassadors were exchanged. US citizens were allowed to trade and live at the open ports but few of them actually did so. Shufeldt's mission was largely ignored by the Arthur administration and the media, and he received little thanks for his pains. He didn't even get a position with Li's naval forces. The other Western powers, however, did see the merits of his achievements and within a few months of the signing on the beach, Britain, Germany, Italy, France and Austria all had their own treaties with Korea. Li could hope that his strategy of using Western 'barbarians' to control Japan was bearing fruit. It was not to last.

The next tributary state to fall under foreign influence was Vietnam, which the Qing and French continued to refer to as Annam. French forces had seized the city of Saigon in 1859 but wanted more. In 1862/3 they forced the Vietnamese Tu Duc Emperor to cede three southern provinces as French Cochinchina. In 1874 France had imposed a further 'Treaty of Peace and Alliance'. Article 2 made a point of 'acknowledging the sovereignty of the King of Anam and his entire independence of all foreign power of any name', while in Article 3, 'the King of Anam engages to conform his foreign policy to that of France'.[61] The treaty ended the old tributary relationship through what was a transparent diplomatic fiction: the notion that Annam was an independent state making its own choices. In reality Vietnam became a protectorate of France. It sent its last tribute embassy to Beijing in 1880.[62] But, again, the French wanted more, particularly trade routes north into Yunnan province: the remote southwest of the Qing domain.

When the Tu Duc Emperor died in July 1883 a political crisis ensued. Vietnam had five emperors in just over a year, most of them being killed in office. Amid the chaos, one emperor signed a treaty accepting a French protectorate over Tonkin, the area adjacent to the frontier with Yunnan. French troops began moving in. This time, the court in Beijing thought it could use military force to prevent another tributary from slipping away. It sponsored various semi-regular units and gangs such as the 'Black Flags' to take on the French.[63] Aware that he also needed diplomatic support, Li Hongzhang turned again to the United States.

By this time the American representative in Beijing was John Russell Young, formerly the correspondent who had accompanied Ulysses S. Grant on his grand tour. Young had used his political connections to have himself sent back to Asia as a diplomat and was looking for a crisis in which to make his name. In August 1883, as the clouds gathered, he reported back to Washington on a revealing conversation he had had with Li.

> *Young*: Why does not China define her territory?
> *Li*: The limits of empire were well defined. There was China and there were the tributaries of China. These tributaries were self-governing, except in the fact that they owed the emperor an allegiance; which was satisfied by acts of tribute and ceremony.
> *Young*: In modern times and under the forms of civilization which now prevailed, there were no such institutions as tributary states: a colony was as much part of the empire as the capital. . . . This is the rule of civilized nations. China should follow it and save herself embarrassments by consolidating her empire and having the world know the exact limits of her territory.
> *Li*: I see no reason why the outside nations should destroy the relations that had existed between China and these outlying nations for ages.[64]

The mismatch in world-views is obvious. Young may have objected to what the French were doing but he agreed with the basis upon which they were doing it.

Young advised Li not to attempt to fight the French military, advice that Li was happy to take since he wanted to preserve his northern fleet to face the challenge from Japan. Li preferred to negotiate and asked Young to be the mediator. The French, however, were not interested; they simply demanded recognition of their territorial claims in Annam and Tonkin and a large financial indemnity. The Qing court refused, so, in August 1884, France reverted to the traditional European practice of naval shelling to induce compliance. Meanwhile, the French forced Vietnam to break its tributary relationship with the Qing. On 30 August 1884 the court, in the presence of French diplomats, destroyed the official seal that the Qing had given to the Vietnamese court in 1804. Six kilograms of beautifully engraved silver were melted into an ugly blob.[65]

The French had forced the Vietnamese to cut their tributary relations with Beijing but it took further shelling to persuade Beijing to give up Vietnam. However, domestic opposition in France and some Chinese successes against French troops in Tonkin dented Paris's ambitions. Young was still trying to mediate but his only success was in persuading Li to abandon his objections to recognising French sovereignty over Vietnam. It was actually the inspector-general of the Maritime Customs, Robert Hart, who persuaded the French to accept a ceasefire in exchange for the recognition of its control over Annam and Tonkin. The treaty was signed at Tianjin on 9 June 1885. Another tributary was gone.

Interestingly, the British took a different approach. In late 1885 they launched the third Anglo-Burmese War and seized those areas of Burma they hadn't taken in the first and second invasions. Britain formally annexed the whole country on 1 January 1886. However, unlike the French, the British allowed Burma to continue to send tribute to Beijing every ten years. The first article of the 'Convention Between Great Britain and China Relating to Burmah and Thibet', signed in Beijing on 24 July 1886, makes this clear, while the second article states that 'in all matters whatsoever . . . England shall be free to do whatever she deems fit and proper'.[66] For the British, 'tribute' was a pointless piece of symbolism which could be tolerated while they got on with the business of empire. For the Qing court, it was the other way around: the symbolism *was* the business. As it turned out, no missions were actually ever sent from British-occupied Burma and another convention, agreed in 1897, formally ended the ritual. For that first decade, however, appearances had been preserved.[67]

In the wake of the Annam debacle, the Beijing conservatives had seized the initiative. A large number of lower- and middle-ranking scholar-officials formed a 'Purists Party' – *Qingliu Dang* – which denounced the passive response to the French and demanded militant action. They had no experience of dealing with foreigners, nor of modern warfare, but they insisted that a return to Confucian values would be sufficient to defend the realm. Under pressure, the Dowager Empress Cixi fired or punished all the members of the *Zongli Yamen* – including Yixin/Gong. Li managed to escape censure largely because of his personal relationship with Cixi. His forces had made her the power behind the throne in 1861 and throughout the years of self-strengthening they remained allies. He also tolerated her extravagance and misuse of state funds.

Some of the results of her extravagance still stand in the northwestern suburbs of Beijing for all to see. On a fine day, the huge Imperial Summer Palace, with its artificial lakes and mountains, stone bridges and monumental temples, draws thousands of visitors: vastly more than would have ever been allowed to see it in Cixi's time. For five years after 1889, millions of *taels* of government revenue that should have been spent on ships were diverted into preparations for the empress's sixtieth birthday, due in 1894. Hidden away on the far western side of the site is the former Naval Academy. These days, the tourist signs in front of the low grey buildings tell the story: 'Built in 1886, it was a special school to train naval officers for the Qing armed forces. It was also utilised as a front behind which Empress Cixi diverted naval funds to rebuild the Summer Palace. . . . The students put on numerous naval manoeuvres for the Empress Dowager on the lake and shouldered the duty of tugging her Imperial Pleasure Boat with a steamboat for pleasure rounds of the lake.' The steamboat is still preserved there, as is a marble pavilion in the shape of a boat. As the naval historian Sarah Paine has noted, the boat-pavilion 'was the Empress Dowager's sole contribution to the Chinese fleet between 1889 and 1894'.[68] The marble boat lasted far longer than the rest of the navy, soon to meet an ignominious end at the hands of the Japanese.

The immediate cause of the war with Japan was the status of Korea. Li's attempts to use the Western barbarians to control the Japanese barbarians had not prevented the militant faction in Tokyo from trying to seize control of the peninsula. Throughout the 1880s the two rival powers had plotted with their supporters inside the Korean elite to foment coups and counter coups. On 3 June 1894 the Korean king, Gojong, requested Chinese troops to help suppress yet another rebellion. This gave the Japanese the excuse they had been looking for. By mid-June, 6,000 Japanese troops were marching on Seoul. Japanese politicians spoke of the country's 'duty to lead the little kingdom along the path to civilisation' and out of its traditional tributary status. On 23 July the Japanese stormed the royal palace in Seoul, took King Gojong hostage and demanded the court introduce a series of reforms. The new government then renounced its status as a tributary of the Qing.[69]

In Beijing, the conservatives demanded action. They were convinced that their mighty great-state could crush the upstart empire across the water. The *Qingliu Dang* scholar-officials cultivated the support of the Guangxu Emperor, now twenty-three years old, and became a war party. Li, on the other hand, knew that his forces were no match for the modernised Japanese and sought to avoid conflict. Instead, he tried to get the Western barbarians to intervene again. They weren't interested. In fact, they felt considerable sympathy with Japan's modernising mission. After decades of failing to persuade the Qing to reform, the Westerners felt that a stinging defeat would prove instructive. It wasn't long in coming. On 25 July the Japanese sank a Chinese troopship and damaged two others. A week later Japan formally declared war, and the Qing responded in kind. In his declaration, the Guangxu Emperor took care to refer to the Japanese by the traditional insult of *wo-ren* – dwarfs – six times.

The war turned out to be a walkover for the dwarfs. In battle after battle, on sea and on land, the Qing forces were no match for the Japanese. By the end of October, Japanese forces controlled the Korean peninsula. In November they captured the naval base at Port Arthur on the eastern side of Bohai Bay and, in February 1895, the other main naval base, at Weihaiwei on the western side. The route to Beijing was wide open. The court's first response was to deny it was all happening. The second was to blame the defeats on Li and his attempts at modernisation. His honours were stripped from him and if it hadn't been for Empress Cixi's realisation that she needed Li's forces to defend the capital, he would have been executed. Instead, he was given the task of negotiating the humiliating surrender and staining his reputation for ever.

On 19 March 1895 Li, together with a retinue of over 100 people, arrived in the Japanese port of Shimonoseki. Among the crowd was an expensively hired adviser, another American, former US secretary of state, John W. Foster.

After leaving office, Foster had acted as a consultant to the Chinese legation in Washington and was contracted again to guide Li through the intricacies of international law in Shimonoseki. Li's initial plea to the Japanese had been for the two sides to ignore international law and work together as members of the 'yellow race' to counter the Westerners. The Japanese declined. They intended to deploy Wheaton and his works to destroy the old tributary order.

Foster may have been hired by Li, but he came from an intellectual world in which the 'natural order' of international relations had no place for tributary systems. He would hammer the final nail into the coffin of the old regional order. On 5 April he drafted, on Li's behalf, a four-point reply to Japan's draft peace treaty. The first point was to agree the full and complete independence of Korea, ending the Qing's final formal tributary relationship. Worse was to follow. Japanese troops had invaded Taiwan on 25 March and the cession of the island was added to the list of Japanese demands. This was even more humiliating than the loss of Korea, since Taiwan was a province, not a tributary. But, faced with overwhelming military force, Li and Foster decided they had no choice but to agree.

On 17 April 1895, almost exactly 100 years after Andreas Everardus van Braam Houckgeest had paid tribute to the Qianlong Emperor, the Qing world was turned upside down. In a small hotel in Shimonoseki, the great-state's leading statesman, Li Hongzhang, viceroy of Zhili, minister of the Northern Sea Trade, grand secretary of the Hall of Literary Flourishing and grand tutor to the crown prince, was obliged to formally recognise that his emperor was not the ruler of 'all under heaven' but simply the head of one, rather weak, state surrounded by many others. Li and his adopted son, acting as representatives of the imperial throne, signed the Treaty of Shimonoseki recognising the independence of Korea, the cession of Taiwan and the payment of 7,500 tonnes of silver to Japan. It was an utter humiliation – so bad that Li couldn't face the court to explain it. Instead, he sent Foster to Beijing.

It was the first time the Grand Council had ever met a foreign envoy. Foster was unimpressed with the encounter. For him, it demonstrated why the Qing Great-State had found itself in the mess that it had, particularly once he discovered that the emperor's tutor, Weng Tonghe, had no idea about the history of European wars and how they had led to the creation of Western international law. Ultimately, however, the Grand Council agreed to face reality: the treaty was the only alternative to continued military humiliation. The court tried to keep details of the Treaty of Shimonoseki secret. Nonetheless, details leaked out and 2,500 scholar-officials signed petitions in opposition. Two of the organisers of the opposition were the outspoken reformists Kang Youwei and Liang Qichao.

The *Qingliu Dang* were determined to pin the blame on Li. They pressed the court into ordering that the person to sign the edict handing over Taiwan to Japan would be Li's nephew and adopted son Li Jingfang. Li was concerned that his relative might be killed by Taiwanese scholar-officials outraged by the treaty's provisions so he insisted that Foster accompany Li Jingfang to the ceremony. On 30 May 1895 the two men rendezvoused with the Japanese off the coast of Taiwan. They didn't even go ashore but signed the edict aboard the Japanese ship *Yokohama Maru*, anchored off the port of Keelung.[70]

The Qing world order was over. In the aftermath of those defeats, the Western ambassadors used the Qing's need for political support to wrest concessions from the court. No longer would they be received as second-class barbarians in peripheral buildings. From 1894 they would be received as equals in the Hall of Literary Flourishing at the heart of the Forbidden City. It had taken a century – from February 1795, when a Qing emperor could believe that a Dutch kingdom had come to offer tribute to his *zhong guo*, to April 1895, when Li Hongzhang, following the counsel of his American advisers, finally conceded that China was now surrounded by independent sovereign states. The formal recognition of this came in 1901, after the suppression of the Boxer Rebellion, when the *Zongli Yamen* was formally renamed the Ministry of Foreign Affairs (*Waiwubu*) and given the same status as the court's traditional six ministries.

Li was the one who was obliged to wield the brush but his role capped a century of failure. The Qing Great-State rotted from within. Given that failure, Li had little choice but to engage with the new rules of the international order. He became the mediator between the power of Western armaments and the norms of the Qing world. He did not do so alone. At each stage in that process he was advised by outsiders – predominantly Americans: Pethick, Grant, Shufeldt, Young and Foster. These men had no way of thinking of the world other than in terms of 'sovereignty', a world in which independent states with formal boundaries dealt with each other on the basis of law.

Li could see that this was only half the picture. He also had legal arguments but in the face of superior firepower, whether European or Japanese, law meant little. In the new world order, only the strong triumphed: law without power meant nothing; might trumped right. Li understood this but his opponents within the court, the conservative scholar-officials, the *Qingliu Dang* and others who saw themselves as the upholders of tradition were never convinced. For them, *tianxia* and the moral superiority it both required and engendered were the natural order.

This, then, is the origin of contemporary China's 'sovereignty fundamentalism': a hybrid of Confucian chauvinism and American legalism. It melds premodern ideas of the cultural pre-eminence of the *zhong guo* with Western ideas of fixed borders and independence. At its heart lies a philosophical difference: the Chinese word for sovereignty, *zhuquan*, carries the literal meaning of 'the authority of the ruler' – it is focused domestically, not internationally. *Zhuquan* mandates the continuation of a morally superior culture within the protection of inviolable boundaries. It is, in effect, *tianxia* with passport controls – *tianxia* in one country. This is not an idea that can tolerate intervention in a country's internal affairs but is rather a mandate for the opposite: the exclusion of other states and their 'international norms', whether on human rights or climate change.

Memories of the dynastic rituals of tribute still underpin ideas about political legitimacy in communist China. The Beijing leadership frequently deploys the performance of rituals of international respect as a critical element of its domestic political messaging. The number and size and status of delegations attending a 'Belt and Road Forum', or a G20 summit, are widely publicised and help to confer a modern 'mandate of heaven' upon the Communist Party. By contrast, critical commentary on the party's performance is kept away from the people. The idea of international delegations traipsing across the ancestral land, 'measuring, reporting and verifying' its carbon emissions and then telling the world that Beijing is not living up to an internationally agreed standard remains anathema. The assertion of sovereignty above all else is therefore a means to avoid disrespect and a loss of domestic legitimacy.

Wang Huning is the brain behind Xi Jinping, just as he was the theoretician behind Xi's predecessors Jiang Zemin and Hu Jintao. He currently sits at the apex of political life in China: on the Standing Committee of the Politburo. As a law professor at Fudan University, his first book was entitled *Guojia Zhuquan* – 'National Sovereignty'.[71] In it he argued that the Chinese word *zhuquan* pre-dates the Western concept of sovereignty.[72] We have come full circle. Wang's predecessors fought in vain to prevent the concept of sovereignty taking root in Beijing. Wang now claims China invented it and wants to own and control its meaning. He has chosen to ignore the roles of Wheaton and Martin, who worked to bring the *zhong guo* into the modern world by re-creating the meaning of *zhuquan*. This 'strategic ignorance' of the foreigners' intermediary roles enables Wang's wider philosophical project: to fill Western concepts with Chinese meaning in order to underpin Beijing's plans for a world based upon the notion of a 'community of common destiny'. It fits neatly with a modern version of *tianxia*, in which Beijing sits, once again, at the top of a regional, or even global, hierarchy. It is a hierarchy open to all, as long as they know their place.

3
THE INVENTION OF THE HAN RACE
zhongzu – race

The residence of the consul-general of the People's Republic of China in San Francisco is one of the smartest properties in the city. Originally built for the developer of the wealthy neighbourhood of Monterey Heights, 85 St Elmo Way sits on the brow of a small hill with views down to the Pacific Ocean. Its garden is shaded by a pair of huge cypress trees and the steps leading to the house are flanked by a pair of large stone lions. In all, an impressive venue for a party. On 5 December 2015 the occasion was a reception for Bay Area parents who had adopted children from China. The Chinese consul-general, Luo Linquan, had what he called a 'special message' for the children who came: 'You grow up speaking English, live in American families and have loving American parents. Yet your black eyes, black hair and dark skin all remind you that you are Chinese. I want to let you know that China, your country of birth, never forgets you,' he told them. He was not appealing to Chinese citizens on the basis of their passports but to foreign citizens on the basis of their ethnicity.[1]

A few months beforehand, another Chinese diplomat had caused an international incident by expressing similar sentiments. The Chinese ambassador to Malaysia, Huang Huikang, organised a walkabout along Petaling Street, the heart of Kuala Lumpur's Chinatown. The timing was deliberate. 25 September 2015 was the day before ethnic-Malay chauvinists were due to march through the area and the community was on edge. Standing amid the busy market stalls, Huang read out a prepared statement. 'With regard to the infringement on China's national interests, violations of legal rights and interests of Chinese citizens and businesses which may damage the friendly relationship between China and the host country, we will not sit by idly,' he told journalists. 'China is forever the natal home of Malaysia's ethnic Chinese.' The shops and stalls along Petaling

Street are not run by Chinese citizens but predominantly by Malaysian citizens of Chinese descent. Ambassador Huang had neither authority over nor responsibility for this community but took it upon himself to speak out for, in his words, members of the 'Chinese race'.[2]

In 2014 the Chinese government's 'Overseas Chinese Affairs Office' announced plans to create a global network of 'Overseas Chinese Service Centres' in sixty countries around the world.[3] At the time of writing there were offices in at least sixty cities: from London and Paris to Houston, Caracas, Cape Town, Yangon and beyond. While many countries maintain consular offices to assist their citizens overseas, the purpose of the Overseas Chinese Service Centres is quite different. In 2018 the responsibility for the Overseas Chinese Affairs Office was transferred from the Chinese government to the 'United Front Work Department' – the Chinese Communist Party organisation that is formally tasked with building support for the Communist Party and neutralising its political enemies. Article 31 of a set of Communist Party regulations issued in September 2015 makes clear that one of the main goals of the United Front 'is to utilise overseas Chinese to help with the development and modernisation of the ancestral land . . . to defeat Taiwan separatism and to promote friendship between the people of China, Chinese people and the world'.[4] The United Front is directly supervised by the fourth most powerful figure in the party's Politburo, and a United Front teaching manual seen by the *Financial Times* newspaper in 2017 made clear that, 'The unity of Chinese at home requires the unity of the sons and daughters of Chinese abroad.'[5] It is clear that the Communist Party intends to use the people it calls 'overseas Chinese' to support its agenda both at home and abroad.

The English phrase 'overseas Chinese' is ambiguous. It can refer both to citizens of the People's Republic of China who are overseas and to people of Chinese ancestry who are citizens of other countries. In Chinese there are different terms for each group, *waiji huaren* and *huaqiao* respectively, but Chinese officials rarely use the first one. In speech after speech they display an understanding of Chineseness that is overtly racial. It is not about which passport someone holds but about their 'blood'.

The term that the United Front regulations use for overseas Chinese is *huaqiao*. As we have seen earlier, the name *hua* emerged as a cultural description that literally means 'efflorescent' or 'civilised', but it has come to refer to Chinese people. *Qiao* has the meaning of 'sojourner' – someone who is out of the country temporarily and who will, one day, return. When Xi Jinping gave his closing speech to the nineteenth National Congress of the Chinese Communist Party in October 2017, he used the phrase *haiwai qiaobao* – literally 'over-seas sojourner-siblings'. The meaning is the same: regardless of how long ago someone's ancestors left home, or for how many generations they have been citizens of another country, they are still *hua* and still have obligations to the ancestral land. Xi told the congress that, 'The point of working with the over-seas sojourner-siblings is to promote the revival of the Chinese nation [*Zhonghua minzu*].'[6]

The leading authority on the history of the overseas Chinese, Professor Wang Gungwu of the East Asian Institute in Singapore, argues that the term *huaqiao* was coined in the early twentieth century for political reasons.[7] Right up until 1893 it had been illegal for subjects of the Qing to leave the empire without permission. Those who had gone abroad to trade or work were commonly regarded as outlaws or even traitors. During the nineteenth century, as the number of people leaving the country illegally began to rise, a more sympathetic attitude emerged among the public. It became common to refer to them as *hua-ren* or *hua-min* – '*hua*-people' – to distinguish them from barbarian foreigners. Official attitudes towards them began to change from the 1870s once the first Qing diplomats were sent abroad and learned about the migrants' often miserable living conditions. One of them, Huang Zunxian, the reformer we met in Chapter 1, who served in Tokyo, San Francisco, London and Singapore, coined the term *huaqiao* to imply that the migrants were only abroad temporarily and through necessity and that they deserved some official protection. From 1902 the Qing court started to require its diplomats to send formal reports on their conditions.

However, the term *huaqiao* only came into general use after 1903 when the revolutionaries who wanted to overthrow the Qing state adopted it as a means of honouring the overseas communities who were their main sponsors. One of their leading propagandists, eighteen-year-old Zou Rong, penned a nationalistic essay, 'The Revolutionary Army' (*Geming Jun*), while a student in Japan. Another Japan-based student, Zhang Binglin, composed the martial 'Song of Revolution'.

In both they exhorted their fellow *huaqiao* to stop enjoying their meaningless wealth, embrace their racial origin and overthrow the Manchu oppressors. Zou's essay was reprinted dozens of times over the following decade and Zhang's song performed on innumerable occasions. The term *huaqiao* became a key part of the revolutionaries' appeal to their funders overseas. It told them they were a part of a global community of *hua*-people and owed allegiance to it.

Partly to try to counteract this appeal, and partly because of moves by the various colonial authorities in Southeast Asia to give the *huaren* local citizenship, the Qing government passed a Nationality Law in 1909. It was based upon blood ties – the principle of *jus sanguinis* – that citizenship was acquired from ancestry, not from the place of birth. It stated that even if *huaren* took local citizenship, they would become Qing subjects if they returned 'home'. In other words, the definition of a Qing subject became a racial one.[8] This created problems for *huaren* in Southeast Asia throughout the following decades. Their dual status as actual citizens of the country in which they lived but also potential citizens of China became a cause for suspicion. It was not until the 1970s that Cold War politics in Southeast Asia obliged most *huaren* to take local citizenship and let their ties with China wither. Around that time, the term *huaqiao* largely dropped out of use within Southeast Asia to be replaced by the less loaded word *huayi* – 'descendants of hua'.[9] However, the racialised notion of overseas Chinese identity persisted within China itself and has returned to prominence with the rise of Xi Jinping and the newly assertive United Front. It is likely to create new problems for the overseas Chinese. On 1 February 2018 China began granting five-year residency permits to overseas Chinese. The visa rules now state that applicants need only one Chinese ancestor to qualify and set no limit on how many generations back that ancestor might have lived in China. Chinese officials frequently describe the overseas Chinese diaspora as numbering 60 million people.[10] The People's Republic now seems to be laying claim to all of them.

These proprietorial attitudes towards overseas Chinese emerged from much earlier arguments, a century ago, about how Chinese-ness should be defined. In the context of the times, and under the heavy influence of European ideas, identity became racialised. Key roles in this process were played by figures we have just encountered: Huang Zunxian and Zhang Binglin. This chapter tells the story of their parts in the invention of two races: firstly the 'yellow race' and then the 'Han race'.

In 1855 long-simmering disputes between communities in the southern province of Guangdong erupted into a vicious civil war that lasted twelve years. The rival groups were known locally as the *Hakka* – literally 'guest' people – and the *Punti* – literally 'original place' people. The two names expose the basis of the conflict: the *Punti* considered themselves the native inhabitants of the province, with long-established rights to its more fertile and prosperous parts. The *Hakka* had migrated into the region over several centuries and been restricted to less fertile and more remote areas. The *Punti* looked down on the *Hakka* migrants in racialised terms: calling them, in effect, dogs. Unlike the *Punti*, *Hakka* women worked alongside their menfolk and did not bind their feet. Hard work had allowed them to improve their social position and, in a nineteenth-century attempt at social reform, the Qing authorities had encouraged some *Hakka* to migrate to the wealthier areas. The result was increased competition for resources – with predictable consequences. Along the west branch of the Pearl River, rival communities armed themselves and eventually attacked one another. Over the following decade the Hakka-Punti war killed well over 100,000 people.[11] The war became enmeshed in the Taiping Rebellion (see Chapter 2) and was only quashed by government forces with considerable violence.

To this day there are neighbouring villages in Guangdong with *Punti* and *Hakka* populations still separated by the legacy of that nineteenth-century war. The *Punti* still look down on the *Hakka* and the *Hakka* still complain of discrimination. The languages they speak, Cantonese and Hakka, are largely unintelligible to one another and the communities observe different religious practices and follow different social customs. They are more different from one another than, for example, Serbs are from Croats in the Balkans. They are, in short, different ethnic groups. In 1905 a new Guangdong school textbook stated explicitly that the two groups were, in fact, different races. In a time of revolutionary upheaval, the implications were potentially genocidal. It provoked prominent members of the *Hakka* community to try to prove that the textbook was wrong: that the *Hakka* had the same origins as the Cantonese/*Punti* and were therefore just as much a part of the same race.[12] The key instigator of this defence was Huang Zunxian, by then a retired diplomat and also a revered poet. It was fitting that this would be Huang's final intervention in public life because, arguably, he was the first person to introduce modern racial thinking into China. He introduced his countrymen to the idea of the 'yellow race'.

Quite why Europeans began to think of East Asians as 'yellow' remains obscure. Michael Keevak of the National Taiwan University has traced the idea to the eighteenth-century botanist Carl Linnaeus, who attempted to classify all forms of life and created a particular category for *Homo asiaticus* whose defining characteristic was 'yellowness'. Then, in the nineteenth century, the French anthropologist Paul Broca attempted to measure and standardise skin colour and declared the 'Mongolians' to be yellow. This, however, was based on the invention of an idea that there was a group of people called 'Mongolians' in the first place. That was an innovation by the German anatomist Johann Friedrich Blumenbach, one of the eighteenth century's most prolific collectors of human skulls. In the 1795 edition of his *De generis humani varietate nativa* he argued that the facial angles of these skulls demonstrated the existence of a racial hierarchy. He declared the existence of five separate races, which were, in order of 'degeneration': Caucasian, Native American, Malay, Mongolian and then African. He associated each race with a particular colour: white, copper, tawny, yellow and black respectively. According to Keevak, this was the moment that the Mongolian 'race' was invented and given the colour yellow. It was a broad and vaguely defined category but Blumenbach was sure that it included both the Chinese and Japanese.[13]

Quite why a Qing official such as Huang Zunxian would think of his own people as part of a 'yellow race' is an even more complicated story. Across East Asia, there were long-standing traditions of venerating ancestors and of tracing family lineages back into the deep past. The Chinese word for lineage is *zu*.[14] One of the leading historians of the period, Pamela Kyle Crossley, has argued that under the Qianlong Emperor, towards the end of the eighteenth century, the Qing Great-State moved towards an overtly racial categorisation of its subjects. The term that it chose to use was also *zu*. She argues that the best English translation for *zu* in this context is 'race', since it carried with it the idea of 'immutable, genealogically-determined identity with fixed cultural, psychological and moral attributes'.[15]

The rulers of the Qing Empire were originally semi-nomadic tribes from the sparsely populated lands along what are now the frontiers of modern China, Russia, Korea and Mongolia. In the early seventeenth century, a leader of one of these peoples – the Jurchen – called Nurgaci, united disparate groups of plains-dwellers under his rule and began to expand his territory southwards. His son and successor, Hung Taiji, continued this process and decreed that the Jurchen should henceforth call themselves *Manju*, or, in English, 'Manchu'. He chose a new name for his dynasty too: Qing, meaning 'pure'. In 1635, to consolidate his power, Hung Taiji divided his subjects into militarised groups, known as 'banners': one set for Manchus, one for Mongols and another for settled people who had become loyal to him. This latter group were named *Han-jun*. *Jun* means 'martial' and the term *Han* was an ethnic description – but it was not a term used by the people who were to be called *Han*. The Singapore-based researcher Yang Shao-Yun has argued that the use of the name *Han* emerged among an Inner Asian people, the *Xianbi*, in the fourth or fifth centuries CE. The *Xianbi* had a folk memory of the much earlier Han Dynasty and used the same name to describe the people living along their southern frontier. From the *Xianbi* the name then spread to other Inner Asian nomadic groups: Khitan, Mongols and Jurchen.[16] As we saw in Chapter 1, Han had not been a term used by the 'Han' themselves; they generally called themselves subjects of a particular dynasty or, more generally, *Hua* – civilised.

So even before the Manchu conquered Beijing and toppled the Ming Dynasty in 1644, they had already created a form of classification within their state structures. The different 'banner' units were kept separate from the civilian population. The categories of *Man* (from *Manju*) and *Han-jun* were not formally defined but there were boundaries between them based upon their members' ancestry. More important was the boundary between the banner units – who were collectively termed *qi* – and the rest of the population, who were termed civilians – *min*. However, from the mid-eighteenth century onwards, the court moved to more formally demarcate a difference between the populations. This may well have been prompted by the proximity with which the conquerors and conquered found themselves living. Discipline among the Manchu was breaking down, rule-breaking was increasing and the court's response was to impose order through separateness. As the historian Edward Rhoads has shown, these rules lasted right into the 1900s: Manchus were obliged to live in separate, usually walled, districts of cities, they were formally banned from engaging in trade and intermarriage between *qi* and *min* was forbidden.[17]

The use of the term *Han* as a racial marker therefore appears to have begun with foreign rulers who invaded the 'Han-lands' from the north: Xianbi, Mongols and Manchu. It was their way of describing their newly conquered subjects. Once they became rulers of the Han, however, they took care to demonstrate their legitimacy to the conquered population by outwardly adopting traditional Sinitic rituals of government in the 'Han-land' areas of their great-states. By following these principles they could proclaim themselves civilised in Confucian terms: uniting themselves and their subjects under the umbrella term *Hua*. But by maintaining their separate and privileged status as *qi*, the Manchu elite created the conditions for a race-based revolution at the beginning of the twentieth century.

By the mid-nineteenth century it was routine for European social theorists of all kinds to see the world in racial terms. Among the most influential was the British naturalist and philosopher Herbert Spencer, who transplanted concepts of evolution from biology into sociology. Spencer's aim was to describe how societies might progress towards perfection. He took ideas from Charles Darwin and Jean-Baptiste Lamarck about the effects of evolutionary pressures upon individuals and applied them to entire groups. It was he, not Darwin, who in 1864 coined the phrase 'survival of the fittest'. Spencer borrowed the subtitle from Darwin's *On the Origin of Species* – 'the preservation of favoured races in the struggle for life' – and made it the focus of his social theory.[18] His entire outlook was founded upon racial thinking: 'The contrasts of races in form, colour, and feature, are not greater than the contrasts in their moral and intellectual qualities', as he put it in his first major work, *Social Statics*, originally published in 1851.[19]

Spencer's ideas travelled far beyond Britain. They were enthusiastically adopted among some in the United States and also in Japan, where they arrived at a time of political ferment. At least thirty-two translations of Spencer's works were published in Japanese between 1877 and 1900 and many more of his shorter articles were republished in journals and magazines.[20] Spencer's ideas nourished the Japanese 'Freedom and People's Rights' movement, a new coalition of merchants and wealthy farmers who were demanding emancipation from the old feudal ways and greater rights for individuals. The traditional elite stood their ground for some time and arguments over Spencer's ideas dominated Japanese political life in the 1870s and 1880s.

Closely observing this subversive spectacle was the third-ranking diplomat at the Chinese Mission to Japan, Huang Zunxian. Huang was unusual in several ways. He was a Hakka from Guangdong and his family had made money in business – particularly money-lending – before losing most of it during the turmoil of the Taiping Rebellion and the Hakka-Punti war. In 1870 he had visited the British colony of Hong Kong and been both impressed and outraged by the opulence and sophistication of a foreign city implanted within the Qing realm. That seems to have triggered feelings of disillusion towards the Qing scholar-officials and their ignorance of the world beyond the oceans. He made this plain in poems he wrote for his friends. By 1876, though, he was living in Beijing and studying for the government exams. His father, working as a civil servant in the Agriculture Department there, took him to Chefoo (Zhifu in Pinyin; now called Yantai), where Huang met Li Hongzhang, who was by then firmly established as governor-general of Zhili and superintendent of the Northern Ports. This introduction to Li and his entourage finally opened the door to the Qing bureaucracy. After nine years of study, Huang passed the official exams.

From the poems he composed at the time, it appears that Huang saw himself as an ally of Li and the self-strengtheners' attempts to modernise the country. In the view of the Japanese scholar Noriko Kamachi, Huang was one of the first scholar-officials to openly challenge the Qing concept of being the 'central state'. 'Now the world is one, stop being so self-important about *zhong guo*,' he wrote in 1876. In this period his poetry looked forward to a new era of friendship between the people of the Qing Empire and foreigners – 'The East and West are one family', read one line. This sense of hope, combined with support from his powerful new friends, drove him to seek work not in the government machine at home but in the Qing's first overseas mission. A friend of his father's, another Hakka, had been made head of the delegation to Japan and insisted that Huang accompany him as counsellor. It was a well-paid job: each month he earned what a junior local magistrate might earn in a year.[21]

Huang arrived in Tokyo in late 1877 as part of the first Qing diplomatic delegation to take up residence there. The establishment of the delegation was, in the eyes of court conservatives, a humiliating step: the rightful order was for tributaries to visit the emperor, not the other way around. But from the moment he arrived, it was clear to Huang that the Japanese had already adopted a European outlook on international relations: Japan saw itself as China's equal. All of this Huang reported back to Li Hongzhang in Tianjin and the *Zongli Yamen* (the putative 'foreign ministry') in Beijing. But Huang did more than draft diplomatic letters. He composed poems and started to write a book on Japan's reforms. Huang could not speak Japanese and few of the officials and intellectuals he met could speak Chinese. However, both sides could understand written Chinese characters so the two sides engaged in 'brush talk': writing their words on paper for the other to read.

Huang became a keen observer, occasional supporter and sometimes critic of the 'Freedom and People's Rights' movement, reading and commenting on the European tracts that they translated and published – which included the work of Herbert Spencer. Among those he held discussions with was Sone Toshitora, a former naval officer turned leader of a pan-Asianist organisation, *Shin-A sha*. Sone believed that Japan and China should stand together against the West and that Japan should take the lead. While Huang agreed with the need for mutual support and took part in some of Sone's activities, he naturally felt that China should be in the lead. Nonetheless, he seems to have absorbed some 'pan-Asian' sentiments; in particular, he started to use the term *Yaxiya* – the Chinese transliteration of the Japanese transliteration of the Western word 'Asia'. He came to believe that Asians were suffering collectively from the predations of the West and that they should stick together to resist.

In the spring of 1879 Huang presented a collection of 154 poems, plus various commentaries on Japan's apparently miraculous modernisation, to the *Zongli Yamen.* It was published by the *Tongwen Guan* (the Translators' College in Beijing) that winter. More importantly, it was republished the following year by a Hong Kong-based Chinese-language newspaper, the *Xunhuan Ribao* (*Hsün-huan Jih-pao*), edited by Wang Tao, one of the most prominent exiled reformers of the period. Huang's views began to reach a wide audience. One of the first poems in the collection described the Chinese and Japanese as being 'of the same culture and the same race' – *tongwen, tongzhong*. This was the Chinese version of a Japanese expression implying the two peoples should resist the whites together. For Huang, though, it had a different meaning: that the Japanese were descended from the Chinese.

The Chinese word that Huang chose as an equivalent to 'race' – *zhong* – was an innovation. (It's a different *zhong* to the *zhong* in *zhong guo*.) As the Sinologist Frank Dikötter has observed, it originally meant 'seed' or 'breed' when applied to plants or animals. Huang used it to refer to different kinds of human being.[22] In another poem, written in Japan but only published later, he explicitly referred to the 'yellow race'. 'The Western nations became stronger and more aggressive; they enslaved blacks and gradually got around to the yellow race,' he wrote in 'Cherry Blossoms'.[23] It was through this circuitous route that Herbert Spencer's ideas about race began to be transferred to a new audience: those who were demanding reforms of the Qing political system.

Huang continued to work on his *Treatises on Japan* for another decade and also to write and publish new poems. However, the next stop on his diplomatic career would radically change his thoughts on race. He came to believe that competition, not cooperation, was the natural international order and that only the fittest would survive. Like Herbert Spencer, he became a 'Social Darwinist'. On 30 March 1882 Huang arrived in San Francisco to take up his post as the Chinese consul-general in the city. Unlike his modern successors, he did not get to live in a fancy part of town. Just over a month after Huang's arrival, President Chester A. Arthur signed the Chinese Exclusion Act into law, banning the immigration of Chinese labourers. These were people who had fled their homeland illegally to escape war and poverty and who had little choice but to endure low wages and poor conditions just to survive. Organised labour saw them as a threat and was pushing for the 60,000 Chinese workers already in California to be expelled en masse. Meanwhile, disorganised labour was perpetrating innumerable abuses on individual Chinese migrants.

In response, Huang wrote a long poem to 'express my indignation'. It shows how his racialised view of the world had hardened by 1882 and includes perhaps the first use of the phrase 'yellow race' by a Chinese writer.

Men of all nations, folk of every country,
Were free to settle in those frontier lands.
The yellow, white, red and Negro races
Would live on equal terms with the American people . . .
On the five continents, each and every race thinks only of its own,
They mutually exclude each other, hate each other and curse each other.
The world today is not a world of great harmony,
Only one's own wit and might can be relied upon for defence against others . . .
Our Celestial Empire and the Yellow Race
Have become a laughing stock to all nations of the world.
(Hopefully we will not be so dull as the African slaves,
Who placidly accept whatever fate brings them.)[24]

Huang performed his consul-general's duties in San Francisco for three increasingly miserable years and then resigned in despair. In September 1885, almost as a coda to his term in office, twenty-eight Chinese miners were murdered by a white mob in Rock Springs, Wyoming. The legacy of American treatment of migrant Chinese would poison relations between the two countries for a long time, providing a pretext for violence against Christian missionaries and other acts of anti-Westernism.

Huang's world-view became even darker. The loss of Vietnam to France in 1885 prompted a poem with the line, 'The weak become the prey of the strong by the slash of a carving knife'. Disillusioned, he spent the next three years grieving for his late mother and working on his *Treatises on Japan*. He finally presented it, along with a recommendation from Li Hongzhang, to the *Zongli Yamen* in 1888. However, the *Yamen* was then under the control of conservatives, following the purge of reformers in the wake of the Sino-French war, and they were not interested in propagating the book's message that the Qing Empire had to follow Japan's example and undergo radical change. Huang was bitterly disappointed. The *Treatises* would only be published – by a private company in Guangdong – in the wake of the Sino-Japanese War seven years later. He consoled himself by sojourning in Beijing for a year in search of a new diplomatic post. He spent long hours in discussions with junior officials who were sympathetic to his ideas on reform, including the thirty-year-old scholar, Kang Youwei. In this way, many of his ideas about Social Darwinism and the racialised world came to be part of the orthodoxy of the reform movement that would develop over the following decade.

Eventually, Huang's lobbying bore fruit and he was appointed counsellor to the Chinese legation in London. He arrived in March 1890 but found he had little to do: minimal correspondence, few overseas Chinese to protect and without enough English to be able to converse with locals. Bored and homesick he jumped at the chance to leave and became consul-general in Singapore in October 1891. There he generated serious friction with the British colonial authorities by, among other activities, issuing Chinese passports to ethnic Chinese who were living under British rule. In a precursor to the disputes of today, it seems his race-based view of the world directly clashed with those of other governments.

It was only in the aftermath of the Sino-Japanese War that Huang became a prominent figure. He was recalled from Singapore during the fighting in November 1894 and spent the next two and a half years working for the governor-general of Liangjiang – the region around and including Shanghai – in charge of his personal 'Office of Foreign Affairs'. This gave Huang plenty of latitude to promote his own ideas and to plot with like-minded officials. He became part of the 'gradualist reform' clique within the bureaucracy, while also maintaining relations with the now-disgraced Li Hongzhang. He met, and became good friends with, the twenty-three-year-old writer Liang Qichao and appointed him editor of a pro-reform magazine that he sponsored and co-funded, *Shi Wu Bao* – the 'Current Affairs Paper'. Its first issue was published on 9 August 1896 and it came out every ten days until it was suppressed two years later. Its circulation rose to 10,000 and its influence – and through it the views of Liang and Huang – spread across the reform-minded elite. They argued for changes in education, state administration and economic affairs. But Huang also managed to stay on excellent terms with key officials in the court. The same month that the magazine was inaugurated, Huang was summoned to a private audience with the emperor. The emperor asked him to explain how Britain and Japan had become stronger than the Qing, and Huang took the opportunity to preach the necessity of new policies. Huang had become one of the most influential reformers in the empire. But it was not to last.

In January 1898 Kang Youwei, the loudest advocate of political reform in the country and Huang's discussion partner, was summoned to the *Zongli Yamen* to explain his proposals for reform. In February, the seventeen-year-old emperor asked to read copies of Huang's *Treatises on Japan* and in June the emperor issued a decree declaring the beginning of what became known as the Hundred Days Reform. Kang was appointed to the *Zongli Yamen* and Huang made minister to Japan. Luckily, before he could take the job, Huang was struck down by dysentery and was on sick leave when the Dowager Empress Cixi and her allies among the court conservatives launched their coup, imprisoning the emperor and crushing the reform movement. The empress ordered Huang arrested in Shanghai but the Western community in the city was outraged at the treatment of the famous reformer and, together with the Japanese government, pressed for the warrant to be cancelled. The court relented and Huang was allowed to retire to his hometown, famous but rusticated. By then, Huang's ideas on the 'yellow race' had spread throughout the reform movement and into the upper reaches of the official bureaucracy. But after 1898, others would take the urge to reform, and the idea of race, in new directions.

The death of his father was tragic for twelve-year-old Yan Fu but it pushed him down a path that, ultimately, made him one of the most important Chinese writers of the late nineteenth and early twentieth centuries. If his father had not been struck down, Yan would probably have joined the scholar-bureaucracy where, in all probability, circumstances would have propelled him to oppose all the ideas that he came to be known for. Instead, he was hurled from a life of prosperity and scholarship into penury and woe. The tutor his father had hired for him was let go, his mother only kept the household together by selling needlework and Yan was married off at the age of fourteen. Unable to afford the necessary schooling in the Confucian classics, a life of obscurity in the steep wooded valleys of Fujian province beckoned.[25]

But then one of his father's old friends stepped in with an offer that was welcome, although very much second best. Shen Baozhen was also from Fujian, had fought with Zeng Guofan against the Taiping rebels and then, like Zeng, become an active supporter of 'self-strengthening' – making use of Western methods to preserve Qing rule. Once the Taipings had been crushed, however,

Shen took leave to formally mourn his mother, in the traditional manner of a devout Confucian. While he was performing his domestic duties, the self-strengtheners convinced the court to hire foreign engineers to teach a new generation of skilled workers how to build ships and weapons. Two modern arsenals were established: one in Shanghai under Li Hongzhang and the other in Fuzhou under Zuo Zongtang (General Tso), the governor-general of Fujian and Zhejiang. Li hired British engineers and military officers while Zuo (who hated the British) hired French ones. Experts from the two countries who had inflicted such a humiliating defeat on the Qing realm in 1860 were now employed by it in order to construct a modern navy that could fight off future attackers.

Zuo needed a Qing official to oversee the foreigners in the shipyard and, in November 1866, Shen was persuaded to mourn only part-time and return to public service.[26] For the next eight years, under his leadership, the Fuzhou shipyard became what the Princeton professor Benjamin Elman called 'the leading industrial venture in late Qing China'.[27] Building ships was only part of the shipyard's work. It was also tasked with training the men who would construct and operate them. The first obstacle to overcome was finding suitable candidates, since most educated families wanted their sons to enter the scholar-gentry rather than have their minds sullied with 'Western learning'. In the end, Shen decided to attract students with a generous stipend and the promise of a well-paid job. It was perfect for the fourteen-year-old Yan Fu.

The availability of teachers meant that naval architects were trained in French while navigators and ships' officers were trained in English. Yan chose to join the 'English School', a decision that proved fateful. His teacher was James Carroll, formerly of the Royal Naval College at Greenwich in England and Yan appears to have studied hard. He graduated in 1871 and then went to sea, sailing as far south as Singapore and as far north as Japan. After six years as a naval officer, his tutors recommended him – along with eleven other officers – for further study at the Royal Naval College. He arrived in 1877, one of a tiny number of Qing subjects in London. There he encountered direct discrimination. Sir Edward Fanshawe, Admiral President of the college, ordered that the visitors live, eat and socialise outside its precincts rather than with the British officers.[28] Yan found more sympathetic company in the person of Guo Songtao, the first Qing ambassador to London, who had only taken up residence there the year before. The two men spent long evenings debating the source of Britain's wealth and power and drawing up radical prescriptions for change back home. In spite of the racism he encountered Yan opted to spend a second year at the college rather than join the crew of a British warship as his contemporaries did. It seems that he preferred to make the most of the opportunities to read and learn then available in London. Yan travelled back home in 1879 to take up a position as an instructor at the Fuzhou shipyard, but his sponsor, Shen, died that year. Li Hongzhang saw an opportunity and he poached Yan to teach at the institution Li controlled – the Northern Naval Academy in Tianjin. He spent a decade there and became its superintendent in 1890.

Fluent in English and fascinated by Britain's rise from obscurity to world domination, Yan spent this decade searching for answers. How could China regain its strength? He found the answers in Herbert Spencer. In 1881 Yan read Spencer's *The Study of Sociology*.[29] The entire book is predicated upon Spencer's racialist ideas. Early on Spencer pokes fun at the idea that 'an Aristotle [might] come from a father and a mother with facial angles of fifty degrees' and argues that the 'genesis of the great man depends on the long series of complex influences which has produced the race in which he appears'.[30] Later on, he argues that war 'has had a large share' in raising races to a higher stage by killing off the less fit. Spencer claimed to be a follower of Charles Darwin but his view of evolution was closer to that of Jean-Baptiste Lamarck: he believed that physical and mental adaptations that developed as a result of changes in behaviour could be passed on to subsequent generations biologically: 'By the unceasing antagonisms between human societies, small and large, there has been a mutual culture of adapted intelligence, a mutual culture of certain traits of character not to be undervalued and a mutual culture of bodily powers.'[31]

In 1892 the British missionary John Fryer (who had briefly worked as a teacher at the *Tongwen Guan* Translators' College in 1863) published what is thought to be the first article in Chinese suggesting a division of humanity into categories based upon skin colour.[32] Fryer had founded and edited a magazine, *Gezhi Huibian* (known in English as the 'Chinese Scientific Magazine') intended to bring Western scientific thinking to Chinese audiences. In his 1892 article, Fryer explained the latest developments in European racial thinking. It posited the existence of five races: Mongolian, Caucasian, African, Malayan and American Indian, each with different skin colours: reddish-brown (*zhe*), white, black, brown and bronze respectively. As Frank Dikötter has pointed out, this could be fitted into existing Chinese ideas about difference. The number five has strong symbolic meaning in Chinese culture, describing the number of senses, flavours, elements and directions. Fryer's 'Mongolians' weren't 'yellow' but in the ferment of the time it didn't take long for these racial ideas to fuse. Traditionally, yellow was the colour of the centre with the 'barbarians of the four quarters' allocated the colours of green, white, red and black. It didn't take much intellectual effort to adapt some of these ideas to the new circumstances.

Yan seems to have languished during the 1880s and early 1890s. Although he had been hired by Li Hongzhang, he seems to have thought the whole 'self-strengthening' approach was a waste of time. Depressed, he turned to opium and bitterness. It was defeat in the Sino-Japanese War that spurred him into action: 'things choked up in my breast, which I had to vomit forth', as he later wrote.[33] The old ways, which had led China into corruption and defeat, must be replaced by new ways based upon Western ideas: 'Science, sincerity and rectitude are made the foundations for ordering society,' he proclaimed.

The dam burst in early 1895. A new journal established by reformers among Tianjin's elite, *Zhibao*, gave Yan the space to publish four essays in rapid succession. Its base in a treaty port gave the publishers and writers protection from the Qing authorities and allowed Yan Fu to let rip with his criticism. Between February and May 1895, the essays introduced readers to Herbert Spencer's ideas on race and what would become known as 'Social Darwinism'. That was not really their primary purpose, though. In the words of the Sinologist James Pusey, Yan Fu 'brought in Darwin not for scientific reasons but as a Western witness to the necessity of change'.[34] Yan wanted reform and, just as in Japan a decade earlier, Spencer's ideas gave him grounds to argue for it. But there was a major difference between Spencer in Japan and Spencer in Yan Fu's writing.

The Japanese reformers liked Spencer because Spencer used Darwin to justify his ideas about the struggle for survival between *individuals*. Yan Fu took the idea of the struggle for survival but turned it into a struggle between *groups*. To explain the ideas, Yan had to create Chinese-language equivalents for the terms used by Social Darwinism. In particular, he needed a translation for 'natural selection'. He chose *wu jing tian ze* – literally, 'living things contend, heaven chooses'. Yan explained the meaning of the phrase as 'only the fit races survive'.[35] This was a distortion of Darwin's original meaning – that the fittest *individuals* passed on their genes to successive generations – but it fitted with Yan's thoughts on social change – that *groups* were the engine of history, a view formed by his observations of British society and his years as a resentful observer of Qing politics.

Yan's purpose is clear from the conclusion of the second essay, 'On the Origin of Strength' (*Yuan qiang*), published sometime between 4 and 9 March 1895. Written in the light of the stunning defeats inflicted upon the Qing forces by Japan, he argued, 'If we want to . . . resist our foreign enemies we must . . . establish a parliament at the capital and let each province and county elect its own officials.' In Yan's view, the only way to make 'the people' willing to fight for the country and defeat its enemies was to give them the power to direct it. The big question was, therefore, who were 'the people'?

To answer the question, Yan borrowed the idea of the 'yellow race' from Huang Zunxian. He complained that the Manchus had ruled their great-state as a separate elite ever since their conquest in 1644 and argued that, in the face of the existential threat from the 'white race', that needed to change. Yan opined that, despite the Qing elite's deliberate strategy of keeping themselves apart from the majority of the population, they were in fact part of the same people, the same race: 'Now on earth there are only four great races: the yellow, the white, the brown, and the black. . . . The *Man* [Manchu], *Meng* [Mongol], and *Han* people of today are all of the yellow race. . . . Therefore *zhong guo* [China] from of old has been ruled by one race only. It has never actually fallen to an alien kind.' The Chinese word that Yan chose for 'race' was the same as the one used by Huang: *zhong*. He used it to argue that the barriers between *Man* and *Han* had to be torn down.

It is interesting to note that Li Hongzhang set sail for the negotiations with Japan at Shimonoseki a few days after 'On the Origin of Strength' was published in *Zhibao*. It is easy to imagine that he took a copy of the journal with him and that this was the reason why he tried to appeal to his Japanese counterparts on the basis of their shared membership of the 'yellow race' at Shimonoseki. The fact that the Japanese gave him short shrift must have demonstrated to Li the weakness of the idea.

Nonetheless, the trope of the 'yellow race' continued to motivate the reformers during the following decade. In August 1896 Yan Fu met Huang Zunxian as he was travelling to Beijing to meet the emperor. Over the following few years, the two men wrote to each other frequently, exchanging ideas on race and reform.[36] In 1897 Yan founded two journals in Tianjin – the daily *Guowen Bao* ('National News Journal') and the weekly *Guowen Huibian* ('National News Collection')[37] – to spread his ideas. In 1898 his 'translation' – really a paraphrasing – of an 1893 lecture by the British social reformer Thomas Huxley on 'Evolution and Ethics' was published as *Tianyan Lun* ('On Evolution'). Huxley was strongly opposed to Spencer's individualism and emphasised, instead, group solidarity. That was even more emphasised in Yan's rendering of it. As Dikötter points out, Yan took Spencer's ideas of competition and Huxley's ideas of cooperation and inflected both with his own ideas about race to argue that 'science' told us that the 'yellow race' is locked in a death struggle with the 'white race' and would end up in the same state as the 'black race' and the 'red race' unless it instituted political reform.

Yan Fu's writings became extremely influential: they came to be seen as the authentic representation of Darwinism in China for many years. It was not until 1919 that a full translation of Darwin's *Origin of Species* was published in Chinese. In the meantime, it was Yan Fu's rendering of the interpretations of Darwin by Huxley and Spencer that set the terms of the debate both for reformists such as Liang Qichao and revolutionaries such as Sun Yat-sen. In the words of James Pusey in his study *China and Charles Darwin*, the way Yan Fu wrote about race 'helped open the door for a generation of unpleasant racial thinking'.[38]

15 April 2018 and the *grande salle* of the University of New South Wales, Leighton Hall, is filled with 600 members of Australia's 'overseas Chinese' community. Against the polished travertine wall hangs a giant image of a mythical figure, or rather a giant image of a real statue in the Chinese city of Xinzheng representing a mythical figure: the Yellow Emperor. This is an annual event organised by the 'Australia Chinese Ayers Association', a group founded, in its

own words, to 'promote understanding between countries'. The only country the association promotes, however, is the People's Republic of China. Among those attending the event or sending messages of congratulation were the former Australian Prime Minister Tony Abbott, the governor of New South Wales and various local mayors and councillors. It is a classic example of the kind of work that the Chinese Communist Party's 'United Front Work Department' undertakes – building links between the motherland, overseas Chinese and local politicians and figures of influence. The main United Front organisation in Australia, the 'Australian Council for the Promotion of the Peaceful Reunification of China', was a supporter of the event, as were several other United Front-linked cultural groups. Among the organisers was Deng Li, a journalist with China's state media, and the event, like others before and since, was duly celebrated on the United Front's own website.[39]

The purpose of the Sydney event was to connect its participants with a much larger gathering taking place around that statue in Xinzheng: a mass worshipping of the mythical Yellow Emperor in his mythical birthplace on his mythical birthday – the third day of the third month of the lunar calendar, 2698 BCE. It was one of six similar gatherings on the same day: others were in Hong Kong, Macao, Taiwan, San Francisco and Vancouver. Ever since they were first held, in 2006, the celebrations in Xinzheng have been aimed at building a sense of community with overseas Chinese. Their official theme is 'same roots, same ancestors, same origins, peace and harmony'.[40] The purpose of the 'core' ceremony in Xinzheng, according to the Chinese state media, was to 'build a spiritual home to pray for the great rejuvenation of the Chinese nation', a message that was broadcast around the world by online news sites and China's overseas broadcasters, CCTV International and Phoenix TV.

In the years since Yellow Emperor worship was inaugurated in Xinzheng in 2006, the organisers have devised a specific form for the festivities, which has become the model for the others around the world. Nine events take place in sequence, including music, dancing and prayers, venerating the Yellow Emperor as the 'Ancestor of the Chinese nation'. It is a classic case of what the British historian Eric Hobsbawm once called 'the invention of tradition'. The Yellow Emperor has been positioned as a globally unifying figure: a poster boy for all Chinese everywhere and an ideological tool for the Communist Party of China.

It is the culmination of a journey that began a century ago with the thoughts of a young hothead from Hangzhou called Zhang Binglin.

We encountered Zhang Binglin in Chapter 1: the classical scholar who became a reformist writer after the 1895 defeat by Japan, and then a revolutionary agitator after the international suppression of the Boxer Rebellion in 1900/01. As we saw, his political evolution was founded upon a dramatic shift in his thinking about race. In short, Zhang invented the idea of the 'Han race'. As the Hong Kong-born professor of Chinese History, Chow Kai-wing, has observed, 'Before 1899, Zhang's characterisation of China's struggle against European powers was primarily based on the idea of war between the "white" and "yellow" races.' He accepted some of the 'Western-origin' theories of the French orientalist Albert Terrien de Lacouperie – that the white and yellow races shared common origins in Mesopotamia – but inverted them by claiming the whites were descendants of the yellows. In 1898, having read the work of Yan Fu, he had published an introduction to Herbert Spencer's racial thinking in a reformist journal, *Changyanbao*.[41] Politically, he followed the reformist arguments of Huang and Yan.[42] But in May 1899, writing from the safety of Japan and then Shanghai, he penned an article referring to the emperor as the 'Guest Emperor', highlighting the 'barbarian' origins of the Qing, and in early 1900 his *Qiushu* ('The Book of Urgency') explicitly called for the overthrow of the Manchu government.

Zhang had an ideological difficulty. The 'Confucian' attitude shared by the court and the reformers was that political legitimacy came from an enlightened culture and that anyone, including barbarians, could become *Hua* by adopting that culture. Manchus could be *Hua* as much as Han. But having decided that the Manchus were the problem, Zhang needed a basis for an argument against culturalism. He found it in a fourth-century BCE historical commentary called the *Zuozhuan*, which – according to Zhang – demonstrated that bonds of kinship were more important than culture. Since 'barbarians' were not of the same 'type', they could not have the same loyalties as the Han. He adopted the word *zu* – meaning 'lineage' – as a marker of difference. Lineage was a vexed issue in the turbulent nineteenth century. The Qing needed its 'bannermen' to demonstrate their ancestry and, as Frank Dikötter has shown, many Han families drew up long family trees as a survival strategy: to demonstrate their pedigree and also to strengthen their kinship connections with neighbours. Around the country, lineage groups were frequently involved in violent feuds, ranging from small inter-village disputes to large-scale conflicts such as the Hakka-Punti war.[43] *Zu*, then, encapsulated a powerful idea. Zhang Binglin took *zu* and enlarged it from the local to the national: the Han became the *Hanzu* and Manchu, the *Manzu*. The two groups were rival lineages and therefore conflict between them became not just thinkable but logical.

Onto this he grafted European ideas about evolution and race. Both the white race and the yellow race were intelligent, he argued in the *Qiushu*, but the yellows were more civilised. The Han belonged to the 'yellow race' but he created the idea of the 'race-surname' – *zhong xing* – to demonstrate that they were different from the Manchus. The term *zhongxing* was a contraction of the characters in 'race-lineage' (*zhongzu*) and 'surname' (*xingshi*). Han and Manchu may have been part of the same *zhong*, but they were not part of the same *zhongzu*, and lineage surnames were a vital way to discern the two. This was not the only innovation in the *Qiushu*. In it he also gave the world his lasting legacy, the notion that the ancestor of all the Han was Huangdi: the Yellow Emperor.

Just after his publication of the *Qiushu* came his decisive split with the reformers. The Eight-Nation Army seized Tianjin on 14 July 1900 and, unlike the reformists, who pledged to defend the Qing court, Zhang denounced it. In a hugely symbolic protest he cut off his 'queue' – the braided pigtail hairstyle imposed on all Qing male subjects on pain of death – in front of a reformers' protest meeting on 3 August. He then wrote an article entitled 'The Correct Discourse on Hatred for the Manchus' for the first revolutionary magazine *Guominbao*, based in Japan. He did not want to kill the Manchus, he wrote, but he did want them expelled back to Manchuria, the northeastern lands of their origin. In this he was a relative moderate among the revolutionaries. There were already some arguing for an anti-Manchu genocide. While Huang Zunxian, Yan Fu and the other reformers were calling for the Qing government to break down the barriers between members of the same 'yellow race', Zhang Binglin and his revolutionary comrades were arguing that the race which mattered was the Han and there was no place for the Manchus.

There was a key difference between Western racism and its 'eastern' counterpart. Whereas most European racialists argued in terms of biology, there were no obvious differences in skin colour or facial angle between Han and Manchu. But Zhang needed a rationale to demarcate the boundary between the two groups he was trying to create. He found it in the logic of the lineage. He made use of his early training as a classical scholar and went searching through the ancient texts. He found an answer in the writings of the second-century BCE historian Sima Qian, who began his account with the life of the Yellow Emperor. For Zhang, the emperor became the *shi zu* – the original ancestor – and the twenty-four surnames of his sons (according to Sima Qian) were the original Han *zhongxing*. Almost 5,000 years later, the entire 450 million-strong *Hanzu* could be imagined as the sons and grandsons of the Yellow Emperor – the *Huangdi zisun*.

Like most successful new political ideas, Zhang's racial-nationalism took pre-existing ideas – the myth of the Yellow Emperor, the importance of the lineage, dislike of the government and so on – and fashioned a new ideology from the amalgam. In the aftermath of the Qing court's failure to resist the allied powers during the 1900 Boxer Rising, the concept became so successful that within just a few years the arguments of reformists such as Huang Zunxian, Yan Fu and Liang Qichao had disappeared into near irrelevance. By December 1906 the new ideas could simply subsume the old ones. Writing in the second edition of *Minbao*, the pro-revolutionary journal that he edited, Hu Hanmin 'borrows Yan Fu's own Social Darwinist categories to prove that the Manchus are simply an inferior people and that China can only flourish when the superior Han race prevails', in the words of Yan's biographer, Benjamin Schwartz.[44] At a meeting that same month to celebrate *Minbao*'s first anniversary, Zhang finished his speech by chanting 'Long live the *Minbao*! Long live the *Hanzu*!' The notion of a 'yellow race' that could contain all the inhabitants of East Asia was jettisoned for a much narrower one that deliberately excluded those outside the freshly imagined *Hanzu*.

The beauty of the 'Han race' idea for the revolutionaries was that it created a huge community of potential supporters who could be mobilised against a declared enemy: the ruling Manchu elite. If the *Manzu* were excluded, then so were the *Mengzu* (Mongols) and the non-Chinese-speaking minorities. Indigenous groups were relegated to the status of 'browns' or 'blacks' for whom Social Darwinism predicted only one fate: they could be ignored in the coming struggle. Increasingly, the revolutionaries – mainly young, male students living in exile in

Japan – mixed old ideas of lineage – *zu* – with new racial ideas of biological race – *zhong*. The fusion of *zhong* and *zu* was made possible by the imaginary figure of the Yellow Emperor: *Huangdi* became the father of the *zhongzu*. However, the question of who was, and was not, a member of the *zhongzu* was not always so easy to answer.

With revolutionary sentiment rising, the Qing government made some belated efforts at reform, including, in 1904, new regulations on primary schooling. They stipulated that schools should promote 'their love of the nation' through, among other things, 'native place education'. Various local literati rushed to publish their own 'gazetteers' of prefectures, sub-prefectures, departments and counties in the hope of promoting their world-view to the younger generation and perhaps making a profit from sales. According to May-bo Ching, history professor at the City University of Hong Kong, the politics of these men traversed the spectrum from traditional scholar-officials to reformers and revolutionaries. While the 'gazetteer' was a long-established publishing format, the Qing administration specified in 1905 that reformed editions needed to include new information. Apart from basic history and geography, each gazetteer should include details about the various races (literally *ren lei* – 'person types') and their clans (literally *shi zu* – surnames and lineages).[45]

The guidelines also specified that gazetteer compilers needed to decide who counted as a subject of the empire – a *qi min* (a new term that submerged the differences between members of banner units – *qi* – and civilians – *min*). There were three criteria: they could not be a believer in 'another religion', such as Christianity or Islam; they had to be employed in one of the four traditional occupations: scholar, artisan, farmer or trader; and they could not be a member of 'another race' – *ta zhong*. The regulations specified that *ta zhong* included the Hui (Muslims), the Miao (Hmong), the Zhuang (Tai) and several other named minorities. By listing these groups as 'outsiders', the Qing state was, in effect, saying that everyone else was an insider, whether Han, Manchu or Mongol. Thus, by 1905, even the Qing state had begun to replace the idea of *zu*, which had structured its military and bureaucracy for almost 300 years, in favour of the reformists' ideas of *zhong* – race.

However, a controversy that year would demonstrate the arbitrariness of the whole concept of a Han race and bring the pioneer of Chinese racial thinking,

Huang Zunxian, back into the public eye one final time. The question of who was, and was not, Han could be extremely divisive, particularly in Guangdong province, where older inhabitants still remembered the Hakka-Punti war. The compilers of different local-level gazetteers took different positions. For example, two counties, Shixing and Xingning, both contained large numbers of Hakka speakers: the Xingning gazetteer mentioned this fact but the Shixing book did not. The issue came to a head when a writer with revolutionary sympathies, Huang Jie, published his 'Textbook of Guangdong Local History'.[46] Huang Jie had co-founded the 'National Essence Society' (*Guoxue baocun hui*) the year before to promote political change, with inspiration from a conservative view of the past. The society's anti-Manchuism combined revolutionary zeal with the Social Darwinist fear that the Han race had to be preserved from the threat of extinction. This, the society argued, could only be done through the mobilisation of ancient culture. Huang Jie and his fellow National Essence Society members saw an opportunity in the education reforms to transform the thinking of the new generation by providing them with 'national essence' textbooks.[47]

Huang Jie's 1905 Guangdong History textbook stated baldly that, 'Among the races of Guangdong are Hakkas and Hoklos who are not Cantonese and not of Han racial stock.' This infuriated Huang Zunxian, then living in quiet banishment in the province, and provoked him into organising, along with fellow Hakka scholar-officials, a 'Society for Investigating the Origin of the Hakka People'. The society used all its influence to lobby the provincial education authority which, eventually, agreed to have the sentence removed from the book. Huang Zunxian died in March 1905 but his struggle continued. Although other textbooks were published that specifically excluded the Hakka from membership of the Han, by 1907 the provincial authorities had agreed to remove all the offending sections. Thus, in his final act, Huang Zunxian demonstrated the emptiness of the notion of a 'Han race' by showing it could be expanded or contracted not by science but by political pressure from influential people. Henceforth, the Hakka and the Hoklo would be Han.

But empty or not, the idea of a Han race became the revolutionaries' most powerful weapon. It enabled them to create alliances between literate officials and illiterate peasants. It was no longer sufficient to be a cultured *Hua*, or a member of the 'yellow race' – change could only come from the Han, the sons and grandsons of the Yellow Emperor. From 1900 onwards, as a result of Zhang Binglin's innovation, the way that Chinese communities referred to themselves began to change. That change endures. The descendants of the *huaqiao* who settled abroad before 1910 generally still refer to themselves as '*Hua*' to this day. They are using a 'culturalist' definition of themselves that Huang Zunxian, Yan Fu and Liang Qichao would have recognised. By contrast, those who live in the People's Republic of China or on Taiwan are far more likely to call themselves '*Han*'.

But it is clear that the Communist Party of China's United Front Department wants to change this. The promotion of the Yellow Emperor ritual among *huaqiao* communities is an obvious example of a political strategy intended to change their identity and allegiances. When a Chinese consul in San Francisco makes an appeal for loyalty to American citizens based upon their genetic inheritance, he is doing so on the basis of Zhang Binglin's racial nationalism. The same is true of the granting of residency visas to descendants of nth-generation emigrants. Rather than simply being proud of being *Hua* and having ancestral connections to villages in faraway provinces, the leadership in Beijing wants these audiences to see themselves as sons and grandsons of the Yellow Emperor and be loyal to his lineage, embodied today in the People's Republic of China.

Given that attendances at United Front-type events generally number only in the hundreds, a tiny fraction of the estimated 60 million 'overseas Chinese', it seems safe to say that this message has only a minority appeal. Yet by recruiting key figures within diaspora communities and by dominating the global narrative about the nature of 'Chinese-ness', the United Front's activities can have a far greater impact around the world than mere numbers might suggest.

4
THE INVENTION OF CHINESE HISTORY
guoshi – national history

Beijing's answer to Silicon Valley is Zhongguancun. A generation ago it was still possible to cycle through parts of it along muddy tracks between paddy fields. These days it is home to ten science parks, from which have sprung Lenovo, Baidu and a hundred other hi-tech giants, most of them unknown outside their home country. Zhongguancun is also an intellectual hub. It is fringed by the huge campuses of Tsinghua and Peking universities, built decades ago in what was then splendid rural isolation to keep the students away from city vices and safely under political control. At its heart sits the people's university, Renmin, originally founded by the Communist Party in 1937 to educate its cadres. And on the fifth floor of one of Renmin University's gleaming towers lives the 'Institute of Qing History'.

Just a year after its victory in the civil war, the Communist Party leadership called on its university to write a history of the Qing Dynasty.[1] As one of the leading American historians of the Qing period, Pamela Kyle Crossley, has pointed out, the instruction would 'complete the traditional arc in which each imperial dynasty declared its legitimacy by writing the history of its predecessor'.[2] The party's directive led to the formal creation of the Institute of Qing History in 1978 and then, in 2002, to something far bigger. Following a proposal from Professor Li Wenhai, formerly the president of Renmin University – and also the secretary of its Communist Party Committee, director of the China Society of History and director of the History Teaching Guidance Committee of the Ministry of Education – the State Council approved the establishment of the 'National Qing Dynasty History Compilation Committee'. The project enjoys the kind of government financial support that makes other historians weep with envy. It has now digitised nearly 2 million pages and images, translated tens of thousands of foreign studies into Chinese, published multi-volume collections of documents and held dozens of academic conferences.[3]

From the outset, the Qing Dynasty History Compilation Committee has been a vehicle for the Communist Party to direct the way that the Qing Dynasty is remembered. Following Xi Jinping's ascent to the apex of power in 2012, however, the party's hand has gripped ever more tightly around the project's throat. There are increasingly strict limits on what can, and more importantly cannot, be said about the seventeenth, eighteenth and nineteenth centuries. The reason is obvious: facing demands for independence in Taiwan and separatist feeling in Tibet and Xinjiang, nothing can be allowed to upset the official national narrative that these places were smoothly, peacefully and organically incorporated into the motherland and that they are therefore integral parts of a nation-state with ancient roots.

Since 2013 foreign historians such as Crossley, Evelyn Rawski, James Millward, Mark Elliott and the many others who tell a different story about the Qing Great-State – that it was a Manchu dynasty and expanded its realm through conquest, violence and oppression – have been denigrated in China, denounced as imperialists and denied access to archives. The same fight has also been taken to independent-minded Chinese historians. In early 2019 the Communist Party's own 'Chinese History Research Committee' warned that, 'A very small number of scholars lack the proper vigilance against Western academic thoughts, and introduce theoretical variants of foreign historical nihilism into the field of Qing historical research.' The phrase 'historical nihilism' has become increasingly common in recent years: it is Communist Party-speak for research that does not support the party's own view of history. The article, by Zhou Qun, deputy editor of the committee's own journal, *Lishi yanjiu* ('Historical Research'), was republished in the *People's Daily* to make sure the message was widely received. Under the headline 'Firmly Grasp the Right of Discourse of the History of the Qing Dynasty', it helpfully reminded readers that, 'Studying history, and learning from history is a valuable experience of the Chinese nation for 5,000 years, and it is also an important magic weapon for the Chinese Communist Party to lead the Chinese people to win one victory after another.'[4] As a description of the Communist Party's view of history, that could hardly be bettered, except perhaps by Mao Zedong himself: 'Make the past serve the present', as he told students in 1964. The ideological war over the events of three and four hundred years ago is alive and apparently still vital to the survival of today's People's Republic. The National Qing Dynasty History Compilation Committee is a bulwark in the party's defences against foreign plots to undermine national unity through the ruse of archival research.

There is a new rigidity to the Communist Party's imposition of an 'ideologically correct' history but the creation and curation of a national story that begins 5,000 years ago pre-dates Mao. It is not, however, 5,000 years old. The belief that there was a place called 'China' and a people called the 'Chinese' in continuous existence for 5,000 years only came into existence itself around the turn of the twentieth century. The idea was born in the minds of political exiles, far from home and dreaming of a new world. For that new world to be created, they first had to create a story about the old world. And the person who did the most to bring this old world story into existence was someone we have already encountered: the radical reforming writer, the father of Chinese journalism, Liang Qichao.

By the time Timothy Richard died, in April 1919, he had become the most famous foreigner in China. He is now largely forgotten in his home country but his picture can still be found in museums in Beijing. It is quite possible that even Xi Jinping has seen it, for Richard has a place in the Communist Party's pantheon as the first person to publish the names of Karl Marx and Friedrich Engels in Chinese. It was an unlikely prospect for a farm boy from the far west of Wales.

Richard was born in 1845 in Ffaldybrenin, a one-chapel village tucked away in the Carmarthenshire hills, into a staunch protestant family. At the age of fourteen, he chose to be baptised in the chilly waters of a nearby river and a decade later he signed up for the ministry at the theological college in the county town of Haverfordwest. Almost immediately, it seems, China became his vocation. After four years of study and a three-month journey by ship, he arrived in Shanghai on 12 February 1870. The Baptist Missionary Society sent him north, to Chefoo/Zhifu (now better known as Yantai) in Shandong province, where he lived among the people, wore local clothes and learnt Chinese. He married another missionary, Mary Martin, in 1878 and they had four children. Their role as organisers and relief workers during the famines of the time earned them respect and, later, protection against the anti-missionary feeling that arose in many other parts of the country.[5]

His attitude to missionary work was very different from many of his colleagues. He sought dialogue and common ground, hoping to convert by example rather than inducement. In 1891 Richard was appointed secretary of the 'Society for the Diffusion of Christian and General Knowledge Among the Chinese' (SDK – also known as the Christian Literature Society for China, or CLS), whose purpose was to translate and circulate materials 'based on Christian principles'. It was the Society's firm belief that their mission was not just religious but social: 'pure Christianity, as a matter of fact, has lifted up every nation that has thoroughly adopted it', as they put it in their annual report of 1898. They were preaching the gospel of Westernisation just as much as the gospel of Christ. The society's explicit strategy was to reach out to 'the future rulers of China', and they found a receptive audience among a section of the elite. The Chinese name that it operated under, which translates as the 'Broad Study Association', made this easier by obscuring its religious nature. One of the SDK's most successful tactics was circulating books and pamphlets to candidates outside the traditional examinations for future scholar-officials.[6] Between 1892 and 1896, it distributed over 120,000 tracts to candidates.[7] For the society's leadership, political and religious reform went hand in hand.

Another tactic was to publish the *Wanguo gongbao*, a Chinese-language magazine carrying a mixture of Christian argument, articles about European progress and calls for political reform, many of them written or translated by Timothy Richard. Throughout 1894 he devoted several issues of the magazine to an abridged version of a particular history book that he believed would have a profound effect on its audience. The book he chose was a 463-page doorstopper: *The Nineteenth Century: A History* by Robert Mackenzie, originally published in London, Edinburgh and New York in 1880. It was not an academic work but one aimed at a new middle class keen to discover its place in the world. About half of the book was focused on Britain, with the rest looking at Europe, particularly France and Russia, as well as Turkey and the United States. There was almost nothing on Asia or Africa outside the British colony of India. Richard's purpose in choosing this tome to translate was to show how Britain and France had emerged from poverty and wartime destruction into the world powers they had become. His audience was similar to Mackenzie's: the urban, literate middle classes. And his prescription was simple: education, reform and liberalisation.

The *Wanguo gongbao* serialised *The Nineteenth Century* between March and September 1894. As each edition appeared, the situation in the Sino-Japanese War grew worse. Every successive defeat became, in effect, physical proof of Mackenzie's message: through reform, even little upstart Japan had become stronger than the sclerotic Qing Great-State. Demand for Mackenzie's writings was so huge that, the following year, the society published a complete edition of *The Nineteenth Century* with the Chinese title of 'The Outline of Occidental New History'. The idea of 'New History' was important to Richard, as he explained in his preface: 'Just as a clear mirror reveals the beautiful and the ugly, so New History reveals what flourishes and what needs to be replaced.' 'New History' was therefore more than a way to learn about the past; it was a guide to instruct modern people, modern nations and modern governments. The translation was a sensation: 4,000 official copies were sold in a fortnight. More importantly, pirated versions were printed all over the country. The historian Mary Mazur estimates that, in all, around a million copies were sold and that the book's influence 'cannot be underestimated'. It was read by almost the entire elite, including the emperor.[8]

While the book was being published, Richard took his proselytising directly to the elite, making a visit to Beijing at the time of the highest-level examinations for prospective scholar-officials, which took place every three years. Many of those taking the *jinshi* already knew Richard from his writings in *Wanguo gongbao*, and some were eager to meet him. In the wake of defeat by Japan, 1895 was a time of ferment in the capital. In April, the reformist scholar Kang Youwei and his pupil Liang Qichao had organised 1,200 of the examination candidates to sign a petition demanding that the emperor reject the humiliating conditions imposed by the Treaty of Shimonoseki (see Chapter 2).[9] Their demands were rejected but that only sharpened the reformists' determination. In August, Kang founded his own newspaper, the first independent journal to be published in Beijing. The model for the paper was obvious; it was the SDK's *Wanguo gongbao*. In fact Kang even gave it the same name to begin with, before changing it to *Zhongwai Jiwen* ('World Report') three months later. Liang, who had just failed the *jinshi* exam for the second time, agreed to be its editor.

On 17 October 1895, Richard and Kang Youwei met for the first time. In Richard's account, Kang came to say that he wanted 'to cooperate with us' in the work of regenerating China.[10] The relationship grew strong enough for Richard to become a founding member of Kang's reformist lobby group, the *Qiang Xue Hui*, or 'Strengthening Study Society', established the following month. At the same time Liang Qichao volunteered to work as Richard's secretary, helping with his translations and his dealings with officials. The two men clearly shared a vision for the future of the country. During late 1895 and early 1896, while working as Richard's secretary, Liang devised and published a bibliography of important texts intended as a guide for reformists. Two of his particular recommendations were Mackenzie's book and the society's *Wanguo gongbao*. As the two men worked alongside each other, Liang's ideas on reform continued to develop. Richard's influence can be seen in many of Liang's later writings, whether on history, political reform or the role of women.[11] When the court banned the *Zhongwai Jiwen*, Liang founded another newspaper, *Shiwu Bao*, in the safety of Shanghai in August 1896. He copied its format from *Wanguo gongbao* and covered many of the same themes and arguments.[12]

This was an intellectual journey that Liang Qichao had been traversing ever since 1890, when he failed the *jinshi* exam for the first time as a seventeen-year-old. While making his way home in disappointment via Shanghai, he had discovered Western maps and reformist ideas which completely changed the direction of his life. By the late 1890s Liang was probably the most influential journalist writing in Chinese and the ideas about history that filled his articles in *Shiwu Bao* were, in turn, heavily influenced by the thoughts of Timothy Richard, and through him, Robert Mackenzie. When the *Qiangxuehui* published its 'New Collection of Tracts of the Times' (*Jing Shi Wen*) in February 1898, thirty-one of the essays were written by Richard, along with forty-four by Liang and thirty-eight by Kang.[13]

Richard also introduced Liang to Social Darwinist ideas at around the same time as Yan Fu's translations of Herbert Spencer and Thomas Huxley (described in Chapter 3) were being published. They inspired Liang to develop his idea of the 'group' – *qun* – and the best way to ensure its survival. During this period, the fear of racial extinction became the spirit that animated the reformers. Liang's 1897 essay 'On Grouping' (*Shuo Qun*) introduced the idea to readers of *Shiwu Bao*.[14] According to Liang, it was groups of people who provided the energy for social change. That meant they were the proper subjects for any writer of history – not the state and its rulers. This implied a complete break with traditional ideas of 'old learning' and indicated the direction in which Liang's thoughts on a Chinese 'New History' were heading.

The schemings of Kang and Liang and their hopes for reform (not to mention those of Timothy Richard) were smashed on 22 September 1898 when Empress Cixi launched her coup. Cixi's allies placed the emperor under house arrest and executed six of the leading reformers but failed to prevent Kang and Liang from escaping to Japan. Richard had been supposed to meet the emperor on that day but seems to have been warned about the danger and worked his contacts to make sure that Kang and Liang received diplomatic protection.[15] Once established in exile, the reformers found themselves in a cauldron of plots and theorising as communities of Chinese students, taking inspiration from the rapid modernisation of Japan, dreamt of change back home. Liang made his home in Yokohama and learnt Japanese. As a result he was able to read many Western books that had already been translated into Japanese but not yet into Chinese. His intellectual horizons expanded once more. In a 1902 article he recommended dozens of titles by authors ranging from Aristotle to the German historian Karl Ploetz. Many of the ideas and terms he both adopted and invented clearly bore the influence of these European thinkers filtered through Chinese and Japanese translations.

Most fundamentally, Liang adopted an exile's view of home. Writing from Yokohama, it was obvious to him that the Qing Great-State did not comprise 'all under heaven' or *tianxia*, but was just one country among many. In an article in 1899 he referred to that country as '*Zhina*', borrowing the Japanese name.[16] Lacking Chinese-language equivalents for the Western concepts intrinsic to the writings of European 'New History', such as 'country' and 'nation', he began to experiment with new words. In October 1899 he wrote that while there was a Chinese term *guo-jia*, meaning state-clan, the survival of the yellow race required a *guo-min* – a state-people. The only way to save the *guo* from 'Social-Darwinist' extinction by the white race was to mobilise the *min* – the people – in its defence. With a *guomin*, the state would belong to the whole people, who would thereby form a nation.[17] Liang developed his idea of the importance of the 'group' into a single-minded focus on the nation as the engine of history. In 1900 he wrote, 'Today's Europe, every single part of it, has benefited from nothing so much as nationalism.'[18] Crucially, in Liang's view, it was the people who should define the state, not the other way around. As we shall see in Chapter 5, all these terms – 'people', 'race' and 'nation' – were new and very loosely defined, and their meanings would shift over the following few years as political battles raged between reformists and revolutionaries. However, Liang's emerging ideas about the *guomin* would go on to define the 'New History' that he wanted to write and how his successors would define 'Chinese history' for the following century and beyond.

In 1901 Liang published what became the founding text for the 'Chinese New History': his 'History of China Introductory Essay' (*Zhongguoshi Xulun*). In it he laid down the intellectual foundations upon which a nation would be defined and built. He writes of a place – no longer called *Zhina* but *Zhongguo* – and he declares that this *Zhongguo* is comprised of a single people with a history that binds them together and makes them different from their neighbours. He tells his readers what should be included in the history of '*Zhongguo*' and what should be left out, and the correct terms in which to discuss it. The term he chooses for 'people' is clearly influenced by the debates about race that are taking place among exiled reformists and revolutionaries (discussed in Chapter 3). It is *minzu* – literally 'people lineage' – but something that could just as easily be translated as 'race'. The Chinese people are therefore the *Zhongguo minzu*. He borrows ideas from German historians to argue that the impact of the *Zhongguo minzu* on history was akin to that of the Aryan/white race.[19]

Liang believed there was an organic connection between history-writing and survival. All groups were in competition but those groups who possessed a history – and for Liang, that meant the white and yellow races – survived, while those who had 'no history' – the blacks, browns and reds – would not. In another essay published at around the same time, he claimed that 'the black, the red and the brown races are inferior to the white as far as micro-organisms in the blood and brain power are concerned. Only the yellow race can compete with the white.'[20]

It was critical for racial survival, therefore, to have a history that reinforced the group. Liang's chosen group was the 'people of *Zhongguo*' and his 'New History' therefore had to be a narrative of continuity. But the concept of *Zhongguo minzu* had to be flexible enough to include all the diverse peoples of the great-state. He tore up the traditional way of writing histories of dynasties and adopted a European classification of 'ancient', 'middle ages' and 'modern'. For him, the ancient period began with the mythical Yellow Emperor in 2700 BCE and ended with the creation of a unified '*zhong guo*' under the Qin Dynasty in 221 BCE. In Liang's words, 'This was the age when *zhong guo* became *Zhongguo*, as the *Zhongguo minzu* developed itself, struggled among itself, and unified itself.' The 'middle ages' started in 221 BCE and continued until the end of the Qianlong Emperor's reign in 1796, when the 'modern' period began. As Professor Xiaobing Tang has noted, this periodisation was based upon Liang's views about the 'natural' geography of *Zhongguo* and he chose it with the frontiers of the Qing Great-State in mind. He described the 'ancient' period as a time when the *minzu* struggled with other groups, such as the Miao. The implication here was that the original *minzu* was a racial group, the Han, even though Liang profoundly disagreed with the *Hanzu* racism of Zhang Binglin who was also active in Japan at the same time.

It is important to understand that in 1901 Liang was not describing an already existing Chinese nation but was actually *creating* one by writing its history. By choosing which groups were included in the *Zhongguo minzu* and which were excluded, he drew a boundary around the nation that has endured to this day. He felt no need to explain *why* he was writing a history of this particular group of people: the necessity appeared simply self-evident. Liang was not writing history for its own sake but in parallel with essays and articles on the need for political reform. History was the foundation of his political work. Liang wanted to modernise but also to preserve the Qing Great-State and he needed an ideology that justified his arguments. He found it in a European view of history, based on a 'Social Darwinist' view of progress in which the authenticity of a nation was provided by its ostensibly ancient roots. The existence of the nation therefore had to be proven by tracing its evolutionary history. It was critical that he demonstrate continuity between a distant past and the present. It did not matter whether members of the original *Zhongguo minzu* actually knew that they were part of that group. What mattered was the link between then and now.[21] He stitched together a narrative based on a mixture of evidence and conjecture, selecting certain stories while leaving out others, and all to justify his modern political agenda. That agenda still defines the Chinese-ness of the People's Republic of China to this day.

Liang's characterisation of middle ages 'Asia' included only those races (*zhong*) who were incorporated into the Qing realm during the seventeenth and eighteenth centuries: the aboriginal 'Miao' (a catch-all term that included the Hmong and other southern hill peoples), the Han (described as the descendants of the Yellow Emperor), plus Tibetans, Mongols, Tungus (Manchus) and Xiongnu (Uighurs or Turks). These 'Asian races' fought the Han but then, Liang argued, united with it to form a single race very different from those outside.[22] These, then, were the historically 'obvious' components of the modern *Zhongguo minzu*. This had equally 'obvious' implications for the territory of *Zhongguo* – it should include all the territories on which those peoples lived: *Zhongguo Benbu* ('China proper', the former Ming realm) plus Tibet, Xinjiang, Mongolia and Manchuria.

Liang then defined the beginning of the 'modern' period as the time when *Zhongguo* became connected to the wider world and was forced into a 'survival of the fittest' competition with the countries of the white race.[23] He argued that racial mixing, not separateness, was the key to survival and that, in particular, the barriers between Han and Manchu needed to be broken down. For Liang, the Han were the core of the *Zhongguo minzu* and clearly superior. The purpose of mixing was to raise up other peoples to their evolutionary level.

This was just a taste of what was to come. In February 1902 Liang founded a bi-weekly paper called *Xinmin Congbao* ('New Citizen Journal'). Each edition sold around 10,000 copies, distributed mainly in Japan but also in China and overseas. Its enormous influence among reformers can be demonstrated by a letter from Liang's friend and sponsor, Huang Zunxian, sent in November 1902, in which Huang says that the ideas and new terms developed in Liang's articles have appeared widely in other newspapers and even been discussed in the Qing bureaucracy's entrance examinations.[24] *Xinmin Congbao* would be the outlet for most of Liang's new thinking until it folded in November 1907. He was explicit about the purpose of this newspaper: it was dedicated to bringing a new nation into existence. The very first edition included the first of six instalments of a major essay in which Liang explained how a new history needed to be written for this new nation. It was called 'New Historiography' – *Xin shixue* (literally, 'new history-study'), and he began it by borrowing the metaphor that Timothy Richard had used in his preface to Mackenzie seven years before: 'The writing of history . . . is the mirror reflecting the nation, it is also the source of patriotism.' He went on to dismiss the traditional twenty-four dynastic histories as merely 'a unique, comprehensive account of people beheading one another' and called for a 'revolution' in history-writing.[25]

Liang was explicit. Without the right kind of history, he argued, 'our nation cannot be saved'. History had to belong to the people, not the rulers. As the American historian Peter Zarrow has observed, *Xin shixue* 'was a history specifically designed to promote national feeling'.[26] Questions of race and grouping were, again, fundamental. Competition between rival races was the engine of progress and the outcome would decide whether a particular race would be 'historical' – dominant, or 'non-historical' – extinct. However, Liang's thinking about race had itself evolved. Instead of the six races he mentioned by name as belonging to the *Zhongguo minzu* in the earlier essay, he named only three: Mongols and Turks were identified separately but the others – Han, Tibetan, Manchu and Miao – were not. In Liang's view, whatever differences may exist between these groups were immaterial, because: '*Zhongguo* is a country of great unity! People are united, language is united, culture is united, religion is united, tradition is united.'[27] He did not give his reasons but the change came at the time he was arguing against the Han racialism of Zhang Binglin, and Liang was making a case for 'yellow race' unity against the bigger enemy of the 'white race'.

Nowhere did Liang justify his racial divisions beyond vague references to language, script and tradition and, as is the case with all such classifications, they are littered with inconsistencies. This is not particularly surprising, given how quickly he was working. Liang's Chinese biographer, Li Guojun, estimates that during 1902 Liang wrote 450,000 characters in *Xinmin Congbao* alone.[28] More fundamentally, however, Liang was inventing a completely new way of looking at the past and experimenting with ideas as he did so. His ideas about the Chinese past were being formed and re-formed, published and republished every week. Some of these ideas were discarded, others came to define a new nation-state.

Liang described certain mountain ranges – the Himalayas, Pamir and Altai – as natural borders of the Chinese nation. Their size had prevented the transmission of the 'high culture' of *Zhongguo* into India and west Asia. However, he describes other equally high ranges, such as the Kunlun, which divides Tibet from the central plains, and the Tian Shan, which runs through the middle of Xinjiang, as 'permeable'. The Mongol people, the Tibetans, Turks, Tungus and the Miao could be found living on both sides of the 'natural borders' but that did not prevent them from being 'naturally' part of the Chinese nation. Nor did Liang think that the other places where these people could be found – south, Southeast or central Asia – should be included within the territory of *Zhongguo*. The logic is inconsistent and, as the Sinologist Julia C. Schneider has shown, it demonstrates that the prime motivation behind Liang's historical ideas was to justify the survival of the Qing Great-State and the extent of its realm.[29]

Liang downplayed similarities that could have provided grounds for a different 'natural' order. Mongols and Tibetans, for example, share a Buddhist culture, together with people in Nepal and northern India. Mongol, Tibetan and Manchu societies share a tradition of shamanism. The Islamic Turkic peoples have cultural connections with peoples all the way west to Istanbul, and highland 'Miao'-type minorities can be found throughout Southeast Asia. These cultures are all quite different from that of the Han people of the central plains, but Liang minimised the differences and emphasised similarities in order to highlight the unity of *Zhongguo*-ness. As a result, his logic would preserve the Qing's 'five ethnicities' (Manchu, Han, Mongol, Turkic and Tibetan), along with their five respective territories.[30] These were choices he made in the early 1900s for clearly political reasons but the consequences of those ideas have long outlasted the Qing Great-State. Chinese 'national history' is, to this day, usually written as a history of a territory that was not actually 'fixed' until the middle of the twentieth century.

Liang developed the link between the writing of history and the construction of a nation in a further essay in 1903. There, Liang expressed his admiration for the ideas of the Swiss-German political theorist Johann Bluntschli, already well known to reformers in Japan. Liang adopted Bluntschli's definitions of the words 'people' and 'nation'. A 'people' was the result of a shared cultural history and therefore did not necessarily correspond to borders.

A 'nation', on the other hand, comprised the inhabitants of a certain country. Liang chose to use the word *minzu* as the equivalent of 'people' and *guomin* for 'nation'. Following Bluntschli, Liang argued that creating a nation – a *guomin* – will automatically create a 'nation-state', a *guojia.*

However, Liang differed from Bluntschli in defining what constitutes a 'people'. Bluntschli mentioned eight criteria: language, religion, physical appearance, way of life, occupation, tradition, living together and political union. However, several of these would, quite obviously, divide a putative *Zhongguo minzu*. Therefore, Liang said, only three were truly important: language, script and tradition. The essential nature of the people would thus be defined in a very traditional way – cultural. All those who adopted the higher culture – its language, script and tradition – were part of the *Zhongguo minzu*. This was simply a nationalist restatement of a traditional Confucian view of culture. But it fitted with Liang's racialised view of the nascent nation. In his 1903 essay he argued, 'This greater nation (*da minzu*) has to take the Han people (*Han ren*) as its centre and its organisation has to be formed by the hands of the Han people. Regarding this fact there is nothing to argue about.'[31] In other words, the future for all the other groups within the Qing realm was to become assimilated. He opposed those who argued for the Han to 'go it alone'. He called that idea 'lesser nationalism', or *xiao minzuzhuyi*, and contrasted it with his own ideas of 'greater nationalism', or *da minzuzhuyi*. The lesser form would split the country, while the greater form would unite it against the threat from outside countries (*guo wai*).[32]

In order to back up his claim for the power of assimilation, Liang created another major historical myth, which survives to this day. To show that Han culture would prevail in the future, he claimed that it had already done so with the Manchus, saying, 'They have already totally assimilated into *Zhongguo*.' This statement was clearly false, given that cities were still divided into separate living quarters for the two groups. The legal ban on marriage between them had only been lifted in 1902 and the two peoples lived largely separate existences. Nonetheless, Liang clung to it as politically expedient. He also projected his argument further back in time to claim that, in addition to the Manchus (1644–1912), previous invaders of *Zhongguo* – the Tabgach (386–535), the Khitan (907–1125), the Jurchen Jin (1115–1234) – had also been converted to its superior culture. He did concede, however, that the Mongols (1279–1368) had failed to change.

Ironically, what Liang's list makes clear is that for more than half the period from 386 CE until Liang's essay was published in 1903, *Zhongguo Benbu* ('China proper') had been ruled by 'barbarians' from the north. During those periods *Zhongguo* had been, in effect, a colony within empires ruled by non-Han peoples. However, in Liang's nationalist rendering of that *longue durée*, this was actually a reverse colonisation: all those foreign rulers had been overawed by superior Han culture and become part of the *Zhongguo minzu*. There was a Chinese essence that had survived unchanged for millennia.

Liang was seeking a narrative of continuity, a history like those European histories he had been absorbing since his encounter with Timothy Richard in 1895. If *Zhongguo* was to become a nation, it would also need a history. A nationalist history, written according to Liang's prescriptions, must stress continuity over discontinuity and naturalness over arbitrariness. The result must convert a collection of contradictory fragments into an evolutionary narrative, telling a story of how 'we' got 'here'. To do this Liang invented the notion of 'assimilative power': the nation progressed and expanded as more and more people became assimilated into its superior culture.[33] He could not accept the Chinese nation as being weak. As he put it in his 1901 introductory essay (*Zhongguoshi Xulun*), 'Seen from the angle of outer appearances, the Han race often lost but seen from the angle of inner spirit, the Han race often won.'[34] In other words, the Han only *appeared* to have been colonised; those who could really see what was going on would understand that throughout its travails the nation remained coherent and strong.

Between 1903 and 1905, Liang's views on the nation developed and his chosen term shifted from the *Zhongguo minzu* to the *Zhonghua minzu*. This seems to have come about as a result of his debate with Zhang Binglin about the nature of the Han race. Liang made clear in an article published in 1905 that, for him, the *Hanzu* were the backbone of the nation, but he disagreed with Zhang by including others within it too. For Liang, the purest ethnicity was the *Hua*, the original descendants of the Yellow and Red emperors. They had subsequently assimilated eight other ethnic groups to form the Han: the Miao and Man, Shu, Ba and Di, Xu and Huai, Wu and Yue, Min, the Hundred

Yue and the Hundred Pu. Liang admitted that the Miao and Pu actually remained unassimilated but he considered them to be part of the Han anyway. The Han were therefore the same thing as the *Zhonghua minzu*. Again, in the face of plenty of evidence to the contrary, Liang denied any differences between the other groups, even though plenty of regional differences in language and tradition existed then and survive to this day.[35]

But in the early 1900s, Liang believed the nation was in an existential struggle with the white race. Talk of division therefore was literally suicidal: strength could only come from intermingling. There could only be one nation and everyone in *Zhongguo* needed to be a part of it: there was no space for separate identities. In his view, it went without thinking that the Han were the core of the Chinese nation and everyone else just had to assimilate. This didn't just apply to other ethnic groups; Liang was equally uninterested in local differences among the Han. Resistance to the outsider was far more important than minor differences between insiders. Liang's vision of the nation was both ethnic and cultural. What kept the *Zhonghua minzu* together and allowed it to overcome invaders was its superior culture. This superior culture assimilated all those with whom it came into contact. The history of the Chinese nation was therefore the story of the progress and expansion of this culture.

Liang never found the time to write his grand national history. His writings moved onto the need to construct the 'new citizen', to arguments over the relative merits of reform and revolution, to the role of women and almost every other topic that was up for debate in the first decade of the twentieth century. But the ideas that Liang introduced – about the nation and the need for a national history to produce the nation – endured. In 1904 his close friend Xia Zengyou wrote the book that Liang never wrote: the first national history of China by a Chinese to be published in China. The two shared similar ideas: Xia frequently wrote articles for Liang's newspaper *Xinmin Congbao* under a pseudonym. Probably because of those articles, and perhaps a recommendation from Liang himself, Xia was commissioned by the privately owned Commercial Press in the treaty port of Shanghai – safely out of reach of the Qing authorities – to write a new history textbook for schools: '*Zuixin Zhongxue Zhongguo Lishi Jiaokeshu*' ('The newest secondary school textbook on Chinese history'). The company was hoping to cash in on a newly created demand since the Qing government had just approved educational reforms setting up a national school system for the first time.

One of the explicit purposes of the regulations was to strengthen students' 'foundation for loving the nation', although the Qing court's idea of nation was, unsurprisingly, somewhat different from Liang's. It used the word *guojia* (state-family), rather than his preferred *minzu*. *Guojia* was a particularly Confucian formulation based on the idea of concentric circles of feeling – radiating outwards from the individual, through their family and lineage to the state.[36] Liang's *minzu* was about loving the nation above all. However, the new regulations followed Liang's ideas in explicitly calling for the learning of 'national history' (*guoshi*). They also stipulated that students should be educated about 'the virtuous rule of the emperors of the current dynasty', which a reformist like Liang would also have agreed with.

Xia's book closely followed Liang's prescriptions for the new national history. His preface referenced Social-Darwinist ideas about evolution to explain why the theme of the book was progress and change. He divided the past into ancient, medieval and modern periods but showed how the continuous thread of the Chinese nation ran right through it, or, as he put it, 'The Han defined the Chinese territorial boundaries.' He specifically emphasised the role of non-Han groups – the Turkic and Mongol peoples – in the formation of the nation. Xia's book naturalised the boundaries of the state with reference to mountain ranges and justified the incorporation of Manchuria, Mongolia, Tibet and Xinjiang within the country's frontiers. The book was sold as a school textbook but its initial audience also included the wider literate population. It remained immensely popular and went on to be a standard work in schools after the 1911 revolution and the creation of the Republic of China. It was even republished in 1933 for a new generation of teachers and students. By then, it may have appeared to its readers that the book was simply describing the natural order of things. But the story of the book demonstrates that the origins of the history it tells lie with the exiled thoughts of Xia Zengyou and Liang Qichao and, further back, with Liang's meeting with Timothy Richard in 1895.

Most foreigners who know Deshengmen in Beijing know it for the bus station from where tours to the Great Wall generally begin. Towering above it is the reconstructed 'Gate of Virtuous Triumph' from which the area gets its name – one of just two remaining original gates into the old city. The wall in which the gates sat was built during the Ming Dynasty but is long gone, removed in the 1960s to build the city's subway and second ring road. The demolition of the city walls was originally motivated by communist demands for progress and then by capitalist demands for profit but it would have been easy to believe that it was intended to be a personal rebuke to Liang Qichao's family. His son, Liang Sicheng, and daughter-in-law, Lin Huiyin, both leading architects, fought throughout the 1940s and 1950s to preserve the walls, and the entire old city, as they were. Sadly for lovers of authentic heritage, they lost. Even the gates and towers that were left behind were rebuilt to make them appear more impressive.

A huge defensive 'arrow tower' stands at Deshengmen as a reminder of the old walls, overshadowing what is now an even bigger road junction. Long before the bus station and the junction were built, this gate was the beginning of the main route to the northwest. Armies once marched through it on their way to the frontier. Perhaps this explains why the area was home to a community of Muslim Hui people, clustered around a small mosque. Until the late 1990s, Deshengmen Road was a one-way street just twenty metres wide, lined with small shops and businesses. Beijing's city planners had bigger ideas, however. In the space of a few years, three-quarters of the population was moved out while the road quadrupled in width. The small businesses were bulldozed and replaced by offices and shopping malls.[37] The mosque survived, at least in name. The Fayuan Mosque was rebuilt in 2003, largely as a tourist attraction, since its original worshippers had been removed from the neighbourhood.

Directly opposite the mosque stands one of the shiny office complexes built in the 2000s. And in pride of place, separated from the arrow tower by rivers of traffic, is the headquarters of 'Hanban', the Confucius Institute. Hanban, or the 'Office of the Chinese Language Council International', to give it its formal name, is an agency of the Chinese Ministry of Education charged with promoting the teaching of Chinese language and culture worldwide. Generously backed by government resources, Hanban now directs more than 500 'Confucius Institutes' in over 140 countries around the world.[38] The work of the institutes is mostly focused on language learning but a particular view on history and culture is also part of the package. The only book on history that Hanban recommends to its students is entitled *Common Knowledge About Chinese History*. Together with its companion volumes about geography, the series is available in at least twelve languages: from English to Norwegian to Mongolian. This is the official 'national history' – *guoshi* – packaged up for consumption by foreigners. And the history that the Confucius Institute chooses to tell still follows the model laid down by Liang Qichao, albeit with a few communist modifications.

Sections are given such titles as 'The period of great feudal unity: the Qin and the Han', 'The period of further development of the unitary multi-ethnic society: the Ming and Qing' and so on. An early topic is 'Ancestors of the Chinese Nation', which tells us that the descendants of the Yellow Emperor and the Red Emperor merged to form the *Huaxia*, who 'were the predecessors of the Han people, and the principal part of the Chinese nation'. By the time we get to the Sui Dynasty in the sixth century, we learn that, 'The Chinese nation, with the Han nationality at the core, had become a relatively stable community, thus the Sui's reunification was a historical trend.' The tautology demonstrates that Liang's difficulties with translating the concepts of 'people' and 'nation' are still alive and well in the People's Republic.

The theme of the first half of the book is the primordial existence of a place called China and a people called the Chinese who have existed across millennia. Even when it wasn't called 'China', or was divided between rival states, it was still somehow 'China'. The underlying premise is continuity. We are told, 'Many institutions initiated in the Qin and Han dynasties [over 2,000 years ago] were inherited continuously by later dynasties.' The three centuries from the end of the Tang state in 907 to the arrival of the Mongols in 1260 are described as a 'chaotic period', but 'China' was there throughout. When the Mongols invade China they miraculously become a Chinese dynasty: 'In 1279 . . . China was unified into one nation once again.' Even more ridiculously, the founders of the Qing Dynasty are described as 'Manchu tribes of northeast China' and their takeover is not even acknowledged to be an invasion.[39]

The book's biases are particularly pronounced when, on rare occasions, it is obliged to deal with 'non-Han' peoples, especially when they invade and rule 'China'. The *Xianbei* people, who founded the Wei state across what is now northern China and Mongolia, apparently discovered that, 'The key to consolidating their ruling was to . . . learn from the Han people.' We're told how the Tibetans used to live in tents but admired the culture of the Tang Dynasty. They received the gifts of Chinese culture through their emperor's marriage to Princess Wencheng. Liang Qichao's concept of 'assimilative power' is still going strong. Unless they are learning from the Han, or fighting against them, the other peoples of northeast Asia are generally absent from the book, as they are from national history.

Of course, there are many more history books published in China and many historians with a far more sophisticated understanding of the past. But this book is the one chosen by the Chinese government to represent its national history abroad. Its narrative is the one found in Chinese school books and forms the foundation of Chinese leaders' frequent references to historical precedents. This is the narrative to which organisations such as the Institute of Qing History are working. Since the coming to power of Xi Jinping, the political space for dissenting views on history – never large to begin with – has been shrunk even further. National history is reduced to a story about the expansion of a superior culture over its inferiors.

How else might we tell the story of this piece of the earth's surface and the peoples who have lived upon it? If we avoid the temptation to assume that China was a primordial territorial unit with 'natural' boundaries, then we need to look at what happened in each period in its own terms, not necessarily as a stage on the way to the present-day situation. The story should be framed in a regional context, highlighting how peoples moved, states rose and fell, frontiers fluctuated, trade flowed and cultures hybridised. If we avoid assumptions about superiority and inferiority, we start to see the flows in the past as multi-directional.

Reading against the grain of the standard histories, we might take the view of the Japanese historian Hidehiro Okada, for example.[40] In his narrative, the earliest recorded inhabitants of this part of East Asia all arrived from elsewhere. The *Xia* people were southerners, perhaps originally from Southeast Asia, who settled the southern and eastern coastal plains. The *Shang* and *Zhou* peoples, on the other hand, seem to have been nomads who arrived from north Asia. The highland *Man* people formed the state of Chu in the early eighth century BCE. In the conventional telling, these groups were the barbarians, separate from the 'Chinese'. Okada argues the opposite: these 'barbarians' were in fact the original inhabitants who adopted a settled, urban lifestyle and thereby made themselves different from their wilder relatives – they lived in towns and were led by an emperor who ruled through a written language. These were the three markers of the early civilisation, not ethnicity. Cities were composed of members of many ethnic groups but by adopting an urban culture the 'citizens' reinvented themselves as a new group. Around 100 BCE the court official, Sima Qian, concocted a revised version of history to please his imperial master. He traced the origin of his emperor's Han dynasty back to 'ancient times', making sure to obscure its heterogenous roots. Sima Qian was a propagandist as much as a historian and a remarkably successful one. The tale he wove is still recycled two millennia later.

The Han state began to disintegrate around 184 CE with the beginning of an uprising by the 'Yellow Turbans' religious sect. The fighting, and the famine that ensued, killed almost 90 per cent of the population, reducing it from 50 million to just 5 million. The remnants of the last Han state then fled south to the Yangtze valley. The land it had left behind was then filled by more migrants from North Asia. They created a new northern state with a new, 'northernised', form of language. This north–south divide lasted for around 200 years until, in 589 CE, the northern Sui state, founded by the *Xianbei* people of central Asia, defeated the southerners.

The Sui were overthrown by what became the Tang Dynasty in 618. They too were partly of *Xianbei* descent. That empire began to fragment in the ninth century and finally collapsed in 907. Its place was taken by several smaller rival states and the following century was characterised by upheaval and war with the northern area once again ruled by Turkic peoples. The Shatuo were replaced by the Khitan (from whom we get the archaic name for China: Cathay), who founded the Liao Dynasty, until they were conquered by the Jurchen, who ruled until 1234. According to Okada, none of these peoples saw themselves as ruling the *zhong guo*. They were Inner Asians for whom China was an imperial appendage. Beijing became the Jurchens' winter capital, away from the extreme cold of Siberia, and doubled as an administrative capital for their subject people. This period is almost entirely glossed over in the 'national history' narrative, which prefers to concentrate on the existence of a rival state, under the Song Dynasty, which controlled the southern part of what is now China, although its territory steadily shrank under pressure from the north.

The Mongols took Beijing in 1215 before extinguishing the Jurchen Jin Dynasty in 1234. Over the following half-century, the Mongols pushed ever further south, squeezing the Song state right back to the coast before finishing it off in a naval battle near Guangdong in 1279. The Mongols named their Chinese administration the 'Yuan Dynasty' in order to make it more culturally acceptable, but it was not a 'Chinese' state so much as an Inner Asian great-state. Although Kublai Khan moved his capital to Beijing in 1271, 'China' was simply one part of a khanate that, in 1279, stretched from the Korean peninsula to the Hungarian plains. With some awareness of the historical irony, Liang Qichao would later honour the Mongols' Yuan Dynasty as the 'unifiers of *Zhongguo*', since they conquered both the Jurchen and the Song states, bringing their territories under the same ruler for the first time since the Tang Dynasty collapsed, nearly four centuries before. Even Liang Qichao had to admit that 'China' is therefore a legacy of the Mongols.

This united Mongol realm lasted just less than a century before local insurrection pulled it apart. A great-state based upon continuous expansion was simply unable to cope with the demands of settled administration. The early fourteenth century was a time of centrifugal chaos and in several places local warlords claimed the mantle of pre-existing empires. One of them, Zhu Yuanzhang, established a new southern capital (*nan-jing*) in Nanjing and declared himself the leader of a new dynasty, the Ming (meaning 'brilliant') in 1368. Although Liang and subsequent 'national history' writers portrayed the Ming as an authentically Chinese dynasty, they played down how much the Ming rulers consciously emulated the Mongols. Indeed, the basic bureaucratic structure of their government, with a Secretariat, Censorate and Bureau of Military Affairs, was borrowed from Kublai Khan's court.

The same was true of regional government. The Mongols had parcelled out the country into personal fiefs: the leader of each locality was the tribal chief who had conquered it. The Ming copied the principle but when their scholars came to write the history of the previous dynasty they erased the details and made the system sound more centrally organised. It was in the interests of the Ming scholar-officials to present themselves as the core of a Confucian state but, says

Okada, the real authority lay with the 'military aristocracy' – the descendants of the generals who had supported Zhu Yuanzhang. This, again, was a pattern directly borrowed from the Mongols. The Ming organised the population along Mongol lines, too. Military families were organised as 'centuries', who were grouped into 'thousands' and then into 'guards'. Surviving census registers indicate that the leaders of the 'guards' were generally of Mongol heritage.

The second Ming emperor did not build a northern capital (*bei-jing*) in Beijing just because he preferred the climate there. The location – at the gateway to Mongolia – was deliberate and strategic. He wished to be both emperor of the Ming and khan of the Mongols. By assuming the mantle of the Yuan, the Ming also extended their control into two areas which had been conquered by the Mongols: the old Tai kingdom of Yunnan and the Korean-populated Liao River basin. In Liang Qichao's version of history, the invading northerners had been 'civilised' and 'Sinicised' by the superior culture of the *Hua* people that they encountered in the *zhong guo*. The basic structure of the Ming (and later the Qing) states tells us that culture flowed both ways. The *Hua* were hybrids.

For the Ming, the 'natural boundaries' of the great-state stretched from the mountains of Yunnan, northwards and eastwards through the mountains of Sichuan, the Altun, the Min and Qilian ranges before joining the less natural frontier of the Great Wall. These boundaries were specifically designed to keep out Tibetans, Turks, Mongols and Manchus – physically but also psychologically. These boundaries lasted for 300 years until the Manchu Qing breached the wall in 1644. For them, as heirs to the Khitan, Jurchen and Mongol civilisations, *Zhongguo* was only a waypoint on the road to regional supremacy. Qing military campaigns would triple the amount of territory ruled from Beijing. If the Mongols created China, as Liang Qichao asserted, the Manchus created 'greater China'.

This is a far from comprehensive account of two millennia but it is an attempt to show how a different history could be written if we chose to see it as a regional story rather than a national one. (For a longer and far more expert account, the book *Demystifying China: New Understandings of Chinese History*, edited by Naomi Standen, would be a good place to start.)[41] Once we understand the 'messiness' of these twenty centuries, we can see that it takes considerable imagination, of the kind that can only be provided by nationalism, to discern within them an essential 'Chinese' nation that endured throughout. At best this version of history is really only an account of a number of urban populations who recognised an emperor and wrote with a particular set of characters.

The search for political legitimacy in each age caused emperors to commission scholar-officials to write official histories that emphasised continuity. Around 800 CE, these official historians formulated an official dogma: *daotong* – 'Transmission of the Way' – in which rulers could seek legitimacy by consciously emulating the mindset of their predecessors as laid down by Confucius and other scribes. As Tim Barrett, professor at the School of Oriental and African Studies in London, has argued, 'The urge to reconstruct could incorporate without strain considerable intellectual innovation.'[42] He notes how the writing of 'histories' during each time period involved considerable manipulation of evidence in order to present a version of the past that accorded with the needs of the present. The invention of paper and scissors allowed for narratives to be cut and pasted at will. In this, the current work of the National Qing Dynasty History Compilation Committee is entirely within precedent. Its job is to edit and re-present the history of the previous dynasty in order to legitimise the current regime and delegitimise its critics through allegations of 'historical nihilism'.

Each ruler needed, and still needs, to claim descent from ancient sages. The result is a narrative that stresses continuity, even where there is little evidence. Disruption is ignored, jumped over, written out of 'history'. The received story is of one dynasty succeeding another divided by 'exceptional' periods of disruption and division. A disinterested survey of the past would discover that, in fact, unity was the exception. But Xi Jinping has declared China to be a great power and great powers need a great history – something like 5,000 years long. And great powers aren't invaded or humiliated; they are winners – always. The nation that Liang Qichao conjured into being, the *Zhonghua minzu*, was always there and always will be.

Just inside the former east gate of the imperial city, which gives its name to the Dongzhimen metro station, is a maze of grey brick alleyways, still lined with benevolently shady trees. The spaces between their trunks are now parking places for the silent-but-deadly electric scooters that menace unwary pedestrians across Beijing. Number 23 Beigouyan Hutong looks just like any other building in this neighbourhood: a bare wall is punctuated with barred windows and a maze of electrical cables festoons its tiled roof. Set into the wall next to its red door, however, is a plaque revealing that this is a protected '*siheyuan*', a traditional courtyard residence. Like most *siheyuan*, this one was divided up by the Communist government. Instead of a single wealthy family, it is now home to a dozen poorer ones. These elderly beneficiaries of the revolution are nonetheless proud that they live in what was once the home of Liang Qichao. One produces a photocopy of an old drawing, showing how the place looked in the early years of the twentieth century, before extra housing replaced elegant gardens and ponds.

Liang returned to Beijing from Japan after the nationalist revolution in 1912, welcomed by the president of the new Republic of China, Yuan Shikai. He was appointed to successive government positions: minister of justice, minister of finance and state counsellor, from where he continued to argue for liberal social change. In December 1913 Liang's return was followed by that of Kang Youwei, after fifteen years in exile. The last time he had seen Beijing was when he fled it in fear of his life in 1898. After being reunited with Liang, almost the next person they went to see was Timothy Richard. At their meeting, Liang expounded on his theory of the three stages of history and his view that the worldwide spread of science, prosperity and democracy would bring about a utopia that unified Western concepts of peace with the Confucian ideal of *datong* – great harmony. Richard was in full agreement. Way back in 1879 he had drafted a scheme for a world federation.[43] In his daughter's account he lobbied heads of state and 'countless' others about the need for it over subsequent decades.[44] Such dreams were, of course, about to be smashed, along with the men's hopes for political reform in China. The new country rapidly collapsed into fiefs controlled by regional warlords. President Yuan even declared himself emperor in 1915. Simultaneously, a more aggressive government in Japan sought to make the most of this weakness with ever more belligerent demands.

As Europe collapsed into the cataclysm of the First World War, Japan was the first to see an opportunity for advantage. With a covetous eye fixed on the

German enclave on the Shandong Peninsula, Japan declared war at the end of August 1914, three weeks after its ally, Britain. However, Liang Qichao recognised that the war was also an opportunity for China. He lobbied the government, arguing that official support for Britain and France might oblige those powers to treat China more fairly after the war. In August 1917 the Beijing government also declared war on Germany. While it had no troops to despatch, it did send around 140,000 civilians to labour in the mud and blood of the Western Front in the last year of the war.

Shortly after the signing of the armistice in November 1918, the victorious powers announced the convening of an international peace conference in Paris to ensure that such a terrible conflict would never happen again. A new world was in prospect: one where peace and justice would prevail and the rights of new nations would be respected. Liang's hopes were lifted. Although not a member of the government, he resolved to lead a personal mission to Paris to lobby for the rights of the Republic of China. He took along six colleagues who had studied in Britain, France, Germany and Japan so they could make their country's case to the negotiators through the world's media.[45] The small band departed Shanghai in December 1918 and arrived in London on 12 January 1919. They were not impressed by the cold and sooty city struggling in the grip of post-war economic depression, 'a picture of impoverishment and desolation', Liang called it.[46] Their hotel room was freezing cold, the food was terrible and the smog made the sun appear 'like blood'. But the delegation was not in London for tourism alone. They had arrived with a particular mission in mind. A quarter-century after their first meeting, Liang Qichao had come to say farewell to Timothy Richard.

Richard had left China for the final time in 1916. Suffering from poor health, he had resigned his position as secretary of the Society for the Diffusion of Christian and General Knowledge at a meeting in Shanghai the year before. A motion of thanks was formally agreed, noting that Richard's name had become a 'household word in China'. His impact on the movements for both Christian mission and political reform had been profound. There were plaudits too, once back in Britain: an honorary doctorate, several valedictory meetings and a few books in his honour. He retired to a small house in the London suburb of Golders Green, where he received some of the great and good of the day: Earl Grey, General Smuts and the Foreign Office minister Lord Robert Cecil among them.[47]

Liang had many pressing matters in mind when he arrived in London but, according to a surviving note of the meeting, the first person that he wanted to see was Timothy Richard. He immediately asked the Chinese legation to arrange the reunion. He made the pilgrimage to Golders Green, dressed in his new Western-style suit, to present Richard with copies of some of his recent writing.[48] Reunited, the two men found common cause once again. Despite his ill health, Richard was still devoting his time to the cause of world peace. Over the years he had doggedly promoted his idea of a world federation to all who would listen. This appeared to be on the verge of coming to pass during the period when Liang came to visit him. He was proclaiming the arguments for a new 'League of Nations' at public meetings and in letters to leading figures. Once again the two men shared their hopes for a peaceful future.

However, not everyone in London was so pleased to see Liang. A younger generation of nationalist Chinese students were alarmed. Because he had spent so long in Japan, and had served President Yuan's dictatorship, they suspected Liang's motives. In February, a group of students sent him a sharp letter warning him that this was no time for deals with Japan. The world had changed, they claimed, and the new 'League of Nations' supported by the 'righteous' United States and 'democratic' Britain and France would ensure that China would be fairly treated. Had China not sent tens of thousands of labourers to work and die on the Western Front? Was the country not therefore deserving of respect and fair treatment?

In March Liang left Britain for France, where he was appalled by the effects of the war, particularly the devastation wrought upon the historic city of Reims.[49] In Paris he observed, lobbied and commented on the peace negotiations that had been under way since mid-January. As it turned out, the 'righteous' and 'democratic' countries betrayed China. Britain and France had already agreed a secret deal with Japan in exchange for Japan joining the war. While Japan was treated as a 'great power' at the talks, China was only granted the status of a 'minor power': less than Belgium, Brazil or Serbia.

The Chinese delegation was also hobbled by a split between supporters of the recognised government in Beijing and Sun Yat-sen's rival Guomindang

(Nation Party) leadership based in Guangzhou. The void in Chinese leadership was filled by exiled student groups protesting outside the conference, distributing pamphlets and organising petitions and letters to the other governments. Unknown to them, the Beijing government had already made a humiliating deal. On 24 September 1918 it had agreed, in effect, to allow Japan to occupy defeated Germany's enclave on the Shangdong Peninsula in exchange for new loans to build railway lines.[50]

The result of the conference was a stitch-up between the 'great powers'. Instead of returning defeated Germany's possessions to the new Republic of China, they handed them to Japan.[51] At a stroke, all those nationalist hopes in a new world order based on sovereign and equal states were crushed. The new order looked very similar to the old. Liang was just as outraged as the younger generation and poured his vitriol into print. It was Liang's telegram about China's treatment at the Versailles Peace Conference that prompted a newspaper article which inflamed public sentiment back home. That led, on 4 May 1919, to student demonstrations in Beijing and the burning of the home of Cao Rulin, the minister of communications who had negotiated the Japanese railway loans the previous year. It also ushered in the next, more radical, phase of Chinese nationalism, what became known as the May Fourth Movement.

Timothy Richard never knew any of this. He underwent surgery shortly after Liang departed London but never recovered. He died in London on 17 April 1919, at the age of seventy-three. The two men had turned the writing of history into a tool for the cause of political reform. In the century since, that way of interpreting the past has been pressed into the service of a nation-state just as Liang had dreamt that it would. It has become the foundation for the Chinese state's sense of self and, just as importantly, for the outside world's sense of China. But it is a partial vision of the past, one that was conjured into being to support a political project and which continues to privilege one idea of the nation above all its rivals. Nationalism is a hallucinogen, whose addicts can see illusions of wholeness where others see only disjuncture and diversity. With official patronage inside China, and uncritical support from outside, the 'Chinese' version maintains its dominance over Tibetan, Turkic, Mongol, Manchu or Miao versions in both history-writing and politics. And, in Beijing, the Institute of Qing History is making sure things stay that way.

5
THE INVENTION OF THE CHINESE NATION
Zhonghua minzu – Chinese nation

In late August 2018 a special visitor was given a guided tour of a Chinese engineering marvel in the Tibetan Himalayas. The Zangmu Dam sits astride the Yarlung Tsangpo River more than 3,000 metres above sea level. When it opened in 2015, it was the highest-altitude hydropower plant in the world, generating 500 megawatts per hour, doubling Tibet's electricity output. The guaranteed supply of power has attracted new customers to the area: mining companies, a high-speed train line that runs close to the border with India and luxury tourism developments. And in their wake have come migrants from the lowlands.

The visitor to the dam that day was the second holiest figure in Tibetan Buddhism, the Panchen Lama. Or perhaps it wasn't, because Gyaltsen Norbu is the Chinese government's chosen Panchen Lama. In 1995 the exiled Dalai Lama chose a different boy, Gedhun Choekyi, to be the Panchen Lama but he was immediately taken away by Chinese officials. Both rival Panchen Lamas are now in Chinese custody. The difference between them is that Gyaltsen Norbu is periodically paraded in front of the national media visiting construction projects and the like, while Gedhun Choekyi has not been seen for twenty-five years. The two men are pawns in the Chinese state's battle for the hearts and minds of the Tibetan population.

According to the official media, the message the Chinese Panchen Lama gave to the people during his visit was that the 'Communist Party's Central Committee, with Comrade Xi Jinping as the core, attached great importance to religious work and gave love to religious people.'[1] He told a gathering of the official Buddhist association that they must 'uphold the party's leadership, resolutely oppose splittism, pay attention to the combination of Buddhism with modern knowledge and policy learning, and be a bridge between the party and the government to unite and connect with the believers'. He was then pictured in front of the Zangmu Dam, endorsing the fruits of 'social development'.

This is exactly the role that the Communist Party expects the Panchen Lama to perform. It was how the previous Panchen Lama played the part, at least for a time. In 1949, while Tibet was still independent, the 10th Panchen Lama was contacted by a party official called Xi Zhongxun and then helped to plan what the Chinese government still calls the 'liberation' of Tibet by the People's Liberation Army in 1950. However, in 1962, after criticising the impact of communist policies on Tibetans, the 10th Panchen Lama was stripped of his title, denounced and imprisoned until 1982. During the last years of his life, however, he was restored to his position and renewed his relationship with Xi Zhongxun. By then Xi had become the country's vice-premier in charge of ethnic, religious and 'United Front' work. The two men cooperated in reversing many of the policies that had caused so much suffering. They also created a local ethnic-Tibetan bureaucracy to loyally administer the autonomous region on Beijing's behalf. When the 10th Panchen Lama died suddenly in 1989, the vice-premier wrote a long eulogy in the party's official newspaper, the *People's Daily*, describing their forty-year friendship and the 'Panchen Lama's love of the Communist Party'. After years of experience working with ethnic minorities in the north and west of the country, Xi Zhongxun had come to the view that it was better to allow minorities to manage their own affairs, so long as they remained loyal to the party. It was a position quite different to the one now espoused by his own son, the current leader of China, Xi Jinping.

On 22 March 2018, Xi Jinping gave the closing speech to the National People's Congress under a title translated into English as 'The Communist Party will always be the backbone of the Chinese people and the Chinese nation'. In most countries, 'nation' and 'people' are taken to be the same thing, but the fact that Xi repeatedly used the two terms coupled together in the phrase '*Zhongguo renmin yu zhonghua minzu*' tells us that there is something different about their meanings in Chinese that disappears when they are translated into English. Readers who have made it this far will be alert to the distinction between *Zhongguo* and *Zhonghua*, despite both being translated into

English as 'China': *Zhong-guo* is a rendering of 'central state', whereas *Zhong-hua* has far stronger ethnic connotations. *Renmin* is generally translated as 'people' but scholars have lengthy arguments about how to translate *minzu*, mainly because of the word's confused origins.

Zhongguo renmin has clear Communist Party associations. In the early years of the People's Republic, it was a standard piece of vocabulary. The 'people of China' are a political entity, members of the four favoured classes that are on the side of the party: workers, peasants, national bourgeoisie and petty bourgeoisie. The national flag represented each one with a small star. The 'people', in this formulation, excluded the party's enemies: landlords, capitalists and supporters of the Nation Party, the *Guomindang* (or Kuomintang/KMT).[2]

Zhonghua minzu, on the other hand, was much more associated with the enemy's language. It underpinned the ideology of the Guomindang and featured prominently in the wartime writings of its leader, Chiang Kai-shek. In his 1943 book *China's Destiny*, Chiang describes a Chinese nation – *Zhonghua minzu* – that is made up of various 'stocks', but who constitute a single race because they are all descendants of the same ancestors.[3] They may have divided into Han, Manchu, Tibetan, Mongol and Hui (Muslim) over the course of the previous 5,000 years, but their unavoidable destiny was to reassimilate into a single Chinese nation. Chiang also asserted that the natural frontiers of the *Zhonghua minzu* exactly coincided with those of the greatest extent of the Qing Great-State.

At the time, the Communist Party of China denounced this formulation. Its collective ideas were strongly influenced by the policies of the Soviet Union and the views of Joseph Stalin. In 1931 the party even declared that 'nations' – and they specifically mentioned Mongols, Hui and Tibetans, among others – had the right to secede from China. However, by the time they took power in 1949, the party had revised its views. By 1950 it was committed to a multi-national republic within its existing boundaries. The best that 'splittist'-minded minorities could hope for was autonomy. Once in power, the People's Republic called upon its anthropologists to classify the *minzu* on the Soviet model and in 1954 the researchers came up with the somewhat arbitrary number of fifty-six, which included Han, Tibetans, Uyghurs, Mongols, Manchus and many far smaller minorities.[4]

It was only in the mid-1980s that the idea of a single *Zhonghua minzu* started to be acceptable among communist theoreticians. A particular pioneer was Fei Xiaotong, one of the anthropologists who had taken part in the original ethnic classification project thirty years earlier. He talked of a 'pluralistic unitary structure': each group might have its own distinctive identities but its primary identity had to be that of *Zhonghua*. This was founded upon a view of the past that was strikingly similar to Chiang Kai-shek's – that the course of Chinese history was the story of distinct ethnic groups fusing into one.

During the 1990s, as orthodox communist ideology retreated, Communist Party pronouncements increasingly featured the word 'nation' alongside 'people'. In October 2000, for example, in a speech marking the fiftieth anniversary of the Korean War, President Jiang Zemin talked of the soldiers defending the 'dignity of the nation'. The following year, the *Zhonghua minzu* made several appearances in a speech by Jiang that officially welcomed capitalists into the party. They had not been part of Mao Zedong's 'people' but they were now to be included within Jiang's 'nation'.[5]

This new thinking was given extra urgency by incidents of ethnic violence and protest in Tibet and Xinjiang during the 2000s. A small number of very influential figures in the PRC came to view the notion of separate *minzu* as a threat to the country's future. Some, such as Professor Ma Rong of Peking University and Professor Hu Angang of Tsinghua University, warned that the encouragement of ethnic difference could lead to the country breaking apart in the same way that the USSR and Yugoslavia had fragmented in the 1990s. As a result they came to advocate a radical alternative – a 'melting pot' approach in which ethnic differences would be eradicated in the interests of the unity of a single 'Chinese nation'.

If followed through, this would be a direct repudiation of the policies implemented by Xi Zhongxun and followed by the PRC for many decades. Significantly, one of the main supporters of this approach appears to be Xi's son, Xi Jinping. This Xi has repeatedly stressed the importance of what he calls the 'five identifications' required of all Chinese citizens. They must identify with the motherland, with the Chinese nation (*Zhonghua minzu*), with Chinese culture, the Chinese socialist road and the Communist Party itself. This can only make sense if Xi believes that there is a single nation with a single culture.

But Han and Tibetans, along with Uyghurs and many other groups, speak different languages, write in different scripts and live different ways of life. So, is there a single Chinese nation or are there several different nations gathered together under a single state? Finding an answer to this question has been a problem for Chinese nationalism right from the beginning.

On 13 January 1897, Sun Yat-sen, later to be the first president of the Republic of China, went to Madame Tussauds in London to see its newly opened tableau: a waxwork of King John signing the Magna Carta.[6] He was there, in effect, to give thanks. Three months earlier, he had been kidnapped and detained in the Chinese legation's building in the city's West End. For twelve days officials tried to pressure Sun into confessing to treachery. They threatened to smuggle him out of the country and execute him, but not necessarily in that order. Sun, however, managed to bribe his British guard in the legation to take a note to his friend and former medical teacher, Dr James Cantlie. Cantlie then obtained a writ of *habeas corpus* from the High Court, obliging the legation to free Sun. Magna Carta, in effect, saved Sun's life.[7]

The British newspapers lapped up the story. Sun became a celebrity, even more so when his book *Kidnapped in London* was published at around the same time as the trip to Madame Tussauds. At a stroke, the Qing authorities had turned a marginal dissident into a global star. Until then, Sun had been making slow progress in building an opposition movement. The *Xing Zhong Hui* – 'Revive the Centre Society' – he had founded in Hawaii two years before (see Chapter 1) had few supporters; the uprising he had co-organised in Guangzhou in 1895 had failed, with most of the plotters captured; and reform-minded scholar-officials wanted little to do with an upstart, missionary-educated agitator like him. In an interview with a British journalist immediately after his release, Sun made clear that his aims were quite different to those of the reformers: 'We changed our idea to creating a revolution and putting the present dynasty out of existence,' he explained.[8] Sun added that he saw the corrupt bureaucratic class as just as much part of the problem as the Qing rulers. He was so radical that Timothy Richard, then visiting London, would have nothing to do with him.[9]

We know in great detail what Sun did during the eight months that he stayed in London because the Chinese government hired a firm of detectives to follow him around. On 5 December 1896 he was granted a ticket for the reading room at the British Museum on the recommendation of Sir Robert Kennaway Douglas, a retired British diplomat who headed the library's oriental department. Sun spent most of his time in the library, reading widely in politics and current affairs.[10] He got to grips with the fashionable ideas of Social Darwinism as promoted by Herbert Spencer and Thomas Huxley. These were the ideas that Yan Fu had partially translated into Chinese two years earlier, which had fired up the thinking of a generation of radicals (see Chapter 3).[11] They would prove to be foundational for Sun's subsequent ideas about nationhood also.

However, as English spring turned to English summer, Sun said goodbye to his host James Cantlie and headed to Canada and then on to Asia. The detectives hired by the legation remained on his tail for the whole journey, informing Beijing of Sun's attempts to raise money and support from the Chinese community in North America, particularly the cities of Vancouver and Victoria. One result of his fundraising success was that he was able to upgrade his cabin from intermediate class to 'stateroom' for the final leg of his journey.[12] Banned from Hong Kong following his role in the Guangzhou Uprising, Sun opted for exile in Japan. He arrived in Yokohama on 10 August 1897 where he was introduced to, and quickly integrated with, Japanese sympathisers of many stripes – from supporters of 'yellow race' pan-Asianism to ultra-nationalists, including several government ministers. This gave him access to plenty of funding from those who, in the aftermath of the Sino-Japanese War and for various different reasons, wanted to see an end to the Qing Dynasty.[13]

Further funding came from the Chinese community in Yokohama, particularly when Sun's supporters set up a new school. They saw the project as a chance to bridge the ideological and cultural gap between the reformers and the revolutionaries. They made a point of reaching out to Liang Qichao and inviting him to be its first headmaster. Liang, however, was too busy editing his reformist newspaper in Shanghai. Instead, Liang's teacher and ally Kang Youwei, a scholar whose radical reinterpretations of Confucianism were already causing a stir, recommended some other candidates. Kang also suggested a name for the school derived from his utopian readings of the classic texts: it was *Datong Xuexiao*, 'Great Harmony School'. The friendly relations between

Kang, the reformist, and Sun, the revolutionary, lasted only a few months, however. As Kang's advocacy became more influential, he became closer to the emperor in Beijing. His links to the exiled revolutionaries became an embarrassment, particularly during the period of the Hundred Days Reform in the summer of 1898. Kang's allies in Yokohama banned Sun from the school he had helped to found and which his supporters funded.

The split continued to worsen until Empress Cixi's coup against the emperor and his reforms on 22 September 1898. Both Kang and Liang had to flee the country. Japanese agents rescued Liang from Tianjin and later collected Kang from Hong Kong. They brought the two men to Yokohama where, for a few months after November 1898, they tried to engineer a political union between reformists and revolutionaries. Kang, however, was still not prepared to work with the 'uneducated bandit' infatuated with Western materialism. Sun was equally hostile to the 'corrupt Confucian' obsessed with pointless theorising.[14] Within months, the Japanese had lost patience with Kang and in March 1899 he left for Canada to seek more sympathetic company among the Chinese communities there.

Kang's departure allowed an unlikely friendship to develop between his reformist acolyte Liang Qichao, who advocated the unity of the 'yellow race' against the whites, and Sun the revolutionary, whose *Xing Zhong Hui* organisation was pledged to 'drive out the Manchus'. Liang's sympathies began to move towards revolution, while Sun adopted many of Liang's ideas about the nation. The two even authored several joint articles in the newspaper that Liang was now editing from Yokohama, *Qingyibao* ('Clear Discussion Newspaper').[15] Their shared obsession was the Social Darwinist fear of yellow race extinction at the hands of whites. Just as importantly, neither man had any time for the Han racialism of people like Zhang Binglin. Liang saw Manchus as part of the same yellow race as the Han, and Sun was opposed to the Manchus as a corrupt elite, not as a racial group. In early 1902 Sun refused to join Zhang in convening a meeting to commemorate the Manchus' 'ruination of China'. In a later speech, Zhang complained that Sun was 'utterly lacking in wholehearted devotion to the idea of saving the Han race'.[16] With common enemies and marooned together in Yokohama, Liang and Sun's ideas developed in symbiosis. While Liang the 'insider' scholar thought about the Chinese nation he wanted to create, Sun the 'outsider' activist was thinking about the future state that he wished to lead. Both dreams, however, hinged upon Liang's idea of the *minzu*.

Liang Qichao coined the term *minzu*, in a 1903 essay, with the literal meaning of 'people-lineage'. Liang chose it as an equivalent for Johann Bluntschli's German-language concept of '*Nation*', by which Bluntschli meant (confusingly) the English word 'people'. Bluntschli's people/*Nation* became Liang's *minzu*. Equally confusingly, Bluntschli used the German word '*Volk*' in the sense of the English word 'nation'. Liang translated nation/*Volk* as *guomin*. For Liang there could be several *minzu* in a state and a *minzu* could even exist across borders. *Guomin*, on the other hand, described the citizens of a state.[17] This confused origin still marks the ideology and policies of the People's Republic of China towards minorities in Tibet, Xinjiang and elsewhere as its modern leaders try to grapple with the same problems that faced the reformists and revolutionaries in the 1900s – how to reconcile their dream of a homogenous people with the reality of a diverse empire.

The ferry from the Canadian city of Vancouver to the southern part of Vancouver Island takes a direct but hair-raising route through the forested islands of the Salish Sea. It zigzags through the straits and narrows, dodging working ships and pleasure yachts, until it pulls into the terminal at Swartz Bay. Just before it reaches the dock, passengers on the port side are treated to a public view of a private fief: Coal Island, now the property of the Shields family, Canadian industrialists. Just over a century ago, however, this secluded isle was the hideout to where Kang Youwei fled to escape the hired assassins of both the Qing Great-State and the Japanese government. Empress Cixi wanted him dead because of his sympathies for the imprisoned emperor, while the Japanese wanted him out of the way so that their chosen revolutionary, Sun Yat-sen, could dominate the exiled political movement. The British government, however, wanted to keep him alive in the hope that his efforts at reform might be successful. They provided protection in Hong Kong, foiled an attempted assassination by Japanese agents in Singapore and gave him a police guard in Canada.

Kang's reputation arrived in the port of Victoria well before him. When the ship carrying him from Japan docked on 7 April 1899, he immediately gave interviews to two local newspapers, calling for political reform in China and requesting the British government intervene in its support. (When these remarks were reprinted in Liang Qichao's newspaper, however, the section about requesting British help was omitted.) He was received by the lieutenant-governor of British Columbia and numerous other dignitaries and gave speeches to large audiences in the Chinatowns of Victoria and Vancouver. For the first time he talked of the need for patriotism to bind the overseas Chinese to their homeland across the ocean.

But while the British government was prepared to protect Kang, it was not willing to force political reform on the Qing Great-State. Kang travelled to London in May and June 1899 to lobby for military intervention but returned to Canada disappointed. Instead, he and Chinese businessmen in Victoria founded the *Baohuanghui* (literally the 'Protect the Emperor Society' but known in English as the Chinese Empire Reform Association) to organise the *huaqiao* (overseas Chinese) community in support of reform. They chose as a motto, '*Bao zhong, bao guo, bao jiao*' ('preserve the race, preserve the state, preserve the faith', by which Kang meant Confucianism). Kang was declared president of the society, with Liang Qichao its vice-president. Kang then retreated to Coal Island to reflect and write.[18] On 19 September 1899, he composed a poem about his place in exile:

> A drifting stranger from twenty thousand *li* away,
> Long white sideburns forty years of age,
> Turning to look at the Milky Way and enjoying the bright moonlight;
> Most rare on Coal Island to chat with fellow villagers;
> Ashamed to shock the neighbours with the troubles and disasters of our party;
> Ashamed of having accomplished nothing for our fellow countrymen;
> Afraid this may be a separation forever from my native place . . .[19]

Aware that he was unwelcome in Japan, Kang spent most of the next few years in different parts of the British Empire. In 1900 he was in Singapore, in 1901 in Penang and Malaya, and in 1902 he wrote his greatest work, *Datongshu* ('Book of the Great Harmony', the same name as the school in Yokohama) while living in the Indian hill station of Darjeeling. The book offered a utopian vision of a future society in which the social boundaries around family, gender, class, nation and occupation would wither and the world could live as one. Kang saw no value in nationalism, instead he wanted to see states merge to form regional federations and then a global state with its own parliament and military.[20] It was, however, a deeply racist vision of the future. Kang foresaw the darker races being transformed through intermarriage, migration and sterilisation. Whites and yellows who married Africans would be awarded medals for their service.[21] Ultimately the new global race would have the physical strength of whites and the mental skills of yellows.

Kang only allowed the first two chapters of *Datongshu* to be published during his lifetime,[22] and in public he continued to advocate a Confucian solution to the problems of the Qing Great-State: all efforts must be made to save the emperor and establish a constitutional monarchy along British lines. Despite his apparent desire for global equality, however, he had no wish to deal with the masses. Instead, he courted the support of *huaqiao* businesspeople abroad and the scholarly elite in his homeland. The first group were encouraged to create new companies through *huaqiao* connections across North America to provide funds for the society, the latter were exhorted to stand fast for the emperor.

Eminent scholar that he was, Kang was nonetheless barred from the United States by the Chinese Exclusion Act introduced by President Arthur in 1882. Unable himself to rally the American *huaqiao* for the 'Protect the Emperor Society', in 1903 Kang instead sent his two closest supporters to do the job. Liang Qichao seems to have had no trouble entering the country and between February and October was feted by Chinese communities across the US and Canada. Kang also despatched his daughter, Kang Tongbi, who founded women's branches of the society in British Columbia, Washington state, San Francisco, Chicago and, on 20 October, in New York City.[23]

Liang travelled around the United States for many months. However, the experience seems to have disillusioned him about the merits of its political system. While he enjoyed the spring flowers of Washington DC and was impressed by the tall buildings of New York, he also observed the overcrowded and insanitary Chinatowns. Comparing American cities with those he knew back home, he drew the conclusion that the fault lay with the Chinese, who were not yet ready for republican democracy. 'Were we now to adopt majority rule, it would be the same as committing national suicide. Liberty, constitutionalism, republicanism, all these would be like wearing fancy summer garb in winter: beautiful to be sure but out of place. . . . In a word, the Chinese people have to accept authoritarian rule for now and do not merit liberty.'[24] He remained convinced that republicanism was the highest form of government but until the Chinese were ready for it, constitutional monarchy would have to be the way forward.

Liang returned to Japan re-committed to a slow transition to democracy and this caused a bitter break with Sun Yat-sen. There would be no more jointly authored articles. The ideological fight between Kang's monarchist *Baohuanghui* and Sun's revolutionary plotters grew worse and became a global fight for the loyalty of *huaqiao* communities in North America, Southeast Asia, Australia and beyond. Initially, the advantage lay with Kang. He had scholarly stature and his message of Confucianism, loyalty to the Qing and gradual change had strong support among the wealthiest overseas Chinese communities. Sun lacked all these advantages so he was obliged to adapt his political message in order to attract more adherents to his revolutionary movement: he added a far more radical strain of nationalism. During 1904 his group distributed thousands of copies of Zou Rong's violently anti-Manchu book, *The Revolutionary Army* (see Chapter 3). In it, Zou called on the Han to 'annihilate the five million and more of the furry and horned Manchu race, cleanse ourselves of the 260 years of harsh and unremitting pain, so that the soil of the Chinese subcontinent is made immaculate'.[25] Up until this point, Sun had been wary of Han-race nationalism. He only seems to have adopted it as a tactic to win supporters away from Kang and Liang's yellow-race nationalism.

The arguments between reformers and revolutionaries, yellow-race supporters and Han-race supporters, dominated the exile community in Japan and the wider *huaqiao* communities in Southeast Asia and North America for the following decade. While Liang wrote and thought, Sun plotted and acted. In the hope of bringing about a revolution, he made all kinds of deals with secret societies, domestic warlords and foreign powers. In late August 1905 Sun made a breakthrough. He, Zhang Binglin and the other rival revolutionaries managed to put aside their differences and form the *Zhongguo Tongmenghui* – the 'China Alliance Society'. On 12 October 1905 Sun outlined the *Tongmenghui*'s ideas in the first edition of its newspaper, *Minbao*. They were: *minzuzhuyi* – nationalism (literally, 'the doctrine of the people's lineage'); *minquanzhuyi* – republicanism (literally, 'the doctrine of the people's sovereignty'); and *minshengzhuyi* – socialism (literally, 'the doctrine of the people's livelihood'). These three 'isms' eventually became known as the 'Three Principles of the People'.

Although they were by now firmly in different political camps, *minzuzhuyi* clearly bears the imprint of Liang's thinking. Liang, in his 1903 essay, chose the word *minzu* to be the equivalent of 'people' and *guomin* for 'nation'. For Liang, a *guomin* could include several *minzu* and, since the future of the yellow race depended upon the unity of all the groups within the Qing Great-State, he argued for a 'greater nationalism', a *da-minzu-zhuyi* to bring them together. Sun, who was more of a doer than a thinker, borrowed from Liang but adapted his terms for political convenience. For him, it was *minzu* that would eventually come to mean 'nation'.

The historian James Leibold has argued that the English word nationalism is not sufficient to explain Sun's meaning.[26] Sun was walking a political tightrope. Zou Rong was far from being the only revolutionary to openly advocate genocide against the Manchus. Some also called for the abandonment of the provinces of Tibet, Xinjiang, Manchuria and Mongolia to their native populations in order to make the future republic a purely Han domain. However, Sun agreed with Liang about the need to preserve the territory of the great-state. As early as 1894, Sun had written to the Qing official Li Hongzhang (see Chapter 2) calling for the court to 'emulate the West by recruiting people to open up the wasteland along the great-state's vast frontier'.[27] In 1900, to demonstrate his commitment to maintaining the territory of the future country (which at that point he called *China*), Sun wrote a long list of all the places that should be included within its frontiers: everywhere under Qing rule, from western Tibet to eastern Manchuria. Sun's priority was that the future republic should inherit and preserve the territory of the Qing Great-State.

Somehow, Sun needed to keep the support of his partner in the *Tongmenghui*, Zhang Binglin, and the other Han racialists while, at the same time, preserving his own dream of a future state that included all the areas populated by non-Han peoples. This was the biggest ideological problem facing the revolutionaries and Sun delegated the search for a solution to a newly arrived student called Wang Jingwei.

Wang was a nineteen-year-old scholar and wannabe-official from Guangdong province sent by the Qing authorities to Hosei University in Japan in late 1904 to study 'Western learning'. Once there, Wang became dedicated to overthrowing his sponsors. He joined the *Tongmenghui* shortly after it was founded and his first contribution to *Minbao* was spread across its first and second editions. It was a lengthy two-part article dedicated to resolving Sun's problem. In it, Wang adopted Liang's distinction between 'people' and 'nation' and asked whether a nation could comprise more than one 'people'. The Manchus were clearly a different *minzu*, he argued, but had not the Han successfully assimilated other *minzus* in the past? Was it not logical that if Manchu rule were ended, then they too would be assimilated? The Han were the 'master race' (*zhu-ren*) into which all the other peoples of the Qing realm would merge to form the new nation.[28]

As a result of his travels in North America, Liang's firm political belief, on the other hand, was that the Qing Great-State needed a gradual programme of reform, not revolution. This obliged him to argue that the division between Han and Manchu was already breaking down, removing the need for revolutionary political change. He claimed that this process of racial amalgamation would create a new *Zhonghua minzu* to save the race and the country. His journey through the United States seems to have persuaded him of the importance of a cultural 'melting pot' and he wrote of the necessity of the various *minzu* to 'smelt together in the same furnace'.[29] Wang Jingwei and Sun, on the other hand, were convinced that the Manchu had not assimilated and therefore had to be overthrown before the *Zhonghua minzu* could be created. What both reformists and revolutionaries had in common was that they regarded ethnic diversity as merely a temporary phenomenon that would be eliminated by the assimilating power of the Han. They also agreed that the overriding priority was to preserve the territory of the great-state. For Sun, for Liang and for the People's Republic today, the organisation of this territory would be distinctly hierarchical. There was a core China – Sun called it *Zhina Benbu* ('China proper') – and there were its four dependencies, or *shudi*: Manchuria,

Mongolia, Tibet and Xinjiang. This would be the political basis upon which Sun would subsequently define his nation and its state. Regardless of which side won the political battle, reformists or revolutionaries, the prescription for the 'non-Han' areas of the Qing Great-State – Tibetans, Uyghurs, Manchus and Mongols – was the same: incorporation into the future state and ethnic assimilation.

As it turned out, the greatest threat to the reformist political movement spearheaded by Kang Youwei and Liang Qichao did not come from their revolutionary rivals but from the Qing court itself. As the 1900s rolled on, Empress Cixi agreed to many of the reforms that Kang had lobbied for, and that she had so dramatically opposed, back in 1898. The ban on Han-Manchu marriage was lifted in 1902, school reforms were announced in 1904, the traditional exams for the bureaucracy were abolished in 1905, and in 1906 officials were sent abroad to study other countries' constitutions. It looked as if radical change was already under way without the need for Kang and Liang. The strength of their arguments began to dwindle and almost entirely collapsed on 14 November 1908 when the Guangxu Emperor, the one their movement had been trying to 'protect', died at the age of thirty-seven. Since his gaoler and aunt, Cixi, died the following day, it was automatically assumed by her critics that, lying on her deathbed, she had arranged to have the emperor poisoned and his two-year-old nephew, Puyi, to be chosen as his successor.

Calling for the little boy emperor Puyi to be 'protected' made little sense to anyone, even Kang Youwei. The emotional content of the reformers' narrative drained away and the initiative shifted to the revolutionaries. After 1909 Kang's wealthy supporters in North America rapidly switched their allegiance to Sun. Sun took their money and used it to launch repeated armed uprisings. All of them were failures but each one increased his prestige. The political situation seemed to have reached stalemate until, on 10 October 1911, troops in the southeastern city of Wuchang rose up. Sun's Revolutionary Alliance actually had nothing to do with the initial mutiny, but as it spread, the movement snowballed and by the end of the year the fate of the Qing Dynasty was sealed.

In the chaos of those two months, the *Hanzu* racism of Zhang Binglin and Zou Rong was expressed in blood on the streets. Taking the slogan *Geming*

Paiman – 'A revolution to expel the Manchus' – literally, Sun's followers inflicted terrible violence upon ethnic Manchus in many places. This started with the initial uprising in Wuchang. The revolutionaries reported that only around twenty of their own fighters were killed, compared to more than 500 Manchus.[30] The historian Edward Rhoads has identified ten cities where massacres took place. Twelve days after Wuchang, the revolution hit Xi'an and around 10,000 people, half the Manchu population, were killed in indiscriminate slaughter. Other mass killings took place in Fuzhou, Hangzhou and Taiyuan, where as many as 20,000 may have died.[31] In Zhenjiang and Nanjing the garrisons surrendered without a fight, yet Manchus were nonetheless killed in large numbers and their residential districts destroyed. Individual Manchus were singled out by the shape of their allegedly flat heads, by the way they spoke or by the unbound feet of the women. Countless numbers were simply killed on the spot.[32]

Many provincial leaders feared that this genocidal violence could become unstoppable and called upon the revolutionaries to denounce and prevent it. It was in this atmosphere that another formulation of the Chinese nation came to the fore: the idea of a 'five-lineage republic' – *wuzu gonghe*. This idea, which came to define the early years of the Republic of China, can be traced back to the pages of another magazine published by exiles in Japan in the 1900s. What made this magazine, the 'Great Harmony Journal' (*Datongbao*), different was that its editors were both reformers and ethnic Manchu. The choice of name clearly showed the influence of Kang Youwei's neo-Confucian ideas but its writers were not utopians. They were frightened by the rise of anti-Manchu thought, and its implications for them and their families. In the seven issues that they published in 1907 and 1908, they sought to address the 'problem' of Han-Manchu relations. They supported constitutional monarchy and parliamentary democracy but, most importantly, they sought to 'unify Manchus, Han, Mongols, Muslims and Tibetans as one *guomin*'. The influence of Liang Qichao's ideas of 'many *minzu* in a single *guomin*' formulation is obvious,[33] but whereas Liang ultimately wanted to smelt all the *minzu* into a single *Zhonghua minzu*, the writers in *Datongbao* wanted the five groups recognised as different *zu* (lineages) and called for equality between them, as groups.

They were working within, but also drastically modifying, a vision of the great-state laid down by the Qianlong Emperor over a century earlier. This was a framework in which five constituencies – Manchus, Han, Mongols, Muslims and Tibetans – each defined by the writing scripts that they used, and each corresponding to a particular territory, could co-exist within the great-state while maintaining their own beliefs and systems of governance. This is what Pamela Crossley has termed 'simultaneous rule'.[34] Tibetans, for example, could be Buddhists and accept the authority of Lamas but still remain subjects of the emperor. In return, the emperor could publicly practise Buddhism, worship in the Lama Temple in Beijing and appear to be a magnanimous leader of the Tibetans. He could also appear as a *khan* to the Mongols and a Confucian ruler to the Han. The system was flexible enough for each group to feel autonomous, yet part of the whole. The innovation that appeared in the pages of *Datongbao* was that instead of a personal loyalty to the emperor, in the modern world the five *zu* should feel loyalty to *Zhongguo*, of which they were all *guomin*.

This was an arrangement, they argued, which could keep the country together both ethnically and territorially. In the final, fevered months of 1911 it was also a compromise that the revolutionaries were forced to accept. They were not in a position to take power since the court still possessed loyal military forces and many of its former commanders had already broken away to create their own independent fiefs. More importantly, the prospect of a Han-dominated republic replacing the multi-ethnic great-state frightened the Mongol princes into declaring independence in December. Tibet was also heading down the independence road with fighting already under way and Xinjiang had become de facto autonomous under a local warlord. More than half the territory of the great-state was slipping out of Beijing's control.

Sun Yat-sen and the revolutionaries knew they had to negotiate to achieve power, both with the Qing court and with the regional warlords. A key intermediary was an ethnic-Manchu reformer, Yang Du, who had also studied in Japan and been one of the supporters of *Datongbao* in 1907/8. He shared the magazine's ideas for reform and ethnic group equality. By 1911 he was back in Beijing and close to both the northern warlord Yuan Shikai, who became the court's prime minister, and to Sun's ideologue, Wang Jingwei.[35] That put him in a pivotal position to influence the compromise that would end the Qing Great-State and herald the Republic. At the time, neither the court nor the revolutionaries believed in a future political arrangement based upon equality between the five *zu*. For the court, the great-state was hierarchical: with the Manchu at the top. The revolutionaries, on the other hand, weren't prepared to politically recognise any groups; everyone was simply part of the single *Zhonghua minzu*.

After travelling across North America and Europe, Sun Yat-sen arrived back in Shanghai on Christmas Day 1911, just as the negotiations were reaching a climax. On 29 December, the revolutionaries' negotiator Wu Tingfang made the crucial concession: the Manchus, Mongols, Muslims and Tibetans would be treated on a basis of equality with the Han.[36] The future state would be a 'five-lineage republic' – *wuzu gonghe*. Neither side had wanted this at the outset, but that was the compromise they came to. As James Leibold has demonstrated, it was the outcome Sun was obliged to accept in the particular circumstances of December 1911.[37] Sun's reward came on 1 January 1912, when he was declared provisional president of the new Republic of China by a congress of revolutionary representatives. However, he made his views on the ethnic composition of the nation very clear in his inaugural speech. 'The essence of the state exists in its people. The uniting of the Han, Manchu, Mongol, Hui and Tibetan territories into a single country also means the uniting of the Han, Manchu, Mongol, Hui, Tibetan and other lineages [*zu*] into a single people (*yiren*). This, you could say, is *minzu* unity.' Sun, like Liang, was still a 'smelter' at heart.

It was only on the very final day of the Qing Dynasty, 12 February 1912, when the court formally abdicated in the name of the boy emperor Puyi, that it used the language of the five peoples – *minzu* – for the first time.[38] It did so in a statement that had been written by the revolutionaries in Shanghai, edited by Yuan Shikai in Beijing and then delivered by the Dowager Empress Longyu, the adoptive mother of the emperor, widow of the emperor's predecessor and niece of Cixi. Yuan added two critical stipulations to the revolutionaries' abdication edict: firstly, that the existing nobility of the Manchus, Mongols, Muslims and Tibetans would be preserved and, secondly, that the minorities' religions would be protected. Thus, two key foundations of ethnic separateness would be maintained by the new Republic.

Sun served just ten weeks as provisional president before giving way to Yuan Shikai, who was threatening to use his military forces against the revolution. Those ten weeks were marked by a dispute that crystallised the fundamental disagreements over the Republic's policy towards race and nation: what should be on the new state's flag? Sun was very clear in his preference. Back in 1895 Sun's childhood friend Lu Haodong had created a banner of a blue sky with a white sun (*qingtian bairi*) for the first attempted uprising against the Qing in Guangzhou. When the uprising failed, Lu had been captured and executed, becoming, in Sun's view, the first martyr of the revolution. Sun had insisted that Lu's flag was the one adopted by the *Tongmenghui* when the revolutionary groups merged in 1905 and had fought all attempts to change it.[39]

The flag was therefore clearly identified with Sun and his organisation and beliefs. But it was only one of several contenders for the role. Some Han nationalists used a flag with eighteen stars, one for each of the (modern) provinces of the former Ming Dynasty, which implicitly excluded any mention of the non-Han regions. Another flag simply bore the Chinese character for 'Han'. In the end, the flag that was adopted by the Republic on 10 January was intended to signify the opposite: the harmonious unity of the five *minzu* in the new state. It was composed of five coloured stripes. The top stripe was red and intended to represent the Han, below it came yellow for the Manchu, blue for the Mongols, white for the Hui Muslims and, finally, black for the Tibetans.

The exact origins of the flag are mysterious. Cultural historian Henrietta Harrison says it was initially used as a naval flag for low-ranking officials and was then adopted by Cheng Dequan, the Qing-appointed but ethnic-Han governor of Jiangsu province (which surrounds Shanghai), who switched sides to the revolution and declared the city of Suzhou independent in November 1911.[40] It was his forces that conquered Nanjing and, despite their nominally multi-ethnic flag, massacred the surrendered Manchu inhabitants.[41] One of Sun's lieutenants, the leader of the *Tongmenghui* in Shanghai, Chen Qimei, also adopted it. He argued that by representing the Manchus on the flag, Qing officials would be able to support the Republic.

The flag, therefore, had two advantages over Sun's preferred choice. It was seen both as non-partisan and also inclusive of the five *minzu*. But from Sun's perspective, both rationales were negatives. He continued to denounce it long after he was forced to resign as president. He objected, ostensibly, to the suggestion that the colours on the flag implied a racial hierarchy, but his real opposition was to the idea of separate *minzu*. In a speech in 1920, he told his audience, 'The term five *minzu* is inappropriate', and urged 'the various *minzus* to meld together into a single *Zhonghua Minzu*, like in America which was originally a mix of different European *minzus* and now forms only a single American *minzu*'.[42]

When Yuan Shikai was formally sworn in as provisional president of the Republic on 10 March 1912, delegates representing each of the five *minzu* bowed before him and the new flag. It was, in effect, a modernised version of the former imperial tribute ceremony, except that under the Qing, tributaries had come from different territories, whereas now they came from different ethnic groups living in what was supposed to be a single territory: the Republic of China. In fact, the Republic was crumbling. A month after the swearing-in, Tibetan troops under the leadership of the Dalai Lama expelled the Chinese garrison. A few months after that, President Yuan despatched a new force to retake control, but it failed to bring the Dalai Lama to heel. Instead, Yuan tried to reanimate the old Qing techniques of rule. He sent two friendly letters to the Dalai Lama conferring old Qing titles upon him. In late October, the Republic's official state bulletin, the *Peking Gazette*, optimistically declared, 'Now that the Republic has been firmly established and the five *minzu* deeply united into one family, the Dalai Lama is naturally moved with a feeling of deep attachment to the mother country.' According to the British diplomatic representative to Tibet, Charles Bell, the Dalai Lama replied by saying he had no wish to receive the titles, adding that he intended to rule Tibet independently.[43] Bell and the British were particularly supportive of the Dalai Lama. They wished to preserve Tibet as a neutral buffer state between the new Republic and their imperial domain in India. The more they could separate Tibet from Beijing's control, the more secure they would feel and they warned Yuan not to attempt a full-scale invasion.

Sun, meanwhile, although pushed from the presidency, was still pursuing his *Zhonghua minzu* dream. He remained immensely popular among the urban population and, despite their differing positions on most issues, Yuan Shikai clearly preferred to have Sun as an ally rather than an adversary. When Sun arrived in Beijing from Shanghai on 24 August 1912 he was greeted almost as if he were still head of state, with an honour guard, a banquet and a huge residence. The following day, Sun, the remaining leaders of the *Tongmenghui* and the leaders of several smaller reformist parties travelled to a Peking Opera

1. A modern-day tribute ceremony. General-Secretary Xi Jinping offers a toast to world leaders at the welcoming banquet of the Belt and Road Forum in the Great Hall of the People in Beijing, 26 April 2019.

2. Emblems of two of the Manchu 'banners' on display at the former mansion of Prince Gong (Manchu name: Yixin) in Beijing. All Manchu and Mongol subjects, along with some Han, were organised into banners – military units – through which the Qing Great-State imposed order.

3. The first American to meet a Qing emperor was Andreas Everardus van Braam Houckgeest. This picture, commissioned by Houckgeest himself, depicts him (seated left, without a hat) meeting the Viceroy of Guangzhou. Houckgeest travelled to Beijing in 1795 to present the tribute of a non-existent Dutch king in order to win trading rights.

4. Former American president Ulysses S. Grant meets Qing statesman Li Hongzhang in 1879. Li asked Grant to intervene in the dispute with Japan over the Ryukyu Islands but Grant ended up siding with Japan.

5. The former offices of the *Zongli Yamen* in Beijing now serve as a complaints office for the Ministry of Public Security. A plaque indicates its former role.

6. The diplomat and poet Huang Zunxian (centre) with some of his family. He was one of the pioneers of 'yellow race' thinking in the late Qing period but later helped ensure the Hakka people were classified as part of the 'Han race'.

7. The evolution of evolutionary thinking in China. Charles Darwin argued that there is a struggle for survival between individuals in a species. The British social reformer Thomas Huxley turned this into a competition between groups. Yan Fu took Huxley's ideas to argue that 'science' demonstrated that the 'yellow race' is locked in a death struggle with the 'white race'.

8. Timothy Richard with his wife Mary (née Martin) and their two eldest daughters Eleanor (top) and Mary Celia. This picture was probably taken in Taiyuan, Shanxi province, in 1883. Richard was a Welsh Baptist missionary who tried to live like the Chinese people he wanted to convert. He combined evangelism with social reform. His translations introduced many members of the Chinese elite to European ideas. Liang Qichao was his translator/secretary for a few key months in the momentous year of 1895 and many of Liang's ideas about writing Chinese history were inspired by Richard.

9. (a) Liang Qichao as a student. His hair is tonsured in the 'queue' style required of all men living under Qing rule. The front part of the head is shaven and the rest is swept back to form a braided ponytail. (b) Liang in exile in Japan, early 1900s. He has cut off his 'queue' and is now dressed in the manner of a modern Japanese/Western gentleman.

10. Liang Qichao's former house in Beijing, near the Dongzhimen metro station, is now home to around a dozen families. One proud resident displays a picture showing how the mansion used to look before it was divided and redistributed.

11. The reformer and scholar Kang Youwei. He helped persuade the emperor to initiate reforms in 1898, which were crushed within 100 days. He then fled into British protection while continuing to agitate for reform and the restoration of the emperor's power.

12. Xi Jinping's father Xi Zhongxun with the 10th Panchen Lama in the city of Xi'an while the latter was travelling to Beijing, 22 April 1951. Xi Zhongxun favoured greater autonomy for national minorities, in complete contrast to his son's current policies.

13. Sun Yat-sen (centre) flanked by his wife Soong Ching-ling and Mikhail Borodin, political adviser from the Soviet Comintern (wearing glasses) in Guangzhou, 1923. At its congress a few weeks later the Guomindang, under Borodin's influence, would modify its principle of nationalism over the objections of Sun and his ideologue Wang Jingwei.

14. Sun Yat-sen flanked by the flags of the nascent Republic of China. On the right, the 'Five Races Under One Union' flag and, on the left, the 'Blood and Iron' eighteen-star flag of the Republican army. On 15 February 1912, the day the Qing court formally abdicated power, Sun journeyed to the Xiaoling tomb of Zhu Yuanzhang, founder of the Ming dynasty, to celebrate the end of 'Tartar' rule with revolutionary supporters.

15. A silk scroll on display in the Shanghai History Museum. Note the Manchu script (left) used alongside the Chinese characters. The document is the 'Imperial Mandate to Parents of Liu Xixiong', dated 1780.

16. Ceremony to mark the new Nationalist government in Nanjing, 18 April 1927. First on the left in the front row sits Chiang Kai-shek. Wu Zhihui sits fourth from left. He chaired the 1913 Conference for the Unification of Reading Pronunciations. As a former anarchist with a penchant for obscenity he was not the best choice for such a sensitive role. Third from the right is Hu Hanmin, editor of the revolutionary journal *Minbao* and one of Sun Yat-sen's ideological advisers.

17. Sun Yat-sen (seated) with a young Chiang Kai-shek, whom he has just appointed as Commandant of the Whampoa Military Academy, standing directly behind him, 1924.

18. KMT leader Chiang Kai-shek with geographer Zhang Qiyun in Taiwan in the 1950s. Zhang was part of the second generation of modern Chinese geographers. It was he who persuaded Chiang to retreat to Taiwan in 1949.

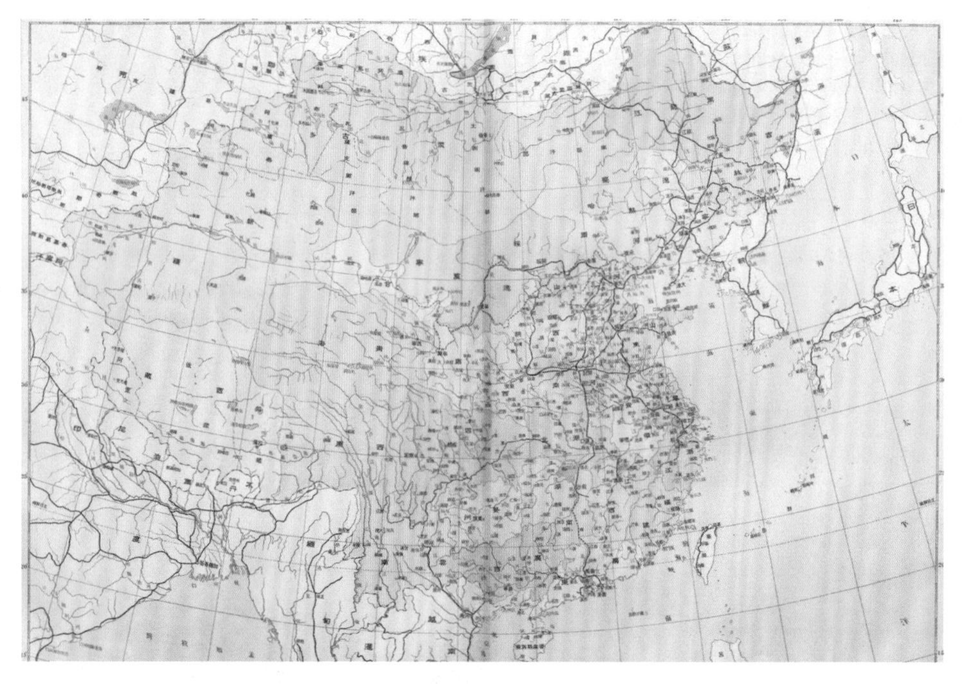

19. In 1934 the *Shenbao* newspaper published an atlas of China to instruct the population about the country. Its cartographers included Outer Mongolia and Tibet within the national territory, despite both being independent at the time, but they did not include Taiwan, which had been ceded to Japan.

20. Bai Meichu, the self-taught geography professor whose poor map-making helped create China's claims in the South China Sea. Bai taught the students who later advised the Republic of China government on which territories to claim after the Second World War. Bai's 1936 *New Atlas of China's Construction* owed as much to his nationalist imagination as to geographical reality.

21. Map of the South China Sea drawn by Bai Meichu for his *New Atlas of China's Construction* in 1936. James Shoal (off Borneo), Vanguard Bank (off Vietnam) and Seahorse Shoal (off the Philippines) are drawn as islands, yet in reality they are underwater features. Almost none of the islands that Bai drew in the central and southern parts of the South China Sea actually exist, yet this map, and Bai's line, remain the basis for China's modern territorial claims.

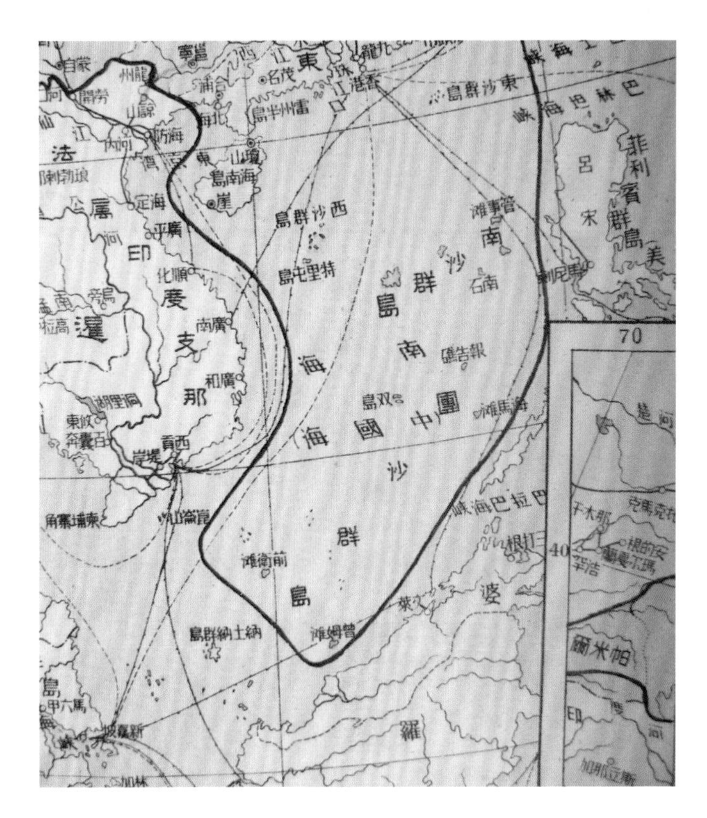

22. The leaders of the Republic of China expedition to the Spratly Islands ready to depart from Nanjing, aboard the ROC ship *Taiping* (formerly the USS *Decker*), 23 October 1946. Third from left at the front is Fleet Commander Lin Zun and fourth from left at the back is geography professor-turned Interior Ministry adviser, Zheng Ziyue. He brought Bai Meichu's ideas about China's claims in the South China Sea into government for the first time.

23. This statue of Chiang Kai-shek stands proudly on Pratas Island. This was where Qing China first staked a claim to any of the South China Sea islands. The building behind the statue holds clues that could unlock the territorial disputes over the sea.

venue, the Huguang Guild Hall, for the founding congress of their new political party, the *Guomin Dang* – the 'Nation Party'.[44]

The Guomindang adopted a five-point political agenda, including, critically, 'the strict implementation of racial assimilation [*zhongzu tonghua*]'. In Sun's view this would take place through a process of melding (*ronghe*), a notion that had its origins in Sun's time in the Reading Room of the British Museum in London, fourteen years before, when he studied the ideas of Social Darwinism. A few days after the congress, Sun demonstrated this in a speech at the Guangdong-Hunan Club in Beijing. 'World evolution depends upon learning how to advance from barbarism to civilisation,' he argued. Darwinian principles would ensure that more civilised *minzu* would be selected by nature over those *minzu* that continued to act like birds and beasts. Since the Han possessed the most 'civilised knowledge', they had a duty to lead the baser minority peoples out of barbarism and into civilisation. He called this duty *ganhua*, which James Leibold translates as 'reforming through examples of moral superiority'. Sun told his audience that the leaders of Tibet and Mongolia had only broken away from the Republic because they did not understand its benefits: 'Their education is still not sufficient . . . we can only gradually help them to see what is right', he told a reporter.[45]

The most effective way to bring about the melding of the *minzu*, according to Sun, was to encourage the migration of civilised Han to the barbarous frontiers. And the key to his plan was the development of railways to the far reaches of the Republic – a plan that he had originally sketched out in the map he had drawn back in 1900. President Yuan Shikai may not have been particularly interested in melding a new nation, but he certainly understood the strategic importance of controlling the frontiers. During the month that Sun was in Beijing, he had thirteen long meetings with Yuan, covering defence, foreign affairs, agricultural reform and industrial development. In the middle of these meetings, Yuan appointed Sun 'director of railways' and gave him a budget of 30,000 yuan per month, along with full powers to plan a national railway network and negotiate loans with foreigners to pay for it. The following week, Sun departed Beijing on Empress Cixi's former train to begin preparations for the task ahead. He told the Australian journalist travelling with him, William H. Donald, that he would build 100,000 kilometres of new track over ten years to connect Xinjiang and Tibet to the rest of the country. When Donald told him that the routes were impossible to build because of the high mountains, Sun apparently asserted that anywhere a yak trail could go, a railway could be built. Sun told a French journalist that the plan would cost an estimated 16 billion francs and that he was seeking foreign lenders to make it happen.[46] For Sun, it was far more important to spend the money on linking the northwestern frontiers to 'China proper', and thereby preserving the territory of the Qing Great-State for the Republic, than on more feasible projects in the Han parts of the country. However, despite his desperation to build it, the lenders did not come. Nonetheless, Sun continued to make his plans, even after July 1913, when Yuan fired him from the job as the political differences between them turned into civil war.[47]

Out of power, and living in semi-retirement in Shanghai, Sun kept on dreaming of railways and nationalism. By the end of the decade he had produced two major pieces of work: his 'Programme for National Reconstruction' (*Jianguo fanglue*) and his far better known 'Three Principles of the People' (*San Min Zhuyi*). The two should be seen as companions. In 'Programme for National Reconstruction' (later published in English as 'The International Development of China') he based his ideas on the American frontier. Sun called for a massive scheme of 'cultivation and colonisation' and the forced transfer of tens of thousands of landless peasants and soldiers to the frontiers to civilise the inhabitants. In 'Three Principles of the People', Sun borrowed Liang Qichao's definitions of two forms of nationalism – narrow and broad – to say that, so far, 'We have achieved only the negative aspect of *minzuzhuyi*', and must go further to achieve the positive side, 'for the *Hanzu* to sacrifice the bloodline, history and identity that they are so proud of and merge with all sincerity with the Manchus, Mongols, Hui and Tibetans in a single furnace to create a new order of the *Zhonghua Minzu*, just as America has produced the world's leading *minzuzhuyi* by melding scores of different peoples: black and white'.

In October 1919 Sun founded a new party as the successor to the Guomindang, the *Zhongguo Guomin Dang* – the China Nation Party – but it was not until January 1924 that it convened its first congress and adopted Sun's 'three principles' as its manifesto. They did so under war conditions, meeting in the Guangzhou National Teachers College in the only part of the country they controlled: the far south. Under the influence of new Soviet advisers sent by Joseph Stalin, the principle of 'nationalism' – *minzuzhuyi* – was modified significantly. It did not call for 'melding' many *minzu* into a single one but promised that they would all be treated equally. This did not represent a change of mind by Sun, however. Documents found in the Russian archives tell us that the wording about separate nations living within a single state was entirely the work of the Soviet advisers and inserted over the objections of Sun and his ideologue Wang Jingwei.[48]

Four days later, Sun delivered the first in a series of speeches at the National Guangzhou University that he had just founded. Away from the Soviet advisers, he directly contradicted the manifesto. He told his audience that, unlike other countries around the world, China has a single *minzu* forming a single *guojia* – a single people forming a single 'state-family' (the Confucian rendering of nation). While admitting that there were, in fact, other *minzu* in the country, he said they could be ignored because they would be assimilated into the superior Han lineage: 'China's *minzu* total four hundred million people. Among these people there are only a few million Mongols, a million Manchus and a few million Tibetans and some hundred thousand Muslim Turks, all totalling no more than ten million non-natives. Thus considering the vast majority, we can say that the four hundred million Chinese people are entirely *Hanzu*, sharing a common bloodline, language, religion and customs – a single pure *minzu*.'[49]

In short, Sun had no time for the Soviet advisers' ideas about minority nations living side by side in nominal equality. He believed in Social Darwinism and the need for the Han race to subsume the minorities into a Chinese race, which could compete with, and defeat, the white imperialists. His faith in Social Darwinism was so strong that he believed the assimilation process would take place of its own accord, without force or compulsion. This led him to argue that this 'natural' process had been going on for centuries and that Manchuria, Mongolia, Tibet and Xinjiang had all become Chinese because their peoples admired the Han people's culture. In his sixth lecture he suggested that this 'assimilative power' could ultimately extend as far as Annam, Bhutan, Borneo, Burma, Korea, Nepal, Taiwan and all the former tributary states, to include them all within a unified greater China.

Sun died in 1925 and a year later Chiang Kai-shek established himself as the Guomindang's military and political leader. By 1928 the Guomindang had captured Beijing and formed a national government. One of its first acts was to abandon the 'five-colour flag' adopted sixteen years before, and replace it with a version of Sun's cherished 'Blue Sky, White Sun' design. Then, at its third congress in 1929, it dropped the 1924 manifesto and its commitment to self-determination for the minorities. It appeared that the party was going to implement Sun's ideal of a single *Zhonghua minzu*. Yet, once again, the practicalities of needing to control the frontiers intervened. Responding to local political leaders' demands and conscious of the threat from foreign powers, the new government of the Republic began the process of creating special provinces in Inner Mongolia and Tibetan-inhabited areas.[50] Later on, it created autonomous regions for 'Inner Tibet' (the Chuanbian Special Autonomous Region) in 1939 and, in 1947, for Inner Mongolia.

However, at the same time, the railway construction that Sun had long promoted began to turn his dream of population 'melding' into reality.[51] In the first forty years of the twentieth century, 25 million Han moved into the three northeastern provinces and, although most of the settlers subsequently left, Manchus became a tiny minority there. The former Manchu homeland, where Han people were officially barred from living until the 1860s, became a Han domain. The Manchu became assimilated and Manchu, which had remained an official language of the Qing Great-State right until its end, almost completely disappeared.

Mongols are also now a small minority in Inner Mongolia, despite the region being declared autonomous. They make up less than a fifth of the autonomous region's population of 24 million. Although they have not been assimilated to the same extent as the Manchu, the numbers still able to speak, read and write Mongolian are declining.[52]

It has been a different story in Xinjiang and Tibet, mainly because they are further from the main population centres, climatically challenging and difficult to build railways to. The track into Xinjiang took well over a decade to construct and the connection to the provincial capital Urumqi only opened in 1966. The province was declared an autonomous region by the People's Republic in 1955 but in the years after, the Han population rose from around 10 per cent of the population to 40 per cent by the time of the 2010 census. The Turkic-speaking, Arabic script-writing, Muslim peoples still form a majority, but only just. The railway connection to Tibet took even longer to complete and only reached the capital, Lhasa, in 2006. As a result, the Han population remains relatively small in the Tibetan Autonomous Region, although it has grown far more quickly in the better-connected, historically Tibetan-populated areas in the provinces of Qinghai and Sichuan. However, in both Xinjiang and Tibet the Han population is concentrated in towns and cities with railway connections, where incomes and living standards are higher.

During the often violent decades since the revolution of 1911/12, Chinese state policy towards the peoples of the four dependent territories has veered, sometimes dramatically, between the rival positions of Yuan Shikai and Sun Yat-sen. There were long periods when differences between the *minzu* were tolerated, even encouraged, and others when the state went into 'smelting' mode to try to eradicate difference in the name of the single *Zhonghua minzu*. Sun's belief was that the job of smelting would be achieved by sheer numbers: 'It does not matter if there are disturbances along the frontier region,' he told a reporter in May 1912. 'They are merely an extremely small minority, not a strong enough force to stir up trouble.'[53] A century later, his chauvinistic optimism has been proven right in some cases but not others.

On 13 August 2018, at around the same time as the Panchen Lama was touring the construction projects of Tibet, a previously obscure Chinese official called Hu Lianhe was making global headlines in Geneva. For his appearance before the United Nations Committee on the Elimination of Racial Discrimination, Hu was blandly listed as a senior official of the United Front Work Department of the Communist Party. 'Crackdown instigator' might have been a better title, for Hu was the brains behind the security campaign in Xinjiang that began in early 2017 and, at the time of his appearance, had led to well over a million Uyghurs and other Turkic-speaking Muslims being detained in 1,200 remote 're-education' camps. This was nothing to worry about, Hu told the committee. The camps were 'vocational education and employment training centres' where extremists could be 'assisted with their rehabilitation and reintegration into society'.[54] Former inmates disagreed, describing the physical and mental torture they had endured at the hands of their interrogators behind the barbed wire.

This vast internment exercise was a response to a number of attacks by Uyghur extremists that had targeted members of the Han population. The final straw seems to have been the killing of five civilians near the strategic town of Hotan in southwestern Xinjiang in February 2017. Local officials were instructed to identify anyone showing signs of 'extremist thought', which might include wearing a headscarf, growing a beard or criticising Chinese-language education. As a result, something like 10 per cent of the adult population was detained in the camps and subjected to months (or longer) of pressure until they convinced their guards that they had abandoned separatism and embraced the teachings of the Communist Party. At the same time, security forces were deployed in huge numbers across the province. Armoured vehicles, paramilitary police on motorbikes and special forces paraded through Hotan, the capital Urumqi and anywhere else that the party felt insecure about its control.

Hu Lianhe is a key figure in the rethinking of *minzu* policy in China. After receiving his PhD from the Communist Party school for his thesis on terrorism, he was recruited by the party's Central Political and Legal Affairs Committee (CPLC) and then seconded to the Counter Terrorism Research Center at a military-run think tank, the China Institute for International Strategic Studies. He became the party's leading adviser on terrorism and was involved in drafting anti-extremism laws. Then, in 2004, he joined Professor Hu Angang, the leading critic of the first incarnation of PRC *minzu* policy, at Tsinghua University. Together, the 'two Hus' wrote over a dozen papers on the need for a new approach.[55] Hu Lianhe claimed to have developed a 'theory of stability', something that requires the 'standardisation of human behaviour'.

The two Hus focused, in particular, on Tibet and Xinjiang, warning that without determined action, the country would lose the allegiance of their indigenous populations and face the same fate as the Soviet Union. In a direct echo of Liang Qichao and Sun Yat-sen a century earlier, they called upon the government to 'embrace the melting pot' and meld the fifty-six *minzu* into a single *Zhonghua minzu*. In a 2011 article, they called on the party to remove all group-based rights, improve connectivity between minority-populated areas and the rest of the country (think railways), increase the use of the standard national language and increase migration across all parts of the country.[56]

On 28 September 2014, this approach received the official blessing of Xi Jinping. Speaking at the 'Central Ethnic Work Forum', he made clear that there would be a change of direction, that the Communist Party would pay more attention to integration and less to institutionalising diversity. 'We should not continue with what is rotten,' he is reported to have told the gathering. The forum approved a new approach to ethnic affairs, a more gentle version of 'melding' officially called 'mingling' – *jiaorong*. It follows the prescriptions of the two Hus; policies to increase labour mobility to bring Tibetans and Uyghurs to work in factories in Han areas of the country, build ethnically mixed communities, boost inter-ethnic marriage and so on.[57]

This was formalised at the 2017 Party Congress, which resolved to include the concept of 'forging a strong sense of collective consciousness for the *Zhonghua Minzu*' in the Communist Party's constitution. However, Xi Jinping and other supporters of the 'second generation' of ethnic policy are fighting against an entrenched opposition. The simple fact that the People's Republic of China still classifies people into different *minzu* tells us that the nationalist project dreamt of by Liang Qichao and Sun Yat-sen has not succeeded, despite more than a century of effort. Yet, as Xi fights the ideological and bureaucratic legacy of Yuan Shikai, Joseph Stalin and his own father, he seems determined to complete a task that began in 1903 with the invention of the idea of a single *Zhonghua minzu* in the first place.

6
THE INVENTION OF THE CHINESE LANGUAGE
guoyu – national language

To its tens of millions of fans, the fishball is the defining taste of Hong Kong. To most foreign palates, its elasticity can be disconcerting. The prolonged pounding of the raw fish flesh forms a spongy paste that vendors mix with rice flour and shape into spheres of springy delight. Some streetside cooks boil them in broth and skewer them on a stick. Others fry them in oil and slaver them with sauce. For the disenchanted, the result is merely gelatinous bycatch, but for the true Hong Konger, street-food fishballs epitomise local city culture.

And there is no better time to enjoy a proper Hong Kong fishball than lunar new year. The seasonal celebrations call back the many mainlanders who have moved to the Hong Kong Special Autonomous Region over the past few years. For native Hong Kongers it's like turning back the clock to a time before 1997, when mainlanders were kept out by high fences and British foot patrols. And there is no better place to enjoy a Hong Kong fishball at lunar new year than Sham Shui Po, a high-rise, working-class district of northern Kowloon, home to many former refugees from the mainland. For three days, unlicensed hawkers set up stalls alongside the buzzing streets to cater for the revellers: low-paid workers selling low-cost snacks. Their business is illegal but typically the police turn a blind eye. It's a festival, after all.

Monday 8 February 2016 was not a typical new year fishball-eating night. By the time Monday evening had turned into Tuesday morning, forty-four police had been injured and twenty-four people had been arrested. It started with a crackdown on 'illegal' stalls, organised by officials from the city's Food and Environmental Hygiene Department. To escape them, the hawkers headed south into Mong Kok, the shopping and entertainment neighbourhood, sometimes described as the busiest place on earth and also as Hong Kong's 'true heart'. They settled on Portland Street, the red-light area parallel with the main shopping district on Nathan Road. It wasn't long, however, before the officials arrived in force, threatening to arrest anyone operating a stall. The hawkers retreated into side alleys. The stage was set for confrontation. A group of protestors appeared and began to escort the hawkers back to Portland Street. They had come prepared, carrying home-made shields, masks and banners. A stand-off ensued, police riot squads were called, and the result was a ten-hour street battle featuring batons, bricks, bottles and two bullets fired into the air.

As the street-cleaning teams swept away the wreckage, it became clear that this was not really a battle over the right to sell illegal fishballs on the street. The 2016 'fishball riot' was a defence of 'localism', an outburst of resistance against a government in Beijing that was perceived to be trying to homogenise national culture and thereby eradicate a way of life that made Hong Kongers feel special. That it happened in a gritty, vice-ridden area with an underworld contested by rival Triad gangs makes establishing the exact cause of events difficult, but there's little doubt that underlying the riot was a strong sense of cultural persecution. Localists, including supporters of a group calling itself 'Hong Kong Indigenous', decided to make the fishball hawkers a symbol of a new identity – a Hong Kong nationalism set in opposition to the mainland's overbearing version. The riot police were deployed as a political hit squad, not against the hawkers but to crush an incipient separatist movement.

When the United Kingdom grabbed the rocky island of Hong Kong as part of its booty from the 1840 'Opium War', the indigenous population consisted of a few fishing villages. In typical fashion, the British set up a colonial administration that operated only in English. Over the subsequent century and a half, hundreds of thousands of mainlanders fled to the city to escape poverty, war and disorder at home, bringing their different regional dialects with them. But it was not until 1974 that the British finally relented to public protest and allowed Chinese to be used as an official language. They did not specify which form of Chinese should be used, however, mainly because there was no dispute: Cantonese was the one spoken by the overwhelming majority of inhabitants.

And in written form, Hong Kongers used traditional Chinese characters, not the simplified ones introduced by the communists on the mainland after 1956.

Officially, there has been no change to this arrangement, even though Hong Kong was handed over to the People's Republic of China (PRC) in 1997. Traditional characters are still used on road signs and public buildings and Cantonese is still spoken in government and the legal system. There are certain terms and certain forms of expression that are only found in Cantonese and they are widespread through official and unofficial language. However, Hong Kong 'localists', like the Mong Kok protestors, believe that the Communist Party leadership in Beijing is intent on changing this. It has never been officially stated, but there is plenty of evidence that a 'stealth' campaign against Cantonese – and against the very idea of a Cantonese identity – is under way.

A year after the handover, the Hong Kong government decided that the official mainland version of Chinese, *Putonghua*, would become a compulsory subject for primary and junior-secondary schoolchildren. It was, however, taught as a 'foreign' language, with perhaps just an hour of class time per week. Ten years later, the city authorities began to incentivise schools to make *Putonghua* the language of instruction. From 2008, schools were given extra funding if they agreed to teach all their subjects through *Putonghua*. Increasingly, Hong Kong parents started to choose these schools for their children, expecting that fluency in *Putonghua* would help them obtain better jobs. This seems to have amplified the generation gap between parents and their offspring, with younger Hong Kongers resenting having to learn in *Putonghua*. For some it seems to have had the opposite effect to the one intended: setting them on a path towards resistance rather than integration with the mainland.

At around the same time, fears for the future of Cantonese also emerged on the mainland. The city of Guangzhou (the 'Canton' in 'Cantonese') was due to host the Asian Games in November 2010. In July of that year, the city committee of the Chinese People's Political Consultative Conference (CPPCC – the body that brings together the Communist Party and other local organisations in a 'united front') recommended that the province's main television stations should change their broadcasting from Cantonese to *Putonghua* in time for the games. PRC law requires all channels transmitted by satellite to be broadcast in *Putonghua* only, so the change would allow Guangzhou TV to benefit from satellite distribution. This, argued the committee, would enable it to be seen by a much larger audience, both inside China and abroad, enhancing the province's international reputation. It would also, according to the committee, allow foreigners who had learnt *Putonghua* to understand the news.[1]

The local *Southern Daily* newspaper group, then known for its independent-mindedness, started covering the story, immediately provoking a reaction in its online discussion forum and elsewhere. Contributors spoke of their pride in speaking Cantonese, of how much closer to classical Chinese it was, of how it was an international language with 100 million speakers around the world and of how ugly *Putonghua* sounded by comparison. Beijing's campaign against Cantonese was presented by some as a campaign against local culture itself, with many saying they believed the ultimate aim of the government was to eliminate Cantonese altogether. There were also criticisms of migrants from other areas who had moved to Guangzhou and not learned Cantonese. The author of the CPPCC proposal was himself one such migrant.[2] Locals had a name for these people: '*bei lao*' – 'northern guy' in *Putonghua*, which in Cantonese sounds very similar to 'northern profiteer'.[3]

On 25 July the protests moved offline, into the real streets of Guangzhou. At least 2,000 people (some say as many as 10,000) gathered outside Jiangnanxi metro station to voice their anger. Another protest involving hundreds of people was held a week later in the city's People's Park, and a solidarity rally was held in Hong Kong at the same time.[4] A pan-Cantonese movement appeared to be taking shape. In response, the Guangzhou authorities backpedalled. The committee's *Putonghua* proposal was rejected by the television station, the channel was kept off the satellite network and the athletes and spectators of the Asian Games were obliged to receive their news in Cantonese.

It was only a tactical retreat, however. On 30 June 2014, Guangzhou TV's hourly news bulletin switched from Cantonese to *Putonghua*.[5] The station also replaced four of its Cantonese-speaking presenters with *Putonghua* speakers. Then, in September, most of its original programming switched to *Putonghua*. One insider told the Hong Kong-based newspaper, the *South China Morning Post*, 'This is being done quietly, without any official promotion or notification to audiences.'[6] The new strategy was compared by its critics to the slow-boiling of the proverbial frog. The result was another victory in the long campaign to assert a single national language over the entire territory of the People's Republic. But it may surprise some readers to know how far from complete this campaign currently is.

In April 2017 the Chinese Ministry of Education and its agency, known in English as the State Language Commission[7] (officially the National Committee for Language and Script Work),[8] set a target for 80 per cent of the PRC's citizens to speak *Putonghua* by 2020. It was absurd: the chances of teaching 140 million people to speak a new language in three years were minimal, but it was an indication of the urgency with which the Communist Party views the work of nation-building. Way back in 1982 a new clause had been inserted into the national constitution mandating the state to 'promote the nationwide use of *Putonghua*'. More than a quarter of a century later, the Ministry of Education's announcement was an admission that the change had had little effect: almost a third of the population, around 400 million people, did not speak the national language. As the protests in Hong Kong and Guangzhou (not to mention the far more serious resistance in Tibet and Xinjiang) demonstrate, the idea of a national language has not been nationally welcomed.

In all these places, language is a proudly held symbol. It is a reminder that there are regional, even national, identities that pre-date the modern 'Chinese' identity that was rolled out from Beijing and Nanjing during the past century. The protests on Hong Kong's streets during 2019, prompted by the population's concerns about becoming subjected to the mainland's unfair legal system, became violent because of the mainland leadership's refusal to allow the regional administration to find compromise with its critics. The political battle behind the scenes was perceived as an attack on Hong Kongers' sense of difference, their sense of self. And that seems to have been deliberate. There is little space in Xi Jinping's China for differences in cultural identity. Language has become a battlefield between the steamroller of nationalism and the bedrock of local difference. But this is far from being a new phenomenon: it goes right back to the original idea of a national language in the first place. And it climaxed with a fight between two Wangs over who was right.

The new home of the Shanghai History Museum is the city's former Race Club. In the early twentieth century the building was a bastion of imperialist cultural power, but it has a new purpose now: to assert a sense of Shanghai-ness stretching back to 'ancient times'. In an understated but radical move, exhibits tell the story of the emergence of a local civilisation rather than a 'national' one: a 'Yangtze Delta culture' rather than a 'Chinese culture'. There is the skull of a man from the 6,000-year-old Majiabang culture and an intricate ivory carving from the 4,000-year-old Liangzhu culture, but not a terracotta warrior anywhere. At each display case parents pore over the explanatory texts and loudly explain their meanings to children in a cacophony of regional tongues: Shanghainese, Cantonese, *Putonghua*, none of which would have been understood by the makers of these ancient artefacts.

Who were the people of Liangzhu? We know very little about them, but geneticists, linguists, archaeologists and anthropologists are starting to put together a picture. The human remains found at the site have been shown to have genetic markers on the male chromosome that place them within the 'Y haplogroup O1'. Although the science is still developing, this haplogroup (a population believed to share a common ancestor) is strongly associated with speakers of the Tai-Kadai and Austronesian-type languages found in Southeast Asia.[9] In other words, the current theory is that the early inhabitants of Shanghai and the Yangtze Delta migrated there by travelling around the coast from Southeast Asia and spoke a language that had more in common with peoples to the south than those to the north. Given the plentiful supply of fish, the ease of travelling by boat and the fertile soils that river deltas provide, it is not surprising that human settlement spread more quickly by sea than over land. The Yangtze people grew rice, which they may have brought with them from Southeast Asia, in contrast to the northerners who cultivated millet around the Yellow River. These Austronesian rice growers had been resident millennia before speakers of other language groups arrived to join or conquer them. New research, led by Professor Kong Qingdong of the Kunming Institute of Zoology, seems to confirm this. His team found that around 10,000 years ago the populations of the Yellow River basin and the lower reaches of the Yangtze and Pearl rivers were genetically separate. His controversial conclusion is that all three locations have an equal claim to be called the ancestors of the Chinese.[10]

The present-day result of this prehistoric settlement is a pattern of language around coastal China that is quite different from that found inland. Shanghainese,

Cantonese, Hokkien (spoken in Fujian province and Taiwan) and many other less well-known tongues are founded upon roots that stretch into the remote past and whose development can only be reconstructed with great care and some conjecture. The current consensus is that the modern languages spoken in the cities of Hong Kong, Shanghai and Xiamen – and most of the spaces in between – are the results of blended influences from southeast and northeast Asia, a process that is still ongoing.[11] Some linguists talk about 'layers' of language almost like layers of rock, with new particles flowing in from many directions, being laid down on top of old structures and mixed up into new formations. So much influence has come from the north over the past two millennia that it can be hard to spot the early layers. Yet there are words, linguistic structures and pronunciations in these southern tongues which have more in common with their Vietnamese and Thai neighbours than with the officially mandated *Putonghua*.

The Chinese linguist Lü Shuxiang, one of the original compilers of the 'Contemporary Chinese Dictionary' in the 1950s, once estimated that there were around 2,000 forms of 'Chinese' spoken across China and Taiwan.[12] While speakers of some can understand speakers of others without too much difficulty, the late American Sinologist Jerry Norman once estimated that as many as 400 are mutually unintelligible.[13] 'A speaker of the Peking dialect can no more understand a person speaking Cantonese than an Englishman can understand an Austrian when each employs his native language,' he later wrote. 'The Hainan Min dialects are as different from the Xi'an dialect as Spanish is from Rumanian.'[14] Exactly how to describe the relationships between these different types of speech is a political as much as a linguistic problem. As the Russian linguist Max Weinreich famously quipped, 'A language is a dialect with an army and a navy.' While it is a commonplace to describe Spanish and Romanian as separate languages, the Chinese government insists that Hainan Min and Xi'an are simply 'dialects' of a single language spoken by a single nation.

There is a term in *Putonghua* that neatly circumnavigates these difficulties: *fangyan* – literally 'regional speech'. Chinese scholars encounter no political problems while using it because it can mean both 'language' and 'dialect'. They commonly recognise seven major *fangyan* spoken in China: *Putonghua*, *Yue* (which includes Cantonese), *Wu* (which includes Shanghainese), *Min* (which includes Hokkien), *Hakka*, *Gan* (in Jiangxi province) and *Xiang* (in Hunan province). There are historical examples of the word *fangyan* being used to describe both the minor differences between local ways of speaking and major differences between local and European languages. The American philologist Victor H. Mair invented the word 'topolect' as an English-language equivalent for *fangyan*. It describes a way of speaking that is tied to a particular place (which can vary in size) but without having to specify exactly how different it is or whether it is the recognised language of a political entity. As a consequence, Mair cautions against using the phrase 'Chinese language' since the choice of which single language is spoken by 'the Chinese' is entirely political. He prefers to speak of a 'Sinitic' group of topolects that bear some relationship to each other but are not necessarily descended from a common root.

Until modern times there was no Chinese word for 'language'. There was a word for script – *wenzi* – and a word for speech – *yuyan* – and their meanings were distinct.[15] Mair argues that the vast majority of Sinitic topolects were never written languages; historically they were spoken by people who were illiterate. The written language – 'classical Chinese' or *wen* – was, by definition, only used by literate people. It was only written and read; there was no spoken form. There was also a form of prestigious speech, known as *guanhua*, used by officials. Its name means, literally, 'official speech'. Foreigners seem to have missed the distinction between the spoken and written forms of officialdom. The result was that both the classical written script, *wen*, and the spoken form, *guanhua*, became jointly known as 'Mandarin'. The term 'Mandarin' comes through the Portuguese word *mandar*, 'to order', but with connections to the Malay word *mantri*, which was itself borrowed from Hindi-Urdu and means 'official'. 'Mandarin', therefore, is a good translation of 'official speech'.[16] The written language, *wen*, was a *lingua franca* that could be read by scholars and officials across the empire. It performed a role equivalent to that of Latin in the Roman Empire – it was a means of communication and control. The vast majority of Roman subjects never read Latin, but the people who ordered their lives did. It was the same with *wen*.

But there was also a key difference between Latin and *wen*. While there was a form of speech used by the elite (*guanhua*), *wen* texts could also be read aloud using completely different word-sounds according to the local topolect. Court decrees and other central announcements would be written as *wen* in Beijing and then, in effect, 'translated' in order to be understood in the cities, towns and villages of the empire. In time, words in local topolects came to be associated with characters in *guanhua* so that they appeared to be referring to the same language. For an equivalent, imagine the European Union decreeing that all European languages had to be written with emojis. English speakers might say 'fish', French speakers 'poisson' and Croatians 'riba', but all would share the same written character.

But even *guanhua* was not the official language of the Qing Great-State. *Guanhua* was only used to communicate within the Sinitic part of the realm ('China proper'). The other parts of the empire used different scripts: Tibetan, Turkic and Mongol. The court used its own language to coordinate its subordinate parts, as can be clearly seen in one display case at the Shanghai History Museum. Exhibit 222 contains the 'Imperial Mandate to Parents of Lu Xixiong', chief editor of the Qing Dynasty's vast encyclopaedia. The mandate, dating from 1780, is a gold and silver silk brocade scroll. The golden end is beautifully adorned with *guanhua* calligraphy, but the silver end is in another script entirely: the administrative language of the Qing court.

Right up until the end of the Qing Great-State in 1912, its official language was not 'Chinese' *guanhua* but Manchu, the language of the people from the northeast who conquered the Ming empire and went on to incorporate Mongolia, Tibet and Xinjiang within their realm. There was always a 'Manchu track' within the Hanlin Academy, the court's secretariat. All government documents had to be written in the language and all memorials to the emperor presented in it. There were separate archives for documents in Manchu and for the other languages. Even after most 'Manchus' had stopped speaking Manchu in their daily life, hundreds of scholar-officials were still busy translating official edicts and reports between Manchu and the other languages. The emperor continued to address officials and envoys in Manchu and disciplined some who were not able to speak it.[17] The scroll delivered to the parents of Lu Xixiong was just one of tens of thousands of examples of official multilingualism. In fact, Manchu was often referred to in *guanhua* as the 'state speech' – *guoyu*. The cultural changes of the early twentieth century and the revolution of 1911/12 would reverse this situation completely. *Guanhua* would become, in effect, the *guoyu* and Manchu would disappear.

Right up until its end, the Qing Great-State had no need for a *national* language because there was no Qing nation. The court only required a *state* language to administer its multi-lingual and multi-ethnic empire. It was not until Sun Yat-sen, Liang Qichao and their contemporaries imagined a *Chinese* nation into existence in the 1890s and 1900s that the question of a national language was even thought about. And the fate of that discussion was strongly influenced by a series of other questions about language that were being raised by other intellectuals at the same time.

Many reformers blamed defeat in the Sino-Japanese War of 1894/5 on the empire's weakness in education. Even junior Japanese soldiers had been able to read orders and maps, unlike their Qing counterparts. But the reformers saw a deeper reason, too: in other countries, mass education had built the nation. One Japanese moderniser, Ueda Kazutoshi, had studied in Berlin and Leipzig in the 1890s where he had come to accept the arguments of German language theorists that the 'mother tongue' represented 'the internalised spirit of the nation'. In 1898 Ueda was appointed to head Japan's Special Education Bureau with a mandate to create a national language that unified speech and writing. This involved standardising and limiting the use of traditional 'Chinese' characters (*kanji*), establishing Tokyo upper-class speech as the common national standard and encouraging the use of this vernacular speech in written works.[18]

Meanwhile, missionaries such as Timothy Richard were preaching the example of Japan in the pages of *Wanguo gongbao* and other outlets (see Chapter 4). Huang Zunxian's *Treatises on Japan*, republished in 1895 (see Chapter 3), was also a major source of inspiration for Qing reformers. Their message was clear: mass education through schools, libraries and newspapers would unite the country and make it strong. Kang Youwei's 1895 reform petition and Liang Qichao's 1896 'Comprehensive Proposal for Reforms' both called for an expansion of education and the need to learn from Japan, and this message had been well received by the Guangxu Emperor. One of his final acts before his aunt's coup against him was to issue an edict calling for more translations from

Japanese and for the despatch of students to Japan for higher education. After Empress Cixi's coup and the crushing of the Hundred Days Reform, there was, indeed, a dramatic exodus to Japan, but only of reformers fleeing for their lives. However, after Cixi herself began to introduce reforms during the 1900s, the government sent increasing numbers of students there on scholarships. For the following decade they had a first-hand view of the impact of language modernisation taking place in Japan under the direction of officials like Ueda Kazutoshi. The more radically minded framed the issue in Social Darwinist terms: as a choice between reform and extinction. As they saw it, language was at the heart of the problem. Some argued that the Chinese language was simply incompatible with national survival: it could not cope with modern concepts, took too long to learn and therefore left too many people illiterate and disempowered.

Huang Zunxian's book had introduced the Japanese version of the German theorists' belief in the need for a 'congruence of speech and writing' to Chinese readers for the first time. He translated the phrase – via Japanese – as *yan wen heyi*. Huang was concerned about the difficulty of learning classical Chinese characters and their remoteness from the language spoken in everyday conversations. He noted that England and France had become strong countries after abandoning Latin and, instead, writing in the language that people spoke. Japan had followed suit after supplementing *kanji* characters with a phonetic script, known in Japanese as *kana*.

However, Huang's argument contained two implications that pointed the future of language reform in two different directions. These were often thought to refer to the same thing but the difference between them would be fundamental to the future creation of a Chinese national language. Huang called both for a modern writing style using traditional Chinese characters and for a way of writing that told speakers how to pronounce the sound of the language – a phonographic script.[19] Understanding that these were, in fact, two quite different problems takes us to the heart of the difficulty that the reformers were facing.

Ideas for a phonographic Sinitic script had actually been circulating for some time. Christian missionaries and foreign diplomats had created their own versions to assist with spreading religion and gathering information. The 'Wade-Giles' system, authored by the British officials Thomas Wade and Herbert Giles, came to be the English standard. It was not sufficiently good for native speakers, however, and their search for alternatives continued. What they all shared was an ambition to exchange traditional Chinese characters, each of which represented a word (technically a 'morpheme'), for symbols which represented the actual spoken sounds of the word. Instead of a character representing a cat or the concept of fear, for example, a phonetic script would indicate the sounds of 'c' and 'at', or 'f' and 'ear'. Despite their variety and ingenuity, however, all the phonetic schemes suffered from the same problem, which was obvious from the start.

Lu Zhuangzhang, a Christian from the city of Xiamen in the coastal province of Fujian, was the first to formally publish a scheme for a phonetic script. Lu had been experimenting with the idea for well over a decade while working as a translator for foreign traders and later for the British missionary, John Macgowan.[20] Lu had helped Macgowan to create a Xiamen–English dictionary in 1883 but then, in 1892, he published his own guide to the topolect entitled '*Zhongguo's* fastest new phonetic writing in the Xiamen *fangyan*'. Lu adapted the letters of the Latin alphabet to invent a total of sixty-two new pronunciation symbols. Fifteen of them indicated the first sound of each syllable and forty-seven represented the final sound. Unfortunately for Lu, the unfamiliar symbols and the sheer complexity were difficult to grasp, and his alphabet failed to make any impact. However, his ideas lived on. In 1895 Timothy Richard's *Wanguo gongbao* published Lu's essay on 'The Foundations of Reform' in which he called for a phonographic script. It argued that the alphabet, and the mass literacy that it facilitated, had made Western societies strong and should be emulated in China. In 1898 Lu sent his phonetic writing scheme to the court for consideration in the Guangxu Emperor's reforms. Again, it failed to win support. Indeed, the official response described it as incomplete and bizarre.[21]

The major problem with Lu's scheme was that, while it may have been a good way to learn to speak in the Xiamen manner, it did not help anyone to speak Beijingese, Cantonese, Shanghainese or any of the other topolects. The same problem afflicted all the other phonographic alphabets developed over the next few years. The Chinese scholar Ni Haishu has identified twenty-nine rival schemes published between 1892 and 1910.[22] His American counterpart Jing Tsu believes there were even more, including a few published by *huaqiao*

(Chinese people living outside China).[23] Some of them used symbols based on Chinese characters, much like the Japanese *kana* script. Others used Roman letters, in the same way that Vietnamese became Romanised at around the same time. But none of them worked for every topolect. The very act of trying to write down pronunciation made obvious what the use of characters concealed – the sheer diversity of local ways of speaking.

The only phonographic alphabet to make a significant impact in this period was proposed by a government insider, a well-connected junior official at the Qing court's 'Board of Rites'. Meet our first Wang: Wang Zhao. Wang's grandfather was a general who had been killed in the First Opium War and the family still had friends in influential circles. However, none of them could protect Wang after he publicly supported the 1898 reforms. Like so many others, he was forced into exile in Japan. Unlike most of them, he realised that he did not enjoy the company of other reformers and smuggled himself back to the port of Tianjin disguised as a monk. There he opened a language school under a pseudonym and began working on his own phonetic alphabet. He published it in 1901 as his 'Northern Vernacular Syllabary' as an aid to help the illiterate write in their local topolect. It seems that, at this stage, this was all that Wang wanted his scheme to achieve. Unlike Lu's script, Wang's was based on traditional Chinese characters, albeit with much simpler forms. Like Lu's, his script had sixty-two symbols but with fifty indicating the first part of the syllable and only twelve describing the ending.

Wang's ambitions then grew. He moved to Beijing and opened a new school there. In 1904 he sought, and received, a formal pardon from the court for his earlier reformist activities, allowing him to move in official circles again. It was typical of Wang that a friend of a friend of his was the son of Yuan Shikai, the governor-general of the province of Zhili, which surrounds Beijing. Yuan became the most important supporter of Wang's syllabary. In 1904 Yuan authorised funding to train teachers, publish reading materials and spread its use among the military. By 1906 Wang's ambitions had grown even greater. In the version of his book published that year, Wang adjusted the preface to pretend that the syllabary was based on an early eighteenth-century pronunciation guide, disguising its real origin in the local peasant topolect. Books and newspapers were starting to be printed with the alphabet and in 1907 its use spread to Beijing.

But then, as the historian Elisabeth Kaske has discovered, the problems started. Although the syllabary could be used in Beijing and the Zhili provincial capital Baoding, it was no use in Tianjin, even though it is just 100 kilometres away. Pronunciation was simply too different. There were attempts to adapt the script and spread its use to Nanjing and other cities, but they withered. No other provincial leaders were as enthusiastic about the system as Yuan Shikai. It seems they recognised the difficulty of creating a phonetic alphabet that could describe the entire country's pronunciations. The central government was equally uninterested. However, that didn't stop wannabe reformers from making new proposals. But whereas the first efforts to create phonetic scripts were for topolects in the south and southeast, Kaske has noted that, after 1908, only scripts for 'Beijing-ese' were proposed.[24]

By then, however, a reaction against the phonetic scripts was gathering support. It began in 1906 with articles in the Shanghai newspaper *Zhongwai Ribao*, arguing that phonetic scripts for regional topolects jeopardised the unity of the country. Shortly afterwards Liang Qichao ended his own support for phonetic scripts and in April 1907 he wrote an article for *Xuebao* entitled 'An Analysis of the Origin of the State Language' (*Guowen yuyuan jie*), which argued that it was the writing of traditional characters that 'unites our country, and the characteristics of our people are unfolded and continued through it'.[25] As we saw in Chapter 5, Liang was the person who did more than anyone to imagine the Chinese nation into existence, and he came to believe that a unified nation required a unified mother tongue – just as the German theorists had explained to Ueda Kazutoshi: one nation with one state and one language. This national mission would be undermined by the existence of phonographic scripts, since they clearly demonstrated that the mother tongue was far from unified.

Instead, the nationalists reframed the entire linguistic question. Since the single Chinese nation and its single Chinese state could only have a single Chinese language, it must be the case that the hundreds of forms of regional speech were simply wayward descendants of a single parent. In the view of these nationalists, all the myriad forms of 'Sinitic' were merely dialects. The idea that these *fangyan* might have different origins was not considered. The nationalists sidestepped the problem of the existence of different languages by asserting that the difficulty was merely one of pronunciation. Those offspring dialects needed to be brought back into the fold.

Western theorising about language was still in its infancy at this time, strongly influenced by the nationalism, racism and imperialism that characterised so much European thinking in the late nineteenth century. Yet these were the ideas that came to guide the Chinese language reformers. In 1898 the radical Zhang Binglin had helped his friend Zeng Guanquan (the grandson of the Qing general Zeng Guofan – see Chapter 2) to translate a typically Social Darwinist essay by Herbert Spencer entitled 'Progress: Its Law and Cause', for the journal *Changyanbao*. Although he spoke no English, Zhang discerned parallels between Spencer's argument about the evolution of language and traditional Chinese concepts of textual analysis. Spencer's purpose was to show how the process of evolution and adaptation naturally transformed a single homogenous population into several heterogenous branches over time. Spencer used the example of language to make his point: common roots had given birth to hundreds of descendant languages over centuries. Zhang Binglin used this insight to argue that the pattern of topolects within 'China proper' (the former Ming realm) was simply the result of diversification from a common ancestor.

Zhang was using these borrowed European ideas for several purposes. His first was to argue that the pattern of language proved the existence of the Chinese nation. In a lengthy article entitled 'New Regional Speech' (*Xin Fangyan*), published over several editions of *Guocui Xuebao* ('National Essence Magazine') between October 1907 and August 1908, Zhang tried to show that words and expressions found in regional dialects were in fact derived from words found in dictionaries from the Han period, two millennia before. Since, Zhang argued, there was a continuous evolutionary link between this ancient language and the heterogenous pattern of the present day, diversity should not be a cause of concern: it was simply a consequence of progress.[26] He explained that his purpose in making this argument was explicitly 'to unite the people'.[27]

However, Zhang's defence of diversity was also a coded attack on 'northern' culture. In the 1904 edition of his anti-Manchu tract *Qiushu*, 'The Book of Urgency', Zhang argued against imposing a standardised Beijing pronunciation on the whole country because, in his view, the northern way of speech had been polluted over the centuries by invasions of 'Tartars' from central Asia. Zhang's 'pick and mix' approach to historical documents allowed him to argue that the purest pronunciation actually came from Hubei province. He inverted the Beijingers' hierarchy: the real centre of Chinese culture was the south. As a consequence, he demanded a national pronunciation based upon the dialects of the region around the former Ming capital of Nanjing, which included his own birthplace, Hangzhou.

Zhang's view of language evolution rested on his wider views about race evolution. In *Qiushu*, Zhang espoused the theories of the University of London professor of Indo-Chinese Philology, Terrien de Lacouperie. De Lacouperie claimed to have found enough similarities between the ancient culture of Mesopotamia and that of early China to assert that the Yellow Emperor was, in fact, a Babylonian king called Kudur-Nakhunte who had migrated east in the twenty-third century BCE. This appeared to explain how a single, original culture had arrived in the *zhong guo* millennia before and become so diverse over subsequent centuries. This was, for Zhang, confirmation of the existence of a single nation since ancient times.

Even though the de Lacouperie theory was rather quickly discredited, this view of national history – that there was a single starting point for a homogenous Chinese culture – endured. Indeed, it became the heart of the entire nationalist project. The idea that there could have been multiple sources of culture, that migration into the *zhong guo* and around the coast may have come from different sources and at different times, was not part of the nationalists' conversation. Instead, they competed to make claims about which source of the single national culture was the most authentic. And, like most of his revolutionary peers at the time, Zhang believed that that single culture was best expressed through the writing of traditional characters.[28]

But this wasn't a view shared by all the revolutionaries. For some, Chinese characters – and everything that they represented – were the problem. They were not interested in creating a new set of characters or introducing an alphabet to make a Chinese language easier to learn. At exactly the same time as Zhang was publishing his lengthy account of the evolution of Chinese topolects, Chinese anarchists sojourning in Europe were calling for all of them to be replaced by the freshly invented language of Esperanto. They saw traditional Chinese characters and the classical language inextricably bound up with the classical texts of Confucianism, traditional ways of thinking and the entire backwards nature of Chinese society. They wanted to change the entire society, and that meant getting rid of the entire Chinese language.

Zhang felt obliged to respond. In print he strongly defended the culture, the language and the characters, although he conceded that there was room for improvement. He suggested adapting the traditional phonetic notation system known as *fanqie* to help learners memorise the sounds of characters, creating an indigenous way to represent (to use the earlier example) the word 'cat' through the sounds of 'c' and 'at'. Zhang then spent some time developing his own version of the *fanqie* system. Like some of the other language reform proposals, Zhang's required two characters: one for the initial consonant and another for the vowel sound. Unlike the others, Zhang based his system on rhymes found in tenth- and eleventh-century texts. Being a language scholar, Zhang insisted that his symbols were far more authentic than any of the rivals. The major downside was that they had little relation to the ways people actually spoke in the early twentieth century. However, after a year of arguments, Zhang and the anarchists called a truce. In 1909 the anarchists conceded that making Esperanto a national language was impractical (although some others continued to make the case for it until the 1930s) and that the pronunciation of Chinese characters had to be standardised across the country. Most importantly, both sides agreed that Beijing pronunciation was disgusting and should not form the national standard.

While the exiled revolutionaries plotted abroad, reformers in Beijing had already begun changing the national education system in line with Western models. In 1902 the first national School Regulations were promulgated, setting out a new curriculum. A revised set, governing the establishment of schools (for boys only), was promulgated in 1904. A Ministry of Education was created in December 1905, and in 1907 a new law allowed the creation of schools for girls. The actual implementation of these new laws and regulations was very uneven, however. They had more effect in provinces controlled by reform-minded officials and where those officials had real authority. Reform also had its limits: the government was continuing to insist that pupils studied the Confucian texts and memorised the classical characters. In some places, particularly in girls' schools, a more modern form of literary writing was allowed, but overall the question of how to speak the characters on the page was left unaddressed.

Then, in April 1909, the Ministry of Education agreed a 'Constitutional Agenda' specifying that officials should begin compiling new Mandarin textbooks the following year. However, late the following year, members of the newly formed national Consultative Assembly demanded a change. Under the influence of the Japanese (and therefore German) national language theorists, they called for Mandarin – *guanhua* – to be renamed '*guoyu*' – national speech. Aware that the 'national speech' was very far from being 'national', they also called for proper studies of its grammar and pronunciation and for the printing of dictionaries and textbooks. But without waiting for the conclusions of these studies, they also called for Wang Zhao's syllabary to be introduced across the country to standardise pronunciation. The difference between 'speech' and 'language' had been erased. The question of what to do about the diversity of regional topolects had been completely reframed. The focus now was on 'the unification of the national language'.[29]

In July and August 1911, in one of its final acts, the Education Ministry of the Qing Great-State convened a 'Central Education Conference' to begin the process of finding an answer to the language question. In their conclusions, the delegates called on the Ministry to actually set up a 'National Language Research Commission', rather than just talking about it. They also agreed to 'the unification of the national language' with a nationally agreed pronunciation. To the great annoyance of the southern delegates, the conference voted to base 'national pronunciation' on the Beijing topolect, albeit with some concessions to regional variation. Ironically, the person put in charge of this process was a native of Zhili province called Gao Yutong, whose local dialect was so incomprehensible to almost all the other participants that one newspaper article questioned whether anyone 'actually understood his two hour speech'.[30] It didn't really matter, however, because within six months of the conference concluding, the Qing Dynasty had been toppled.

But the issue did not go away: instead, it became more emotive. Under the Qing, the language question had been a discussion about efficiency, learning and the best way to strengthen the state. Under the Republic, it became one of fundamental identity. The nationalists – spanning the political spectrum from Liang Qichao to Sun Yat-sen to Zhang Binglin – had summoned a nation into existence and, in their view, a nation needed both a nation-state and a national language. This was an imperative that many, but not all, nationalist movements across the globe shared in this period. India, for example, still has no single 'national language' to this day. In India, different states have the right to choose their own official language with the result that the national constitution recognises twenty-two regional languages plus English. This was not an outcome that Chinese nationalists were prepared even to think about. After decades of internal decay and imperialist land-grabs, with Tibet and Outer Mongolia declaring independence and regional warlords breaking away from central control, their overwhelming demand was for unity. They recognised the tension between strong regional, even national, identities and their desire to create a single Chinese nationality. Language was one way to impose a single identity on a nation – even if that nation did not yet know that it existed.

Just five months after the declaration of the new Republic, the new Ministry of Education convened a 'Provisional Education Conference'. To some extent it was a continuation of the previous conference a year earlier: many of the participants were the same. The atmosphere was, however, completely different. The Confucian Classics had been removed from the school curriculum and replaced by a new ethos of 'pragmatic, militarist and aesthetic' education. Among the conference's conclusions was a 'Proposal for the Adoption of a Phonographic Script', which was really a demand for the Ministry to convene another conference to resolve, once and for all, the problem of pronunciation. This would be the event at which the issue would come to a head.

The idea for the conference came from Wu Zhihui, one of the Paris-based anarchists who had called for the abolition of Chinese and its replacement by Esperanto. Wu hated Confucianism and tradition, and had a reputation as a 'renowned reviler'. In various articles during the 1900s, he had referred to the Manchus as a 'dog-fucked race', to the Empress Cixi as a 'whore' and a 'withered old hag', and to the articles of Liang Qichao as 'pure farting' and 'rotten dog shit'.[31] This was the man whom the Ministry of Education chose to lead the new Republic to linguistic consensus.

Wu had a simple plan of action, originally outlined in a 1909 article. Firstly, a committee of wise men would decide upon a system of phonetic symbols to represent the authentic sounds of the language. Secondly, the experts would decide how each and every one of the thousands of Chinese characters should be correctly pronounced. The result would be a systematic, democratically agreed guide to 'national pronunciation'. The reality would, of course, be far from simple. The 'Conference for the Unification of Reading Pronunciations' opened in Beijing on 25 February 1913 with the best intentions. By the time it concluded, on 22 May, it had witnessed a struggle for regional supremacy combined with a monumental clash of egos and created a legacy of linguistic bitterness that would endure for decades.

Eighty experts were summoned to Beijing. The original plan had been to invite two delegates from each province to ensure fairness but in the end most of the participants were chosen because of their expert status or political connections. About half were selected by the ministry and the rest by their provincial governments, although not all of them turned up. On the first day, forty-seven middle-aged men, dressed in a mixture of Western-style suits and traditional gowns, gathered in the Ministry of Education building just outside the western wall of the Forbidden City. Among them were some of the most active participants in the language debates over the previous two decades, including the first 'script reformer' Lu Zhuangzhang and the well-connected author of the Beijing syllabary, Wang Zhao. Several had their own phonetic script systems to promote, some of which used Latin letters, some used Japanese *kana*-style markers and others various forms of shorthand. This was the first problem. Each man wanted to go down in history as the man whose idea revolutionised the teaching and writing of Chinese.

After long and bitter arguments, the system that eventually won the support of the whole conference was largely based on the one proposed by Zhang Binglin. This was mainly because more than a quarter of the delegates were radicals from the eastern coastal provinces of Zhejiang and Jiangsu, from where Zhang originated. Over the previous decade, compared to most of the other delegates, they had had more contact with missionaries and other purveyors of foreign ideas, spent time in exile in Japan and had played greater roles in the revolutionary movement. They arrived at the conference with a clear set of ideas, notably support for Zhang's nationalistic approach to language. They would not agree to a Western or Japanese-style phonetic script, the solution had to be 'authentically' Chinese. This persuaded the conference to select a system based on 1,000-year-old texts.

Having agreed on the symbols, the next task was to agree on the sound that each symbol stood for. This is when rival regional identities really started to make things difficult. There could be no logical or neutral way to resolve disputes over the different ways to say a word like 'fish' in different topolects. This was not a question of 'pronunciation', as the nationalist language reformers liked to pretend – this was about choosing one topolect word over another. The delegates from the eastern coastal provinces of Jiangsu and Zhejiang, including the conference organiser and chair Wu Zhihui, regarded the Beijing topolect as disgusting – too polluted by 'Tartar' influences. In one article, Wu had previously compared it to the barking of a dog. In this, Wu was supported by another Jiangsu delegate, a translator and philosopher. Meet our second Wang, Wang Rongbao. Wang had once studied at the Translators' College of the *Zongli Yamen* and then in Japan.[32] In 1906 he had been the Qing official who drafted the rejection letter for Lu Zhuangzhang's ideas of script reform, calling them 'bizarre'.[33] More recently he had arranged the words of the Republic's new national anthem. Wu and Wang were at the head of the Jiangsu lobby, arguing for their own eastern topolect to become the agreed national pronunciation.

In the opposite corner was our first Wang, Wang Zhao, who had earlier been selected as vice-chair of the conference. He became, in effect, the spokesperson for the speakers of Beijingese. First Wang may have lost the fight over the choice of phonetic script but he was on stronger ground when it came to the choice of pronunciation, not least because of his personal friendship with Yuan Shikai, the former governor of Zhili who had once promoted Wang's syllabary and who was now president of the Republic. But Second Wang, Wang Rongbao, was not giving up the fight. As the conference progressed, the struggle between the two main linguistic rivals – the *Wu* topolect native to Jiangsu and Zhejiang and Beijingese – boiled down to a personal fight between the two Wangs.

The arguments went on for over a month, without resolution. The situation became so bad that, during one vexed session, the chairman, Wu Zhihui, suddenly shouted, 'I can't stand this,' and resigned. His place was taken by Wang Zhao. It was then that this Wang pulled a dirty trick. He called a meeting of all the delegates except those from Jiangsu and Zhejiang. He told them that the easterners were attempting to turn their topolect into the national language and that the northerners and southerners had to unite to prevent what he called 'a national disaster'. Having created a 'blocking caucus' he then called a meeting of the entire conference, which agreed to change the voting system. Instead of each delegate having an equal vote, each province would have one. At a stroke, the power of the Jiangsu-Zhejiang group was decimated. The result was uproar.[34]

First Wang then tried to pressure the easterners into silence by threatening to also walk out. He riled his opponents by sarcastically denouncing the event as the 'Jiangsu-Zhejiang Conference'. Then, when it seemed things could not get worse, they did. It was, fittingly, a difference of dialect that caused the critical confrontation which tilted the political balance at the conference. At one point Second Wang was discussing whether to call a rickshaw with another delegate from Jiangsu. The word for rickshaw in Shanghainese is '*huangbao che*'. To First Wang's northern ear, it sounded like '*wangba dan*' – the word for 'bastard' (literally 'turtle's egg') in Beijingese. He was enraged. First Wang rolled up his sleeves and prepared to fight Second Wang on the floor of the conference. Second Wang then fled the meeting, never to return. And that was the end of the blocking power of the eastern/Shanghainese/*Wu* topolect. The way was now clear for northern pronunciation to become the standard for the national language.

Over the following weeks the committee voted on the new 'pronunciation' of 6,500 characters. In some cases this really was just about pronunciation, but in many others it was the choice of one topolect word over others. With the voting system now favouring the northerners, the outcome was largely a foregone conclusion. The result was not, however, a total victory for Beijingese. Although most *Wu* topolect words and pronunciations were excluded, the conference did make an allowance for localised versions of phonetic spellings. Notation for an extra tone not found in Beijingese was also included, which went some way to mollifying speakers of the Nanjing topolect. There were some other changes, which resulted in a compromise. The end result was a set of pronunciations that resembled the old *guanhua* Mandarin rather than a specifically Beijingese topolect. Some called it 'Blue-Green Mandarin' – neither one thing nor the other.[35]

Under First Wang's leadership, the conference went on to make a number of demands of the Ministry of Education: that it should immediately promulgate the agreed phonetic alphabet, create bureaus to make sure everyone learned it and make it the standard means of instruction in schools. However, by mid-1913, the Republic of China's politics were in crisis. Song Jiaoren, one of the most charismatic leaders of the Guomindang, had been assassinated in March, while the conference was taking place. It was widely assumed that President Yuan Shikai had ordered the killing. Then, in July, in a reminder of the continuing power of regional identities, seven southern provinces – those where the revolutionaries remained strongest, including Jiangsu, Zhejiang and Guangdong – rose up against President Yuan. Their 'second revolution' was swiftly crushed, however, and in its aftermath the Yuan government imposed a renewed conservatism with more emphasis on Confucianism and very little on national language policy. Outside the small group of language activists, the resolutions of the Pronunciation Conference were forgotten. But in June 1916 Yuan died and for just over a decade the Republic was fractured into fiefs run by rival warlords. The chances of imposing a national language against these regional powers were minimal. As a result, the regional topolects would continue to be spoken largely without interference. It would be years before the nationalist language reformers were in a position to actually enforce the outcomes of the 1913 conference.

In July 1916 a junior textbook compiler within the Ministry of Education, Li Jinxi, along with several other frustrated officials, founded an 'Association for the Study of the National Language' (*Guoyu Yanjiuhui*) to press for change that the government had little ability to enforce.[36] They wrote articles for newspapers but had minimal impact on policy. In February 1917 the Association opened up its membership to the public and quickly recruited most of the major players in the earlier national language discussions. Liang Qichao joined, as did the former minister of education turned principal of Peking University, Cai Yuanpei, who became its secretary. Just as with the pronunciation conference, many of the members came from the provinces of Jiangsu and Zhejiang; indeed, its headquarters were in the Jiangsu migrants' school in Beijing.

In November 1918 the Ministry of Education, in effect, incorporated the Association. The Association's vice-chair, Zhang Yilin, was appointed to head what was called the 'Preparatory Committee for the Unification of the National Language' (*Guoyu Tongyi Choubeihui*). It held its first meeting on 21 April 1919 and agreed three priorities: the promotion of the phonetic alphabet agreed by the 1913 conference, the replacement of classical writing (*wenyan*) by the vernacular style known as *baihua*, and the compilation of a single national dictionary to include every Chinese word written between ancient times and the present.[37] The committee was riding the crest of a new wave of thought. Two weeks after its first meeting, on 4 May, students gathered at the Tiananmen gate of the Forbidden City in protest at the terms of the Versailles peace agreement. From there they marched east to the house of Cao Rulin, the director of the state bank, and burnt it down. The 'May 4th Movement' then swept through the cultural realm, throwing out old ideas and bringing in new ways of writing and making art. Many of its leading figures were familiar faces from the revolutionary end of the new language movement.

Among them was Hu Shi, another easterner, who had been sent to study agriculture in the United States at the age of nineteen. While at Cornell University, he abandoned farming and transferred to philosophy and literature and then went on to further study at Columbia University. In 1917 he brought home his newly acquired ideas about language and nation and was given a position in Peking University's philosophy department from which to espouse them. Over the following decades, Hu became the leading advocate for a single national language.

Shortly after arriving in Beijing, he wrote an article entitled 'A Tentative Proposal for Reforming Literature', outlining eight demands for modern writing. It was published in 'New Youth' magazine, edited by Chen Duxiu, one of Hu's colleagues at Peking University. Most of the article was an argument for writing 'in the manner of speech' – what had become known as *baihua*. But towards the end he hinted at his support for the northern base of *baihua* by referring to some of the stories that had already been written in its vernacular form such as 'The Water Margin' and 'Journey to the West'. He followed this, in April 1918, with an article on 'Constructive Literary Revolution – A Literature of National Speech', in which he coined the slogan which encapsulated his mission, 'Only with a national language literature can there be a literary national language.' Then, in 1922, Hu founded his own magazine, *Guoyu Yuekan* ('National Language Monthly'). In a special edition dedicated to the problem of reforming Chinese script, he argued, 'In promoting reform in speech and writing, scholars and writers should understand that it is their duty to observe the trend in the speech of the people, to accept the people's proposals for reform, and to give them formal recognition.'

All of these interventions were dedicated to Hu's dream of uniting Chinese text and speech in order to create a truly national language on the model of Western nation-states. But speaking many years later, Hu admitted he had been biased right from the beginning: he had assumed that the 'national' language would be a northern topolect all along. In those 1958 comments he outlined his argument: 'If one were to draw a straight line from Harbin in the northeasternmost reaches [of China] all the way to Kunming [in southwest China], this straight line would be more than 4,000 miles long. All along these 4,000 miles, no one would feel the need to change his speech, because the language he speaks is the most common language in the world. This is *guoyu*. This is our capital . . . left by our ancestors.'[38] Hu Shi's imaginary line would, in effect, divide northern and western 'China proper' from its southern and eastern parts. Linguistically, Hu Shi's line does two things. Firstly, it claims that there is a single way of 'northern speaking', despite all the differences that exist along that 4,000-mile axis. Secondly, it specifically excludes six of the seven commonly acknowledged topolects: *Yue*, *Wu*, *Min*, *Hakka*, *Gan* and *Xiang* (not to mention Tibetan, Mongolian and other 'minority' languages). Hu's message to them was, in effect, 'If you want to be part of the nation, you have to speak Beijingese.'

Nonetheless, a consensus was forming among the language reformers. By 1926 the 'Preparatory Committee for the Unification of the National Language' had decided upon the answer to the main question that it faced. According to one of its members, Zhao Yuanren, the committee simply 'decided that we had better take the speech of Beijing city. And so we just found out how people [in Beijing] actually spoke.'[39] What made this possible was a change of heart among the Jiangsu-Zhejiang caucus. Many of the leading figures, including people like Hu Shi, seem to have decided that the task of imposing a compromise language that no one spoke naturally would be far more difficult than choosing one that was close to something already spoken by more than half the population. It was a logical decision, and echoed the policies of language reformers in Japan, Germany and elsewhere who had turned the way of speaking in their capitals into national languages. The language nationalists in Beijing were going to attempt to reverse the process described by Zhang Binglin (and Herbert Spencer) and homogenise diversity back into a single national language. There was no question of allowing regional topolects to take wing as alternative languages.

In 1928 the 'warlord era' came to an end with the victory of Chiang Kai-shek's Guomindang. For the first time the Nationalists were truly in charge of government and the language reformers had the power to give some effect to their pronouncements. Cai Yuanpei returned to office as the head of the University Council, which had replaced the Ministry of Education, and in December the Preparatory Committee was re-established and re-energised. As the Nationalists attempted to actually create the single nation they had been arguing over during the previous decades, the national language question moved once again to the fore. A 'Vocabulary of National Pronunciation' was published in 1932 which laid down the 'new national pronunciation' – *xin guoyin* – of thousands of characters in the Beijing topolect. The new national language – *guoyu* – had arrived, defined as the sound of Beijing topolect with the grammar and vocabulary of the north. The work is still far from complete. The process had to begin again after the Communist victory in 1949 and events then closely echoed what happened after 1912. Just as then, the new rulers made language reform a priority. The first meeting of the new China Script Reform Association (*Zhongguo Wenzi Gaige Xiehui*) was held just ten days after the People's Republic was declared.[40] It gave itself a list of tasks that was strikingly similar to the tasks given to the language conference in 1913: find a system to write down the sound of the language phonetically, simplify Chinese characters and regularise a unified language for China on the basis of the northern dialect. In October 1955 the Association was made a central government institution, renamed the China Script Reform Committee (*Zhongguo Wenzi Gaige Weiyuanhui*) and made the recommendations which led to the formal definition of the new national language. On 6 February 1956, after six years of discussion, the government decreed the definition of *Putonghua* or 'common speech'. It was almost exactly the same as that decided upon by the Preparatory Committee for the Unification of the National Language thirty years before: '*Putonghua* has the northern dialects as its base dialect, the Beijing phonological system as its norm of pronunciation, and looks to exemplary modern works in *baihua* for its grammatical norms.'[41] The parameters had been set a generation earlier, the direction of travel was the same – and resistance would be just as hard to overcome.

On 26 October 1955, three months before the formal adoption of *Putonghua*, an article in the Communist Party of China's official newspaper directed the people to understand the relationship between regional topolects and *Putonghua*. It said, '*Putonghua* serves the people of the whole country, and dialects serve the people of an area. To spread *Putonghua* does not mean to wipe out dialects artificially, but to reduce the scope of dialect use progressively. This is in line with the objective laws of social progress.'[42] It wasn't clear who wrote these 'objective laws of social progress' but they probably inspired the authors of a law promulgated in Shanghai in 1985 which decreed that henceforth city schooling would be conducted entirely in *Putonghua*. In 1992 the regulations were strengthened to encourage pupils to report their fellows for speaking Shanghainese. Campaigns were organised to eliminate Shanghainese phrases on signs and in other areas of public life. And, yet, Shanghainese survives.

However, the success of the pro-*Putonghua* campaign, combined with the migration of millions of 'outsiders' from other provinces into Shanghai, created a 'localist' reaction. Concerns about the decline of regional culture prompted some local figures to call for efforts to preserve it. In 2010 the city authorities began to quietly encourage the teaching of Shanghainese. In 2013 an artist with the Shanghai Farce Troupe, Qian Cheng, proposed a motion to the Shanghai Committee of the Chinese People's Political Consultative Conference calling for the teaching of Shanghainese to preschool children. In response the Municipal Education Commission began a pilot project, in 2014, with twenty public kindergartens and around 100 schools using Shanghainese.[43] It was a sign of how dominant *Putonghua* had become over the previous fifteen years that the local topolect had to be reintroduced in the form of a second language, rather than the native tongue that it had been a generation earlier. However, the 'Shanghai Heritage Project' has to be careful. Since the Ministry of Education has specified that academic subjects can only be taught in *Putonghua*, the use of Shanghainese is limited to games, greetings and other social aspects of school life.[44]

While the central government seems prepared to accept the preservation of some local topolects, there are also limits to its tolerance. In 2017 a well-known promoter of Cantonese, author and Guangzhou TV presenter Rao Yunsheng, appeared to cross the line. He tried to introduce a textbook to teach spoken and written Cantonese at Wuyang primary school in Guangzhou. His book included a form of phonetic romanisation to help children read and learn. According to local media reports, Mr Rao said that local authorities had stepped in to prevent its use. He was unable to comment any further.[45] It seems that while teaching children to speak a regional topolect might now be more permissible, teaching them to read it as a written language remains forbidden.

In both Shanghai and Guangzhou, it was regional prosperity that created the problems for national language policy. Both became economically strong and therefore able to assert a degree of autonomy from central government. At the same time, both attracted large numbers of migrants from other parts of the country, unable to speak the local topolect. The central government urged the cities to integrate the new arrivals through the promotion of *Putonghua*, and thereby simultaneously integrate the city with the nation. However in both cities this created a backlash among local people resentful at the loss of regional distinctiveness. This caused demands for local authorities to take steps to protect regional identity, bringing the city governments into collision with national instructions.

China's national language policy appears to be simultaneously succeeding and failing. While *Putonghua* is the national language of schooling, and the number of people able to speak it is rising, the policy also seems to be provoking rearguard efforts to defend the regional topolects. Increasingly, the battle is taking place in areas of life that the central government finds difficult to control, particularly the Internet. Online fora buzz with discussions about local identity and the problems of migrants in a cat-and-mouse game with the regulators. In Shanghai in the 2010s, some local topolect speakers took to referring to incomers as 'YPs', *ying pan*, meaning 'hard disk'. The largest local producer of computer hard disks was a company called West Data and the initials 'WD' indicated the word *wai di*, meaning 'non-local'.[46] In response to examples like these, in 2014, the official communications regulator, the State Administration of Press, Publications, Radio, Film and Television, issued a formal ban on the use of puns and word play in broadcasts. It too was mocked, and enforcement was minimal.[47]

Cantonese speakers have become experts in avoiding the censors. They can use the Cantonese phrase for 'northern guy' as a sound-alike for 'northern profiteer'. If they want to criticise the Communist Party, they can use the phrase 'grass mud horse' – *cao ni ma*, which sounds like 'fuck your mother' in Cantonese. Since the party is often described as the 'mother' of the people, the phrase also suggests 'fuck the party'. If they want to criticise party propaganda they might sarcastically use the Cantonese pronunciation of the name of a patriotic TV series, 'Bravo, My Country' – *lai hoi liu, ngo dik gwok* – which was itself derived from a phrase used by communist organisations on social media, 'Bravo, my brother' – *li hai le, wo de ge*.

It looks as though the outlook for the topolects will depend on how economically important they are. There are plenty of speakers of Shanghainese and Cantonese who have sufficient resources – financial and political – to organise a defence. However, not all regional ways of speaking will so easily resist the march of *Putonghua*. The coming to power of Xi Jinping and his 'Chinese Dream' of national unity suggests that the impetus to impose the national language across the country will continue. The China State Language Commission sees a direct connection between its work and the official call for 'the great rejuvenation of the Chinese people'. In its 'Outline of the National Medium and Long-Term Plan for Language and Script Reform and Development (2012–2020)', the Commission asserted, 'The comprehensive establishment of a moderately prosperous society, the construction of a common spiritual home for the Chinese people, the enhancement of the country's cultural soft power, and the acceleration of the modernisation of education all put forward new requirements for the language and script enterprise.'[48]

This seems to encapsulate the twin urges that have been driving the reformers' efforts to construct a single national language over the course of more than a century. One is the desire to make the state more effective, and its people stronger, through a language that promotes literacy among the masses and communication between diverse communities. The other is the nationalistic desire to construct a 'common spiritual home'. Buried deep within the language project is the fear that China might be simply too diverse to hold together. This is a fear with deep roots, yet it remains too sensitive to be spoken out loud. We can only hear its echoes when Xi and his fellow leaders talk about the need for a 'culturally harmonious country' and constantly call for 'unity'. Disharmony and disunity are the concerns-who-must-not-be-named. The idea that Hong Kong or Taiwan – or Guangzhou or Shanghai – might have their own identities that are stronger than their Chinese national identity is literally unimaginable for those who lead the People's Republic.

To admit such seditious thoughts is to open the intellectual gates to the return of chaos: to the warlord era of the 1910s and 1920s, or further back to times of rival warring states. National disintegration may be far away but must be constantly fought against nonetheless. In 1991 the governor of Guangdong province, Ye Xuanping, was perceived as too strong a local figure by the central Communist Party leadership. They made sure that he was promoted, against his will, to a largely ceremonial position in Beijing as a means of removing him and his clan from the regional power structures. Something similar happened in 2012 in Chongqing city when the local Communist Party secretary, Bo Xilai, was stripped of his position because of concerns that his local fief was beyond the control of central government. The fear that centrifugal forces might tear apart the new 'great-state' is ever present, giving rise to the centre's constant stressing of unity through appeals to a single culture.

This impetus can be traced back through a line of language reformers from Huang Zunxian in the late nineteenth century, through the two Wangs who came to blows in 1913, to members of the Preparatory Committee for the Unification of the National Language and their communist successors in the China Script Reform Association, which then evolved into the China State Language Commission of today. Behind them all stood the linguistic nationalists in Japan and Germany from whom the idea of a 'national language' – *guoyu* – emerged, in the formulation 'one state, one nation, one language'. And, as the protestors of Hong Kong know well, that slogan has been given new energy under the leadership of Xi Jinping.

7
THE INVENTION OF A NATIONAL TERRITORY
lingtu – territory

14 May 2018 began like any other Monday for the executives at Gap China, but within hours the usual concerns of managing an expanding chain of clothing stores in a fast-moving market had been replaced by panic. By the time everyone had gone home, the company bosses had been forced to publish a grovelling apology. They went to bed fervently hoping they had done enough to defuse a swelling online protest caused by a $7.99 T-shirt on sale in a factory outlet store 11,000 kilometres away. That Monday the executives received a brutal induction into contemporary China's territorial neuroses.

A few months earlier, Gap had issued a series of T-shirts intended to allow customers to show a bit of local pride. The range included shirts with the names of 'China', 'Japan', 'San Fran' and 'Paris' printed on the front and back. Most of the designs were illustrated with a flag of the relevant country, but the China version was different: it had a map. A keen-eyed Chinese patriot, picking up some discount clothing after a trip to the Canadian side of Niagara Falls, noticed that the map on the 'China' T-shirt failed to include the full extent of the country's territorial claims. As they demonstrated with the help of an annotated photo, the Gap map omitted the islands of the South China Sea, areas in the Himalayas occupied by India and, most egregiously, the island of Taiwan.

The nationalistic tourist's post on the Chinese social media site Weibo might have gone unnoticed had it not been picked up by the popular blogger 7sevennana. Until that point she had been best known for commenting on computer games while wearing low-cut tops. In May 2018 she repositioned herself as a patriot. When she forwarded the T-shirt photo to her thousands of followers she added her own message to Gap: 'If you earn Chinese money, why can't you be careful about China's territorial issues?' Very rapidly Gap found itself in trouble. As that Monday wore on, calls for a boycott of Gap stores began to spread on Weibo. The government's army of online censors made no attempt to stop them. Many of the boycott supporters asserted that Gap must have deliberately chosen to humiliate the country by choosing a map rather than a flag for the design. Perhaps it was because the T-shirt was printed in India or Taiwan, they suggested. The accusations mounted.

For a company with 136 stores, including a 1,900-square-metre flagship on Shanghai's West Nanjing Road, not open for even a year, not to mention 200 China-based manufacturing subcontractors,[1] the implications were obvious. Commercial realities required corporate contrition. Before the day was out, Gap China had loudly declared in its own Weibo statement that it 'respects the sovereignty and territorial integrity of China', that the T-shirt 'mistakenly failed to reflect the correct map of China' and that the company 'sincerely apologised for this unintentional error'. The T-shirts were pulled from the shelves in China and from online stores everywhere else. The boycott threats disappeared and the Weibo patriots patted themselves on the back for a job well done.

Such incidents are becoming increasingly common. Gap is far from the only company to have found itself in trouble for failing to recognise China's territorial claims. In January 2018 the Marriott hotel chain also had to apologise after listing Taiwan and Tibet as separate countries in a customer survey. At around the same time, several foreign airlines that listed Taiwan as a separate 'country' were forced to amend their websites. In March 2019 MAC, the cosmetics brand owned by Estée Lauder, had to apologise after an email sent to customers in the United States failed to include Taiwan on a map of China.[2]

On 27 April 2017 China's rubber-stamp parliament tightened up the country's 'Surveying and Mapping Law' to, among other things, 'raise public awareness of national territory'. The spokesman for the Standing Committee of the National People's Congress, He Shaoren, told journalists that incorrectly drawing the country's boundaries 'objectively damages the completeness of our national territory'.[3] In February 2019 the government went even further with specific rules covering the printing within China of maps in books or magazines intended for sale in overseas markets. Each map would require permission from provincial officials and none would be allowed to be distributed within the country. The possibility that a Chinese citizen might see a map showing an unauthorised version of China's territorial claims was perceived as such a threat to national security that it justified the involvement of the 'National Work Group for Combating Pornography and Illegal Publications', according to the regulations.[4] To prove the point, in March 2019 the authorities in the port city of Qingdao destroyed 29,000 English-language maps destined for export because they showed Taiwan as a separate country.[5]

China is far from being the only country with concerns about its borders. What is striking, however, is the extent to which anxiety about those borders has become a national neurosis. Government statements explicitly connected the mapping laws and regulations of 2017 and 2019 to the state's 'patriotic education' campaign. Part of their purpose was to guide the teaching of schoolchildren in the correct view of the country. Messages from the national leadership obsessively remind the population that the only way to be a Chinese patriot is to fervently seek the 'return' of Taiwan to control by the mainland; to insist that China is the rightful owner of every rock and reef in the South China Sea; demand that Japan hand over the Diaoyu/Senkaku islands; and insist on maximalist claims in the Himalayas. The official media constantly remind citizens of the state's territorial claims, exhort them to personally identify with those claims and nurture feelings of hurt and shame towards unresolved border disputes. Paranoia about national boundaries in China is not merely an obsession of online gamers or Weibo patriots, it is central to the state itself. The speeches of Xi Jinping make clear that his vision of national rejuvenation can only be complete when all the territory claimed by China is under Beijing's control.

But the story of how certain territories came to be regarded as 'rightfully' Chinese while others did not is far from simple. During the twentieth century, some areas that were held to be 'natural' parts of the country, such as Outer Mongolia, were let go while others that had been abandoned, notably Taiwan, were reclaimed. When the Qing Empire collapsed in 1911, most of its borders were more imaginary than real. Except in a few places, where Russian, French or British empires had forced them to be demarcated, they had never been formally defined. In the decades after the revolution, the national elite in Beijing had to 'fix' a national territory for the first time. This was a process that had to take place on the ground but also in the national imagination. Maps had to be drawn but, just as importantly, the world-view expressed on those maps had to be inculcated in the minds of the people. Anxiety about the vulnerability of those borders was deliberately generated, right from the beginning. There were fears of foreign threats but there were also expansionist dreams and political calculations. The story of the invention of modern China's territory – and its territorial anxieties – begins a century ago, in the aftermath of war and with the arrival of the Western science of geography. It ends with the rediscovery of Taiwan, its reconnection with the mainland and then its separation.

The last major piece of territory to be formally renounced by the Qing court was signed away on 17 April 1895. The treaty that Li Hongzhang agreed in the Japanese port of Shimonoseki ceded Taiwan, and the Pescadore Islands off its coast, 'to Japan in perpetuity and full sovereignty' (see Chapter 2). Just over a month later, the acting governor of the island, a mainlander, and a few other officials and merchants, declared independence in the name of the 'Taiwan Republic' rather than submit to Japanese rule. They hoped to elicit support from Britain and France but the Europeans saw no advantage in intervening and the Republic collapsed just eleven days after being declared. Resistance, nonetheless, continued. It took a further five months for Japanese forces to occupy all the cities and a further five years before the last vestiges of banditry were completely crushed.[6]

Throughout this long campaign the Qing court declined to offer any support to its former subjects in its former province. In fact, material support for the rebel Republic was explicitly banned by a court edict in May 1895.[7] The fate of Taiwan was simply not important enough to Beijing to risk further conflict with Japan. Half a century after the first 'Opium War', the Qing court had been forced to accept the binding nature of international treaties. It had signed away its rights to the territory and that was the end of it. Taiwan's fate did not become a cause célèbre, however. While the sundering of the island from the body of the great-state was a major blow to the prestige of the court, it barely disturbed the general population. The mainland's relationship with Taiwan in 1895 could be described as, at best, 'semi-detached'. Even after its partial annexation in 1684, the Qing had treated the island as a dangerous frontier, notable mainly for its wild aborigines and deadly diseases. The court only declared it to be a province 200 years later, in 1885, after the war with France. Taiwan remained a province for just a single decade, before it was ceded to Japan at Shimonoseki.[8]

In the aftermath of the treaty-signing, Qing officials almost entirely ignored developments in Taiwan. The island was lost, in the same way that other pieces of territory signed away by other treaties had been lost. In 1858 the Qing had ceded 500,000 square kilometres of land north of the Amur River to Russia through the Treaty of Aigun.[9] They had then been forced, through other 'unequal treaties', to allow European powers to establish micro-colonies all around the coast. Taiwan appeared to have gone the same way; there was no feasible way of wresting it back from Japan's clutches. The 2 million or so Qing subjects on the island, mostly speakers of the Hokkien and Cantonese topolects, along with the aboriginal population, became colonial subjects of Japan.

Surprisingly, perhaps, the same insouciance about Taiwan's fate also characterised the revolutionary movement. Sun Yat-sen and his comrades made no demands for the return of the island to Qing control. At no point, so far as we know, did Sun concern himself with the resistance to Japanese rule, even though it continued to smoulder. For Sun, Japanese-controlled Taiwan was more important as a base from which to overthrow the Qing Dynasty than as a future part of the Republic. We can see this in his behaviour during 1900. That year, Sun left Japan and travelled around Southeast Asia seeking support for a planned uprising in Guangdong province. He was disappointed: neither the established reformists nor local community leaders took him seriously. Instead, when Sun returned to Nagasaki he became part of a Japanese plot to seize the port of Amoy (modern-day Xiamen). Under Tokyo's patronage, Sun based himself in Taiwan and ordered his revolutionary forces to mass around their main support base in Guangzhou. But, in a typically rash move, Sun changed the plan at the last minute, diverting the fighters to Amoy, where he intended to join them accompanied by a shipment of Japanese weapons. The Japanese, however, had become concerned about provoking a Russian reaction and backed out of the entire scheme. Sun's rebel force found itself isolated and outgunned and was destroyed.[10]

Despite the betrayal in Amoy, Sun continued to regard the Japanese government as his main sponsor, and the revolutionary movement continued to ignore the issue of Taiwan. The reformists had little interest in the island either. When a leading Taiwanese activist, Lin Xiantang, met Liang Qichao in Japan in 1907, Liang advised him not to sacrifice lives in opposing Japanese rule, since the mainland would not be able to help. Since neither could speak the other's topolect, Liang had to communicate with Lin through 'brush talk'. This only made Liang's message more poignant: '(We were) originally of the same root, but are now of different countries.'[11] The Qing court, the revolutionaries and the reformists all took the same view: Taiwan had been ceded by treaty and lost to China. It seems remarkable, given the passion that the island's political status generates today, but the island virtually disappeared from political discussions in the decade before the revolution of 1911/12. Even after the revolution, when Sun had no more need of Japanese support, he and his supporters continued to ignore the fate of Taiwan.

While some revolutionaries were prepared to cede the peripheral territories of the Qing Great-State in order to create a pure 'Han' state in the heartland, Sun and Liang shared a determination to ensure the Republic inherited all the territory of the former empire. The 'non-Chinese' areas (Manchuria, Mongolia, Tibet and Xinjiang) made up more than half of its territory and contained vital natural resources. But in order to express their desire to defend the national territory, Sun, Liang and their supporters had to create new words with which to describe it.

There were several words for 'place' in Chinese, but none that equated to territory, with its connotations of ownership and sovereignty. The traditional term was *jiangyu*, which literally meant the boundary (*jiang*) of the imperial realm (*yu*). In dynastic times the *yu* stretched as far as the emperor's authority and so, in theory at least, could have included tributary and vassal states.[12] Its meaning was vague and certainly did not imply the existence of a defined border.

A new word for 'territory' came into Chinese from Japanese, specifically from a Japanese translation of a text by the British Social-Darwinist Herbert Spencer (see Chapter 3). In his 1883 translation of Spencer's *Political Institutions*, Sadashiro Hamano chose the two *kanji* characters *ryo-do* – literally 'governed-land' – as equivalents for 'territory'. As president of Keio University, Hamano was an authoritative figure and his translation soon spread into general use. Fifteen years later, when Liang Qichao translated Tokai Sanshi's nationalistic novel *Strange Encounters with Beautiful Women* from Japanese into Chinese for his newspaper *Qingyibao*, he used the same characters.[13] In classical Chinese they are pronounced *ling-tu* but have exactly the same meaning – 'governed-land'. *Lingtu* therefore carries the clear meaning of a sovereign country, enclosed within a defined border.

From there, the word was picked up by one of Sun Yat-sen's followers, Hu Hanmin. One of Hu's roles in the revolutionary *Tongmenghui* movement was to provide the theoretical justifications for Sun's policies.[14] Hu expounded on the political implications of *lingtu* in a lengthy article ('Anti-foreign Sentiments and International Law' – *Paiwai yu guojifa*), printed over several editions of the revolutionaries' newspaper *Minbao* during 1904 and 1905. He was arguing that territorial sovereignty – *lingtu zhuquan* – was the foundation of international law and that, logically, the revolutionaries needed to oppose the 'unequal treaties' demanded by foreign powers. Hu's ideas – and his new words – were largely based on a 1,000-page book by a Japanese legal scholar, Takahashi Sakue, entitled *International Law in Peace Time*, published the year before. Takahashi's tome was, in turn, a summary of several Western works printed over the previous couple of decades.[15] In other words, the revolutionary movement's new-found territorial passions were the direct descendants of late nineteenth-century European nationalisms.

The progeny of this Euro-Asian ancestry emerged in the Republic of China's constitutional debates a decade later. The 'Provisional Constitution' written by Sun Yat-sen's allies immediately after the revolution and approved by the freshly-installed president, Yuan Shikai, on 11 March 1912, set out in relatively precise detail what it believed the territory of the Republic should be. It said, in effect, that the new state inherited the boundaries of the Qing Great-State as they stood when the revolution broke out. Article 3 stated simply that 'The territory of the Chinese Republic consists of 22 provinces, Inner and Outer Mongolia, and Tibet.'[16] The choice of '22' provinces was highly significant since Taiwan was the twenty-third. Given that the constitution text was still laying claim to Outer Mongolia, despite its declaration of independence three months earlier, Tibet despite the ongoing insurrection there, and Xinjiang despite its de facto independence at the time, this seems to be clear proof that the Republic had formally abandoned any claim to Taiwan.

However, in May 1914, when Yuan Shikai, the former Qing general who had forced Sun Yat-sen from office in 1912, imposed a new 'Constitutional Compact' on the country, the definition of the national territory was changed. Article 3 became the apparently tautological 'The territory [*lingtu*] of the Chinese Republic remains the same as the domain [*jiangyu*] of the former empire'.[17] New words notwithstanding, the 1914 constitutional definition of territory merely begged a further question about the exact extent of the domain of the former empire.

After Yuan died in 1916, the Compact was suspended and the first constitution was reinstated. So, from 29 June 1916, the definition of the national territory reverted to the '22 provinces, Inner and Outer Mongolia, Tibet and Xinjiang'. But seven years later, the Republic returned to tautology. The constitution approved on 10 October 1923 replaced Article 3 with the words 'The territory [*guotu* – literally 'state land'] of the Republic of China is based on its inherent domain [*jiangyu*]'.[18] Once again, no definition of that territory or domain was provided. Eight years after that, the new 'Provisional Constitution' promulgated by the Guomindang government of Chiang Kai-shek on 1 June 1931 struck a compromise. Article 1 combined vagueness and specificity by stating, 'The territory [*lingtu*] of the Republic of China consists of the various provinces and Mongolia and Tibet',[19] but the number of provinces was left undefined. By 1931 Qinghai had been forcibly reincorporated into the state and given the status of a province. Mongolia and Tibet had been independent of the Republic for almost two decades by this time but Chiang still claimed them nonetheless. Notably, Taiwan was still not a consideration. The last Republican constitution promulgated before the civil war doesn't even attempt to define the national territory. The version approved on 25 December 1946 merely says, in Article 4, 'The territory of the Republic of China according to its existing national boundaries shall not be altered except by resolution of the National Assembly.'[20]

This constitutional back-and-forth demonstrates that throughout this period and even beyond, there was considerable difficulty in deciding exactly where the country's boundaries should be drawn. Some fundamental questions needed to be answered first, chiefly: where were the boundaries of the Qing

Great-State that the Republic had ostensibly inherited in 1912? The Nationalist modernisers thought there was a simple answer to that question based on a view of borders they had acquired through contact with foreign powers and experts. The reality was far from simple.

The Qing Great-State had constructed, in effect, a multi-ethnic federation in which five 'script regions' – Chinese, Manchu, Mongol, Tibetan and Turkic – were ruled separately through different structures and according to different rules. It was an approach known in Chinese as *jimi* – loose rein – although Qing methods of government would have varied depending on the peoples they were dealing with.[21] The mission of revolutionaries like Sun Yat-sen, however, was to create a single unitary nation-state ruled from the centre through a single set of structures and rules. As we saw in Chapter 5, Yuan Shikai, who had risen to power through the old imperial system, was far more familiar with the traditional techniques of rule than with the new ideas of the Western-educated nationalists. His conservative instincts led him towards a more 'fuzzy' definition of the state, while the modernisers' search for clarity on the national question led them to seek something more precise. But the more they tried to impose unity on strong local rulers, the more the warlords broke away, causing the fragmentation of the very state they were trying to unify.

The Qing Empire had only formally defined its borders in places where it had been forced to do so by other powers: from the 1689 Treaty of Nerchinsk, which drew a line with Russia in the northeast, through to the 1894 Convention with Great Britain, partially demarcating the boundary with Burma in the southwest.[22] Elsewhere, the situation was far from clear: how far did the boundary of the realm – the *jiangyu* – stretch? At the end of the Qianlong Emperor's reign in 1796, the Qing court was accepting tribute from thirteen rulers whose territory lay even further west than Xinjiang province and also from a Gurkha ruler beyond Tibet even though none were under Qing rule.[23] So did the *jiangyu* include them? On the other hand, even within the Qing domain, the court exerted control over remote and thinly populated regions through local rulers whose own control, and loyalty, were not absolute. The Kham area of eastern Tibet, for example, had long been ruled by autonomous chieftains who were only nominally subordinate to the rulers based in Lhasa and, through them, even more nominally to the emperor in Beijing.[24] Although

Qing officials were based in a few strategic places, wide areas were left unsupervised. A military campaign to impose central rule on Kham in 1745/6 was a costly failure. 'Loose rein' rule was reinstated.

As a result, we should see the Qing's efforts to control central Asia in the nineteenth century not so much as attempts to defend 'their' territory from the predations of outsiders but as moves in a constant competition (a 'Great Game') for territory and influence between three empires: the Qing from the east, the Russian from the north and west and the British from India in the south. Throughout the nineteenth and early twentieth centuries, all three were battling for the support of, or domination over, dozens of local rulers, warlords and other kinds of leaders – spiritual and temporal. We can see one effect of this increased competition in the change of meaning of the Chinese word *bianjiang*. The Australia-based historian James Leibold has shown how, in the eighteenth and early nineteenth centuries, it was used to refer to an intermediate zone between two states. During the later nineteenth century, however, in certain places it came to mean the line of a defined border.[25]

The Manchu Qing court, inheritors of Inner Asian traditions of rule, had known how to play this game. They had relations with other Inner Asian peoples stretching back generations. The new Republic, however, was attempting to impose a completely different political order based upon a Western template of sovereignty and hard borders. Its leaders were obliged to find an answer for the *bianjiang wenti* – the border question. How were they to 'fix' the national territory when the state was in the process of falling apart? But there was also a bigger question: how could the new state make its citizens feel loyal to each other and to places that they had never seen, would almost certainly never visit and yet which were assumed to be vital for national survival? Both of these missions were given to a new class of special agents: the geographers.

The man regarded as the father of the modern academic discipline of geography in China was born the youngest of six children on the outskirts of Shaoxing, a city best known for its rice wine at the mouth of the Qiantang River, south of Shanghai. The rich soils and wealthy markets of the river delta had been good to Zhu Kezhen's family. Ancestors had worked the paddy fields for generations, but as the coastal cities expanded and the number of urban mouths rose,

Kezhen's father realised there was a better living to be made as a trader rather than a grower of rice. By the age of three, Kezhen had become his parents' favourite child. While his siblings were prepared for lives of manual labour, Kezhen was directed towards intellectual pursuits. He was sent to a private school in Shanghai, 150 kilometres away, and then even further north, to Tianjin, to attend the Tangshan Mining College.[26]

Having benefited from the natural advantages of his local environment and the economic boom of the coastal region, Zhu Kezhen would next receive a windfall from international politics. In the aftermath of the 1900 uprising known in the west as the Boxer Rebellion, the Qing government had been forced to pay compensation of 450 million *taels* of silver to the Western powers. The United States government had demanded $25 million, a sum which even its own diplomats in Beijing regarded as excessive – perhaps twice as much as the actual damage suffered by American citizens and their government during the violence. Over the course of the 1900s, pressure rose on Theodore Roosevelt's administration to do something to alleviate the huge burden of debt imposed on the Qing government. By 1909 a compromise emerged: the excess, around $11 million, was to be put into a fund to pay for the education of Chinese students. This, it was thought, would benefit both Chinese students and American universities while also diverting future members of the Chinese elite away from Japan and towards the United States.[27] One of the first to be diverted was Zhu Kezhen, the twenty-eighth recipient of a Boxer Indemnity Scholarship.

In 1910, at the age of twenty, Zhu arrived at the University of Illinois to study agronomy. But he hadn't travelled to the United States to become a better farmer. He wanted to be a scientist and, after receiving his degree, enrolled for a PhD in meteorology at Harvard. There, his supervisor was Robert DeCourcy Ward, America's first professor of climatology. Ward's views went much wider than the weather, however. In 1894 he had co-founded the Immigration Restriction League and his academic opinions combined meteorology with eugenics: he believed that climate determined civilisation. He claimed that in the seasonality of the temperate zone of the planet 'lies much of the secret—who can say how much of it?—of the energy, ambition, self-reliance, industry, thrift, of the inhabitant'. In the tropics, by contrast, the climate was enervating, and 'voluntary progress toward a higher civilisation is not reasonably to be expected'.[28] As a result it was entirely justified, in Ward's view, for white people from the temperate zone to develop the tropical areas of the globe, even with slave labour if necessary. He was particularly impressed with the ability of Chinese 'coolie' labour to work in all conditions. Zhu lapped up all these theories, gained his PhD and returned to China in 1919 to become the first professor of geography at the Normal University of Wuchang, moving to Southeastern Normal University in Nanjing the following year.[29]

At Nanjing he passed on these ideas to the second generation of Chinese geographers, the ones who would devote their careers to helping build the new state. In the words of one historian of this period, Zhihong Chen, 'Ward's influence was evident in Zhu's works.'[30] The American professor's environmental determinism gave a new 'scientific' basis to the prevailing Han racism of the time and helped set the parameters for the emerging discipline of geography. According to Zhu, China's temperate latitude had blessed its people (the *Zhongguo-ren*) with an intermediate skin colour and an unusually strong ability to adapt to all kinds of environments. In his reasoning,

> People who are used to tropical climates cannot bear winter in the temperate zone . . . Those who are used to temperate climates cannot stand tropical or frigid weather . . . But we Chinese are exceptional! No matter how hot or cold an environment is, there are Chinese footprints. . . . [W]hen the Panama Canal was excavated, only our Chinese people kept working tirelessly and efficiently, when foreign workers could not even work. This is why foreigners call the Chinese 'the yellow peril'. This is also a ray of morning sunshine for us Chinese in the future!

Among Zhu's many students at Nanjing during the 1920s was Zhang Qiyun (often spelt Chang Chi-yun). Over the following three decades Zhang would personify the search for China's national territory. He would help define it, propagate it, survey it, advise the government on securing it but then, ultimately, flee it. Over the course of an academic and then political career he would place his insights at the service of the national struggle for survival. In the process he bound his fate, and that of his political masters, to Taiwan.[31]

Zhang Qiyun joined Zhu Kezhen's first ever geography class in 1920. He graduated three years later and joined the staff of the Commercial Press in Shanghai where the brother of one of his classmates was an established editor.[32] The editor was Chen Bulei who would also go on to play a major role in nationalist politics. Together, Zhang, Chen and Zhu formed an influential clique at the intersection of academia, journalism and propaganda. Together, the trio brought geography into the centre of Chinese political thinking and put it at the service of the Guomindang's nationalist mission.

Zhang spent the next four years writing the geography textbooks used in most Chinese schools during the later 1920s and beyond.[33] His memoirs show that Zhu was a strong influence on their content. Then, after Chen Bulei became the editor of the country's third largest circulation newspaper, *Shangbao* ('Commercial News'), he commissioned Zhang to write commentaries on geographical topics. In 1927, on Zhu's recommendation, Zhang was appointed a geography lecturer at Zhongyang (National Central) University in Nanjing.

The next ten years, the 'Nanjing decade', was a time of profound change in both the politics and the educational systems of the Republic of China. The Guomindang captured Nanjing and Shanghai in March 1927 and within eighteen months the party was nominally in control of the whole country. With Chiang Kai-shek installed as chairman, the Nationalist Government began to impose its vision of national unity on the country: a vision that owed more to Sun Yat-sen's ideas of a homogenous *Zhonghua minzu* than to Yuan Shikai's toleration of difference. The ideology of 'the nation of five races', which had guided the state since 1912, was dropped. On 29 December 1928, as a mark of intent, the national flag was formally changed from the coloured stripes of the 'five races', which had flown since the birth of the Republic, to a red flag incorporating in the top left corner the *Tongmenghui*'s original 'Blue Sky, White Sun' flag favoured by Sun Yat-sen. It remains the flag of the Republic of China (on Taiwan) to this day. This new nationalism determined the Republic's entire approach to the border question and the situation of minorities living in the frontier areas.

In the view of the new government, the frontier had to be 'saved' by making sure its inhabitants became loyal citizens of the Republic. Although this was supposed to be the era of 'self-determination' – US President Woodrow Wilson had declared it to be so in 1918 – the Guomindang had no intention of offering such a choice to the inhabitants of Tibet, Xinjiang, Mongolia or Manchuria. In their eyes, the right of self-determination was reserved for the Chinese nation in its struggle against foreign powers. This was no mere academic debate but rather a life-and-death struggle, since one of those powers, Japan, was already deploying the 'self-determination' argument for its own imperial ends. Japanese officials highlighted the ethnic differences within the former Qing Great-State to argue that those groups had a right to self-determination and to secede from a Han-dominated Republic. They claimed to be upholding this principle as they, in effect, annexed Manchuria in 1931 and encouraged separatism in Mongolia and Xinjiang.

Under these circumstances, the Guomindang weaponised the study of history and geography. In 1928 the director of the Nanjing government's Ministry of Propaganda, Dai Jitao (who was simultaneously president of Zhongshan University in Guangzhou), called for the establishment of geography departments at all the country's major universities, arguing that they would play a vital role in national defence. The first one was established in 1929 at Zhongyang University, where Zhang was already on the staff. Over the following eight years, geography departments were established at nine other major universities. Most of them were staffed by former students of Zhu Kezhen.[34] The output of these departments was dedicated to serving the state and its frontier mission. The Chinese historian Ge Zhaoguang has described this period in academia as 'national salvation crushing enlightenment' (*jiuwang yadao qimeng*). Many experts who had spent the 1920s researching the differences between ethnic groups and the contested history of the country's frontiers either changed their public views or went quiet during the late 1930s, as the threat from Japan grew. They included such well-known geographers, historians and anthropologists as Liu Yizheng, Gu Jiegang and Fei Xiaotong. They, and others, chose 'national salvation' over 'enlightenment'.[35]

Up until 1927 school education had been controlled by local elites and varied widely in content and quality. Even before they had taken power across the whole country, the Guomindang leadership had recognised the importance that education would play in their efforts to construct the new nation. The party's Fourth Plenum in January 1928 declared that 'education is indeed a life-or-death matter for Chinese citizens' and must play a central role in the party's war on 'erroneous ideologies' (such as communism).[36] A few months later, in May 1928, just after the establishment of the Guomindang's 'National Government' in Nanjing, the party convened the 'First National Conference on Education'. The conference resolved to adopt a new national curriculum for schools based upon Sun Yat-sen's 'Three Principles of the People': Nationalism, Democracy and People's Livelihood. Within months, the GMD had captured Beijing and very quickly set about imposing a new 'temporary curriculum' nationwide. From 1929 all schools were expected to imbue their pupils with strong feelings of patriotism, mobilised in particular through the teaching of history and geography.[37] Pupils were expected to study the various regions of the country, 'in order to foster the national spirit'.

A major contribution to this patriotic education movement was the series of textbooks written by Zhang Qiyun. In 1928 the Commercial Press published one as *Benguo Dili* – 'Our Geography'. Its key message was that China formed a natural unit despite its enormous size and variety. Using his geographical training, Zhang divided up the country into twenty-three 'natural' regions based on their environments and the inhabitants' ways of life. He then compared them, telling pupils that, for example, the Yangtze Delta was good for farming but had no minerals; Shanxi was rich in coal but too dry for agriculture; Manchuria was forested while Mongolia was good for grazing, and so on. He then told the young learners that this diversity was actually proof of the need for national unity, since each different part was an essential part of a coherent whole.[38]

Yet the 'whole' that Zhang portrayed in the textbook was a territory that, in reality, did not exist. The book contained various maps of the country drawn on blank backgrounds so that the rest of the world disappeared from view. The simple black line marking the national boundary encompassed huge areas that were not actually under the control of the government: the independent states of Mongolia and Tibet. Zhang portrayed them as a natural part of the Republic nonetheless. How reality would be reconciled with the map was not explained to the pupils. Remarkably, given present-day politics, there was a significant omission: Taiwan was not drawn in any of the national maps in the textbook. It seems that, in Zhang's view, the 'natural' shape of the Republic was exactly the same as the shape of the Qing Empire at its collapse in 1911. Mongolia was included, Taiwan was not. The rocks and reefs of the South China Sea did not feature at all.

These were not marginal ideas; Zhang's *Benguo Dili* book had a huge impact. Ten editions were printed before July 1930, a further seven after 1932 and it was honoured as one of the country's three most important textbooks of the time.[39] It was far from being the only example. Dozens of geography textbooks were printed during the 1920s and 1930s and they all ignored Taiwan, while stressing the importance of Mongolia and Tibet. Zhang himself, in another textbook he co-wrote in 1933, *Waiguo Dili* – 'The Geography of Foreign Countries' – described the people of Taiwan as 'orphans' deserted by their birthmother, the Chinese nation *Zhonghua minzu*, and abused by their step-mother, Japan.[40]

Zhang, and the other authors of these books, were nationalists who sought to evince emotions of loyalty to a state and its territory in the hearts of their young audiences. They faced a problem that was both pedagogic and deeply political. How could they persuade a child in a big coastal city, for example, to feel any connection with a sheep herder in Xinjiang? Why should they even have a connection? The general purpose of human geography was to explain how varying environments had created groups with differing cultures. Nationalism, however, required all these different groups to feel part of a single culture and loyal to a single state. It was up to nationalist geographers to resolve the puzzle. They found two main ways to do so. One group of textbook authors simply stated that all Chinese citizens were the same: they were members of a single 'yellow' race and a single nation and no further explanation was needed. A second group, however, acknowledged that different groups did exist but were nonetheless united by something greater. Within this group some authors made use of 'yellow race' ideas, some used the idea of a shared, civilising *Hua* culture, while others stressed the 'naturalness' of the country's physical boundaries.

The textbook writers argued that the answer to the 'border question' was to 'civilise' the inhabitants. One, Ge Suicheng (who was employed by the rival, but equally nationalistic, Zhonghua Publishing Company), found himself facing the same dilemma as the Guomindang government. Both needed to emphasise the theoretical equality of all ethnic groups while simultaneously making the case for their melding into a single Chinese nation based on 'Han' culture.[41] In Ge's view, the study of geography should make the different peoples of the state love their particular home areas but also connect them emotionally to the wider national territory. But in the meantime, in the words of his textbook, 'We should urgently promote the acculturation of the Mongols, Hui [Muslims] and Tibetans so that they are not lured by the imperialists, [and we should] move [Han] inhabitants to the border areas for colonisation . . .'[42]

Zhang Qiyun's 1928 textbook was also deeply imprinted with racial chauvinism. One part of the book's message to its millions of young readers was that the country was on a journey from barbarism to civilisation and that the wild frontier, where the minorities lived, needed to be tamed and developed. The book included a table of various ethnic groups showing how assimilated they were to the 'main body' (*zhuti*) of the Han. In a description of the Miao people of the southwest, Zhang wrote, 'They maintain the customs of great antiquity and are totally incompatible with the Han people. Eliminating their barbarism and changing their customs and habits is the responsibility of the Han people.' For Zhang, the Han provided the 'norm' against which the other groups needed to be measured in order to judge their level of civilisation: they had to be made 'Han'. He shared Zhu Kezhen's opinion that climate was the determining factor in the spread of civilisation. In his 1933 textbook he observed that in southwestern Yunnan province, the native population lived in the hot and humid lowlands while the Han people (*Han-ren*) lived on the cooler plateaus. In the mountains of the northwest, on the other hand, the Han lived in the valleys where it was warm while the natives lived at altitudes where it was colder. It was only natural, therefore, that the 'temperate-dwelling' *Han-ren*, free of 'degenerating' environmental influences, should exert their influence over the minorities – the *tu-ren*.[43] Other textbooks made the same point, stressing Sun Yat-sen's arguments that the Han made up 90 per cent of the country's population and that it was only natural that the other groups would assimilate (see Chapter 5).[44]

These arguments can be traced back to those made by Liang Qichao a couple of decades before (see Chapter 4). Liang created a story of continuity: the expansion of a civilised territory outwards from its cradle in the Yellow River valley. The new geographers tried to write the final chapter, its diffusion to the very edges of the Republic. They also borrowed from Liang the idea that certain rivers and mountain ranges formed 'natural' boundaries to the state. This was the argument deployed by Ge Suicheng in his 1933 textbook and Lü Simian (who worked at both the Commercial Press and Zhonghua Publishing). The most poetic technique was simply to compare the shape of the imagined country to that of a begonia or mulberry leaf turned on its side. The port of Tianjin became the petiole of the leaf with a central 'vein' running west as a line of symmetry all the way to Kashgar in Xinjiang and beyond. The symmetry only made sense, of course, if Outer Mongolia and Tibet were included and Taiwan was excluded. The historians Robert Culp and Peter Zarrow have documented many examples of other geography textbooks which use different, sometimes contradictory arguments and analogies to persuade students of the 'naturalness' of the Republic's putative borders.[45]

An ever-present theme in these textbooks was the threat of foreigners eating away at the country's edges. It was reinforced through school lessons about territory 'lost' during the previous century. Teachers could make use of a peculiarly Chinese form of nationalist cartography – the 'map of national humiliation'. Dozens of such maps were published by the Commercial Press, Zhonghua Publishing and other companies during the 1910s, 1920s and 1930s, sometimes within textbooks and atlases and sometimes as posters for display in classrooms and public buildings. They typically portrayed, often in bright colours, land 'conceded' to neighbouring states over the previous century.[46] There was a clear political purpose behind the making of these maps. They served to delegitimise the Qing Dynasty – by demonstrating its failure to 'defend the country' and thereby legitimise the revolution. But they also deliberately generated a sense of anxiety about the vulnerability of the nation's border in order to promote loyalty to the new Republic. It seemed to work with a young Mao Zedong. He later told the American journalist Edgar Snow that hearing about national humiliation made him an activist.[47] It wasn't just Mao. This was the birth of the national territorial neurosis.

The geographers took the nationalist idea of 'territory' – *lingtu* – and projected it back to the time of 'domain' – *jiangyu* – when there were few fixed borders. A map of national humiliation in Ge Suicheng's 1933 textbook showed vast areas of central Asia, Siberia and the island of Sakhalin as territory 'lost' to Russia. The map may have displayed different areas as 'territory', 'tribute states' or 'vassal states' but all were categorised as inherently 'Chinese', nonetheless. The idea that, at the time they were 'lost', these territories might have been contested areas with no clear allegiance to any particular empire was not part of the lesson. They were presented simply as 'Chinese' lands that had been stolen. Ge Suicheng called on the young citizens reading his textbook to do what they could to recover all this lost territory. But did this mean this 'lost' territory should be included within the rightful boundaries of the state, or not? Was the shape of the country at that time natural, or not? These questions were not even posed in the textbook, let alone answered. What was important for authors like Ge was to encourage students to feel the sense of loss, a collective sense of 'national humiliation', and thereby develop a patriotic attachment to the country. Anxiety about territorial loss was a fundamental part of the nationalist education project right from the beginning.

The anxiety was compounded because no one, not even the geographers, knew where the borders actually were. The historian Diana Lary has shown how, in the southwestern province of Guangxi, the exact line of the border was almost irrelevant. Although it had been formally agreed with the French colonial rulers of Indochina in 1894, as far as the Republican officials were concerned the border was just somewhere in the mountains: high, remote and difficult to reach. The state had generally managed minority groups in southern highlands through a system known as *tusi*, in which local leaders were held responsible for the actions of their people.[48] Borders were largely irrelevant. So long as they didn't trouble the authorities, the mountain peoples were generally left alone. In Lary's words, 'The Chinese world stopped well before the borderlands.'[49] (Things would change. This is the same border that thousands of Chinese and Vietnamese soldiers died fighting over in 1979.)

In 1928 the original geographer Zhu Kezhen declared that Chinese cartography was about a century behind its European counterpart. At the time, most of the publicly available maps were still based on 200-year-old surveys from the early Qing period.[50] In January 1930 the government issued official 'Inspection Regulations for Land and Water Maps' (*Shuilu ditu shencha tiaoli*), instructing the Ministry of Internal Affairs, the Foreign Ministry, the Marine Ministry, the Ministry of Education and the Committee of Mongolia and

Tibet to work together to regularise the country's cartography. Nothing actually happened, however, until 7 June 1933, when the official 'Land and Water Maps Review Committee' held its first meeting.[51] (See Chapter 8 for more on the Committee.)

In the absence of government action, a few academics and private organisations tried to fill the gap. In 1930 senior staff at the influential Shanghai-based newspaper *Shenbao* discussed organising an expedition to the frontier to celebrate the paper's sixtieth anniversary. They asked two well-known members of the National Geological Survey of China, Ding Wenjiang and Weng Wenhao, and a cartographer, Zeng Shiying, to lead the effort. However, during the planning meeting it became clear that no one knew where the actual frontier was. Ding told the gathering: 'If we want to organize a successful research trip of China's frontiers, we first need a map. . . . No one has yet drawn a complete and accurate map of the entire country. Before we organize the trip, we should therefore first work on sketching a map of China.' The anniversary plans therefore evolved into a project to publish a new national atlas. The result was the publication by the newspaper of *New Maps of the Chinese Republic* (*Zhonghua minguo xinditu*) in 1934.[52]

The atlas was well produced and a best-seller. In the absence of any government-produced equivalent it became the national standard until well into the 1950s.[53] However, its depiction of the frontier areas was, in most places, a work of fiction. As was now standard in Chinese maps of this time, Tibet and Outer Mongolia were depicted as integral parts of the state while Taiwan was not. The neat black dashed-and-dotted line that ran around the Republic was more an expression of desire than reality. As Owen Lattimore, the American scholar who explored these areas in the 1920s and 1930s, wrote, 'The linear frontier as it is conventionally indicated on a map always proves, when studied on the ground, to be a zone rather than a line.'[54] In the more recent words of another American historian, James Millward, the frontier was a process, not a place.[55] Wide areas were open to disagreement and conflict.

In December 1928 the government had ordered every province and county to compile a new 'gazetteer' – *fangzhi* – of the area under its administration. Gazetteers were an established tool of local government going back centuries but this new incarnation was intended to be drawn up according to modern geographic practice: produced with the help of newly trained experts using accurate maps and statistics. There was to be a particular focus on 'frontier' areas, where the government's control was weak.[56]

This focus on gazetteers chimed with Zhang Qiyun. He had just co-founded a new academic journal, *Dili Zazhi* ('Geography Review') to promote human geography in secondary schools.[57] In early 1929 Zhang authored an article in *Dili Zazhi* arguing that this new generation of gazetteers would help to foster 'homeland feeling' among the people. This, in his view, would be a positive development because, 'Homeland feeling is the basis for nationalism.' In another edition of *Dili Zazhi* he called for the middle school geography curriculum to be based on Sun Yat-sen's Principle of Nationalism. He became increasingly influential: his 'Tentative Suggestions for Middle School Geography Course Standards', published later in 1929, were adopted by the Ministry of Education as the basis of the new curriculum. They had two main components: explaining the natural conditions and social customs of every place in the country in order to foster nationalist spirit, and explaining the international situation in which the country found itself. As a result, he argued, 'patriotism and the desire to save the nation will automatically grow'.[58] Promoting nationalism became the purpose of Zhang's geographical activities.

These contributions brought Zhang's work to the attention of senior figures in the Guomindang, and in December 1930 he was invited to join the party by its executive committee, probably at the suggestion of his former editor, Chen Bulei. Chen had joined the Guomindang in February 1927, and had swiftly become the party's leading propagandist.[59] Zhang declined the invitation, but on 1 November 1932 he became one of the forty or so founding members of the government's 'National Defence Planning Commission',[60] created in response to the Japanese invasion of Manchuria in September 1931, and also to counter increasing unrest in Xinjiang. Its primary purpose was to advise on strategic issues such as military preparedness and the economy. Zhang was given two roles on the Commission, evidence of the dual roles played by geographers during the period. Initially, he was placed in charge of preparing the country's geography textbooks, with a mission to inculcate the youth with the right values for national survival. Under Zhang, the geography curriculum became more explicit, emphasising the need to protect China's territorial integrity.[61] Then, in September

1934, Zhang was deployed as 'head of geography' for a two-year-long investigation of the country's northwestern frontier: the provinces of Shaanxi, Gansu, Ningxia and Qinghai.[62]

It was an academic mission with strategic importance. With Tibet having achieved de facto independence and Xinjiang ruled by warlords, the Nanjing government needed to know whether the surrounding provinces might also try to break away. The geographers were also tasked with drafting a plan for the economic development of the region to connect it more closely to the heartland. The whole enterprise was supposed to be a low-profile operation but in December 1934, while researching in Gansu, Zhang revealed himself to be more of an academic than a politician. He delivered a speech about the work of the National Defence Planning Commission, stressing the importance of the region's economic development for national security. In it he compared his own work to that of a Ming Dynasty scholar, Gu Yanwu, who, three centuries earlier, had prepared a document, *Tianxia junguo libingshu* ('On the Strengths and Weaknesses of Various Places of All Under Heaven') to help secure the northwestern frontier from invasion.[63] This led to a deluge of newspaper coverage of activities that were supposed to be secret and Zhang found himself in considerable trouble.

Four months later the Commission was reorganised into the 'National Resources Commission' and placed under the government's Military Committee and Zhang was sent back to academia. It was not long, however, before the Guomindang geography network had him rehabilitated. His old friend Chen Bulei was, by then, working as Chiang Kai-shek's chief-of-staff.[64] In April 1936 Chen lobbied Chiang to appoint Zhu Kezhen as head of Zhejiang University in Hangzhou. The week after Zhu took up the post he offered Zhang the position of head of the university's Department of History and Geography.[65] Perhaps in gratitude, Zhang finally agreed to join the Guomindang in July 1938, on Chen Bulei's recommendation. For the next ten years he would combine his political career with his academic one, while remaining a senior figure at Zhejiang University.[66]

Meanwhile, the national situation was becoming ever more critical. Japan had invaded 'China proper' in July 1937 and by the end of the year its forces had captured Beijing, Shanghai and Nanjing. As the crisis grew deeper, Chiang

Kai-shek urged the use of geography and history as tools to spread Guomindang ideology among the country's youth. On 28 August 1938 Chiang gave a speech to the first graduation ceremony for the Central Training Corps (a paramilitary organisation intended to indoctrinate army officers and senior civil servants) in the city of Hankou, in which he told his audience:

> If our people do not know the glory of our national history, how can they fully perceive our humiliation today? If they are not familiar with the geography of our nation, how can they find the resolve to restore our lost territory? From today forward, we must not tread this disastrous path any longer: we must absolutely give special emphasis to history and geography education, to stimulate the citizens' patriotic spirit to defend the country, and launch our people's brilliant and dazzling new destiny!

As a result, the curricula of universities, and then middle and high schools, were revised to include more history and geography, 'to stimulate students' determination and resolve to rejuvenate our national people'.[67]

In December 1939, with Japanese forces advancing south and east, Zhang was invited to talks with Chiang about evacuating Zhejiang University to a safer location. However, it seems the two didn't actually meet until over a year later. On 15 March 1941 they had dinner in Chongqing, along with Chen Bulei. According to their diaries, the group talked about 'history and geography education . . . as well as frontier issues'. The geographer and the generalissimo struck up a strong friendship: they came from the same hometown, and Chiang described Zhang in his diary as 'lovely'. For Zhang, the main result was a grant of $50,000 to establish a new academic journal, *Sixiang yu shidai* ('Ideas and Times'). After this, Zhang became, in effect, Chiang Kai-shek's geopolitical adviser. In 1942 he published a book on 'The International Development of China' and another on 'The Northeastern Problem' (referring to the Japanese occupation of Manchuria). During 1942 and 1943 he wrote a series of articles on 'The Military History of China' for the journal of the 'Society of Contemporary Thought', expounding on the importance of geographical circumstances to military success.[68] Then, in June 1943 and on Zhu's recommendation, Zhang was sent to the US as part of an academic delegation invited by the Department of

State. His original six-month stay was extended until the autumn of 1945. His publications there included one entitled 'Climate and Man in China' that harked back to Zhu Kezhen's original studies decades before[69], and the first pamphlet for a newly established think tank in New York, the Sino-International Economic Research Center, on 'The Natural Resources of China'.[70] He became a key figure in explaining the geography of China to American officials while also offering ideas to the Guomindang government on future policy.[71]

The Japanese invasion had, unsurprisingly, forced Chiang Kai-shek to pay more attention to geopolitics. During the early part of 1938 the Japanese started to occupy the area between Beijing and Nanjing, and on 25 March they attempted to seize the crucial transport hub of Tai'erzhuang, about halfway between the northern and southern capitals. The battle happened to coincide with an Extraordinary National Congress of the Guomindang, called by Chiang Kai-shek to approve his de facto military control of the government. On 1 April the congress did so, appointing him 'director-general' of the party. As the fighting raged in Tai'erzhuang, the meeting in Hankou discussed the government's foreign policy and handling of the war.[72] In the speeches and resolutions we see the emergence of Chiang's geopolitical ideas. In his speech on 'The Anti-Japanese Resistance War and the Future of Our Party', Chiang argued, 'We must enable Korea and Taiwan to restore their independence and freedom, and enable them to solidify the national defence of the Republic of China and consolidate the base for peace in East Asia.' Significantly, although he noted that Taiwan had been part of China's sovereign territory (*lingtu*) in the past, he did not call for either territory to be incorporated into China.[73] What was important was the two territories' strategic position and their potential role as buffer states on the country's frontier.

In retrospect, what is remarkable is how uncontroversial this was at the time. The Communist Party had long supported independence for Taiwan, rather than reincorporation into China. At its sixth congress in 1928, the party had recognised the Taiwanese as a separate nationality. In November 1938 the party plenum resolved to 'build an anti-Japanese united front between the Chinese and the Korean, Taiwanese and other peoples', implicitly drawing a distinction between Taiwanese and Chinese. At this time, in the Communist view, the

Taiwanese were a separate *minzu*.[74] This continued into the early 1940s with articles by both Zhou Enlai, in July 1941, and Marshal Zhu De, in November 1941, describing the future liberated Taiwan as a separate nation-state. Even when the Communist Party declared war on Japan in December 1941, its announcement listed the people of Taiwan separately from the Chinese.[75]

This view of Taiwan's separateness formed a consensus in Chinese politics at least until 1942. Three things seem to have changed the situation. Firstly, the United States entered the war, in December 1941, and it became possible to imagine the defeat of Japan. It was only then that the Guomindang government formally declared war on Japan and unilaterally renounced the Treaty of Shimonoseki. As a result, Chiang's thoughts turned to post-war geopolitics. Secondly, Chiang was looking for ways to divert Japanese war efforts by promoting unrest in areas under its control, such as Taiwan.[76] And thirdly, a tiny number of Taiwanese, who had fled Japanese colonialism for exile on the mainland, were actively lobbying the Guomindang to think of Taiwan as part of China.

Dozens of small Taiwanese exile organisations had been formed in China during the 1920s and 1930s, but they only began to unite and gain political influence after the start of the war with Japan. Being able to speak Japanese made these activists very useful in both intelligence and propaganda work, something that gave them access to the military leadership. Many of them had also been trained in the latest medical methods by the Japanese and provided hospital services behind the front lines. One doctor, Weng Junming, who had joined Sun Yat-sen's *Tongmenghui* in 1912 as a nineteen-year-old student, became a key figure. In September 1940, following lobbying by Weng Junming, the Guomindang formed a 'Taiwan Party Headquarters Preparatory Committee' and put Weng in charge. In February 1941 an alliance of several small Taiwanese groups came together to create the Taiwan Revolutionary League which, in June 1942, was formally recognised by the Guomindang.[77]

It was at this moment that the Guomindang's discussion of Taiwan changed radically. In mid-1942 it began to use the term retrocession (*guangfu*), a word with particular nationalistic significance. *Guangfu* had been used during the Tang Dynasty (618–906) to describe the regaining of control over land previously conquered by foreigners. Comparing themselves to the Tang Dynasty gave the Guomindang a useful propaganda boost during the dark times of war with Japan and increasing hostility with the Communist Party. It is interesting to note, however, that the party felt it had to make a case for *guangfu* – it was by no means a logical step. Research by the historian Steve Phillips shows that they did so in several ways: by appealing to ideas of racial solidarity (that Taiwanese are of the Han bloodline), historical precedent (the two centuries of rule by the Qing), the illegitimacy of the Treaty of Shimonoseki and the assertion that *guangfu* was something that the Taiwanese population wanted.[78]

It seems from Chiang's writings, however, that his own desire to incorporate Taiwan into the Republic was primarily driven by geopolitics. In November 1942 he began drafting his post-war manifesto, the book-length *China's Destiny* (*Zhongguo zhi mingyun*) with the help of ghostwriters, of whom the most important was Chen Bulei.[79] The text also shows the strong influence of geographers. Zhang Qiyun had been personal friends with Chiang for about two years by this stage and did not leave for the United States until June 1943, three months after the book had been published.[80] *China's Destiny* talks about the country forming 'a self-contained unit' and 'each region [having] its own particular soil and natural resources' and with a 'division of labour . . . largely determined by their physical conditions'. The echoes of Zhang's earlier textbooks are clear. The book then moves on to the question of national defence. 'If even one area is occupied by a different race [*yizu*], then the entire nation and entire state loses the natural barriers for self defence. Therefore Taiwan, Penghu, the four northeast provinces, inner and outer Mongolia, Xinjiang and Tibet are all strongholds for the protection of the nation's survival.'[81] There is a chauvinistic vision of the country here: in order to defend 'China', the surrounding areas need to be incorporated into its defences, regardless of their ethnic composition.

It appears, therefore, that during 1942 Taiwan became important to Chiang and the Guomindang both as a bulwark against foreign invasion and as evidence of its commitment to ending national humiliation. Chiang also began to press for other territories to be 'returned' to the Republic. He lobbied Indian nationalists to win support for his claim on Tibet and sought the early return of Hong Kong's New Territories from Britain.[82] The British were not prepared to concede either point, but they were willing to see Japan give back Manchuria and

Taiwan. The compromise was sealed at the Cairo Conference between Chiang, Churchill and Roosevelt in November 1943. Thus it was that Taiwan's *guangfu* was arranged.

And so it came to pass in 1945. On 9 September, General Isayama Haruki, the Japanese chief of staff in Taiwan, flew to Nanjing to formally surrender. Guomindang forces finally arrived on the island on 25 October. However, there were many people on Taiwan who had no wish to be incorporated into the Republic. Some had benefited from the Japanese occupation, some objected to the corruption of the Guomindang, while others were simply hostile towards incomers from the mainland. To compound the problem, local feeling was ineptly handled by Chen Yi, the official whom Chiang had appointed as the island's new governor-general, and discontent grew. Protests finally exploded on 28 February 1947 and were met with extreme violence. By the end of March, at least 5,000 Taiwanese (some say 20,000) had been killed by Chen Yi's mainland forces. All of this undermined the nationalist proclamations of unity that had underpinned the calls for *guangfu*.

Nonetheless, within two years of the massacres, the island became critical to the survival of the Guomindang. As the Communist Party gained the upper hand in the civil war, Chiang Kai-shek's thoughts turned to the question of survival. Where was the best place for his government to retreat to? He favoured the southwest, around his wartime capital Chongqing, or the island of Hainan. In late 1948 he consulted his geopolitical adviser, Zhang Qiyun. Zhang turned his understanding of the country's regional geography into a wish-list for the party's last redoubt. It required a place that could be easily defended but was within striking distance of the mainland; that was fertile for agriculture and large enough to feed several million people, possessed of well-developed infrastructure and an industrial base, and was largely free of Communist Party supporters. In his geographer's opinion, the best option was Taiwan.[83]

Zhang was right. Chongqing and Hainan fell but Taiwan held out. Ultimately then, the reason why Taiwan has a different government from the People's Republic, and why there are increasingly loud calls for the island to formally declare its independence, is because of the advice of a geography professor from Zhejiang University. Zhang himself finally departed Shanghai for Taiwan in May

1949, with Communist forces about to storm the city. His teacher and mentor Zhu Kezhen, who had fallen out with the Guomindang, opted to remain in Shanghai and live under Communist Party rule. The two never met again. Once on Taiwan, Zhang became a senior figure in Chiang's reorganised Guomindang. He was initially put in charge of administrative and logistical matters,[84] and became, in turn, a member of the first National Assembly, general-secretary of the Guomindang's Central Committee and then minister of education. His final work was the establishment of the 'Chinese Culture University' in Taipei, dedicated to making the island more Chinese – a form of intellectual *guangfu*.

Tuesday 26 March 2019 was a proud day for the director and staff of the London School of Economics. A new sculpture by the Turner Prize-winning artist Mark Wallinger was being unveiled right outside the recently completed student centre. Wallinger's work was entitled *The World Turned Upside Down*, a literal description of the piece. It featured a globe, about four metres high, resting on the North Pole, with Antarctica nearest the sky. The title was a reference to England's seventeenth-century Civil War, and the upending of an old order. In Wallinger's words: 'This is the world, as we know it from a different viewpoint. Familiar, strange, and subject to change.' Wallinger's work has often addressed nationalism. His 2001 commission at the Venice Biennale, *Oxymoron*, included British flags with the usual red, white and blue replaced by the green, white and orange of the Irish tricolour. The LSE's director, Minouche Shafik, told journalists covering the launch of the globe sculpture that the work reflected the mission of academia, where research and teaching 'often means seeing the world from different and unfamiliar points of view'.

But one group of students was not prepared to see the world from a different point of view. Within hours of the unveiling, a few students from the People's Republic of China noticed that Taiwan had been coloured pink while the PRC had been coloured yellow and that Taipei had been marked with a red square, indicating a national capital, rather than the black dot used for provincial cities. They protested to the director and demanded that the work be changed. In their view, the artist's intent was irrelevant: Taiwan should be just as yellow as the mainland. The LSE was facing a 'Gap moment'. Students from the PRC make up 13 per cent of the total student body at the LSE,[85] so a boycott could have been ruinous. At the same time, the school's Taiwanese students and their supporters also rallied. They pointed out that Taiwan's president, Tsai Ing-wen, was a graduate of the LSE, a fact that had been trumpeted by the school when she was elected. Two days later, the artwork had expanded to include a notice stating, 'The LSE is committed to . . . ensuring that everyone in our community is treated with equal dignity and respect.'[86]

A crisis meeting was called, chaired by Shafik and including representatives from the school's Directorate, Internal Communication Office and Faith Centre, plus two Chinese students, one Taiwanese, as well as an Israeli and a Palestinian (who were upset about the depiction of the Middle East). The Chinese students then tried to broaden the discussion, saying they were also upset about the depiction of the Chinese-Indian border. According to the Taiwanese student present, Shafik apparently 'took out her notebook' at this point.[87] Wallinger himself avoided media comment except for one interview with the LSE student newspaper, *The Beaver*, in which he said, 'There are a lot of contested regions in the world, that's just a fact.' The arguments continued for several months until, in July 2019, the LSE and Wallinger made a minor concession. They added an asterisk next to the name 'Rep. China (Taiwan)' on the work and also a sign below it stating 'There are many disputed borders and the artist has indicated some of these with an asterisk.'[88] But Taiwan remained a separate colour: the LSE and the artist held their nerve. They did not 'do a Gap' and the sculpture continues to represent political reality rather than an idealised version of 'maximum China' imagined by its patriots online and offline.

Borders and formally defined territories are a modern, European invention imposed on, and adopted by, Asian elites over the course of a violent century. The new Chinese nationalism that emerged from the ruins of the Qing Empire manifested itself as a desire to be a 'normal country', equal to the industrial powers and part of an international system. The nationalists made a choice without really realising they had done so. By choosing to exert a Chinese claim over a multi-ethnic domain, a decision predicated upon a new Han chauvinism, they obliged the Republic to extend its reach into the furthest, most marginal regions. This was, in effect, a new colonialism: expanding 'Han' Chinese rule into places it had never reached before. The geographers' maps and surveys led the way and their textbooks and national humiliation maps built support for the project back in the heartland. The geographers and the Guomindang worked together to make the imaginary boundaries real and create a national territory – a *lingtu* – both on the ground and in the minds of the citizens. They did so by generating a fear of loss, of humiliation, that continues to animate Chinese policy to this day.

The Republic of China only formally recognised the independence of Mongolia under the terms of the 1946 Sino-Soviet Treaty of Friendship, and following a referendum in which the Mongolians nominally exercised their right of self-determination. The border between China and Russia, ostensibly agreed in 1689 with the Treaty of Nerchinsk, was only finally settled on 14 October 2008 with a deal on islands in the Amur River. The border between Guangxi province and Vietnam, although agreed in 1894, was only formally demarcated in 2009. Tibet was forcibly incorporated into the People's Republic of China in 1950, bringing a Chinese state face-to-face with India for the first time. As the T-shirt buyers of Niagara Falls know well, the continuing lack of agreement in the Himalayas has the capacity to provoke full-scale war between two nuclear-armed militaries. Taiwan's separateness is an ongoing crisis. And then there are the maritime boundaries. But that's another chapter.

8
THE INVENTION OF A MARITIME CLAIM
ansha – shoal

Late May 2019, the Sapura Esperanza drilling barge is at work in the southern part of the South China Sea. The barge floats about 100 metres above an area of seabed officially defined by the Malaysian authorities as exploration block SK320. Three thousand metres below the seabed lies the Pegaga gas field. Once this well, known as F14, is drilled and prepared, the gas will be pumped down a thirty-eight-inch pipeline, at a rate of half a billion cubic feet per day, to the city of Bintulu, about 250 kilometres away, where it will generate electricity for the people and businesses of the state of Sarawak.

Managing a three-kilometre-long drill pipe while floating in the middle of the South China Sea is a tricky operation; the last thing the engineers want is distractions. But early that May morning, an unwelcome visitor arrived: China Coast Guard vessel CCG 35111. The ship was not passing through on its way to a friendly port; CCG 35111 had come to intrude and harass. It circled the drilling barge at high speed, impeding the passage of support vessels in clear violation of international maritime rules. For about a month, since the barge had begun drilling, the Royal Malaysian Navy had been expecting something like this. As a result, its patrol vessel, the KD *Kelantan*, was already on station. At the time the Chinese vessel was detected, KD *Kelantan* was on the eastern side of a reef known as the Luconia Breakers, part of the larger series of rock formations known collectively as the Luconia Shoals, named after a British ship that plotted their location in 1803.[1] Malaysia calls it Beting Hempasan Bantin. Navigating carefully through the dangerous shallows, the KD *Kelantan* moved to put itself between the Chinese ship and the drilling barge. CCG 35111 got the message and moved away. But the next day it returned, and again the next day. For three days, the two played cat-and-mouse around the coral reef before the Chinese ship moved to a safe distance. Even then it did not move away entirely but sat on the horizon watching the drilling operation continue until CCG 35111 was replaced, three days later, by an even bigger China Coast Guard vessel.

There has been at least one China Coast Guard ship on station near Luconia Shoals since the middle of 2013. On the surface it may be hard to see why: it is an inhospitable spot of the earth's surface. Occasionally shingle builds up to form a small sandbank on one of the reefs, but it can be washed away again in a single storm. European navigators marked this part of the sea 'dangerous ground' on their maps and largely kept clear. Yet there are reasons for countries to covet this piece of water: the reefs are rich in fish and the rock beneath is even richer in gas and oil. That is one of the reasons why, in 1982, almost every country agreed rules for dividing up the world's underwater resources. The United Nations Convention on the Law of the Sea (UNCLOS) allotted each state with a coast an 'Exclusive Economic Zone', stretching up to 200 nautical miles (approximately 400 kilometres) out from their shores. UNCLOS was supposed to prevent disputes such as the one playing out around the Luconia Shoals. And yet the China Coast Guard is there, 1,500 kilometres from Hainan Island, the nearest piece of undisputed Chinese land.

China claims the Luconia Shoals as part of its national territory, even though there is no territory actually there, beyond a shifting sandbank. Its claim becomes even more surreal 120 kilometres to the southwest at a place called the James Shoal, probably named after one of the 'White Rajahs' of Sarawak, Sir James Brooke. There is no land there at all, just a piece of shallow sea, around twenty-two metres deep. And yet the James Shoal is officially the southernmost point of Chinese territory. Even today, a typical task in a Chinese school geography class is to measure the distance between the country's furthest extremities: from the border with Russia in the north to a patch of sea 100 kilometres off the coast of Borneo. Teachers don't explain to their children why this piece of non-territory should rightfully belong to China. Almost no one in China actually knows. A typical response to the question is to say that it has been Chinese 'since ancient times'. The real story is that it only became part of China's territorial claim in the South China Sea because of a series of screw-ups by Chinese officials in the 1930s. No Chinese government even thought of claiming the James Shoal and the Luconia Shoals before 1946.

It is not just Malaysia that finds itself the subject of unwelcome attention. China has obstructed oil and gas drilling at other underwater features, too. Off the southeastern coast of Vietnam is an area of shallow sea called the Vanguard Bank, named after a British brig which spotted it in 1846.[2] It too is rich in oil and gas and it too has been the site of several maritime confrontations between Vietnam and China since the early 1990s. The Philippines finds itself in the same situation, near a feature called Sea Horse Shoal, spotted by a ship of the same name in 1776. The Philippines won a ruling from an International Arbitral Tribunal in 2016 making clear that it was the legitimate owner of all the marine resources in the area. China refused to accept that ruling and, according to the Philippines president, Rodrigo Duterte, his Chinese counterpart Xi Jinping threatened him with the prospect of war if the Philippines tried to develop the natural gas known to be nearby.

China has never made clear the exact legal basis of its claim to the marine resources so close to other countries' coasts. All we know is that it has something to do with a line that first appeared on Chinese maps in 1948. In its original incarnation, this 'U-shaped line' around most of the South China Sea was comprised of eleven dashes. In 1953 two of the dashes in the Gulf of Tonkin were dropped, probably as part of a deal with the communist party in Vietnam, giving us the 'nine-dash line' of today's headlines. In recent years, China has raised the status of this line to a near religious level by printing it in passports and legislating to ensure that every map published in the country includes it. Leaders vow to defend every inch of it and threaten war on anyone who tries to violate it. But how did this line come to be drawn and why did it take the shape that it did? The most tragic part of the South China Sea disputes is that the world could witness a superpower conflict simply because of poor translation and bad map-making in the middle part of the twentieth century.

11 June 1907,[3] Liu Sifu is assembling bombs in a hurry. He was awake late into the previous night, writing farewell letters to his girlfriend and some of his female relatives, and overslept. Now Liu is hunched over a table on the third floor of a house in Guangzhou, mixing up fulminate of mercury and pouring it into metal casings. The house, arranged for him by a local teacher, belongs to a small private school and sits just around the corner from the *yamen*, the

office of the most senior official in the region, the governor-general of the Liangguang (the 'Two Guangs': Guangxi and Guangdong).[4] Liu is not here for the governor-general, however, but for his expected guest.

The guest has been singled out for assassination because, at that moment, troops under his command are on the verge of crushing a rebel insurrection just outside the city of Huizhou, about 120 kilometres east of the governor-general's *yamen*. Brigade-General Li Zhun has become a particular object of hate for the revolutionaries. The previous month, his troops had suppressed another uprising, in Huanggang. In the words of the historian Edward Rhoads, General Li is 'fast becoming the dominant military figure' in Guangdong.[5] He makes a point of reporting to the governor-general on the first and fifteenth day of each lunar month. The revolutionaries know this and are ready.

But before their plan can unfold, some of the fulminate of mercury that Liu is hurriedly handling in his third-floor room explodes. Zhang Gushan, the schoolteacher who has arranged the room and is acting as lookout, rushes upstairs. He finds Liu lying on the bed, covered in blood and missing his left hand. Still just conscious, Liu instructs Zhang to gently submerge the remaining bombs in the urine in his chamber pot and to hide the farewell letters. By the time the authorities arrive, the exact purpose of the bombers' activities that morning has been hidden. Nonetheless, Liu is arrested and, once his lower arm has been amputated, jailed without trial. General Li Zhun, on the other hand, survives intact. Yet another revolutionary plot fails. It's becoming quite a habit.

While all this is unfolding in Guangzhou, the opening act of a much quieter drama is being staged 450 kilometres to the southwest. The island of Pratas sits like a pearl mounted on a ring-like reef in the sea between Hong Kong and Taiwan. It is a near-perfect desert island: the highest point is just a few metres above the waves, the beaches are fringed with a few palm trees and a lagoon fills and empties with the tide; turtles and fish can be caught in the shallows. The currents are dangerous, however, and the coral is sharp. Sometimes, brave fishermen come here to rest and repair their nets but there is no fertile land and minimal fresh water. The British naturalist Cuthbert Collingwood visited it in 1867, while sailing with HMS *Serpent*, and reported it was 'occasionally visited by Chinese fishermen', and found a dilapidated wooden temple.[6] The only other visitors are birds: millions of them. It is the birds that make Pratas an attractive prize for one Japanese entrepreneur.

Japan's industrial workforce needs cheaper rice, its rice farmers need fertiliser and Pratas is covered with it. The island is metres deep in guano, petrified bird droppings rich in nitrogen, phosphate and potassium. In 1910 the German chemists Fritz Haber and Carl Bosch will perfect their catalytic process for manufacturing ammonia. Until then, guano is what keeps the fields green in the industrialised world. The trade has already brought fleeting wealth, and permanent environmental destruction, to dozens of islands across the Pacific, and Japanese merchants are willing to take big risks for the prize. So in mid-1907, Nishizawa Yoshiji, an entrepreneur from Osaka, lands on Pratas seeking a fortune. He brings along over 100 workers, who set up accommodation, offices and railway tracks on the island to shift the guano from where the birds have dropped it, down to the beach.

As the shipments start arriving in Osaka, rumours start to spread about what is really happening on Pratas. From early September 1907, worried articles appear in Western newspapers suggesting that a naval base could be under construction. The Americans are particularly concerned, given the proximity of Pratas to their recently acquired colony of the Philippine Islands. So when the United States' secretary of war, William H. Taft, visits Shanghai in December 1907 (on his way back from attending the inauguration of the first Philippine Assembly) he receives an urgent telegram from Washington instructing him to ask the Qing government what it knows about the matter. By all accounts, the officials know absolutely nothing about the matter but apparently insist that the island 'indisputably' belongs to the Qing Empire.[7]

Yet, nothing was done about the presence of a foreign merchant stealing the empire's guano resources for well over a year. The press reports dried up and the authorities turned their attention to more pressing maritime matters. Shortly before Secretary Taft's visit, the British authorities in Hong Kong resolved to do something about the worsening piracy problem in the waters around their colony. As order slowly collapsed across Guangdong it was sometimes hard to tell which criminals were revolutionaries, which were bandits and which had official connections. There was little trust in the provincial authorities and the merchants of Hong Kong were demanding action. As a result, the British and other European powers announced they would despatch gunboats to patrol the West River, leading inland from Guangzhou.

This provoked a huge reaction from sections of the citizenry. On 22 November 1907 a group of students founded the 'Society to Recover the Nation's Rights' to campaign against the British operation. They were joined by the 'Guangzhou Merchants' Self-Government Society' and enjoyed the tacit support of the governor-general. The crisis was only resolved in January 1908, when the governor-general appointed General Li as provincial naval commander with the rank of admiral and a mission to crack down on piracy. The British then decided to withdraw their gunboats, something that was greeted as a huge victory by the nationalists. Admiral Li became the hero of the hour. His prestige only grew higher when, the following month, he led an operation to seize a cargo of weapons being smuggled to the revolutionaries aboard a Japanese freighter, the *Tatsu Maru*.

However, the Japanese government demanded a formal apology for the seizure of the *Tatsu Maru*, plus the payment of an indemnity and the punishment of the officials involved. As a result, 20,000 people joined a protest in Guangzhou on 18 March, organised by the Self-Government Society. Despite this, the Qing authorities did agree to apologise, to make a symbolic salute of the Japanese flag and to release the ship. But they refused to release the impounded guns and ammunition. Instead, they paid the Japanese government 21,400 yen in compensation.[8] Two days later, the Self-Government Society designated the date that the *Tatsu Maru* was released as 'National Humiliation Commemoration Day'.[9] It also declared a boycott of Japanese goods, which the central government banned, under pressure from Japanese diplomats. The crisis fizzled out, but the resentment remained.

Li Zhun was at the heart of this episode and the Japanese wanted him punished. However, the Qing governor-general valued him as an effective commander and the British valued his efforts against piracy so he remained in post. He spent the rest of 1908 suppressing unrest in Guangdong and Guangxi and became increasingly popular in both Hong Kong and Guangzhou. He was happy to give interviews to the English-language press and clearly relished the subsequent publicity. Shortly after the *Tatsu Maru* incident, he was asked by a journalist about the reports from Pratas. The *Singapore Free Press and Mercantile*

Advertiser reported, 'When asked as to whether the statement Japan had seized an island to the South of Hongkong, known as the Pratas Island is true, the Admiral [Li Zhun] replied that he was making investigations and did not care to say much on that question.'[10] In fact, almost a year went by before he said anything at all.

The Qing navy barely existed in the 1900s. The results of two decades of 'self-strengthening' policies, intended to create dockyards, skilled technicians and modern maritime forces (policies which had the unintended consequence of allowing translations of Western social and political theory to reach Chinese audiences – see Chapter 3) were literally sunk, or captured, during the 1894/5 war with Japan. The surviving ships were too small to do more than patrol rivers or the immediate coastline. The only organisation with the ability to sail further afield was the Imperial Maritime Customs Service, which, although a government agency, was a hybrid organisation, mainly run by foreigners. (As we saw in Chapter 1, this organisation, too, was responsible for introducing many Western ideas into Chinese society.)

In the absence of a genuine navy, the Customs Service was given the task of investigating developments on Pratas. The trigger seems to have been complaints from fishermen chased away from the island by Mr Nishizawa's workers. A customs cutter was despatched to Pratas, arriving on 1 March 1909 carrying a young British officer, Hamilton Foote-Carey.[11] After a brief discussion, the ship returned to port. Two weeks later it came back, accompanied by a Chinese gunboat carrying the heroic admiral, Li Zhun. They were appalled to see over 100 labourers mining guano under a Rising Sun flag. Nishizawa, however, would not be moved. He had found the guano, and since no one occupied the island, he claimed it was his.

When this news reached Guangdong, with anti-Japanese feeling already running high, crowds poured onto the streets. The main Hong Kong newspaper, the *South China Morning Post* (*SCMP*), noted drily that 'The local Chinese mind has been agitated somewhat' and that 'the Chinese in the south are not taking the matter kindly'. On 19 March the paper reported that the governor-general 'has deemed it expedient in the interests of peace, to prohibit the vernacular [Chinese-language] press making further reference to the subject of an inflammatory nature or otherwise'. The Self-Government Society and others began to revive the anti-Japanese boycott, despite its illegality. With its exports coming under pressure, the Japanese government agreed to negotiate over the fate of Pratas. If the Qing authorities could prove that they owned it, then Tokyo would recognise their claim.

This set off a hunt that continues to this day: a search for evidence to prove that islands in the South China Sea belong to China. It became a passionate cause for nationalist agitators and officials alike. Some went to interview fishermen, seeking details of voyages, but Admiral Li Zhun went to the archives, seeking documents. In his own account, published many years later, he said it was not easy: 'We searched old Chinese maps, books, and the Guangdong Provincial Gazetteer and could not find such a name [Pratas]. Observer Wang Xuecen, who reads extensively, informed me: "In the time of the Qianlong emperor [1735–1796], the general of Gaoliang, Chen Lunjiong, wrote a book titled Record of Sea Nation Observations, in which the name of that island is recorded." We used that book to negotiate with the Japanese about the return of the island.' In other words, the only evidence the Qing authorities could muster was a book that was at least a century old. However, the Japanese side were willing to accept it, so long as Nishizawa was compensated for having to abandon his operation.

There were then five months of negotiations over the value of this compensation. In October, the governor-general agreed to pay 160,000 silver dollars to Nishizawa in exchange for him abandoning his activities and Japan recognising Qing sovereignty. Nishizawa agreed to pay $20,000 for destroying a fishermen's temple he had found on the island. Honour was satisfied all round. The governor-general hoped to recoup the cost by taking over the guano operation and directing the profits towards Guangzhou. However, the practicalities of economic development were more difficult than he realised. Almost a year later, in August 1910, the Guangdong provincial authorities attempted to restart guano extraction on Pratas. Lacking the necessary knowledge, they contracted Nishizawa's firm to run it on their behalf![12]

While all this was going on, Admiral Li came to hear of another maritime territory previously unknown to him: the Paracel Islands, southwest of Hong Kong in the direction of Indochina. According to Li's later account, he had only been informed of their existence by the commander of the 'Left Fleet',

Lin Guoxiang, an experienced sailor. Admiral Li lobbied the governor-general to pay for an expedition to the Paracels to try to prevent any Japanese guano-miners making inroads there. However, Li's naval forces didn't have the ability to sail that far so, once again, the Customs Service was asked to step in. At the end of March 1909, the Customs' cruiser *Kaiban* transported three of the governor-general's officials to the islands. When it returned to Hong Kong on 15 April, it apparently 'caused wonder in the local population by exhibiting 20 or so enormous turtles brought back from these deserted islands', according to the French consul.[13] The interest in these rare creatures and general atmosphere of surprise demonstrate how little Chinese officials and the general public knew about the islands before 1909. Aside from a few fishermen, almost no one had cared about their existence until the Japanese showed up. That had now dramatically changed.

In the wake of this mini-success, Admiral Li persuaded the governor-general to pay for a second expedition to the Paracels. This would have two purposes: the voyage would make a formal claim of sovereignty over the islands, and the ensuing flag-waving would generate huge support for the officials seen to be standing up against the foreigners. The mission would involve three 'small Cantonese gunboats' (as the French consul described them) – the *Fupo*, *Chinhao* and *Kwongkum* – with 106 people aboard, including the admiral himself, the regional supervisor (*daotai*), the secretary of the provincial finance department and the provincial salt commissioner: in all, a high-status delegation. Also on board was a German radio engineer named Herr Brauns, whose job was to send back details of the flotilla's progress to the media in Hong Kong, plus a journalist from the Hong Kong-based newspaper of Sun Yat-sen's pro-revolution *Xingzhonghui*, the *Zhongguo Ribao/Chung kuo jih pao*. Admiral Li wanted the expedition to be front-page news. Something that wasn't mentioned in the coverage was that the expedition was actually guided by a second German: the deputy head of the trading house Carlowitz & Co., based in Hong Kong. Europeans were generally far more familiar with the Paracels than the local officials, since they frequently sailed past them while travelling to and from home. They regarded the islands more as a threat to shipping than a nationalist cause célèbre.

The three-boat flotilla left Guangzhou around 14 May 1909, and stopped in Hong Kong until 21 May. It then headed on to Hainan Island, staying close to shore, with stops in Haikou, Sama Bay and Yulinkan, where they were delayed by a typhoon. At this point, the *Kwongkum* had to return to Haikou. The other two ships made a dash for the Paracels, and spent three days exploring the archipelago. Li Zhun declared Chinese sovereignty over them in a manner familiar to the imperial powers: firing cannon volleys, hoisting flags and giving the islands new Chinese names. One island was named *Fubo* and another *Chenhang* after the ships. Another was called *Ganquan* because of the presence of a well, and others were named after senior officials. This was remarkably similar to the actions of the British, almost exactly a century before, who had named some of the Paracel Islands after their ships (including Antelope Reef and Discovery Reef) and others after managers of the East India Company: Drummond, Duncan, Money, Pattle and Roberts.

The return of the ships to Hong Kong on 9 June should have been an opportunity for Li and the Guangdong authorities to proclaim their patriotic credentials. However, the *South China Morning Post* reported the 'extreme reticence' of the officials who took part in the expedition to talk to its correspondent.[14] It seems they were underwhelmed by what they had discovered. Rather than the land of opportunity that they had imagined, it turned out that the Paracel Islands were small and barren. By late June, expectations were so low that the Guangdong authorities were proposing 'converting the inhabitable portions of the Paracels into a penal settlement, the convicts to be employed in agricultural pursuits and timber working on Tree Island', according to the *SCMP*.[15] Even this desperate idea failed to get anywhere. The governor-general was transferred to a new post and everyone forgot about the whole thing.

However, the mission to claim the Paracels for China had served its purpose. It helped to shore up a collapsing regime in Guangdong and rally the people against the foreigners for a few weeks. That three-day public-relations exercise still forms the foundation of China's territorial claim in the South China Sea today. But it would be the last time any Chinese official visited the islands for almost two decades. They had more important things to do. In the meantime, other Japanese guano merchants landed on the islands, completely ignoring the question of sovereignty. The 'Southern Prosperity Industries Company' and others extracted large amounts of fertiliser without anyone on the mainland taking any action throughout the 1910s and 1920s.

Admiral Li, meanwhile, went back to his regular job of suppressing insurrection. By 1911, according to Edward Rhoads, 'Among the revolutionaries, Li was easily the most hated official in Kwangtung [Guangdong]. His forces had been involved in the suppression of every one of their uprisings since 1907.' He was about to become their target once again. In late 1909, a few months after Admiral Li's voyage to the Paracels, his would-be assassin, Liu Sifu, was released from prison. Liu's relatives, who were scholar-officials, had pulled strings to get him transferred to their home province and then, two years after the bomb attempt, freed. Rather than reforming him, prison had turned Liu into an ideological anarchist. Shortly after his release he returned to Hong Kong and helped to found a new organisation, the China Assassination Corps. Before it could launch its first operation, however, a lone revolutionary tried to shoot Li while he visited an aircraft demonstration in Guangzhou. Since he couldn't get a clear shot at Li, the gunman killed another official, who turned out to be a Manchu general, Fuqi. As a result, security was tightened, making it harder to get closer to Li.

On their third attempt, on 13 August 1911, Liu's band got close enough to Li's sedan-chair to throw a bomb. Some of Li's guards were killed but the admiral suffered just two broken ribs.[16] His injuries were sufficient to take him out of public life for a few months, which, by one report, he spent writing Chinese characters on fans to present to well-wishers and attending his siblings' weddings.[17] He was still on sick leave when the revolution broke out. An army mutiny in the city of Wuchang on 10 October spread to surrounding areas and, one after another, provinces declared their independence from the Qing Empire. Despite the worsening political situation, Li ignored a series of summons from the new governor-general, Zhang Mingqi, to help with defending the regime. This was personal. Zhang had previously stripped Li of command of the province's reserve forces and Li saw no reason to go to his aid now. There is also some suggestion that Li became more sympathetic to Han nationalism around this time and decided he could no longer support the Manchu regime.[18]

Two weeks later, the general sent by Beijing to replace the assassinated Fuqi was himself assassinated within minutes of arriving in Guangzhou by a bomb built under the anarchist Liu's direction.[19] The city began to panic. Fears of attack by rebel bands, of potential massacres of Manchus by Han racists, and of robbery and looting led to shops being boarded up and people leaving the city. Li Zhun's response was to negotiate a surrender with the people who had been trying to kill him for the past four years. He made contact with two prominent Chinese figures in Hong Kong, who had connections with the revolutionaries. Within days, he was in correspondence with Sun Yat-sen's leading ideologue Hu Hanmin, who had just returned to Hong Kong from Saigon. On 7 November Li and Hu met and agreed a deal in which Li would surrender Guangzhou to the revolutionaries in exchange for his life and that of his family. On 9 November the governor-general fled to the safety of British Hong Kong and Admiral Li became, for one day, his successor. He took part in the handover ceremonies to the revolutionaries and then he too fled to Hong Kong. He had spent almost a decade trying to suppress the revolution but at the end he handed them their first major success.

This was not the end of Li Zhun's career. He knew how to survive and he soon found ways to make himself useful to the new regime. In an ironic twist, the new revolutionary government made him 'Commissioner for Pacification' in his old province, Guangdong, in August 1913.[20] In July 1914 he was appointed the military commander of Fujian province and the following month, following the outbreak of the First World War, made commissioner of the defence inspectorate.[21] There was no such good fortune for the guano miners of Pratas Island, however. After taking formal ownership of the reef in 1909, the Guangdong authorities had attempted to restart production on the island. However, during the 1911/12 revolution the workers were completely forgotten about. The mainland authorities failed to resupply them and they starved to death.[22]

The French colonial authorities in Indochina had observed Admiral Li's claim-making in the Paracels with detached bemusement. At the time, they had very little interest in the islands but that was about to change. During the eighteenth and nineteenth centuries the Vietnamese court had licensed fishermen to salvage cannon and other valuables from ships wrecked on the reefs. But after the French occupation (which began in Saigon in 1859 and reached the Qing frontier in 1887) those expeditions seem to have ceased. It wasn't until an enterprising marine biologist, Armand Krempf, sought to bolster his indifferent scientific reputation with research into coral formation that the French authorities started to take an interest. Krempf and his fellow researchers from the Oceanographic Institute of Indochina made their first voyage to the Paracels in 1925. Soon afterwards, entrepreneurs caught a whiff of guano and a few industrialists began to petition the French colonial government for permission to exploit the islands.[23] In December 1928 the governor-general of Indochina, Pierre Pasquier, wrote to the French Minister of Colonies in Paris, calling for the islands to be annexed.[24] Paris was unwilling to do so, afraid of a possible reaction against French interests in China.

However, Krempf's 1931 expedition to the islands included a mining engineer who estimated that the remaining guano on Roberts Island alone, even after the activities of Japanese firms, would meet Indochina's needs for twenty years.[25] At around the same time, the governments of both France and Britain were becoming increasingly concerned about Japan's military interests in the islands and the potential threat to their colonies in Southeast Asia. These two motivations appear to have been sufficient for Paris to overcome its reservations and, on 4 December 1931, to formally claim sovereignty over the Paracels. The Chinese government took nearly eight months to respond but, on 27 July 1932, the Chinese legation in Paris was instructed to formally reject the French claim. Their note made the point that the Paracels were the southernmost point of Chinese territory.

Then, on Bastille Day the following year, 14 July 1933, the French government announced that it had annexed six of the Spratly Islands, a completely separate group of islets 750 kilometres south of the Paracels. There was uproar in China, but also confusion. It is obvious from newspaper reports and government documents of the time that neither Chinese officials nor the general public had any idea where the Spratlys actually were. There was a general assumption that they were the same features – the Paracels – over which France and China were already in dispute. An official telegram sent from the Chinese Ministry of Foreign Affairs to the Chinese consul in Manila on 17 July 1933 contains the questions, 'Where exactly are these islands? Are they the Paracels?' A similar telegram was sent by the ministry to the navy, whose response was surprising, given present-day assertions that China has governed the islands 'since ancient times'. Chen Shaokuan of the Navy Ministry replied, telling the Foreign Ministry: 'There are no "nine islands" at 10°0′ N 150°0′ E between the Philippines and Vietnam. The nine islands between the Philippines and Vietnam are further north. These islands are the *Xisha* [Paracels] and are very close to Qiongzhou [Hainan] Island.'[26] Further confusion was created in some quarters by mentions of another group of islands, the *Qizhou*, or 'seven islands' (known in English as the Taya Islands), which actually lie northeast of Hainan, 300 kilometres north of the Paracels.

American records show that the Chinese consul in Manila, Kuang Guanglin (K. L. Kwong), visited the US Coast and Geodetic Survey office there on 26 July and was surprised to discover that the Spratlys and Paracels were separate archipelagos. This information was transmitted back to the Chinese government, who were still in a quandary about what to do. While they deliberated, the newspapers filled with protest letters, news of demonstrations and criticism from officials unhappy with the Guomindang government's leadership. The contrast between Chinese and foreign coverage of the issue was stark. While Chinese officials and journalists appear confused, the *SCMP* and other international newspapers were more familiar with the geography of the South China Sea. In several articles they pointed out that the Paracels and Spratlys were different archipelagos, a clarity that was quite absent from discussions in China.

At around this time, Admiral Li Zhun, who had retired, returned from obscurity to make an intervention that left a legacy of confusion that persists to this day. On 15 August, a month after news of the annexation broke, the Shanghai-based newspaper *Shenbao* published a long article featuring an account of Li's original (1909) voyages to Pratas and the Paracels. A week later, on 21 August, *Guowen zhoubao* ('National News Weekly') reported that Li 'came to our news agency and talked to the reporter about it in person' and also printed what it claimed to be his original report in which he 'discovered the 11 coral islands' of the Paracels. By the end of the month, almost every Chinese newspaper had printed some version of Li's account. As a result, almost every Chinese newspaper reader was told that the islands the French had just annexed were the Paracels.

By this time, the Republic's Foreign Ministry had received information from its staff in Manila and Paris and was aware that the Paracels and Spratlys were different. Significantly, it decided that China had no grounds to claim the

Spratlys and so would not object to the French annexation. It would settle for the Paracels. This put the government at odds with the mass of public opinion, which had already convinced itself, through the intervention of Admiral Li, among others, that China had annexed the Spratlys back in 1909. China now had two maritime claims: the government's, which only encompassed the Paracels, and that of the angry public, which had already begun to extend as far as the Spratly Islands, even if they did not fully understand this. This confusion would have profound consequences right into the twenty-first century.

To try to clear up this confusion, the government ordered a previously dormant body to investigate. The 'Land and Water Maps Review Committee' had been set up in 1930 in order to try to regularise the country's cartography and define its borders (see Chapter 7) but never actually met until June 1933, just before the French annexation of the Spratlys was announced. Once the crisis subsided, the committee was given the job of making sure that similar misunderstandings would not happen again.

The committee did not have the capacity to undertake its own surveys, however. Instead, it undertook a table-top exercise: analysing maps produced by others and forming a consensus about names and locations. According to the committee's own journal, it examined 630 Chinese maps and 120 books on national history and an unspecified number of foreign maps. When it came to the South China Sea, it is clear from the committee's conclusions that its leading references were British, something which had far-reaching consequences. On 21 December 1934 the Review Committee held its twenty-fifth meeting and agreed on Chinese names for 132 features in the South China Sea. All of them were translations or transliterations of the names marked on British maps. In the Paracels, for example, Antelope Reef became *Lingyang jiao* and Money Island became *Jinyin dao* – both direct translations. The names that Admiral Li had given to the Paracels in 1909 were ignored. In the Spratlys, North Danger Reef became *Beixian*, another translation from the English. Spratly Island became *Si-ba-la-tuo* (a phonetic transliteration of the name of the English sea captain, Richard Spratly), and Luconia Shoals was transliterated as *Lu-kang-ni-ya*.

We know exactly where the committee's list of island names came from because it contains several mistakes which are only found in one other document: the 'China Sea Directory' published by the UK Hydrographic Office in 1906.

This British list is the origin of all the names now used by China. Some of the names on the list had Chinese origins, such as Subi Reef in the Spratlys, while others had Malay origins (such as Passu Keah in the Paracels), but more than 90 per cent were coined by British navigators. Translating these names caused some difficulties and a legacy that disturbs the region to this day.

It is clear that the committee members were confused by the English words 'bank' and 'shoal'. Both words mean an area of shallow sea: the former describes a raised area of sea bed, the latter is a nautical expression derived from Old English meaning 'shallow'. However, the committee chose to translate both into Chinese as *tan*, which has the ambiguous translation of 'sandbank', a feature that might be above or below water. Sea Horse Shoal, off the Philippines, was dubbed *Haima Tan*; James Shoal, just 100 kilometres off the coast of Borneo, was given the name *Zengmu tan*, and Vanguard Bank, off the south-eastern coast of Vietnam, was given the name *Qianwei tan*. *Zengmu* is simply the transliteration of 'James', *Haima* is the Chinese for seahorse, *Qianwei* is a translation of 'vanguard' and *tan*, as mentioned above, is the erroneous translation of 'bank' and 'shoal'. As a result of this bureaucratic mistake, these underwater features, along with several others, were turned into islands in the Chinese imagination. This screw-up, ultimately, is the reason why the Sapura Esperanza was harassed while drilling for gas near the James Shoal eighty-five years later. China is prepared to go to war over a translation mistake.

As a final flourish, in April 1935 the Review Committee printed a map of the South China Sea with all the 'new' names included. The map had an ambiguous title, *Zhongguo nanhai ge daoyu tu*, which could be translated both as 'Map of China's Islands in the South Sea' and also 'Map of Islands in the South China Sea'. There is no evidence that, even at this point, the committee was actually asserting a territorial claim to the Spratlys. There was no boundary line marked on the map and no indication about which features the committee considered to be Chinese and which not. Its members chose to use the name *Nansha* – 'southern sands' – to refer to the Macclesfield Bank, a submerged feature that actually lies in the centre of the sea. The officials appear to have done this because, at the time, it was the southernmost feature claimed by China. It became the third point of a triangle marked by *Dongsha* (East Sand/Pratas), *Xisha* (West Sand/Paracels), and now *Nansha* (South Sand/Macclesfield Bank).

The committee conferred the Chinese name *Tuansha* on the Spratlys. The name vaguely translates as 'area of sand'. In 1935 neither the committee nor the Chinese government was prepared to stake a claim to the Spratlys.

The man who caused China to claim non-existent islands hundreds of kilometres from its shores was a Manchu who probably never went to sea in his life. Bai Meichu was born into relatively humble origins in 1876 in what is now Hebei province, 200 kilometres due east of the Forbidden City. Growing up in Lulong county, his early life must have been surrounded by trauma: the great famine of 1876–9, which first stirred Timothy Richard's radical conscience; the Sino-Japanese War of 1894/5 and the Boxer Uprising of 1899–1901. Bai was part of the last generation to be trained for the old scholar-bureaucracy: his family had enough money to have him privately schooled and, at the age of fifteen, he earned the title of *xiucai*, the first rung on the traditional ladder to success. Before he could climb it, however, that ladder was pulled away as the Qing Great-State entered its final decline. Bai was part of a generation that was caught up in a time of extreme uncertainty. To borrow Antonio Gramsci's phrase, the old world was dying all around him but the new could not yet be born.

Bai was sent to one of the newly established 'modern' schools, Jingsheng College in Yongping (now known as Lulong) in Hebei, which taught both Chinese and Western subjects. He was among the first to experience the clash between traditional ideas of geography as expressed in the ancient texts and the new ideas arriving through the missionaries and the treaty ports. In later life he described reading the 'Classic of Mountains and Seas', the 'Tribute of Yu' and the 'Shangshu', but these 2,000-year-old documents were a poor guide to the changes that Bai was witnessing all around him. Once, he might have expected to study them to pass the necessary exams to join the bureaucracy, but in September 1905 the imperial examination system was abolished. Instead, that same year, and at the age of twenty-nine, Bai enrolled at Beiyang Normal School, whose purpose was to train teachers for a new, reformed education system.

He graduated in 1909 with the honorary title of '*juren*', a throwback to the old examination system. He became a schoolteacher and then a teacher of teachers at the Women's Normal School in Tianjin. There he taught, among others, Deng Yingchao, a future senior cadre in the Communist Party and the wife of Zhou Enlai. At the same time, he was becoming a pioneer in the new subject of geography. This was not yet geography as the later generation of Zhu Kezhen and Zhang Qiyun would come to define it (see Chapter 7) but a hybrid of old ideas and new nationalism. In 1909 Bai became one of the founders of the 'China Earth-Study Society' (*Zhongguo Dixue Hui*). According to the historian Tze-ki Hon, none of its members had any professional training in the subject. Instead, they recruited members from the old literati. They were, like Bai, people who had once expected to join the scholar-bureaucracy but were now struggling to adapt. Many of them found less prestigious jobs, teaching in secondary schools and girls' schools.[27]

Members of the China Earth-Study Society were profoundly influenced by Social-Darwinism. In the first issue of their 'Earth-Study Journal' (*Dixue Zazhi*) they collectively declared: 'The cause [of the rise and fall of power] is due to the level of geographical knowledge of each group. Thus, the level of geographical knowledge has a direct impact upon a country, and it can cause havoc to a race. It is indeed [a manifestation of] the natural law of selection based on competition.' In other words, the size of any group's territory ebbed and flowed depending on its relative civilisation. In the view of the society, China had advanced early but then retreated in the face of Western advances. The only way to regain strength was to master geography. In the words of Bai himself in 1913, 'Loving the nation is the top priority in learning geography, while building the nation is what learning Geography is for.'[28] In August 1917, in recognition of his patriotic efforts, Bai was hired to work at Beijing Normal University.

These geographers put themselves at the service of the nation, both before and after the 1911/12 revolution. In return they received significant financial support. Bai himself petitioned the new Republican government with ideas for reforming local government boundaries and about where it should site the national capital (he favoured Beijing over Nanjing). A turning point for Bai, like so many other intellectuals of the time, was the outcome of the Versailles peace conference in 1919. The decision to hand over the former German enclave in Shandong to Japan enraged students and members of the Earth-Study Society alike. Their journal carried several articles denouncing the decision and urging the government to prevent the expansion of Japanese influence on the peninsula. Bai's students remember him as being a passionate advocate for the nation's rights. His lectures are said to have been most affecting for the students at the Tianjin Women's Normal School.

At around this time, Bai became a mentor to a young Li Dazhao, who had also studied at Jingsheng College and would become one of the founders of the Communist Party in 1921. On New Year's Day 1919 Li introduced him to another young radical, Mao Zedong, and the three spent hours discussing the problems of the nation's territory. It seems unlikely, but Bai, the old-school classical scholar, and Li, the new communist revolutionary, remained firm friends right up until Li's killing in 1927. It is possible that some of Bai's energetic views on geography and national territory were passed directly into the communist movement.[29]

In 1923 the Society was similarly outspoken in demanding the government reclaim the ports of Dalian and Lushun (Port Arthur) at the expiry of the Russian lease on them. Bai continued this work for the rest of his life. Between 1928 and 1930 he wrote a long, serialised essay on the Pian Ma border dispute with the British. Although tiny, this patch of land on the Yunnan-Burma frontier was, for Bai, hugely symbolic. He urged the government to use force to claim it so that 'the weaknesses of our citizens will not be exposed in front of the world'. Bai was becoming increasingly bellicose. He no longer saw territorial arrangements as reflections of the ebb and flow of civilisation but as the result of conspiracies by predatory states to rob the weaker ones. The defence of far-flung borders became critically important, particularly as knowledge about mineral resources in remote areas became more widely known. In his view, it was up to the Chinese people to protect the nation's land.

But Bai's style was increasingly out of fashion, particularly with the arrival of the new, professionally trained geographers such as Zhu Kezhen and Zhang Qiyun (whom we met in Chapter 7), who founded their own societies and had very little to do with the old China Earth-Study Society. In September 1925 Bai published a 4 million-character book on the regional geography of China, but it was denounced by the new-style geographers for its unscientific method. Bai, it seems, was still strongly influenced by the classics he had studied at school. In

1929 he lost his teaching post at Beijing Normal University and moved to the women's equivalent, instead. In 1935 he left university teaching altogether. By chance he came across the 'Programme for National Reconstruction' (*Jianguo fanglue* – see Chapter 5) that Sun Yat-sen had published in 1920, during his time in the political wilderness. From Bai's own account, this book inspired him to devote his remaining years to Sun's mission: using geography to enable national reconstruction.

In 1936 Bai gave the world his lasting legacy: a line drawn through the South China Sea. It was included in a new book of maps, the *New Atlas of China's Construction* (*Zhonghua jianshe xin tu*) that Bai published for use in schools. He included some of the new information about place names and frontiers agreed upon by the government's Maps Review Committee, which had been published the year before. As was typical of maps of this period, the atlas was, in many places, a work of fiction. A bright red border line stretched around the country, neatly dividing China from its neighbours. Within the line were Mongolia, Tibet and Manchuria plus several other areas that weren't actually under the control of the Republican government. However, the fictitiousness reached spectacular levels when it came to the South China Sea.

It is clear that Bai was quite unfamiliar with the geography of the South China Sea and undertook no survey work of his own. Instead, he simply copied other maps and added in dozens of errors of his own making – errors that continue to cause problems to this day. Just like the Maps Review Committee, he was completely confused by the portrayal of areas of shallow water on British and other foreign maps. Taking his cue from the names on the committee's 1934 list, he drew solid lines around these features and coloured them in, visually rendering them on his map as islands when in reality they were underwater. He conjured an entire island group into existence across the centre of the sea and labelled it the *Nansha Qundao* – the 'South Sands Archipelago'. Further south, parallel with the Philippines coast, he dabbed a few dots on the map and labelled them the *Tuansha Qundao*, the 'Area of Sand Archipelago'. However, at its furthest extent he drew three islands, outlined in black and coloured in pink: *Haima Tan* (Sea Horse Shoal), *Zengmu Tan* (James Shoal) and *Qianwei Tan* (Vanguard Bank).

Thus the underwater 'shoals' and 'banks' became above-water 'sandbanks' in Bai's imagination and on the physical rendering of the map. He then added an innovation of his own: the same national border that he had drawn around Mongolia, Tibet and the rest of 'Chinese' territory snaked around the South China Sea as far east as Sea Horse Shoal, as far south as James Shoal and as far southwest as Vanguard Bank. Bai's meaning was clear: the bright red line marked his 'scientific' understanding of China's rightful claims. This was the very first time that such a line had been drawn on a Chinese map. Bai's view of China's claims in the South China Sea was not based upon the Review Committee's view of the situation, nor that of the Foreign Ministry. It was the result of the confusion generated by Admiral Li Zhun's interventions in the Spratly crisis of 1933, combined with the nationalist imagination of a redundant geographer without formal academic training. This was Bai Meichu's contribution to Sun Yat-sen's mission of national reconstruction.

Bai's map was not a state document, though; it was simply the work of a private individual, albeit an influential one. The government continued to regard the Paracel Islands as the southernmost point of Chinese territory right up until the Second World War. In 1943 the RoC Ministry of Information published its *China Handbook 1937–43*, a comprehensive guide to the country's geography, history, politics and economics. On its opening page it stated, 'The territory of the Republic of China extends from [the Sajan Mountains in the north] . . . to Triton Island of the Paracel Group.' But this view of China's maritime territory would change dramatically over the following three years. And this change was orchestrated by two of Bai Meichu's former students.

In 1927, while he was chair of the Department of History and Geography at Beijing Normal University, among the students Bai had taught were Fu Jiaojin and Zheng Ziyue. After graduating, Fu went on to further study at the University of Leipzig and, upon returning to China in 1938, was appointed professor at Fudan University in Shanghai. Zheng, on the other hand, went on to the University of Tsukuba in Japan before being appointed head of geography at Northwest University in Xi'an. The type of geography taught in Germany and Japan during the 1930s was, to say the least, heavily imbued with trenchant views on the need for nations to expand their territory. This seems to have been the view that Fu and Zheng espoused in 1946 when both men were seconded from their academic jobs to the Department of Territorial Administration of the RoC Ministry of the Interior. Fu became the department's director-general and Zheng its 'director of geography'. Their job was to decide how much territory China should claim in the aftermath of the Second World War.[30]

One of the first tasks Professor Zheng undertook was to draw a 'Location Sketch Map of the South China Sea Islands' for a meeting of representatives from various government ministries on 25 September 1946. The meeting had been convened specifically for the purpose of deciding which islands China should claim, but Zheng's map more or less answered the question for them. His 'sketch map' copied the line drawn on Bai Meichu's map as far east, south and west as the imaginary islands of Sea Horse Shoal, James Shoal and Vanguard Bank. The only major difference was that Zheng's line was not solid but comprised of eight dashes. Almost every rock and reef in the South China Sea was encompassed within it. In view of this development, some names had to be changed. It no longer made sense for the 'Southern Sands' – the *Nansha* – to be located in the central part of the sea, so the name was moved south to become the Chinese name for the Spratlys. The central area was renamed the *Zhongsha* – the 'Central Sands' – even though there aren't, in fact, any islands there at all! This is why, to this day, the Chinese government talks of four island groups in the South China Sea, even though only three actually exist. The significance of Zheng's map is that it was the very first document produced by the Chinese government to include a U-shaped line around the South China Sea. It did so because it was based upon the map drawn by Bai Meichu a decade earlier.

A couple of months after the meeting, Zheng accompanied the very first Chinese naval mission to the islands of the South China Sea. The mission was only possible because of the recent arrival of ships and training provided by the United States and Britain. The new flotilla was intended to help the Republic fight the communist threat but was, instead, diverted to take part in a flag-waving exercise to shore up the government's nationalist legitimacy. On 12 December 1946 Zhang was part of the first ever official Chinese landing party on Itu Aba, the largest of the Spratly Islands. The island was then officially renamed after the ship that had carried them there, the *Taiping* (which had begun its life as the USS *Decker* before being retired from the US Navy).

But the issue was still not settled. The commander of the expedition to the Spratlys, Lieutenant Colonel Lin Zun, sent his report to Navy Command Headquarters in February 1947. In it he disputed the notion that the Spratlys belonged to China. He noted that they were more than 500 nautical miles from Hainan and only 200 nautical miles from the Philippines and thus the scope for 'receiving' them should be further studied. Discussions within the government continued for a further two months, until a meeting at the Ministry of the Interior on 14 April settled the matter. It resolved that the southernmost point of Chinese territory was the James Shoal, and that China should proclaim sovereignty over both the Paracel Islands and the Spratly Islands. But this decision came too late for the 1947 edition of the *China Handbook*. It stated that 'the southernmost . . . boundaries remain to be settled . . . and the sovereignty of the Tuansha Islands [here the old name was still used] on the south are contested among China, the Commonwealth of Philippines and Indochina'.

In fact, the arguments continued inside government, with Lieutenant Colonel Lin Zun continuing to argue that the Spratlys should be divided between China and the newly independent Philippines. A further meeting was held on 10 June. According to the Taiwanese academic Hurng-Yu Chen, 'Director-General of the Ministry of the Interior Fu Chiao-chin . . . stated that the publications on the sovereignty of the islands in the South China Sea by Chinese institutions and schools prior to the Anti-Japanese War should serve as a guidance regarding the territorial restoration issue.' In other words, the government would be guided by putative claims made in newspapers in the 1930s. The meeting agreed that the entire Spratly archipelago should be claimed, but given that only Itu Aba (Taiping Dao) had been physically occupied, the claim should wait until other islands had actually been visited. This never happened, but the claim was asserted nonetheless.

A key part of asserting the claim was to make the names of the features in the sea sound more Chinese. In October 1947 the RoC Ministry of the Interior issued a new list of island names. Most of the 1935 translations and transliterations were replaced by new, grand-sounding titles. For example, the Chinese name for Spratly Island was changed from *Si-ba-la-tuo* to *Nanwei* (Noble South) and Scarborough Shoal was changed from *Si-ka-ba-luo* (the transliteration) to *Minzhu jiao* (Democracy Reef). Vanguard Bank's Chinese name was changed from *Qianwei tan* to *Wan'an tan* (Ten Thousand Peace Bank). The name for Luconia Shoals was shortened from *Lu-kang-ni-ya* to just *Kang*, which means 'health'. This process was repeated across the archipelagos, largely concealing the foreign origins of most of the names. A few did survive, however. In the Paracels, 'Money Island' kept its Chinese name of *Jinyin Dao* and Antelope Reef remained *Lingyang Jiao*. To this day the two names celebrate a manager and a ship of the East India Company respectively.

It was at this point that the ministry seems to have recognised its earlier problem with the translations of 'shoal' and 'bank'. Whereas in the past it had used the Chinese word *tan* to stand in for both (with unintended geopolitical consequences), in 1947 it coined a new word, *ansha* – literally 'hidden sand' – as a replacement. This neologism was appended to several submerged features, including James Shoal, which was renamed *Zengmu Ansha*.

In December 1947 the 'Bureau of Measurements' of the Ministry of Defence printed an official 'Location Map of the South China Sea Islands', which was almost identical to the 'Sketch Map' that Zheng Ziyue had drawn a year and a half before. It included the 'U-shaped line' made up of eleven dashes encircling the area down to the James Shoal. In February 1948 that map was published as part of the Atlas of Administrative Areas of the Republic of China and the U-shaped line – with an implicit claim to every feature within it – became the official position.

It was not until 1948, therefore, that the Chinese state formally extended its territorial claim in the South China Sea to the Spratly Islands, as far south as James Shoal. Clearly something had changed in the years between July 1933, when the Republic of China government was unaware that the Spratly Islands existed, and April 1947, when it could 'reaffirm' that the southernmost point of its territory was James Shoal. What seems to have happened is that, in the chaos of the 1930s and the Second World War, a new memory came to be formed in the minds of officials about what had actually happened in the 1930s. It seems that officials and geographers managed to confuse the real protest issued by the RoC government against French activities in the Paracels in 1932 with a non-existent protest against French activities in the Spratlys in 1933. Further confusion was caused by the intervention of Admiral Li Zhun and his assertion that the islands annexed by France in 1933 were indisputably

Chinese. The imagined claim conjured up by the confusion between different island groups in that crisis came to be the real territorial claim.

The island of Pratas is now a conservation zone, and peace reigns where picks and shovels once clanged on the guano. Trees have regrown and preparations are under way for an influx of tourists to the 'Dongsha Atoll National Park'. In contrast to the difficult journeys of a century ago, it is now possible to reach the island by scheduled flight. One departs every Thursday from the city of Kaohsiung in southern Taiwan, although visitors need special permission to buy a ticket and must pledge not to reveal details of defensive installations. Life may be peaceful on Pratas, but it remains on the frontline of superpower confrontation. The island is under the control of Taiwan, but for the Beijing leadership it is just one more piece of Chinese territory that must, one day, be controlled by the People's Republic. The Taiwanese leadership have highlighted their 'civilianisation' of the island. It is no longer garrisoned by marines but by coastguards. But these are a special kind of coastguard: armed with mortars and machine guns to deter potential invaders.

Flying over the huge reef, passengers can see a few small vessels down below: fish-poachers often play cat-and-mouse with the coastguard boats. Perhaps they have heard the old expression, 'If you want to get rich, go to Dongsha'. These days it is a delicate game for the Taiwanese. Do they rigidly enforce the conservation rules and risk a confrontation, or turn the occasional blind eye? In 1909 Pratas was the frontline in China's emerging territorial ambitions; it was where the South China Sea disputes really began. Asserting control over it was the first successful pushback after more than half a century of reverses at the hands of foreign powers. Today it is a frontline again.

The island on the western side of the reef is shaped like a crocodile's head. The runway takes up most of the 'upper jaw', half-enclosing a shallow lagoon, once again home to turtles and passing seabirds. The 'skull' is home to a typhoon-proofed village. Camouflaged towers protrude from the trees, along with the accommodation for the coastguards and their visitors. A new research centre hosts marine biologists from around the world and a post office has been freshly installed to demonstrate the state's administrative control. Visitors can send postcards back home from a mailbox guarded by a cheerful-looking plastic shark. Not far away is a new science exhibition explaining the natural history of the coral reef and its rich marine life. Overlooking the parade ground (which doubles as a rainwater trap) stands a golden statue of Chiang Kai-shek in his sun hat, and behind him is a little museum in what looks like a scaled-up child's sandcastle.

This museum holds, in effect, the key to resolving the South China Sea disputes. In its assertion of Chinese claims to the islets, it actually demonstrates the difference between nationalist cartography and real administration. Bai Meichu may have drawn a red line around various non-existent islands in 1936 and claimed them as Chinese, but no Chinese official had ever visited those places. The maps and documents on the museum walls tell the story of the RoC expedition to Itu Aba in December 1946 and of a confrontation with some Philippine adventurers in 1956, but in the absence of any other evidence, the museum demonstrates that China never occupied or controlled all of the islands. In the Paracels it occupied one, or just a few, until 1974, when People's Republic of China (PRC) forces invaded and expelled the Vietnamese garrison. In the Spratlys, the RoC occupied just one or two. The PRC took control of six reefs in 1988 and another in 1994.

In the meantime, the other countries around the South China Sea – Vietnam, the Philippines and Malaysia – took control of other features. The real history of physical presence in the archipelagos shows how partial any one state's claim actually is. The current mess of rival occupations is, with some exceptions, the only one that has ever existed. Understanding this opens a route to resolving the South China Sea disputes. By examining the historical evidence of occupations, the rival claimants should be able to understand that there are no grounds for them to claim sovereignty over everything. They should recognise that other states have solid claims to certain features and agree to compromise. As the legal phrase goes, *uti possidetis, ita possideatis* – 'as you possess, thus may you [continue to] possess'. Why should this be so difficult? Ultimately, it is because of the emotional power that these territorial claims continue to exert. And those emotions first stirred in Guangzhou in 1909.

CONCLUSION
Zhongguo Meng – China Dream

What do you give a Communist Party general-secretary who has everything? This was the problem Angela Merkel faced when she hosted Xi Jinping in Berlin in late March 2014. To resolve the issue, her staff selected an unusual gift: a map printed in Germany in 1750. The map was a copy of one drawn by the French cartographer Jean-Baptiste Bourguignon d'Anville for an atlas published in Paris in 1735. This was itself a copy – of an atlas prepared for the Qing Dynasty Kangxi Emperor in 1718. That atlas was definitely an original, the result of ten years of remarkable surveying work undertaken by Qing officials, advised by Jesuit priest-scientists sent by the King of France – which is how copies came to be made in Paris seventeen years later. Original copies of the Bourguignon d'Anville map sell for high prices in international auction houses: several thousand dollars apiece. The 1750 German edition is less valuable. Merkel's office probably paid around $500 for it, plus framing.[1] The emperor's original maps are priceless.

The Kangxi-Jesuit atlas was given the Chinese title of *Huangyu quanlan tu* – 'Overview map of the imperial realm'. The court saw no need to specify which country was being portrayed, since the country did not have a name: 'imperial realm' was sufficient. Only the French translation required the cartographers to add names to states. The Kangxi-Jesuit atlas included detailed maps of each Qing province, along with another showing the entire realm and its surroundings: from the Caspian Sea in the west to the island of Sakhalin in the east. But this was not the map chosen by Merkel's officials to give to Xi. Instead they presented their guest with a copy of another one entitled, in Latin, *Regni Sinae* – 'China Kingdom'.

The photographs of the presentation in the chancellor's office show an animated Angela Merkel pointing out some detail of the map while a stony-faced

Xi Jinping watches at a distance. It is unlikely that he was upset by the choice of the cheaper, German, edition of the map, or by what it portrayed. He was far more likely to have been irritated by what it did not show. The *Regni Sinae* map was subtitled *Sinae Propriae* – 'China Proper' – and included only the former provinces of the Ming Dynasty. It therefore excluded most of the other territories acquired by the Qing: Manchuria, Mongolia, Tibet and Xinjiang. To make things worse, Taiwan was outlined in a separate colour.

The Chinese delegation did not know how to react. Protocol required appropriate gratitude, but this was not a gift to be celebrated back home. Was it simply an innocent gesture of goodwill or a deliberate snub by the German government? The editors of the Chinese state media were in a quandary and resolved it in the traditional manner of a one-party state: they faked the news. They reported the gift of the map but then replaced the picture of the actual map that Merkel had presented to Xi with one of a completely different map, one that portrayed a much larger territorial claim. This was actually drawn over a century later, in 1844 by a British map-maker John Dower, and included the Qing's eighteenth-century conquests of Tibet and Xinjiang within the empire's frontiers.[2] In fact, the map showed frontiers drawn much wider than the current borders of the People's Republic. This inaccuracy was not a problem for the Chinese media. Even Professor Wang Yiwei, chair of the School of International Studies at the prestigious Renmin University, was taken in. He wrote an article for the Yale Global website about the significance for Germany-Russia relations of Merkel giving Xi a map showing Russian territory within Chinese borders.[3]

On the surface this might just appear to be an amusing anecdote, but it also demonstrates the anxiety and paranoia that lurk just beneath the surface of contemporary China's politics. If Xi had given Merkel a map of eighteenth-century Prussia that excluded most of western Germany, the object would have been treated as an interesting curio. The People's Republic's sense of self, on the other hand, is far too fragile to admit that the shape of the country may have been different 300 years ago. No debate over the state's 'core interest' of territorial integrity is permitted and the result is absurd denials of any historical evidence that underpins a different story of the past. The only acceptable version of history is the invented version that suits the needs of the Communist Party's current leadership.

The party depends on these invented narratives. As it retreated from Maoist communism in the late twentieth century, it searched for new ways to generate the loyalty of its citizens. One key foundation of its right to rule became 'performance legitimacy': the delivery of ever-higher living standards to most of the country's population. However, proletarians and bourgeois cannot live by bread alone and the party also sought a new guiding idea to fill their souls and lead them in the right direction. The new people's opium would be nationalism – not the kind that makes mobs march through the streets, but an official kind, defined by those at the top and stressing homogeneity and obedience.

As the British sociologist Anthony D. Smith argued long ago, national identities are founded upon historical myths. The myths have a social purpose: they divide believers from non-believers. It doesn't matter how absurd the myth is; believing in it makes someone an insider and gives them an identity that distinguishes them from the outsiders. It may well be that some genetic mutation in the distant past endowed human brains with the capacity to believe in absurd myths, and thereby accidentally gave them an evolutionary advantage. A genetic mutation that strengthens group identity and cohesion is likely to give members of that group greater chances of survival than those of a lone dissenter sitting out in the wilderness.[4] As Herbert Spencer would surely have acknowledged, natural selection should ensure the myth-believing mutation is more likely to be passed to subsequent generations than the DNA of the dissenter.

For a Leninist state seeking, above all, political obedience from a population of well over a billion people, official nationalism has proved a very useful tool. The Communist Party of China has repurposed the original nationalist project begun in the 1890s by people like Liang Qichao and Sun Yat-sen. Then, a relatively small number of people – mainly young men cast adrift in a newly uncertain world – spent decades developing the new national myths that would motivate subsequent generations. These myths would define who was in and who was out of the Chinese nation. Like nationalists everywhere, Liang, Sun and the other characters in this book insisted on a 'flattening' of differences within the new country in order to emphasise the differences with people outside.

During the 1930s, through newspapers, school classrooms and control over public debate, the Guomindang were able to inculcate a new set of collective memories in the citizens of the new Republic. These were not, by and large, complete inventions; they generated their emotional power by mobilising many pre-existing beliefs and repurposing them in the service of the nationalist cause, as we have seen in this book. New ideas about race, history, nation, language and territory were presented as simply updated, more scientific revisions of old truths. These ideas offered the chance of collective advancement for the nation and personal renewal for members of the in-group: who would not want to join?

So when the Communist Party suffered a near-catastrophic crisis of legitimacy in 1989 after the protests of Tiananmen Square and the subsequent massacre, it was not surprising that it turned to nationalism to re-adhere Chinese society to its leadership. The 'Patriotic Education Campaign' was first introduced two years after Tiananmen, in August 1991. Guidelines issued three years later declared that the campaign was intended to 'boost the nation's spirit, enhance cohesion, foster national self-esteem and pride, consolidate and develop a patriotic united front to the broadest extent possible, and direct and rally the masses' patriotic passions to the great cause of building socialism with Chinese characteristics'.[5] In the words of Zheng Wang, who first analysed the campaign, it 'represents a major shift in Beijing's identity politics', primarily by presenting China as the perennial victim and the West as its perennial aggressor.[6] The new curriculum played down the history of the Chinese civil war and the Communist Party's twentieth-century conflict with the Guomindang (thereby sending a new message of national unity across political divides) and, instead, emphasised other divisions by highlighting earlier conflicts between 'China' and the Western powers.

The directors of the Patriotic Education Campaign copied some of the techniques of the early nationalists to impart the new collective memory, and turbocharged them with the power of a one-party state. They used newspapers, textbooks and public discourse to set the parameters of what could, and could not, be said about the past. They also recruited television, film and online media to the cause and used party discipline and the force of the law to ensure adherence. One example will stand for many. When, in 2006, the Communist Youth League's weekly magazine *Freezing Point* published an article critical of the new turn in official history, it was closed down for two months. The article, by Yuan Weishi, a retired philosophy professor, compared the new version of history being taught in the country's schools to 'drinking wolf's milk'. 'If these innocent children swallow fake pills, then they will live with prejudices for their own lives and go down the wrong path,' he argued. The party didn't agree and only allowed the magazine to reopen if it printed a long article rebutting the professor's position.

Under Xi Jinping, the party has doubled down on the narrative. On 29 November 2012, shortly after being anointed party general-secretary, Xi delivered a speech at the National Museum of China in Tiananmen Square in which he unveiled his big idea, the 'China Dream' [*Zhongguo Meng*]. He declared, 'Achieving the great rejuvenation of the Chinese nation [*Zhonghua minzu*] is the greatest dream of the Chinese nation in modern times.' Many explanations have been offered for what Xi means by 'national rejuvenation' but one of the most authoritative comes from Yan Xuetong, dean of the Institute of International Relations at Tsinghua University in Beijing, who says its goal is 'resuming China's historical international status'.[7]

As we have seen in this book, there are many loaded ideas packed into that five-word phrase. What does Yan mean by 'resuming' or 'China' or 'status'? Which period of history is his reference point? In the same interview, he glibly mentions the Han Dynasty of 2,000 years ago, the Tang Dynasty of 1,000 years ago and the early part of the Qing Dynasty, 300 years ago. It requires a nationalist imagination to regard these three utterly different states as all representing an essential, timeless 'China'. It demonstrates how every group that chooses to see itself as a nation constructs myths around itself and, if they are successful, reconstructs the state around those myths. Earlier East Asian states ('dynasties') did exactly this: they sought to present themselves as the legitimate successors to their discredited predecessors. The Communists, like the Nationalists before them, are no different.

Where is all this invention taking China? China's self-image as a wronged but virtuous civilisation, the natural centre of a hierarchical arrangement of Asian states, is already causing it to act in ways that are oppressive to its people, worrying to its neighbours and destabilising to regional peace and security. The People's Republic is now an ethnocracy – a racially defined state – still in thrall to the nationalist myths constructed in the late nineteenth and early twentieth centuries. Under Xi Jinping, the Communist Party has worked to impose ever tighter boundaries around legitimate expressions of Chinese-ness.

Xi and his fellow leaders have put increasing emphasis on the 'four identifications', and added a fifth. They insist that all Chinese citizens must identify with the motherland, with the Chinese nation (*Zhonghua minzu*), with Chinese culture, the Chinese socialist road – and now with the Chinese Communist Party itself. It hardly needs saying that the party regards any suggestion that a Tibetan or a Uyghur might prefer to live under another government, that a Mongol might not be willing to embrace a homogenising view of the nation, that speakers of regional topolects might prefer not to speak *Putonghua*, or that any of them might reject the leading role of the Communist Party, as treasonous. As we are seeing in Hong Kong (at the time of writing), Xi Jinping's problem is that the more worried the Communist Party becomes about national fragmentation, the more it tries to impose national unity, and the more it generates a reaction in the opposite direction. In the end, its only answer appears to be coercion, physical force and mass surveillance, as the forced incarceration of over a million Uyghurs in 're-education centres' during 2019 demonstrates.

Enforced monoculturalism has formed a major strand of the Chinese nationalist project from its emergence at the end of the nineteenth century. But the problem of how to define the 'Chinese Nation' has dogged thinkers and politicians alike for decades. For long periods, under Soviet influence, the Communist Party was prepared to tolerate difference, delaying the creation of a single homogenous nation into the far future. However, in the wake of the breakups of the Soviet Union and Yugoslavia, some Chinese theoreticians argued vociferously for a new approach – a 'melting pot' in which differences would be eradicated in the interests of national unity. Xi Jinping seems to have listened to them.

After Tiananmen, as orthodox communist ideology retreated, Communist Party pronouncements increasingly featured the word 'nation' alongside the more traditional 'people'. Whereas the 'people' only included socialists, the 'nation' could include people of all class backgrounds, so long as they followed Beijing's definitions of what the 'nation' believed. Since Xi came to power in late 2012, the party has doubled down on national uniformity. The more the People's Republic of China stresses its own version of the past, the less room there is for alternative versions. One consequence is that life becomes ever more difficult for minorities or dissenters of any kind. They are seen as both a threat to the narrative and an impediment to modernisation and treated accordingly.

What should we call this new political ideology, one that features a single 'core' leader, insistent demands for national homogeneity, intolerance of difference, rule by party not by law, corporatist economic policies, a focus on discipline and an ideology based on racial exceptionalism – all backed up by a massive surveillance state? China's Communist Party has long talked of building 'socialism with Chinese characteristics'. Xi Jinping now seems more interested in building 'national-socialism with Chinese characteristics'.

The China that presents itself to us in the twenty-first century is more like the West than it, or the West, generally acknowledge. Rather than being a standard-bearer of 'Asian values', it is in fact a state in a Western mould complete with missions of identity, sovereignty, nationalism and territorial aggrandisement. This is not surprising when we look at how it emerged: it is, in essence, a foreign construction. There were two crucial conduits. The first phase was dominated by foreigners inside the Qing realm: missionaries, military men and diplomatic envoys. The second, and more important, phase was dominated by the exiles and *huaqiao* outside the Qing realm – whether in Japan, the United States or Southeast Asia. They looked back on their homeland with sensibilities acquired abroad. They were the ones who translated foreign ideas about a place called 'China' into a place called *Zhongguo*. When we look at China today we see the concretisation of Western views of a country that were adopted and interpreted by a modernising elite and then presented by them to a newly defined people called 'the Chinese'.

European states spent a blood-soaked century – 1848 to 1945 – working through the questions of nations and states and nation-states. Their attempts to make the state fit the nation led to two world wars; their attempts to make the nation fit the state frequently resulted in genocide. Eventually, European governments agreed to attenuate their nationalist urges and form cooperative supra-national structures in order to avoid future destruction. They also decentralised power and created federal systems to give more space for minorities. The result has been decades of peace, freedom and an upsurge in prosperity.

The People's Republic of China does not seem ready to learn from that experience. The question the world faces is whether its leadership is heading in the opposite direction: down a darkly familiar path towards fascism.

The problems China's neighbours face stem from the country's two contradictory views of the past. In the first, China sees itself in imperial terms, as the natural centre of East Asia, where borders are immaterial to power. In the second, China sees itself in Westphalian terms, determined to incorporate every scrap of territory, every rock and reef, within the homeland's 'sacred' national border. The neighbours would prefer things the other way around: a more Westphalian attitude to power – keep it within your own borders – and a less fundamentalist attitude towards territorial disputes – compromise in the interests of peace.

China's economic and military power makes its neighbours nervous, but the anxiety is made worse by Beijing's imperial attitudes to its periphery. In July 2010, at a meeting of the ASEAN Regional Forum in Hanoi, the Chinese foreign minister, Yang Jiechi, looked directly at his Singaporean counterpart, George Yeo, and reminded him that 'China is a big country and other countries are small countries, and that's just a fact.' There are clearly plenty of people, at all levels of Chinese society, who believe their state is more than simply 'first among equals', but use a particular vision of the past as justification for a new imperial outlook. It is made worse by expressions of Han chauvinism towards foreigners and also by treating 'overseas Chinese' in these countries as 'racial allies' and as tools of state policy.

Understanding the origins of China's territorial fundamentalism will be critical for regional peace. The aggressive pursuit of claims to tiny rocks and submerged reefs, the elevation of Taiwan's status to a question of existence and the frequent provocations in the Himalayas can all be traced back to the determination of Liang and Sun to inherit the Qing realm's frontiers. However, a careful sifting of the evidence reveals that these 'sacred' boundaries are largely twentieth-century innovations dreamed up by nationalist imaginations.

This is one of the ironies of China's contemporary situation. While it rejects foreign interference in its affairs, its obsession with sovereignty and its fundamentalist attitudes towards territory are distinctly foreign ideas. In the name of 'national rejuvenation', Xi Jinping's China is adopting the attitudes and behaviour of the imperial powers whose legacy he is supposed to be erasing. The country's present-day interests are being sabotaged by its pursuit of objectives derived from a skewed vision of history. China's future development requires peaceful relations with its eastern and southern neighbours, but those neighbours will not trust a country that seems intent on changing the territorial status quo. And while the leadership in Beijing insists that this territory has belonged to China 'since ancient times', readers who have made it this far will understand that this view of the frontier and the idea of absolute sovereignty is a distinctly modern invention.

In the early twentieth century, the country's urban populations wrestled with the problem of what it meant to be Chinese. They had never called themselves by such a name before and it was far from clear who was included in its definition. The imperial powers of Europe and Japan gave them an answer – by encroaching on territory that nationalist advocates claimed was the rightful home of their people. The narrative of loss implicitly demanded restitution: some future act that would restore the 'amputated' territory to the homeland and collectively redeem the nation. To be authentically Chinese, to belong to this nation, meant being outraged by this seizure of land and seeing it as an assault on the dignity of everyone in the group. Nationalist claims to territory became the marker of belonging. Evidence played a subordinate role to emotion. We are still living with the impact of those emotional claims.

How should the region and the world respond to these historical myths? They need to be taken seriously as drivers of Chinese behaviour but not as statements of historical truth, still less as a guide to the correct order of society or regional relations. Too many people have already been taken in: there are plenty of foreign commentators happy to parrot lines about '5,000 years of superior civilisation' or 'the unity of the Han race', without any understanding of where these concepts come from. As a result, they give Chinese nationalism a free pass. A country that believes it has a superior civilisation, that its population evolved separately from the rest of humanity and that it has a special place at the top of an imperial order will always be seen as a threat by its neighbours and the wider world. Chinese nationalism is subject to a critique just as much as any other form: German, Turkish or British, for example. I hope the stories in this book will help fortify readers with counter-arguments. They must, to quote Mao, seek truth from facts. It may well be that when PRC officials talk about questions of territory, nation, race and history, the most effective response will be laughter and derision.

What does Xi Jinping's 'China Dream' offer to the world? It increasingly feels like a dream from the 1930s: a recipe for destructive nostalgia. It is founded upon a view of the past forged a century ago in very particular circumstances and influenced by European concepts that Europe has now mostly dispensed with. The desire for homogeneity at home and respect abroad has resulted in suppression at home and threats abroad. Xi's China is not a happy place. It is dogmatic and coercive, anxious and unsure, fearful that its unity may come unzipped at any moment. The myths will hold it together for a while, but the fracture lines within the *Zhonghua minzu* were there from the start.

DRAMATIS PERSONAE

Bai Meichu (Pai Mei-ch'u), 1876–1940. One of the founders of the *Zhongguo Dixue Hui* ('China Earth-Study Society'). Geography professor and originator of the 'U-shaped line' in the South China Sea.

Chiang Kai-shek (Pinyin: Jiang Jieshi), 1887–1975. Nationalist politician, revolutionary, military commander, president of the Republic of China 1928–75.

Cixi, Dowager Empress, 1835–1908. The effective 'power behind the throne' from 1861 until 1908. A Manchu, she became a concubine of the Xianfeng Emperor and mother of the Tongzhi Emperor and then adoptive mother and gaoler of her nephew, the Guangxu Emperor.

Guangxu Emperor (Kuang-hsü Emperor), 1871–1908. He instituted the 'Hundred Days Reform' in 1898 but was then pushed from power by his aunt, Empress Dowager Cixi. He died while under house arrest, possibly poisoned on Cixi's orders.

Hu Hanmin, 1879–1936. Editor of the revolutionary journal *Minbao*. One of Sun Yat-sen's ideological advisers.

Huang Zunxian (Huang Tsun-hsien), 1848–1905. Qing diplomat who served in Tokyo, San Francisco, London and Singapore. Coined the term *huaqiao*. Author of the book *Treatises on Japan*. Co-founder, along with Liang Qichao and Tan Sitong, of the reformist journal, *Qiangxue Bao*. Ethnic Hakka.

Kang Youwei (K'ang Yu-wei), 1856–1928. Radical scholar, reformist, mentor of Liang Qichao. Co-founder of the *Baohuanghui* (known in English as the Chinese Empire Reform Association), author of *Datongshu* ('Book of the Great Harmony').

Li Hongzhang (Li Hung-chang), 1823–1901. Statesman of the late Qing. Governor-general of Zhili (the province surrounding Beijing) and superintendent of the Northern Ports. Negotiated in foreign crises during the 1890s and signed the Treaty of Shimonoseki with Japan in 1895.

Li Zhun (Li Chun). As brigade-general in Guangdong province in 1907 he suppressed revolutionary movements. Appointed admiral in 1908 and led naval expeditions to Pratas and the Paracel Islands in 1909. Switched sides to support revolutionaries in 1911.

Liang Qichao (Liang Ch'i-ch'ao), 1873–1929. Nationalist reformer, journalist and editor of several reformist publications. Co-founder of the *Baohuanghui*.

Liu Shipei, 1884–1919. In 1904, at the age of twenty, Liu published *Rangshu* – 'The Book of Expulsion', an anti-Manchu tract. He declared himself to be an anarchist but later became an official in the Qing bureaucracy.

Qianlong Emperor (Ch'ien-lung), 1711–1799. Fourth emperor of the Qing Dynasty. His reign is generally regarded as the apogee of the Qing Great-State.

Sun Yat-sen (Pinyin: Sun Zhongshan), 1866–1925. He co-founded the revolutionary group *Xing Zhong Hui* in 1894. In 1905 this merged with other groups to form the *Zhongguo Tongmenghui* – the 'China Alliance Society'. In 1912 he was appointed the provisional president of the Republic of China but was forced from office by Yuan Shikai after just ten weeks.

Wang Jingwei (Wang Ching-wei), 1883–1944. Sent from Guangdong province as a nineteen-year-old to study at Hosei University in Japan in 1904. He joined the *Tongmenghui* and became Sun Yat-sen's ideological adviser.

Wang Rongbao (Wang Jung-pao), 1878–1933. Language reformer from the eastern province of Jiangsu. He studied at the *Tongwen Guan* and then in Japan.

Wang Zhao (Wang Chao), 1859–1933. Language reformer from the northern province of Zhili. Originator of the 'Northern Vernacular Syllabary' published in 1901.

Xi Jinping (Hsi Chin-p'ing), 1953–. General-secretary of the Communist Party of China.

Yan Fu (Yen Fu), 1854–1921. Translator responsible for introducing the writings of Herbert Spencer and Thomas Huxley into urban China.

Yuan Shikai (Yüan Shih-k'ai), 1859–1916. Northern military commander and then president of the Republic of China 1912–16.

Zeng Guofan (Tseng Kuo-fan), 1811–1872. Senior Qing bureaucrat and military leader who took a leading role in defeating the Taiping rebels. Early believer in 'self-strengthening', mentor of Li Hongzhang.

Zhang Binglin (Chang Ping-lin), 1869–1936. He took the name Zhang Taiyan in 1901 to honour 'Ming loyalists' and demonstrate his opposition to Manchu rule. Author of the anti-Manchu tract *Qiushu*, 'The Book of Urgency'. In 1903 he insulted the emperor in a newspaper article and was jailed for three years in Shanghai. On his release he became the primary voice for a more racialist approach to revolutionary politics. In 1906 he was appointed editor-in-chief of *Minbao*, the newspaper of the revolutionary *Tongmenghui*.

Zhang Deyi (Chang Te-yi), 1847–1918. In 1862 he became one of the first language students at the *Tongwen Guan*. During 1866–71 he was a participant in Qing delegations to Europe and the United States.

Zhang Qiyun (Chang Chi-yun), 1901–1985. A leading figure in the second generation of Chinese geographers. He became an informal geopolitical adviser to Chiang Kai-shek.

Zhu Kezhen (Chu Coching), 1890–1974. The 'father of modern Chinese geography'. Studied in the United States 1910–19 and taught the second generation of Chinese geography professors during the 1920s and 1930s.

Zou Rong (Tsou Jung), 1885–1905. Anti-Manchu revolutionary, author of a violently nationalistic essay *Geming Jun* – 'The Revolutionary Army' – while an eighteen-year-old student in Japan.

NOTES

INTRODUCTION

1. Xi Jinping, Report at the 19th National Congress of the Communist Party of China, *China Daily*, 18 October 2017, Xinhua, http://www.chinadaily.com.cn/m/qingdao/2017-11/04/content_35234206.htm
2. Geremie R. Barmé, *The Forbidden City*, Cambridge, MA: Harvard University Press, 2011.
3. Timothy Brook, *Great State: China and the World*, London: Profile Books, 2019.

1 THE INVENTION OF CHINA

1. Xi Jinping, Toast at the Welcoming Banquet of The Second Belt and Road Forum for International Cooperation, Beijing, 26 April 2019, https://www.chinadaily.com.cn/a/201904/27/WS5d9d3688a310cf3e3556f508.html
2. Matthias Mertens, 'Did Richthofen really coin "The Silk Road"?', *The Silk Road*, vol. 17 (2019); Tamara Chin, 'The Invention of the Silk Road, 1877', *Critical Inquiry*, 40/1 (2013), pp. 194–219, doi:10.1086/673232.
3. C. R. Boxer (ed.), *South China in the Sixteenth Century: Being the Narratives of Galeote Pereira, Fr. Gaspar de Cruz, O.P., Fr. Martin de Rada, O.E.S.A.*, London: The Hakluyt Society, second series, 106, 1953.
4. Matteo Ricci, *China in the Sixteenth Century: The Journals of Matthew Ricci, 1583–1610*, compiled by Nicholas Trigault, translated from the Latin by Louis Gallagher, New York: Random House, 1953, pp. 6–7.
5. Richard J. Smith, *Mapping China and Managing the World: Culture, Cartography and Cosmology in Late Imperial Times*, New York: Routledge, 2013.
6. Peter K. Bol, 'Middle-period Discourse on the Zhong Guo: The Central Country', in *Hanxue Yanjiu (Chinese Studies)*, Taipei: Center for Chinese Studies, 2009, pp. 61–106.
7. Denis Twitchett, John King Fairbank and Michael Loewe, *The Cambridge History of China: Volume 1, The Ch'in and Han Empires, 221 BC–AD 220*, Cambridge: Cambridge University Press, 1987, p. 31.
8. Constance A. Cook and John S. Major, *Defining Chu: Image and Reality in Ancient China*, Honolulu: University of Hawaii Press, 1999, p. 4.
9. Pamela Kyle Crossley, 'The Rulerships of China: A Review Article', *American Historical Review*, 97/5 (1992), pp. 1471–2.
10. Junsei Watanabe, 'Manchu Manuscripts in the Toyo Bunko', in Luís Saraiva (ed.), *Europe and China: Science and Arts in the 17th and 18th Centuries*, Singapore; Hackensack, NJ: World Scientific, 2013, p. 187.
11. Cristina Costa Gomes and Isabel Murta Pina, 'Making Clocks and Musical Instruments: Tomás Pereira as an Artisan at the Court of Kangxi (1673–1708)', *Revisita de Cultura* (International Edition), 51 (2016).
12. Ibid., p. 9.

13. Joseph Sebes, 'The Jesuits and the Sino-Russian Treaty of Nerchinsk (1689) The Diary of Thomas Pereira, S. J.', *Bibliotheca Instituti Historici*, vol. XVIII (1962), pp. 114 and 207.
14. Arif Dirlik, 'Born in Translation: "China" in the Making of "Zhongguo"', *Boundary* (2015).
15. Lydia Liu, *The Clash of Empires: The Invention of China in Modern World Making*, Cambridge, MA: Harvard University Press, 2004, p. 76.
16. Hans van de Ven, *Breaking with the Past: The Maritime Customs Service and the Global Origins of Modernity in China*, New York: Columbia University Press, 2014.
17. Zhang Deyi (trans. Simon Johnstone), *Diary of a Chinese Diplomat*, Beijing: Chinese Literature Press, 1992, p. 11.
18. Zhang Deyi, *Sui Shi Fa Guo ji* ('Random Notes on France'), Hunan: Renmin chuban she, 1982, p. 182; Liu, *Clash of Empires*, p. 80.
19. Luke S. K. Kwong, 'What's In A Name: Zhongguo (Or "Middle Kingdom") Reconsidered', *Historical Journal*, 58/3 (2015), p. 799; Elisabeth Kaske, *The Politics of Language in Chinese Education: 1895–1919*, Leiden: Brill, 2008, p. 80.
20. Nicolas Tackett, *The Origins of the Chinese Nation: Song China and the Forging of an East Asian World Order*, Cambridge: Cambridge University Press, 2017, p. 3; Liu, *Clash of Empires*, p. 76, quoting Zhang, *Riben Guo Zhi*.
21. Julia C. Schneider, *Nation and Ethnicity: Chinese Discourses on History, Historiography, and Nationalism (1900s–1920s)*, Leiden: Brill, 2017, pp. 69–70.
22. John Fitzgerald, *Awakening China: Politics, Culture, and Class in the Nationalist Revolution*, Stanford, CA: Stanford University Press,1996, p. 117.
23. Viren Murthy, *The Political Philosophy of Zhang Taiyan: The Resistance of Consciousness*, Leiden: Brill, 2011, p. 67.
24. Ibid., p. 76.
25. Schneider, *Nation and Ethnicity*, p. 145.
26. Ibid., chapter 3.
27. Yunzhi Geng, *An Introductory Study on China's Cultural Transformation in Recent Times*, Berlin: Springer, 2015, p. 146.
28. Frank Dikötter (ed.), *The Construction of Racial Identities in China and Japan*, Hong Kong: Hong Kong University Press, 1997, p. 45.
29. Schneider, *Nation and Ethnicity*, pp. 222–3.
30. Harold Schiffrin, *Sun Yat-Sen and the Origins of the Chinese Revolution*, Berkeley, CA: University of California Press, 1968, chapter 2.
31. 驱逐鞑虏 [Qūzhú dá lǔ], 恢复中华 [Huīfù zhōnghuá] – with the Xingzhonghui's anti-Manchu oath rendered similarly with only a slight change to: 驱除鞑虏 [Qūchú dá lǔ], 恢复中华 [Huīfù zhōnghuá].
32. Tze-ki Hon, *Revolution as Restoration: Guocui Xuebao and China's Path to Modernity, 1905–1911*, Leiden: Brill, 2013, p. 3.
33. Kenji Shimada, *Pioneer of the Chinese Revolution: Zhang Binglin and Confucianism*, Stanford, CA: Stanford University Press, 1990, p. 20; Murthy, *Political Philosophy of Zhang Taiyan*, p. 110.
34. Liu, *Clash of Empires*, p. 77.
35. Schneider, *Nation and Ethnicity*, p. 154.
36. Ibid., p. 158.
37. Arif Dirlik, 'Born in Translation: "China" in the Making of "Zhongguo"', paper presented at Institute for Social Sciences of the University of California Davis, co-hosted by Kreddha, 22–24 September 2016.

2 THE INVENTION OF SOVEREIGNTY

1. John Vidal and Jonathan Watts, 'Agreement Finally Reached: Copenhagen 9.30 a.m., Saturday 19 December 2009', *The Observer*, 20 December 2009.
2. John M. Broder and Elisabeth Rosenthal, 'Obama Has Goal to Wrest a Deal in Climate Talks', *New York Times*, 17 December 2009.

3. Mark Lynas, 'How do I know China wrecked the Copenhagen deal? I was in the room', *The Guardian*, 22 December 2009.
4. Robert Falkner, 'The Paris Agreement and the New Logic of International Climate Politics', *International Affairs*, 92/5, pp. 1107–25 (2016).
5. François Godement, *Expanded Ambitions, Shrinking Achievements: How China Sees the Global Order*, London: European Council on Foreign Relations, 2017, p. 10.
6. Opening ceremony of the 19th CPC National Congress, http://live.china.org.cn/2017/10/17/opening-ceremony-of-the-19th-cpc-national-congress/
7. Jonathan Spence, *The Search for Modern China*, New York: W. W. Norton & Co., 2001, p. 122.
8. George R. Loehr, 'A. E. van Braam Houckgeest: The First American at the Court of China', *Princeton University Library Chronicle*, 15/4 (Summer 1954), pp. 179–93.
9. André Everard Van Braam Houckgeest, *An Authentic Account of the Embassy of the Dutch East-India Company, to the Court of the Emperor of China, in the Years 1794 and 1795* (Vol. 1), Cambridge: Cambridge University Press, 2011, p. 250. https://books.google.co.uk/books?id=KGxCAAAAcAAJ&dq
10. J. K. Fairbank, 'Tributary Trade and China's Relations with the West', *Far Eastern Quarterly*, 1/2 (February 1942), p. 135.
11. Zhiguang Yin, 'Heavenly Principles? The Translation of International Law in 19th-century China and the Constitution of Universality', *European Journal of International Law*, 27/4 (1 November 2016), pp. 1005–23.
12. Alejandra Irigoin, 'A Trojan Horse in Daoguang China? Explaining the Flows of Silver In and Out of China', LSE Working Paper No. 173/13, London School of Economics, 2013.
13. Jonathan Spence, *Chinese Roundabout: Essays in History and Culture*, New York: W. W. Norton, 1992, pp. 233–5.
14. Takeshi Hamashita, 'Tribute and Treaties: East Asian Treaty Ports Networks in the Era of Negotiation, 1834–1894', *European Journal of East Asian Studies*, 1/1 (2001), p. 61.
15. James M. Polachek, *The Inner Opium War*, Cambridge, MA: Harvard University Press, 1992, p. 2.
16. Alicia E. Neve Little, *Li Hung-Chang: His Life and Times* [1903], Cambridge: Cambridge University Press, 2010, p. 1.
17. Pär Kristoffer Cassel, *Grounds of Judgment: Extraterritoriality and Imperial Power in Nineteenth-Century China and Japan*, Oxford; New York: Oxford University Press, 2012.
18. Tobie Meyer-Fong, 'Urban Space and Civil War: Hefei, 1853–1854', *Frontiers of History in China*, 8/4 (2013), pp. 469–92.
19. Dong Wang, *China's Unequal Treaties: Narrating National History*, Lanham, MD: Lexington Books, 2005, p. 17.
20. S.C.M. Paine, *The Sino-Japanese War of 1894–1895: Perceptions, Power, and Primacy*, Cambridge: Cambridge University Press, 2005, pp. 70–71.
21. Ssu-yü Teng and John King Fairbank, *China's Response to the West: A Documentary Survey, 1839–1923*, Cambridge, MA: Harvard University Press, 1979, p. 47.
22. Richard J. Smith, *Robert Hart and China's Early Modernization: His Journals, 1863–1866*, Cambridge, MA: Harvard University Press, 1991, p. 99.
23. Pamela Kyle Crossley, *Orphan Warriors: Three Manchu Generations and the End of the Qing World*, Princeton, NJ: Princeton University Press, 1990, p. 143.
24. Smith, *Robert Hart and China's Early Modernization*, p. 100.
25. Kwang-ching Liu, 'The Confucian as Patriot and Pragmatist: Li Hung-chang's Formative Years, 1823–1866', *Harvard Journal of Asiatic Studies*, vol. 30 (1970), pp. 5–45.
26. Teng and Fairbank, *China's Response to the West*, p. 53.
27. Liu, 'The Confucian as Patriot and Pragmatist', p. 18.
28. Ibid., p. 30.
29. William Charles Wooldridge, 'Building and State Building in Nanjing after the Taiping Rebellion', *Late Imperial China*, 30/2 (2009), pp. 84–126.

30. Melissa Mouat, 'The Establishment of the Tongwen Guan and the Fragile Sino-British Peace of the 1860s', *Journal of World History*, 26/4 (2015), p. 741.
31. Ibid.
32. Smith, *Robert Hart and China's Early Modernization*, p. 283.
33. Yin, 'Heavenly Principles?', p. 1013.
34. Lydia Liu, *The Clash of Empires: The Invention of China in Modern World Making*, Cambridge, MA: Harvard University Press, 2004, p. 116.
35. Ibid., p. 128.
36. William A. Callahan, *Contingent States: Greater China and Transnational Relations*, Minneapolis; London: University of Minnesota Press, 2004, pp. 76–7.
37. Liu, *Clash of Empires*, p. 123.
38. Teng and Fairbank, *China's Response to the West*, p. 98.
39. Rune Svarverud, *International Law as World Order in Late Imperial China: Translation, Reception and Discourse 1847–1911*, Leiden: Brill, 2007, p. 91.
40. http://www.dartmouth.edu/~qing/WEB/WO-JEN.html
41. David Pong, *Shen Pao-chen and China's Modernization in the Nineteenth Century*, Cambridge: Cambridge University Press, 2009, p. 146.
42. Knight Biggerstaff, 'The Secret Correspondence of 1867–1868: Views of Leading Chinese Statesmen Regarding the Further Opening of China to Western Influence', *Journal of Modern History*, 22/2 (June 1950), pp. 122–36.
43. J. L. Cranmer-Byng, 'The Chinese Perception of World Order', *International Journal*, 24/1 (Winter 1968–9), pp. 166–71.
44. Chris Feige and Jeffrey A. Miron, 'The Opium Wars, Opium Legalization and Opium Consumption in China', *Applied Economics Letters*, 15/12 (2008), pp. 911–13.
45. Jennifer Rudolph, *Negotiated Power in Late Imperial China: The Zongli Yamen and the Politics of Reform*, Ithaca, NY: Cornell University East Asia Program, 2008, p. 222.
46. 'American Who Advised Li-Hung-Chang is Dead', *New York Times*, 21 December 1901.
47. 'Li Hung-Chang's American Secretary For 25 Years: A Power Behind The Throne In China', *St Louis Post-Dispatch*, 5 August 1900.
48. Michael H. Hunt, *The Making of a Special Relationship: The United States and China to 1914*, New York: Columbia University Press, 1983, p. 118; Chad Michael Berry, 'Looking for a Friend: Sino-U.S. Relations and Ulysses S. Grant's Mediation in the Ryukyu/Liuqiu 琉球 Dispute of 1879', thesis, University of Ohio, 2014, https://etd.ohiolink.edu/!etd.send_file?accession=osu1397610312&disposition=inline
49. Richard J. Smith, 'Li Hung-chang's Use of Foreign Military Talent: The Formative Period, 1862–1874', in Chu, Samuel C. and Kwang-ching Liu (eds), *Li Hung-chang and China's Early Modernization*, London: M.E. Sharpe, 1994, p. 137.
50. J. K. Fairbank and Merle Goldman, *China: A New History*, Cambridge, MA: Harvard University Press, 2006, p. 196.
51. J. L. Cranmer-Byng, 'The Chinese View of Their Place in the World: An Historical Perspective', *China Quarterly*, 53 (January–March 1973), pp. 67–79.
52. Jennifer Wayne Cushman, *Fields From the Sea: Chinese Junk Trade with Siam During the Late Eighteenth and Early Nineteenth Centuries*, Ithaca, NY: Cornell University Press, 1993, pp. 137–41.
53. Takeshi Hamashita 'The Tribute Trade System and Modern Asia', chapter 6 in Kenneth Pomeranz (ed.), *The Pacific in the Age of Early Industrialization*, Farnham: Ashgate, 2009.
54. Hyman Kublin, 'The Attitude of China during the Liu-ch'iu Controversy, 1871–1881', *Pacific Historical Review*, 18/2 (May 1949), pp. 213–31.
55. Liu, *Clash of Empires*, p. 106; Svarverud, *International Law as World Order*, p. 93.
56. Li Hongzhang, 'Fu He Zi'e' 覆何子峨 ('Reply to He Zi'e [He Ru Zhang]'), 30 May 1878, in Li Wenzhong gong quanzi: Yeshu han'gao 李文忠公全集:譯署函稿 (Complete Works of Li Wenzhong [Li Hongzhang]: Translation Office Letters), vol. 5, Taipei: Wenhai chubanshe (1962), 8/4, p. 191.

57. The Sino-Japanese Friendship, Commerce and Navigation Treaty, 13 September 1871, http://www.fas.nus.edu.sg/hist/eia/documents_archive/tientsin-treaty.php
58. Letter from Ulysses S. Grant to Adolph E. Borie, 6 June 1879, *The Papers of Ulysses S. Grant*: October 1, 1878–September 30, 1880, p. 146, https://books.google.co.uk/books?id=3zBLjHeAGB0C&l
59. Hunt, *Making of a Special Relationship*, p. 121.
60. Charles Oscar Paullin, 'The Opening of Korea by Commodore Shufeldt', *Political Science Quarterly*, 25/3 (September 1910), pp. 470–99.
61. *The Directory and Chronicle for China, Japan, Corea, Indo-China, Straits Settlements, Malay States, Sian, Netherlands India, Borneo, the Philippines, &c*, Hongkong Daily Press Office, 1882, p. 319; U.S. Government Printing Office, 1876 House Documents, Volume 15; Volume 284, p. 263.
62. Oscar Chapuis, *The Last Emperors of Vietnam: From Tu Duc to Bao Dai*, Westport, CT: Greenwood Press, 2000, p. 61.
63. Bradley Camp Davis, *Imperial Bandits: Outlaws and Rebels in the China-Vietnam Borderlands*, Seattle: University of Washington Press, 2016.
64. 'Peking Dispatch no. 230 (confidential)', 8 August 1883, quoted in Robert Hopkins Miller, *The United States and Vietnam 1787–1941*, Forest Grove, OR: University Press of the Pacific, 2005, pp. 95–6.
65. K. W. Taylor, *A History of the Vietnamese*, Cambridge: Cambridge University Press, 2013, p. 475.
66. *The Directory and Chronicle for China, Japan, Corea, Indo-China, Straits Settlements, Malay States, Sian, Netherlands India, Borneo, the Philippines &c*, Hongkong Daily Press Office, 1888.
67. J.J.G. Syatauw, *Some Newly Established Asian States and the Development of International Law*, The Hague: Martinus Nijhoff, 1961, p. 123; Frank Trager, 'Burma and China', *Journal of Southeast Asian History*, 5/1 (1964), p. 39.
68. Paine, *Sino-Japanese War of 1894–1895*, p. 191.
69. Ibid., p. 121.
70. Niki Alsford, *Transitions to Modernity in Taiwan: The Spirit of 1895 and the Cession of Formosa to Japan*, London: Routledge, 2017.
71. Yi Wang, 'Wang Huning: Xi Jinping's Reluctant Propagandist', www.limesonline.com, 4 April 2019, http://www.limesonline.com/en/wang-huning-xi-jinpings-reluctant-propagandist
72. Haig Patapan and Yi Wang, 'The Hidden Ruler: Wang Huning and the Making of Contemporary China', *Journal of Contemporary China*, 27/109 (2018), pp. 54–5.

3 THE INVENTION OF THE HAN RACE

1. Lia Zhu, 'Families Thanked For Opening Homes', *China Daily USA*, 7 December 2015, http://usa.chinadaily.com.cn/us/2015-12/07/content_22653417.htm
2. Yap Jia Hee, 'Chinese Ambassador Visits Petaling Street on Eve of Rally', *MalaysiaKini*, 25 September 2015, https://www.malaysiakini.com/news/313484; ChinaPress.com.my, '"亲望亲好，邻望邻好" 黄惠康：两国关系良好', 28 September 2015, http://www.chinapress.com.my/20150928/親望親好鄰望鄰好黃惠康兩國關係良好
3. China News Network, 'The Overseas Chinese Affairs Office Will Build 60 "China Aid Centers" Around the World', 19 March 2014.
4. Xinhua, 'Central Committee of the Communist Party of China Issues "Regulations on Chinese Communist Party United Front Work (Trial)"', 22 September 2015, translation, http://www.xinhuanet.com/politics/2015-09/22/c_1116645297_5.htm
5. James Kynge, Lucy Hornby and Jamil Anderlini, 'Inside China's Secret "Magic Weapon" for Worldwide Influence,' *Financial Times*, 26 October 2017, https://www.ft.com/content/fb2b3934-b004-11e7-beba-5521c713abf4
6. Xi Jinping, 'Secure a Decisive Victory in Building a Moderately Prosperous Society in All Respects and Strive for the Great Success of Socialism with Chinese Characteristics for a

New Era,' 19th National Congress of the Communist Party of China, Beijing, 18 October 2017, http://www.xinhuanet.com//politics/19cpcnc/2017-10/27/c_1121867529.htm
7. Wang Gungwu, *Community and Nation: Essays on Southeast Asia and the Chinese*, Singapore: Heinemann Educational Books (Asia), 1981, pp. 123–5.
8. Wang Gungwu, 'A Note on the Origins of Hua-ch'iao', in Wang, *Community and Nation*, pp. 118–27.
9. Huang Jianli, 'Chinese Overseas and China's International Relations', in Zheng Yongnian (ed.), *China and International Relations: The Chinese View and the Contribution of Wang Gungwu*, London: Routledge, 2010, p. 147.
10. An Baijie, 'Overseas Chinese Can Help Build Belt, Road', *China Daily*, 13 June 2013, http://www.chinadaily.com.cn/china/2017-06/13/content_29719481.htm
11. Harry J. Lamley, 'Hsieh-Tou: The Pathology of Violence in Southeastern China', *Ch'ing-shih wen-t'I*, 3/7 (1977), pp. 1–39, https://muse.jhu.edu/ (accessed 14 January 2019).
12. May-bo Ching, 'Literary, Ethnic or Territorial? Definitions of Guangdong Culture in the Late Qing and Early Republic', in Tao Tao Liu and David Faure (eds), *Unity and Diversity: Local Cultures and Identities in China*, Hong Kong: Hong Kong University Press, 1996. p. 58; Jessieca Leo, *Global Hakka: Hakka Identity in the Remaking*, Leiden: Brill, 2015, p. 47.
13. Michael Keevak, *Becoming Yellow: A Short History of Racial Thinking*, Princeton, NJ: Princeton University Press, 2011, pp. 57–65.
14. Chow Kai-wing, 'Imagining Boundaries of Blood: Zhang Binglin and the Invention of the Han "Race" in Modern China', in Frank Dikötter (ed.), *The Construction of Racial Identities in China and Japan*, London: Hurst & Co., 1997.
15. Pamela Kyle Crossley, 'The Qianlong Retrospect on the Chinese-martial (*hanjun*) Banners', *Late Imperial China*, 10/1 (June 1989), pp. 63–107.
16. Yang Shao-Yun, 'Becoming Zhongguo, Becoming Han: Tracing and Reconceptualizing Ethnicity in Ancient North China, 770 BC–AD 581', MA thesis, National University of Singapore, 2007.
17. Edward Rhoads, *Manchus and Han: Ethnic Relations and Political Power in Late Qing and Early Republican China, 1861–1928*, Seattle: University of Washington Press, 2000, chapter 1.
18. Herbert Spencer, *The Principles of Biology*, volume 1, London: Williams & Norgate, 1864–7, p. 444.
19. Herbert Spencer, *Social Statics*, New York: D. Appleton & Co., 1865, p. 46.
20. Michio Nagai, 'Herbert Spencer in Early Meiji Japan', *Far Eastern Quarterly*, 14/1 (1954), pp. 55–64. Nagai was later Japan's minister of education.
21. Noriko Kamachi, *Reform in China: Huang Tsun-hsien and the Japanese Model*, Cambridge, MA: Harvard University Press, 1981, pp. 3–29.
22. Frank Dikötter, *The Discourse of Race in Modern China*, Oxford: Oxford University Press, 2015, p. 41.
23. Kamachi, *Reform in China*, p. 300, fn 49.
24. J. D. Schmidt, *Within the Human Realm: The Poetry of Huang Zunxian 1848–1905*, Cambridge: Cambridge University Press, 1994, p. 246.
25. Benjamin I. Schwartz, *In Search of Wealth and Power: Yen Fu and the West*, Cambridge, MA: Harvard University Press, 1964, pp. 22–6.
26. David Pong, *Shen Pao-chen and China's Modernization in the Nineteenth Century*, Cambridge: Cambridge University Press, 2009, pp. 108–28.
27. Benjamin A. Elman, 'Toward a History of Modern Science in Republican China', in Jing Tsu and Benjamin A. Elman (eds), *Science and Technology in Modern China, 1880s–1940s*, Leiden: Brill, 2014, p. 22.
28. Junyu Shao, '"Chinese Learning for Fundamental Structure, Western Learning for Practical Use?" The Development of Late Nineteenth Century Chinese Steam Navy Revisited', unpublished PhD thesis, King's College, London, 2015, p. 117.
29. Schwartz, *In Search of Wealth and Power*, p. 33.
30. Herbert Spencer, *The Study of Sociology*, London: Henry S. King & Co., 1873, pp. 34–5.
31. Ibid., pp. 193–4.

32. Melissa Mouat, 'The Establishment of the Tongwen Guan and the Fragile Sino-British Peace of the 1860s', *Journal of World History*, 26/4 (2015), p. 745.
33. Schwartz, *In Search of Wealth and Power*, p. 33.
34. James Reeve Pusey, *China and Charles Darwin*, Cambridge, MA: Harvard University Press, 1983, p. 8.
35. Ibid., p. 61.
36. Schmidt, *Within the Human Realm*, p. 17.
37. Schwartz, *In Search of Wealth and Power*, p. 82.
38. Pusey, *China and Charles Darwin*, p. 67.
39. 'Àodàlìyǎ huáqiáo huárén jǔxíng gōng bài xuānyuán huángdì dàdiǎn' (Australian overseas Chinese hold a ceremony to worship the Xuanyuan Yellow Emperor), 16 April 2018, http://www.zytzb.gov.cn/gathwxw/42451.jhtml
40. Chen Mingjie, 'Major Ceremonies to Worship the Yellow Emperor Held Majestically Around the Globe', *China Times*, 16 April 2018, https://www.chinatimes.com/cn/newspapers/20180416000149-260302
41. Dikötter, *Discourse of Race*, p. 101.
42. Chow, 'Imagining Boundaries of Blood'.
43. Dikötter, *Discourse of Race*, p. 70.
44. Schwartz, *In Search of Wealth and Power*, p. 184.
45. May-bo Ching, 'Classifying Peoples: Ethnic Politics in Late Qing Native-place Textbooks and Gazetteers', in Tze-ki Hon and Robert Culp (eds), *The Politics of Historical Production in Late Qing and Republican China*, Leiden: Brill, 2007, pp. 69–70.
46. Ching, 'Literary, Ethnic or Territorial?'; Ching, 'Classifying Peoples', pp. 69–70.
47. Laurence A. Schneider, *Ku Chieh-kang and China's New History: Nationalism and the Quest for Alternative Traditions*, Berkeley, CA: University of California Press, 1971, pp. 34–5.

4 THE INVENTION OF CHINESE HISTORY

1. http://www.iqh.net.cn/english/Classlist.asp?column_id=65&column_cat_id=37 (accessed 2 March 2020).
2. Pamela Kyle Crossley, 'Xi's China Is Steamrolling Its Own History', ForeignPolicy.com, 29 January 2019.
3. Zhou Ailian and Hu Zhongliang, 'The Project of Organizing the Qing Archives', *Chinese Studies in History*, 43/2 (2009), pp. 73–84.
4. 'Firmly Grasp the Right of Discourse of the History of the Qing Dynasty', *People's Daily*, 14 January 2019, http://opinion.people.com.cn/n1/2019/0114/c1003-30524940.html (accessed 2 March 2020).
5. Thomas Jansen, *Timothy Richard (1845–1919): Welsh Missionary, Educator and Reformer in China*, Swansea: Confucius Institute at the University of Wales – Trinity Saint David, 2014.
6. Society for the Diffusion of Christian and General Knowledge Among the Chinese, Eleventh Annual Report, Shanghai, 1898.
7. Eunice Johnson, *Timothy Richard's Vision: Education and Reform in China, 1880–1910*, Eugene, OR: Pickwick Publications, 2014, pp. 67–8.
8. Mary Mazur, 'Discontinuous Continuity: New History in 20th Century China', in Tze-ki Hon and Robert Culp (eds), *The Politics of Historical Production in Late Qing and Republican China*, Leiden: Brill, 2007, p. 116; Johnson, *Timothy Richard's Vision*, p. 65.
9. Xiantao Zhang, *The Origins of the Modern Chinese Press: The Influence of the Protestant Missionary Press in Late Qing China*, London: Routledge, 2007, pp. 67–8.
10. Johnson, *Timothy Richard's Vision*, p. 60.
11. Harriet T. Zurndorfer, 'Wang Zhaoyang (1763–1851) and the Erasure of "Talented Women" by Liang Qichao', in Nanxiu Qian, Grace Fong and Richard Smith (eds), *Different Worlds of Discourse: Transformations of Gender and Genre in Late Qing and Early Republican China*, Leiden: Brill, 2008.

12. Yuntao Zhang, 'Western Missionaries and Origins of the Modern Chinese Press', in Gary D. Rawnsley and Ming-yeh T. Rawnsley (eds), *Routledge Handbook of Chinese Media*, London: Routledge, 2018, pp. 73–4
13. Johnson, *Timothy Richard's Vision*, p. 69.
14. *Shiwu Bao*, No. 26, 1897.
15. Joseph Richmond Levenson, *Liang Ch'i-ch'ao and the Mind of Modern China*, Cambridge, MA: Harvard University Press, 1953, pp. 31–2.
16. Xiaobing Tang, *Global Space and the Nationalist Discourse of Modernity: The Historical Thinking of Liang Qichao*, Stanford, CA: Stanford University Press, 1996, p. 15.
17. Rebecca E. Karl, *Staging the World: Chinese Nationalism at the Turn of the Twentieth Century*, Durham, NC; London: Duke University Press, 2002, pp. 69–70.
18. Tang, *Global Space*, pp. 34–5.
19. Ibid., p. 33.
20. Xu Jilin, 'Tianxia-ism, the Distinction Between the Civilised and Uncivilised, and Their Variations in Modern China', in Gao Ruiquan and Wu Guanjun (eds), *Chinese History and Literature: New Ways to Examine China's Past*, Singapore: World Scientific Publishing, 2018, p. 137.
21. Peter Zarrow, 'Old Myth into New History: The Building Blocks of Liang Qichao's "New History"', *Historiography East and West*, 1/2 (2003), p. 228.
22. Schneider, Julia C., *Nation and Ethnicity: Chinese Discourses on History, Historiography, and Nationalism (1900s–1920s)*, Leiden: Brill, 2017, p. 98.
23. Tang, *Global Space*, pp. 44–5; Rebecca E. Karl, 'Creating Asia: China in the World at the Beginning of the Twentieth Century', *American Historical Review*, 103/4 (1998), p. 1098.
24. Tang, *Global Space*, p. 47.
25. Ibid., p. 62.
26. Zarrow, 'Old Myth into New History', p. 211.
27. Schneider, *Nation and Ethnicity*, p. 106.
28. Tang, *Global Space*, p. 242.
29. Schneider, *Nation and Ethnicity*, pp. 107–8.
30. Ibid., p. 108.
31. Ibid., p. 87.
32. Ibid., p. 90.
33. Ibid., p. 98.
34. Ibid., p. 100.
35. Ibid., p. 121.
36. Tze-ki Hon, 'Educating the Citizens', in Tze-ki Hon and Robert Culp (eds), *The Politics of Historical Production in Late Qing and Republican China*, Leiden: Brill, 2007, p. 83.
37. Lü Junhua, 'Beijing's Old and Dilapidated Housing Renewal', *Cities*, 14/2 (1997), pp. 59-69.
38. Xinhua, 'Over 500 Confucius Institutes Founded in 142 Countries, Regions', *China Daily*, 7 October 2017, http://www.chinadaily.com.cn/china/2017-10/07/content_32950016.htm
39. Office of the Chinese Language Council International, *Common Knowledge About Chinese History*, Beijing: Higher Education Press, 2006, pp. 123, 138.
40. Hidehiro Okada, 'China as a Successor State to the Mongol Empire', in Reuven Amitai-Preiss and David O. Morgan (eds), *The Mongol Empire and Its Legacy*, Leiden: Brill, 1999, pp. 260–72.
41. Naomi Standen (ed.), *Demystifying China: New Understandings of Chinese History*, Lanham, MD: Rowman & Littlefield, 2013.
42. Tim Barrett, 'Chinese History as a Constructed Continuity: The Work of Rao Zongyi', in Peter Lambert and Björn Weiler (eds), *How the Past was Used: Historical Cultures, c. 750–2000*, Oxford: Oxford University Press, 2017, chapter 11.
43. Johnson, *Timothy Richard's Vision*, p. 124.
44. Eleanor Richard, 'A Foster Father of the League of Nations', *Peking and Tientsin Times*, March 1919.
45. Limin Bai, 'Reappraising Modernity after the Great War' (blog post), 17 September 2015, National Library of New Zealand.

46. Tang, *Global Space*, p. 175.
47. Richard, 'A Foster Father'.
48. Handwritten page from Dr Wyre Lewis's box at the National Library of Wales relating to Liang Ch'i-ch'ao's visit to Timothy Richard at Golders Green in London. Many thanks to Eunice Johnson, Jennifer Peles, Peter Thomas and Meryl Thomas for locating this document.
49. Jonathan D. Spence, *The Gate of Heavenly Peace: The Chinese and Their Revolution*, Harmondsworth: Penguin, 1982, p. 115.
50. Bruce Elleman, *Wilson and China: A Revised History of the Shandong Question*, Armonk, NY: M.E. Sharpe, 2002, pp. 24–9
51. Erez Manela, *The Wilsonian Moment: Self-Determination and the International Origins of Anticolonial Nationalism*, Oxford: Oxford University Press, 2007, pp. 114–17.

5 THE INVENTION OF THE CHINESE NATION

1. United Front Work Leading Group Office of the Tibet Autonomous Region Committee of the Communist Party of China, 'Panchen Erdeni Visits Shannan for Buddhist Activities', 28 August 2018, http://www.xztzb.gov.cn/news/1535419327828.shtml (accessed 2 March 2020).
2. W.J.F. Jenner, 'Race and History in China', *New Left Review*, 1 September 2001, p. 55.
3. Chiang Kai-shek, *China's Destiny*, Westport, CT: Greenwood Press, 1985, p. 13.
4. Thomas Mullaney, *Coming to Terms with the Nation: Ethnic Classification in Modern China*, Berkeley, CA: University of California Press, 2011.
5. Jenner, 'Race and History in China', p. 77.
6. Lai To Lee and Hock Guan Lee (eds), *Sun Yat-Sen, Nanyang and the 1911 Revolution*, Singapore: Institute of Southeast Asian Studies, 2011, pp. 18–19.
7. Patrick Anderson, *The Lost Book of Sun Yatsen and Edwin Collins*, London: Routledge, 2016, pp. 22–3.
8. *Daily News*, 'The Politics of Sun Yat-sen: Why His Head is in Peril', 26 October 1896, quoted in Anderson, *Lost Book of Sun Yatsen*, p. 15.
9. Harold Schiffrin, *Sun Yat-sen and the Origins of the Chinese Revolution*, Berkeley, CA: University of California Press, 1968, p. 128.
10. Marie-Claire Bergère (trans. Janet Lloyd), *Sun Yat-sen*, Stanford, CA: Stanford University Press, 1998, pp. 65–6.
11. James Leibold, 'Positioning "Minzu" Within Sun Yat-Sen's Discourse Of Minzuzhuyi', *Journal of Asian History*, 38/2 (2004), p. 168.
12. Schiffrin, *Sun Yat-sen*, p. 139.
13. Ibid., p. 148.
14. Bergère, *Sun Yat-sen*, pp. 77–8.
15. Leibold, 'Positioning "Minzu" ', p. 170.
16. Kenji Shimada, *Pioneer of the Chinese Revolution: Zhang Binglin and Confucianism*, Stanford, CA: Stanford University Press, 1990, p. 28.
17. Julia C. Schneider, *Nation and Ethnicity: Chinese Discourses on History, Historiography, and Nationalism (1900s–1920s)*, Leiden: Brill, 2017, pp. 80–82.
18. Cheng Zhongping, 'Kang Youwei's Activities in Canada and the Reformist Movement Among the Global Chinese Diaspora, 1899–1909', *Twentieth-Century China*, 39/1 (2014).
19. 'Jane Leung Larson, 'Kang Youwei: A Drifting Stranger from 20,000 Li Away', *Baohanghui Scholarship* (blog) 2 June 2013, https://baohuanghui.blogspot.com/2013/06/a-drifting-stranger-from-20000-li-away.html (accessed 2 March 2020).
20. Jonathan D. Spence, *The Gate of Heavenly Peace: The Chinese and Their Revolution*, Harmondsworth: Penguin, 1982, pp. 35–6.
21. Frank Dikötter, *The Discourse of Race in Modern China*. Oxford: Oxford University Press, 2015, p. 56.
22. Marc Andre Matten, *Imagining a Postnational World: Hegemony and Space in Modern China*, Leiden: Brill, 2016, p. 241.

23. 'Life and Legacy of Kang Tongbi', Barnard, https://barnard.edu/headlines/life-and-legacy-kang-tongbi
24. Xiaobing Tang, *Global Space and the Nationalist Discourse of Modernity: The Historical Thinking of Liang Qichao*, Stanford, CA: Stanford University Press, 1996, p. 139.
25. Zou Rong, *The Revolutionary Army: A Chinese Nationalist Tract of 1903*, Paris: Éditions de l'École des Hautes Études en Sciences Sociales, 1968, p. 58.
26. Leibold, 'Positioning "Minzu" ', p. 174.
27. Ibid., p. 186.
28. So Wai Chor, 'National Identity, Nation and Race: Wang Jingwei's Early Revolutionary Ideas, 1905–1911', *Journal of Modern Chinese History*, 4/1 (2010), pp. 63–7.
29. Leibold, 'Positioning "Minzu" ', p. 176.
30. Ma Mingde, 'Tang Hualong in the 1911 Revolution', in Joseph W. Esherick and C. X. George Wei (eds), *China: How the Empire Fell*, London; New York: Routledge, 2013, p. 141.
31. James Leibold, 'Xinhai Remembered: From Han Racial Revolution to Great Revival of the Chinese Nation', *Asian Ethnicity*, 15/1 (2014), p. 3.
32. Edward Rhoads, *Manchus and Han: Ethnic Relations and Political Power in Late Qing and Early Republican China, 1861–1928*, Seattle: University of Washington Press, 2000.
33. Ibid., pp. 114–16.
34. Pamela Kyle Crossley, *A Translucent Mirror: History and Identity in Qing Imperial History*, Oakland, CA: University of California Press, 1999.
35. Gray Tuttle, *Tibetan Buddhists in the Making of Modern China*, New York: Columbia University Press, 2007, p. 61.
36. Rhoads, *Manchus and Han*, p. 214.
37. Leibold, 'Positioning "Minzu" ', p. 180.
38. Tuttle, *Tibetan Buddhists*, p. 62.
39. Tjio Kayloe, *The Unfinished Revolution: Sun Yat-Sen and the Struggle for Modern China*, Singapore: Marshall Cavendish International (Asia), 2018.
40. Henrietta Harrison, *The Making of the Republican Citizen: Political Ceremonies and Symbols in China 1911–1929*, Oxford: Oxford University Press, 2000, p. 101.
41. Li Xizhu, 'Provincial Officials in 1911/12', in Joseph W. Esherick and C. X. George Wei (eds), *China: How the Empire Fell*, London; New York: Routledge, 2013.
42. Leibold, 'Positioning "Minzu" ', p. 181.
43. Tuttle, *Tibetan Buddhists*, p. 64.
44. Bergère, *Sun Yat-sen*, p. 228.
45. Leibold, 'Positioning "Minzu" ', pp. 184–6.
46. Bergère, *Sun Yat-sen*, p. 236.
47. Richard Louis Edmonds, 'The Legacy of Sun Yat-Sen's Railway Plans', *China Quarterly*, 421 (1987).
48. Leibold, 'Positioning "Minzu" ', p. 197.
49. Ibid., p. 191.
50. James Leibold, *Reconfiguring Chinese Nationalism: How the Qing Frontier and its Indigenes Became Chinese*, Basingstoke: Palgrave Macmillan, 2007, p. 58.
51. Edmonds, 'Legacy of Sun Yat-Sen's Railway Plans'.
52. Chien-peng Chung, 'Comparing China's Frontier Politics: How Much Difference Did a Century Make?', *Nationalities Papers*, 46/1 (2018), p. 166.
53. Leibold, 'Positioning "Minzu" ', p. 183.
54. Xinhua, 'Slandering Xinjiang as "No Rights Zone" Against Fact, Chinese Official Told UN Panel', ChinaDaily.com, 14 August 2018, http://www.chinadaily.com.cn/a/201808/14/WS5b7260a6a310add14f385a92.html
55. James Leibold, 'Hu the Uniter: Hu Lianhe and the Radical Turn in China's Xinjiang Policy', *ChinaBrief*, 18/16 (10 October 2018).
56. James Leibold, 'The Spectre of Insecurity: The CCP's Mass Internment Strategy in Xinjiang', *China Leadership Monitor*, Hoover Institution (1 March 2019).

57. James Leibold, 'A Family Divided: The CCP's Central Ethnic Work Conference', *ChinaBrief*, 14/21, Hoover Institution (7 November 2014).

6 THE INVENTION OF THE CHINESE LANGUAGE

1. Xinhua, 'Proposal for News in Mandarin Angers Guangzhou Citizens', 9 July 2010, http://www.china.org.cn/china/2010-07/09/content_20463001.htm; Sihua Liang, *Language Attitudes and Identities in Multilingual China: A Linguistic Ethnography*, Cham: Springer, 2015, pp. 5–6.
2. Xuesong Gao, '"Cantonese is Not a Dialect" : Chinese Netizens' Defence of Cantonese as a Regional Lingua Franca', *Journal of Multilingual and Multicultural Development*, 33/5 (2012), p. 459.
3. Ibid., p. 459.
4. Verna Yu and *SCMP* Reporter, 'Hundreds Defy Orders Not to Rally in Defence of Cantonese', *South China Morning Post*, 2 August 2010, https://www.scmp.com/article/721128/hundreds-defy-orders-not-rally-defence-cantonese
5. Rona Y. Ji, 'Preserving Cantonese Television & Film in Guangdong: Language as Cultural Heritage in South China's Bidialectal Landscape', *Inquiries Journal*, 8/12 (2016), http://www.inquiriesjournal.com/articles/1506/3/preserving-cantonese-television-and-film-in-guangdong-language-as-cultural-heritage-in-south-chinas-bidialectal-landscape
6. Mimi Lau, 'Guangdong TV News Channel Quietly Changing from Cantonese to Putonghua', *South China Morning Post*, 11 July 2014, https://www.scmp.com/news/china/article/1552398/guangdong-tv-news-channel-quietly-changing-cantonese-putonghua
7. Xinhua, 'China to Increase Mandarin Speaking Rate to 80%', 3 April 2017, http://english.gov.cn/state_council/ministries/2017/04/03/content_281475615766970.htm
8. Minglang Zhou and Hongkai Sun (eds), *Language Policy in the People's Republic of China: Theory and Practice Since 1949*, Boston; London: Kluwer Academic Publishers, 2004, p. 30.
9. Dan Xu and Hui Li, 'Introduction', in Dan Xu and Hui Li (eds), *Languages and Genes in Northwestern China and Adjacent Regions*, Singapore: Springer, 2017, p. 3.
10. Stephen Chen, 'Beyond the Yellow River: DNA Tells New Story of the Origins of Han Chinese', *South China Morning Post*, 23 May 2019.
11. Jerry Norman, *Chinese*, Cambridge: Cambridge University Press, 1988, chapter 1.
12. Victor H. Mair, 'What is a Chinese "Dialect/Topolect"?', *Sino-Platonic Papers*, 29 (September 1991).
13. Norman, *Chinese*, pp. 2; 183.
14. Ibid., pp. 15–16.
15. Elisabeth Kaske, *The Politics of Language in Chinese Education: 1895–1919*, Leiden: Brill, 2008, p. 32.
16. Mair, 'What is a Chinese "Dialect/Topolect"?', pp. 11–12.
17. Murata Yujiro, 'The Late Qing "National Language" Issue and Monolingual Systems: Focusing on Political Diplomacy', *Chinese Studies in History*, 49/3 (2016), pp. 108–25.
18. Kaske, *Politics of Language*, pp. 24–6.
19. Ibid., pp. 91–3.
20. John DeFrancis, *Nationalism and Language Reform in China*, Princeton, NJ: Princeton University Press, 1950, p. 33.
21. Yixue Yang, 'Language Reform and Nation Building in Twentieth-Century China', *Sino-Platonic Papers*, 264 (December 2016), pp. 74–6.
22. Ni Haishu, 'Qieyinzi', in *Zhongguo da baike quanshu, Yuyan wenzi*, Beijing/Shanghai: Zhongguo da baike quanshu chubanshe, 1988, pp. 315–17, http://www.chinaknowledge.de/Literature/Script/qieyin.html
23. Jing Tsu, *Sound and Script in Chinese Diaspora*, Cambridge, MA: Harvard University Press, 2010, p. 23.
24. Kaske, *Politics of Language*, p. 146.

25. Quoted in ibid., p. 122.
26. Ibid., p. 366.
27. Ibid., pp. 356–7.
28. Ibid., p. 378.
29. Ibid., p. 292.
30. Ibid., p. 293.
31. Christopher Rea, *The Age of Irreverence: A New History of Laughter in China*, Oakland, CA: University of California Press, 2015, pp. 97–101.
32. Kaske, *Politics of Language*, pp. 407; 410.
33. DeFrancis, *Nationalism and Language Reform*, p. 57.
34. Tsu, *Sound and Script*, p. 194; S. Robert Ramsey, *The Languages of China*, Princeton, NJ: Princeton University Press, 1987, pp. 7–8.
35. DeFrancis, *Nationalism and Language Reform*, p. 66.
36. Kaske, *Politics of Language*, p. 428; Peter Peverelli, *The History of Modern Chinese Grammar Studies*, Berlin: Springer, 2015, p. 28.
37. Kaske, *Politics of Language*, p. 463; Peverelli, *History of Modern Chinese Grammar Studies*, pp. 28–9.
38. Quoted in Tsu, *Sound and Script*, p. 196.
39. David Moser, *A Billion Voices: China's Search for a Common Language*, London: Penguin Books, 2016, p. 27.
40. John DeFrancis, 'Language and Script Reform in China', in Joshua A. Fishman (ed.), *Advances in the Sociology of Language, vol. II: Selected Studies and Applications*, The Hague; Paris: Mouton, 1972, p. 458.
41. Harriet C. Mills, 'Language Reform in China: Some Recent Developments', *Far Eastern Quarterly*, 15/4 (August 1956), pp. 521–7.
42. *People's Daily*, 26 October 1955, quoted in Longsheng Guo, 'The Relationship Between Putonghua and Chinese Dialects', in Minglang Zhou and Hongkai Sun (eds), *Language Policy in the People's Republic of China: Theory and Practice Since 1949*, Boston; London: Kluwer Academic Publishers, 2004, pp. 45–6.
43. Yanyan Li, 'The Teaching of Shanghainese in Kindergartens', PhD dissertation, Benerd School of Education, 2015, pp. 49–52.
44. Qing Shao and Xuesong (Andy) Gao, 'Protecting Language or Promoting Dis-citizenship? A Poststructural Policy Analysis of the Shanghainese Heritage Project', *International Journal of Bilingual Education and Bilingualism*, 22/3 (2019), pp. 352–64.
45. Mark MacKinnon, 'Mandarin Pushing Out Cantonese', *Globe and Mail* (Toronto), 20 November 2009, https://www.theglobeandmail.com/news/world/mandarin-pushing-out-cantonese/article4293285; He Huifeng, 'Why Has Cantonese Fallen Out of Favour with Guangzhou Youngsters?', *South China Morning Post*, 12 March 2018, https://www.scmp.com/news/china/society/article/2136237/why-has-cantonese-fallen-out-favour-guangzhou-youngsters
46. Shao and Gao, 'Protecting Language', p. 357.
47. Moser, *A Billion Voices*, p. 90.
48. Quoted in Natalia Riva 'Putonghua and Language Harmony: China's Resources of Cultural Soft Power', *Critical Arts*, 31/6 (2017), pp. 92–108.

7 THE INVENTION OF A NATIONAL TERRITORY

1. Gap Inc., Gap Inc. Company-Operated Store Count by Country 2017, http://www.gapinc.com/content/dam/gapincsite/documents/Gap%20Inc.%20Company%20Owned%20Store%20Count%20by%20Country.pdf; Gap Inc., Gap Inc. Factory List April 2019, https://www.gapincsustainability.com/sites/default/files/Gap%20Inc%20Factory%20List.pdf (accessed 2 March 2020).
2. 'MAC Apologizes for Omitting Taiwan on Map of China in Promotional Email', *Global Times*, 10 March 2019, http://www.globaltimes.cn/content/1141581.shtml

3. Christian Shepherd, 'China Revises Mapping Law to Bolster Territorial Claims', Reuters, 27 April 2017.
4. Zhang Han, 'China Strengthens Map Printing Rules, Forbidding Publications Printed For Overseas Clients From Being Circulated in the Country', *Global Times*, 17 February 2019.
5. Laurie Chen, 'Chinese City Shreds 29,000 Maps Showing Taiwan as a Country', *South China Morning Post*, 25 March 2019, https://www.scmp.com/news/china/society/article/3003121/about-29000-problematic-world-maps-showing-taiwan-country
6. A. J. Grajdanzev, 'Formosa (Taiwan) Under Japanese Rule', *Pacific Affairs*, 15/3 (September 1942), p. 312; Andrew Morris, 'The Taiwan Republic of 1895 and the Failure of the Qing Modernizing Project', in Stéphane Corcuff and Robert Edmondson (eds), *Memories of the Future: National Identity Issues and the Search for a New Taiwan*, Armonk, NY: M.E. Sharpe, 2002; Harry J. Lamley, 'The 1895 Taiwan Republic: A Significant Episode in Modern Chinese History', *Journal of Asian Studies*, 27/4 (1968), pp. 739–62
7. Alan M. Wachman, *Why Taiwan? Geostrategic Rationales for China's Territorial Integrity*, Stanford, CA: Stanford University Press, 2007, p. 69.
8. Ibid., pp. 50–60.
9. S.C.M. Paine, *Imperial Rivals: China, Russia, and Their Disputed Frontier*, Armonk, NY: M.E. Sharpe, 1996, p. 352.
10. Marie-Claire Bergère (trans. Janet Lloyd), *Sun Yat-sen*, Stanford, CA: Stanford University Press, 1998, pp. 92–6.
11. Shi-Chi Mike Lan, 'The Ambivalence of National Imagination: Defining "The Taiwanese" in China, 1931–1941', *China Journal*, 64 (2010), p. 179.
12. Marc Andre Matten, *Imagining a Postnational World: Hegemony and Space in Modern China*, Leiden: Brill, 2016, p. 126.
13. Jingdong Yu, 'The Concept of "Territory" in Modern China: 1689–1910', *Cultura: International Journal of Philosophy of Culture and Axiology*, 15/2 (2018), pp. 73–95.
14. So Wai Chor, 'National Identity, Nation and Race: Wang Jingwei's Early Revolutionary Ideas, 1905–1911', *Journal of Modern Chinese History*, 4/1 (2010), p. 73.
15. Matten, *Imagining a Postnational World*, pp. 88–9.
16. Republic of China, 'The Provisional Constitution of the Republic of China', *American Journal of International Law*, 6/3, Supplement: Official Documents (July 1912), pp. 149–54.
17. William L. Tung, *The Political Institutions of Modern China*, The Hague: M. Nijhoff, 1964, p. 326.
18. Matten, *Imagining a Postnational World*, p. 152. But see Tung, *Political Institutions of Modern China*, p. 332, for an alternative translation.
19. Matten, *Imagining a Postnational World*, p. 152; Tung, *Political Institutions of Modern China*, p. 344.
20. Tung, *Political Institutions of Modern China*, p. 350; Matten, *Imagining a Postnational World*, pp. 152–3.
21. James Leibold, *Reconfiguring Chinese Nationalism: How the Qing Frontier and its Indigenes Became Chinese*, Basingstoke: Palgrave Macmillan, 2007, p. 4.
22. Frank Trager, 'Burma and China', *Journal of Southeast Asian History*, 5/1 (1964), pp. 38–9.
23. Ning Chia, 'Lifanyuan and Libu in the Qing Tribute System', in Dittmar Schorkowitz and Ning Chia (eds), *Managing Frontiers in Qing China: The Lifanyuan and Libu Revisited*, Boston: Brill, 2016, p. 168.
24. Yingcong Dai, *The Sichuan Frontier and Tibet: Imperial Strategy in the Early Qing*, Seattle: University of Washington Press, 2011, p. 124.
25. Leibold, *Reconfiguring Chinese Nationalism*, p. 11.
26. Chiao-Min Hsieh and Jean Kan Hsieh, *Race the Rising Sun: A Chinese University's Exodus During the Second World War*, Lanham, MD: University Press of America, 2009, p. 103.
27. Michael H. Hunt, 'The American Remission of the Boxer Indemnity: A Reappraisal', *Journal of Asian Studies*, 31/3 (May 1972).
28. Zhihong Chen, '"Climate's Moral Economy": Geography, Race, and the Han in Early Republican China', in Thomas S. Mullaney et al. (eds), *Critical Han Studies: The History,*

Representation, and Identity of China's Majority, Berkeley, CA: University of California Press, 2012, p. 76–8.
29. Hsieh and Hsieh, *Race the Rising Sun*, p. 104.
30. Chen, '"Climate's Moral Economy"', p. 90.
31. Zhihong Chen, 'The Frontier Crisis and the Construction of Modern Chinese Geography in Republican China (1911–1949)', *Asian Geographer*, 33/2 (2016).
32. Timothy Cheek, *The Intellectual in Modern Chinese History*, Cambridge: Cambridge University Press, 2015, p. 134.
33. e.g. Zhang Qiyun, *Chuzhong jiaokeshu rensheng dili* [Human Geography for Junior Middle Schools], 3 volumes, Shanghai: Shanghai Commercial Press, 1925.
34. Chen, 'Frontier Crisis', p. 156; Zhihong Chen, 'Stretching the Skin of the Nation: Chinese Intellectuals, the State and the Frontiers in the Nanjing Decade (1927–1937)', PhD dissertation, University of Oregon, 2008, p. 197.
35. Ge Zhaoguang, *What is China? Territory, Ethnicity, Culture and History*, Cambridge, MA: Belknap Press, 2018, pp. 86–93.
36. Chiu-chun Lee, 'Liberalism and Nationalism at a Crossroads: The Guomindang's Educational Policies 1927–1930', in Tze-ki Hon and Robert Culp (eds), *The Politics of Historical Production in Late Qing and Early Republican China*, Leiden: Brill, 2007, p. 303.
37. Hsiang-po Lee, 'Rural-Mass Education Movement In China, 1923–1937, PhD thesis, University of Ohio, 1970, pp. 60–61.
38. Robert Culp, *Articulating Citizenship: Civic Education and Student Politics in Southeastern China, 1912–1940*, Cambridge, MA: Harvard University Press, 2007, pp. 85–7.
39. Fangyu He, 'From Scholar to Bureaucrat: The Political Choice of the Historical Geographer Zhang Qiyun', *Journal of Modern Chinese History*, 10/1 (2016), p. 36.
40. Lan, 'The Ambivalence of National Imagination'.
41. Peter Zarrow, *Educating China: Knowledge, Society and Textbooks in a Modernising World, 1902–1937*, Cambridge: Cambridge University Press, 2015, p. 239.
42. Culp, *Articulating Citizenship*, p. 81.
43. Chen '"Climate's Moral Economy"', pp. 80–81.
44. Zarrow, *Educating China*, p. 242.
45. Culp, *Articulating Citizenship*, chapter 2; Zarrow, *Educating China*, chapter 8.
46. William A. Callahan, 'The Cartography of National Humiliation and the Emergence of China's Geobody', *Public Culture*, 21/1 (2009).
47. Wachman, *Why Taiwan?*, p. 86.
48. Laura Hostetler, *Qing Colonial Enterprise: Ethnography and Cartography in Early Modern China*, Chicago: University of Chicago Press, 2001, pp. 117–20.
49. Diana Lary, 'A Zone of Nebulous Menace: The Guangxi/Indochina Border in the Republican Period', in Diana Lary (ed.), *The Chinese State at the Borders*, Vancouver: University of British Columbia Press, 2007.
50. Chen, 'Stretching the Skin', pp. 196–7.
51. Li Jinming and Li Dexia, 'The Dotted Line on the Chinese Map of the South China Sea: A Note', *Ocean Development & International Law*, 34 (2003), p. 289.
52. *Shenbao, Zhonghua minguo xinditu* (New Maps of the Chinese Republic), Shanghai: *Shenbao,* 1934, preface.
53. Chen, 'Stretching the Skin', p. 205; *Shenbao*, 'New Maps'; Chi-Yun Chang, 'Geographic Research in China', *Annals of the Association of American Geographers*, 34/1 (March 1944), p. 47.
54. Owen Lattimore, 'The Frontier In History' (1955), in Owen Lattimore, *Studies in Frontier History: Collected Papers, 1928–1958*, London: Oxford University Press, 1962, pp. 469–70.
55. James A. Millward, 'New Perspectives on the Qing Frontier', in Gail Hershatter, *Remapping China: Fissures in Historical Terrain*, Stanford, CA: Stanford University Press, 1996, pp. 114–15.
56. Chen, 'Frontier Crisis', p. 153.
57. The other co-founder was a colleague of his at Zhongyang University, Hu Huanyong, also a former student of Zhu Kezhen.

58. Chen, 'Frontier Crisis'.
59. Dahpon D. Ho, 'Night Thoughts of a Hungry Ghostwriter: Chen Bulei and the Life of Service in Republican China', *Modern Chinese Literature and Culture*, 19/1 (2007), p. 14; Cheek, *Intellectual in Modern Chinese History*, p. 134.
60. He, 'From Scholar to Bureaucrat', pp. 35–51.
61. Zarrow, *Educating China*, p. 221.
62. Chen, 'Stretching the Skin', p. 203.
63. Chen, 'Frontier Crisis, p. 155.
64. Ho, 'Night Thoughts of a Hungry Ghostwriter', p. 14.
65. He, 'From Scholar to Bureaucrat', p. 37.
66. Ibid., p. 41.
67. Li Xiaoqian, 'Predicament and Responses: Discussions of History Education in Early Modern China', *Chinese Studies in History*, 50/2, (2017), p. 161.
68. Chi-Yun Chang, 'Geographic Research in China', pp. 58–9.
69. Chi-Yun Chang, 'Climate and Man in China', *Annals of the Association of American Geographers*, 36/1, 1946, pp. 44–73.
70. Chang Ch'i-yün, 'The Natural Resources of China', No. 1. Sino-international Economic Research Center, 1945.
71. He, 'From Scholar to Bureaucrat', p. 43.
72. Nelson Trusler Johnson, Letter from the Ambassador in China to the Secretary of State, 26 April 1938, *Foreign Relations of the United States Diplomatic Papers, 1938, The Far East, volume III, document 154*, https://history.state.gov/historicaldocuments/frus1938v03/d15414232
73. Frank S. T. Hsiao and Lawrence R. Sullivan, 'The Chinese Communist Party and the Status of Taiwan, 1928–1943', *Pacific Affairs*, 52/3 (1979), p. 463; Steve Phillips, 'Confronting Colonization and National Identity: The Nationalists and Taiwan, 1941–45', *Journal of Colonialism and Colonial History*, 2/3 (2001); Steve Tsang, 'From Japanese Colony to Sacred Chinese Territory: Putting the Geostrategic Significance of Taiwan to China in Historical Context', unpublished paper, 2019.
74. Hsiao and Sullivan, 'Chinese Communist Party', p. 446.
75. Wachman, *Why Taiwan?*, pp. 88–90.
76. Xiaoyuan Liu, *Partnership for Disorder: China, the United States, and their Policies for the Postwar Disposition of the Japanese Empire, 1941–1945*, Cambridge: Cambridge University Press, 1996, p. 65.
77. J. Bruce Jacobs, 'Taiwanese and the Chinese Nationalists, 1937–1945: The Origins of Taiwan's "Half-Mountain People" (Banshan ren)', *Modern China*, 16/84 (1990).
78. Phillips, 'Confronting Colonization'.
79. Among others who assisted was Tao Xisheng, a former professor who served on several key committees within the government, then defected to Wang Jingwei's pro-Japanese government and then returned to the GMD in early 1940. Until 1925, he was a relatively unknown legal historian and an editor at the Commercial Press.
80. It was published on 10 March 1943.
81. Phillips, 'Confronting Colonization'. NB the Chinese text is different from the English-language version published in 1947.
82. Melvyn C. Goldstein, *A History of Modern Tibet*, Berkeley, CA: University of California Press, 2007, pp. 314–49; Simon L. Chang, 'A "Realist" Hypocrisy? Scripting Sovereignty in Sino-Tibetan Relations and the Changing Posture of Britain and the United States', *Asian Ethnicity*, 26 (2011), pp. 325–6.
83. Chen Ching-Chang (陳錦昌), 'Record of Chiang Kai-shek's retreat to Taiwan' (蔣中正遷台記), Taipei: Xiangyang wenhua, 2005, p. 50.
84. He, 'From Scholar to Bureaucrat', p. 46.
85. LSE Undergraduate and Postgraduate Students Headcount: 2013/14–2017/18, https://info.lse.ac.uk/staff/divisions/Planning-Division/Assets/Documents/Student-Statistics-2018.pdf

86. CNA, 'Lúndūn zhèng jīng xuéyuàn gōnggòng yìshù jiāng bǎ táiwān huà wéi zhōngguó wàijiāo bù kàngyì', 7 April 2019, https://www.cna.com.tw/news/firstnews/201904040021.aspx (accessed 2 March 2020).
87. Isabella Pojuner, 'China-Taiwan Tension Feeds LSE Globe Furore', BeaverOnline, 6 April 2019, https://beaveronline.co.uk/china-taiwan-tension-feeds-lse-globe-furore
88. Keoni Everington, 'LSE ignores Chinese cries, adds asterisk next to Taiwan on globe', Taiwan News, 10 July 2019, https://www.taiwannews.com.tw/en/news/3742226 (accessed 2 March 2020).

8 THE INVENTION OF A MARITIME CLAIM

1. James Horsburgh, *India Directory*, vol. 2, London: William H. Allen & Company, 1852, p. 369.
2. Bureau of Navigation, Navy Department, 'A List of the Reported Dangers to Navigation in the Pacific Ocean, Whose Positions are Doubtful, Or Not Found on the Charts in General Use', Washington: Government Printing Office, 1866, p. 71.
3. 1st of the 5th lunar month 1907.
4. Edward S. Krebs, *Shifu, Soul of Chinese Anarchism*, London: Rowman & Littlefield, 1998, p. 44.
5. Edward J. M. Rhoads, *China's Republican Revolution: The Case of Kwangtung, 1895–1913*, volume 81, Cambridge, MA: Harvard University Press, 1975, pp. 111 and 114.
6. Cuthbert Collingwood, *Rambles of a Naturalist on the Shores and Waters of the China Sea: Being Observations in Natural History During a Voyage to China, Formosa, Borneo, Singapore, etc in Her Majesty's Vessels in 1866 and 1867*, London: John Murray, 1868, p. 147.
7. 'US Concern Over Pratas', *Hong Kong Daily Press*, 7 December 1907, p. 2.
8. Wong, Sin-Kiong, 'The Tatsu Maru Incident and the Anti-Japanese Boycott of 1908: A Study of Conflicting Interpretations', *Chinese Culture*, 34/3 (1993), pp. 77–92.
9. Rhoads, *China's Republican Revolution*, pp. 135–7.
10. 'The French in South China', *Singapore Free Press and Mercantile Advertiser*, 20 April 1908, p. 5.
11. 'The Pratas', *China Mail*, 16 March 1909, p. 4; 'The Pratas Island Question', *Japan Weekly Chronicle*, 15 July 1909, p. 106; 'A New Pilot for Lower Yangtze', *North China Daily News*, 28 May 1926, p. 18.
12. *Straits Times*, 23 December 1910, p. 7.
13. Monique Chemillier-Gendreau, *Sovereignty over the Paracel and Spratly Islands*, The Hague; Boston: Kluwer Law International, 2000, pp. 200–203.
14. 'Paracels Islands: Chinese Official Mission Returns', *South China Morning Post*, 10 June 1909, p. 7.
15. 'Local News', *South China Morning Post*, 21 June 1909, p. 2.
16. Rhoads, *China's Republican Revolution*, p. 211; Krebs, *Shifu*, p. 68.
17. 'Li Chun Recovering Rapidly', *Hong Kong Telegraph*, 13 September 1911, p. 4.
18. Mary Man-yue Chan, *Chinese Revolutionaries in Hong Kong, 1895–1911*, MA thesis, University of Hong Kong, 1963, p. 233.
19. Ibid., pp. 230–32.
20. Woodhead, H.G.W., and H. T. Montague, *The China Year Book*, London: G. Routledge & Sons, 1914, p. 575.
21. 'Promotion for Li Chun', *China Mail*, 23 July 1914, p. 7; 'Li Chun', *China Mail*, 7 August 1914.
22. Li Zhun, 'Li zhun xun hai ji' (On Li Zhun's patrol of the sea), *Guowen zhoubao* (National News Weekly) 10, 33 (Aug.), 1933, p. 2.
23. Gerard Sasges, 'Absent Maps, Marine Science, and the Reimagination of the South China Sea, 1922–1939', *Journal of Asian Studies* (January 2016), pp. 1–24.
24. Chemillier-Gendreau, *Sovereignty over the Paracel and Spratly Islands*, p. 107.
25. Sasges, 'Absent Maps', p. 13.

26. Republic of China Ministry of Foreign Affairs, 外交部南海諸島檔案彙編 (Compilation of archives of the South China Sea islands of the Ministry of Foreign Affairs), Taipei, 1995, p. 28.
27. Tze-ki Hon, 'Coming to Terms With Global Competition: The Rise of Historical Geography in Early Twentieth-century China', in Robert Culp, Eddy U, Wen-hsin Yeh (eds), *Knowledge Acts in Modern China: Ideas, Institutions, and Identities*, Berkeley, CA: Institute of East Asian Studies, University of California, 2016.
28. Wu Feng-ming, 'On the new Geographic Perspectives and Sentiment of High Moral Character of Geographer Bai Meichu in Modern China', *Geographical Research (China)*, 30/11, 2011, pp. 2109–14.
29. Ibid., p. 2113.
30. Tsung-Han Tai and Chi-Ting Tsai, 'The Legal Status of the U-shaped Line Revisited from the Perspective of Inter-temporal Law', in Szu-shen Ho and Kuan-Hsiung Wang (eds), *A Bridge Over Troubled Waters: Prospects for Peace in the South and East China Seas*, Taipei: Prospect Foundation, 2014, pp. 177–208.

CONCLUSION

1. https://www.swaen.com/antique-map-of.php?id=22295
2. Marijn Nieuwenhuis, 'Merkel's Geography: Maps and Territory in China', *Antipode*, 11 (June 2014), https://antipodefoundation.org/2014/06/11/maps-and-territory-in-china/
3. Wang Yiwei, 'Economic Interests Attract China to Russia, Not Edgy Policies', *YaleGlobal*, 3 February 2015, https://yaleglobal.yale.edu/content/economic-interests-attract-china-russia-not-edgy-policies
4. See, for example, Dean H. Hamer, *The God Gene: How Faith Is Hardwired into Our Genes*, New York: Doubleday Books, 2004.
5. Zheng Wang, *Never Forget National Humiliation: Historical Memory in Chinese Politics and Foreign Relations*, New York: Columbia University Press, 2014, p. 99.
6. Zheng Wang, 'National Humiliation, History Education, and the Politics of Historical Memory: Patriotic Education Campaign in China', *International Studies Quarterly*, 52 (2008), p. 784.
7. http://www.chinafile.com/library/books/China-Dreams

A GUIDE TO FURTHER READING

This book would not have been possible without the pioneering research of dozens of academics. If you are interested in reading more deeply about any of the topics of this book, these are the authors (and books) upon whom I relied.

INTRODUCTION

Barmé, Geremie R., *The Forbidden City*, Cambridge, MA: Harvard University Press, 2011

Brook, Timothy, *Great State: China and the World*, London: Profile Books, 2019

Mullaney, Thomas S., et al. (eds), *Critical Han Studies: The History, Representation, and Identity of China's Majority*, Berkeley, CA: University of California Press, 2012

Waley-Cohen, Joanna, 'The New Qing History,' *Radical History Review*, 88 (2004)

1 THE INVENTION OF CHINA

Bol, Peter K., 'Middle-period Discourse on the Zhong Guo: The Central Country', in *Hanxue Yanjiu (Chinese Studies)*, Taipei: Center for Chinese Studies, 2009, pp. 61–106

Boxer, C. R. (ed.), *South China in the Sixteenth Century: Being the Narratives of Galeote Pereira, Fr. Gaspar de Cruz, O.P., Fr. Martin de Rada, O.E.S.A.*, London: The Hakluyt Society, second series, 106, 1953

Chin, Tamara, 'The Invention of the Silk Road, 1877', *Critical Inquiry*, 40/1 (2013), pp. 194–219, doi:10.1086/673232

Cook, Constance A., and John S. Major, *Defining Chu: Image and Reality in Ancient China*, Honolulu: University of Hawaii Press, 1999

Costa Gomes, Cristina, and Isabel Murta Pina, 'Making Clocks and Musical Instruments: Tomás Pereira as an Artisan at the Court of Kangxi (1673–1708)', *Revisita de Cultura* (International Edition), 51 (2016)

Crossley, Pamela Kyle, 'The Rulerships of China: A Review Article,' *American Historical Review*, 97/5 (1992)

Dikötter, Frank (ed.), *The Construction of Racial Identities in China and Japan*, Hong Kong: Hong Kong University Press, 1997

Dirlik, Arif, 'Born in Translation: "China" in the Making of "Zhongguo" ', *Boundary* (2015)

—, 'Born in Translation: "China" in the Making of "Zhongguo" ', paper presented at Institute for Social Sciences of the University of California Davis, co-hosted by Kreddha, 22–24 September 2016

Fitzgerald, John, *Awakening China: Politics, Culture, and Class in the Nationalist Revolution*, Stanford, CA: Stanford University Press, 1996, p. 117

Geng, Yunzhi, *An Introductory Study on China's Cultural Transformation in Recent Times*, Berlin: Springer, 2015

Hon, Tze-ki, *Revolution as Restoration: Guocui Xuebao and China's Path to Modernity, 1905–1911*, Leiden: Brill, 2013
Kaske, Elisabeth, *The Politics of Language in Chinese Education: 1895–1919*, Leiden: Brill, 2008
Kwong, Luke S. K., 'What's In A Name: Zhongguo (Or "Middle Kingdom") Reconsidered', *Historical Journal*, 58/3 (2015)
Liu, Lydia, *The Clash of Empires: The Invention of China in Modern World Making*, Cambridge, MA: Harvard University Press, 2004
Murthy, Viren, *The Political Philosophy of Zhang Taiyan: The Resistance of Consciousness*, Leiden: Brill, 2011
Ricci, Matteo, *China in the Sixteenth Century: The Journals of Matthew Ricci, 1583–1610*, compiled by Nicholas Trigault, translated from the Latin by Louis Gallagher, New York: Random House, 1953
Schiffrin, Harold, *Sun Yat-Sen and the Origins of the Chinese Revolution*, Berkeley, CA: University of California Press, 1968
Schneider, Julia C., *Nation and Ethnicity: Chinese Discourses on History, Historiography, and Nationalism (1900s–1920s)*, Leiden: Brill, 2017
Sebes, Joseph, 'The Jesuits and the Sino-Russian Treaty of Nerchinsk (1689) The Diary of Thomas Pereira, S. J.', *Bibliotheca Instituti Historici*, vol. XVIII (1962)
Shimada, Kenji, *Pioneer of the Chinese Revolution: Zhang Binglin and Confucianism*, Stanford, CA: Stanford University Press, 1990
Smith, Richard J., *Mapping China and Managing the World: Culture, Cartography and Cosmology in Late Imperial Times*, New York: Routledge, 2013
Tackett, Nicolas, *The Origins of the Chinese Nation: Song China and the Forging of an East Asian World Order*, Cambridge: Cambridge University Press, 2017
Twitchett, Denis, John King Fairbank and Michael Loewe, *The Cambridge History of China: Volume 1, The Ch'in and Han Empires, 221 BC–AD 220*, Cambridge: Cambridge University Press, 1987
Ven, Hans van de, *Breaking with the Past: The Maritime Customs Service and the Global Origins of Modernity in China*, New York: Columbia University Press, 2014
Watanabe, Junsei, 'Manchu Manuscripts in the Toyo Bunko', in Luís Saraiva (ed.), *Europe and China: Science and Arts in the 17th and 18th Centuries*, Singapore; Hackensack, NJ: World Scientific, 2013
Zhang, Deyi (trans. Simon Johnstone), *Diary of a Chinese Diplomat*, Beijing: Chinese Literature Press, 1992
—, *Sui Shi Fa Guo ji* ('Random Notes on France'), Hunan: Renmin chuban she, 1982

2 THE INVENTION OF SOVEREIGNTY

Alsford, Niki, *Transitions to Modernity in Taiwan: The Spirit of 1895 and the Cession of Formosa to Japan*, London: Routledge, 2017
Berry, Chad Michael, 'Looking for a Friend: Sino-U.S. Relations and Ulysses S. Grant's Mediation in the Ryukyu/Liuqiu 琉球 Dispute of 1879', thesis, University of Ohio, 2014
Biggerstaff, Knight, 'The Secret Correspondence of 1867–1868: Views of Leading Chinese Statesmen Regarding the Further Opening of China to Western Influence', *Journal of Modern History*, 22/2 (June 1950), pp. 122–36
Broder, John M., and Elisabeth Rosenthal, 'Obama Has Goal to Wrest a Deal in Climate Talks', *New York Times*, 17 December 2009
Callahan, William A., *Contingent States: Greater China and Transnational Relations*, Minneapolis; London: University of Minnesota Press, 2004
Cassel, Pär Kristoffer, *Grounds of Judgment: Extraterritoriality and Imperial Power in Nineteenth-Century China and Japan*, Oxford; New York: Oxford University Press, 2012
Chapuis, Oscar, *The Last Emperors of Vietnam: From Tu Duc to Bao Dai*, Westport, CT: Greenwood Press, 2000

China Internet Information Center, 'Opening ceremony of the 19th CPC National Congress' 17 October 2017, http://live.china.org.cn/2017/10/17/opening-ceremony-of-the-19th-cpc-national-congress (accessed 2 March 2020)

Cranmer-Byng, J. L., 'The Chinese Perception of World Order', *International Journal*, 24/1 (Winter 1968–9), pp. 166–71

—, 'The Chinese View of Their Place in the World: An Historical Perspective', *China Quarterly*, 53 (January–March 1973), pp. 67–79

Crossley, Pamela Kyle, *Orphan Warriors: Three Manchu Generations and the End of the Qing World*, Princeton, NJ: Princeton University Press, 1990

Cushman, Jennifer Wayne, *Fields From the Sea: Chinese Junk Trade with Siam During the Late Eighteenth and Early Nineteenth Centuries*, Ithaca, NY: Cornell University Press, 1993

Davis, Bradley Camp, *Imperial Bandits: Outlaws and Rebels in the China-Vietnam Borderlands*. Seattle: University of Washington Press, 2016

Fairbank, J. K. 'Tributary Trade and China's Relations with the West', *Far Eastern Quarterly*, 1/2 (February 1942)

—, and Merle Goldman, *China: A New History*, Cambridge, MA: Harvard University Press, 2006

Falkner, Robert, 'The Paris Agreement and the New Logic of International Climate Politics', *International Affairs*, 92/5, pp. 1107–25 (2016)

Feige, Chris, and Jeffrey A. Miron, 'The Opium Wars, Opium Legalization and Opium Consumption in China', *Applied Economics Letters*, 15/12 (2008), pp. 911–13

Godement, François, *Expanded Ambitions, Shrinking Achievements: How China Sees the Global Order*, London: European Council on Foreign Relations, 2017

Hamashita, Takeshi, 'Tribute and Treaties: East Asian Treaty Ports Networks in the Era of Negotiation, 1834–1894', *European Journal of East Asian Studies*, 1/1 (2001), p. 61

—, 'The Tribute Trade System and Modern Asia', chapter 6 in Kenneth Pomeranz (ed.), *The Pacific in the Age of Early Industrialization*, Farnham: Ashgate, 2009

Hunt, Michael H., *The Making of a Special Relationship: The United States and China to 1914*, New York: Columbia University Press, 1983

Irigoin, Alejandra, 'A Trojan Horse in Daoguang China? Explaining the Flows of Silver In and Out of China', LSE Working Paper No. 173/13, London School of Economics, 2013

Kublin, Hyman, 'The Attitude of China during the Liu-ch'iu Controversy, 1871–1881', *Pacific Historical Review*, 18/2 (May 1949), pp. 213–31

Little, Alicia E. Neve, *Li Hung-Chang: His Life and Times* [1903], Cambridge: Cambridge University Press, 2010

Liu, Kwang-ching, 'The Confucian as Patriot and Pragmatist: Li Hung-chang's Formative Years, 1823–1866', *Harvard Journal of Asiatic Studies*, vol. 30 (1970), pp. 5–45

Liu, Lydia, *The Clash of Empires: The Invention of China in Modern World Making*, Cambridge, MA: Harvard University Press, 2004

Loehr, George R., 'A. E. van Braam Houckgeest: The First American at the Court of China', *Princeton University Library Chronicle*, 15/4 (Summer 1954), pp. 179–93

Lynas, Mark, 'How do I know China wrecked the Copenhagen deal? I was in the room', *The Guardian*, 22 December 2009

Meyer-Fong, Tobie, 'Urban Space and Civil War: Hefei, 1853–1854', *Frontiers of History in China*, 8/4 (2013), pp. 469–92

Miller, Robert Hopkins, *The United States and Vietnam 1787–1941*, Forest Grove, OR: University Press of the Pacific, 2005

Mouat, Melissa, 'The Establishment of the Tongwen Guan and the Fragile Sino-British Peace of the 1860s', *Journal of World History*, 26/4 (2015), p. 741

Paine, S.C.M., *The Sino-Japanese War of 1894–1895: Perceptions, Power, and Primacy*, Cambridge: Cambridge University Press, 2005

Patapan, Haig, and Yi Wang, 'The Hidden Ruler: Wang Huning and the Making of Contemporary China', *Journal of Contemporary China*, 27/109 (2018), pp. 54–5

Paullin, Charles Oscar, 'The Opening of Korea by Commodore Shufeldt', *Political Science Quarterly*, 25/3 (September 1910), pp. 470–99
Polachek, James M., *The Inner Opium War*, Cambridge, MA: Harvard University Press, 1992
Pong, David, *Shen Pao-chen and China's Modernization in the Nineteenth Century*, Cambridge: Cambridge University Press, 2009
Rudolph, Jennifer, *Negotiated Power in Late Imperial China: The Zongli Yamen and the Politics of Reform*, Ithaca, NY: Cornell University East Asia Program, 2008
Smith, Richard J., *Robert Hart and China's Early Modernization: His Journals, 1863–1866*, Cambridge, MA: Harvard University Press, 1991
—, 'Li Hung-chang's Use of Foreign Military Talent: The Formative Period, 1862–1874', in Samuel C. Chu and Kwang-ching Liu (eds), *Li Hung-chang and China's Early Modernization*, London: M.E. Sharpe, 1994
Spence, Jonathan, *Chinese Roundabout: Essays in History and Culture*, New York: W. W. Norton, 1992
—, *The Search for Modern China*, New York: W.W. Norton & Co., 2001
Svarverud, Rune, *International Law as World Order in Late Imperial China: Translation, Reception and Discourse 1847–1911*, Leiden: Brill, 2007
Syatauw, J.J.G., *Some Newly Established Asian States and the Development of International Law*, The Hague: Martinus Nijhoff, 1961
Taylor, K. W., *A History of the Vietnamese*, Cambridge: Cambridge University Press, 2013
Teng, Ssu-yü, and John King Fairbank, *China's Response to the West: A Documentary Survey, 1839–1923*, Cambridge, MA: Harvard University Press, 1979
Trager, Frank, 'Burma and China', *Journal of Southeast Asian History*, 5/1 (1964)
Vidal, John, and Jonathan Watts, 'Agreement Finally Reached: Copenhagen 9.30 a.m., Saturday 19 December 2009', *The Observer*, 20 December 2009
Wang, Dong, *China's Unequal Treaties: Narrating National History*, Lanham, MD: Lexington Books, 2005
Wang, Yi, 'Wang Huning: Xi Jinping's Reluctant Propagandist', www.limesonline.com, 4 April 2019
Wooldridge, William Charles, 'Building and State Building in Nanjing after the Taiping Rebellion', *Late Imperial China*, 30/2 (2009), pp. 84–126
Yin, Zhiguang, 'Heavenly Principles? The Translation of International Law in 19th-century China and the Constitution of Universality', *European Journal of International Law*, 27/4 (1 November 2016), pp. 1005–23

3 THE INVENTION OF THE HAN RACE

Ching, May-bo, 'Literary, Ethnic or Territorial? Definitions of Guangdong Culture in the Late Qing and Early Republic', in Tao Tao Liu and David Faure (eds), *Unity and Diversity: Local Cultures and Identities in China*, Hong Kong: Hong Kong University Press, 1996
—, 'Classifying Peoples: Ethnic Politics in Late Qing Native-place Textbooks and Gazetteers', in Tze-ki Hon and Robert Culp (eds), *The Politics of Historical Production in Late Qing and Republican China*, Leiden: Brill, 2007
Chow, Kai-wing, 'Imagining Boundaries of Blood: Zhang Binglin and the Invention of the Han "Race" in Modern China', in Frank Dikötter (ed.), *The Construction of Racial Identities in China and Japan*, London: Hurst & Co., 1997
Crossley, Pamela Kyle, 'The Qianlong Retrospect on the Chinese-martial (hanjun) Banners', *Late Imperial China*, 10/1 (June 1989), pp. 63–107
Dikötter, Frank, *The Discourse of Race in Modern China*, Oxford: Oxford University Press, 2015
Elman, Benjamin A., 'Toward a History of Modern Science in Republican China', in Jing Tsu and Benjamin A. Elman (eds), *Science and Technology in Modern China, 1880s–1940s*, Leiden: Brill, 2014

Huang, Jianli, 'Chinese Overseas and China's International Relations', in Zheng Yongnian (ed.), *China and International Relations: The Chinese View and the Contribution of Wang Gungwu*, London: Routledge, 2010
Kamachi, Noriko, *Reform in China: Huang Tsun-hsien and the Japanese Model*, Cambridge, MA: Harvard University Press, 1981, pp. 3–29
Keevak, Michael, *Becoming Yellow: A Short History of Racial Thinking*, Princeton, NJ: Princeton University Press, 2011
Kynge, James, Lucy Hornby and Jamil Anderlini, 'Inside China's Secret "Magic Weapon" for Worldwide Influence', *Financial Times*, 26 October 2017, https://www.ft.com/content/fb2b3934-b004-11e7-beba-5521c713abf4
Lamley, Harry J., 'Hsieh-Tou: The Pathology of Violence in Southeastern China', *Ch'ing-shih wen-t'I*, 3/7 (1977)
Leo, Jessieca, *Global Hakka: Hakka Identity in the Remaking*, Leiden: Brill, 2015
Mouat, Melissa, 'The Establishment of the Tongwen Guan and the Fragile Sino-British Peace of the 1860s' in *Journal of World History*, 26/4 (2015)
Nagai, Michio, 'Herbert Spencer in Early Meiji Japan', *Far Eastern Quarterly*, 14/1 (1954)
Pong, David, *Shen Pao-chen and China's Modernization in the Nineteenth Century*, Cambridge: Cambridge University Press, 2009
Pusey, James Reeve, *China and Charles Darwin*, Cambridge, MA: Harvard University Press, 1983
Rhoads, Edward, *Manchus and Han: Ethnic Relations and Political Power in Late Qing and Early Republican China, 1861–1928*, Seattle: University of Washington Press, 2000
Schmidt, J. D., *Within the Human Realm: The Poetry of Huang Zunxian 1848–1905*, Cambridge: Cambridge University Press, 1994
Schneider, Laurence A., *Ku Chieh-kang and China's New History: Nationalism and the Quest for Alternative Traditions*, Berkeley, CA: University of California Press, 1971
Schwartz, Benjamin I., *In Search of Wealth and Power: Yen Fu and the West*, Cambridge, MA: Harvard University Press, 1964
Spencer, Herbert, *The Principles of Biology*, London: Williams & Norgate, 1864–7
—, *Social Statics*, New York: D. Appleton & Co., 1865
—, *The Study of Sociology*, London: Henry S. King & Co., 1873
Wang, Gungwu, *Community and Nation: Essays on Southeast Asia and the Chinese*, Singapore: Heinemann Educational Books (Asia), 1981
Yang, Shao-Yun, 'Becoming Zhongguo, Becoming Han: Tracing and Reconceptualizing Ethnicity in Ancient North China, 770 BC–AD 581', MA thesis, National University of Singapore, 2007

4 THE INVENTION OF CHINESE HISTORY

Bai, Limin, 'Reappraising Modernity after the Great War' (blog post), 17 September 2015, National Library of New Zealand
Barrett, Tim, 'Chinese History as a Constructed Continuity: The Work of Rao Zongyi', in Peter Lambert and Björn Weiler (eds), *How the Past was Used: Historical Cultures, c. 750–2000*, Oxford: Oxford University Press, 2017
Crossley, Pamela Kyle, 'Xi's China Is Steamrolling Its Own History', ForeignPolicy.com, 29 January 2019
Elleman, Bruce, *Wilson and China: A Revised History of the Shandong Question*, London; New York: M.E. Sharpe, 2002
Handwritten page from Dr Wyre Lewis's box at the National Library of Wales relating to Liang Qichao's visit to Timothy Richard at Golders Green in London
Hon, Tze-ki, 'Educating the Citizens', in Tze-ki Hon and Robert Culp (eds), *The Politics of Historical Production in Late Qing and Republican China*, Leiden: Brill, 2007
Jansen, Thomas, *Timothy Richard (1845–1919): Welsh Missionary, Educator and Reformer in China*, Swansea: Confucius Institute at the University of Wales – Trinity Saint David, 2014

Johnson, Eunice, *Timothy Richard's Vision: Education and Reform in China, 1880–1910*, Eugene, OR: Pickwick Publications, 2014
Karl, Rebecca E., 'Creating Asia: China in the World at the Beginning of the Twentieth Century', *American Historical Review*, 103/4 (1998)
—, *Staging the World: Chinese Nationalism at the Turn of the Twentieth Century*, Durham, NC; London: Duke University Press, 2002
Levenson, Joseph Richmond, *Liang Ch'i-ch'ao and the Mind of Modern China*, Cambridge, MA: Harvard University Press, 1953
Lü, Junhua, 'Beijing's Old and Dilapidated Housing Renewal', *Cities*, Vol. 14, No. 2, pp. 59–69, 1997
Manela, Erez, *The Wilsonian Moment: Self-Determination and the International Origins of Anticolonial Nationalism*, Oxford: Oxford University Press, 2007
Mazur, Mary, 'Discontinuous Continuity: New History in 20th Century China', in Tze-ki Hon and Robert Culp (eds), *The Politics of Historical Production in Late Qing and Republican China*, Leiden: Brill, 2007
Office of the Chinese Language Council International, *Common Knowledge About Chinese History*, Beijing: Higher Education Press, 2006
Okada, Hidehiro, 'China as a Successor State to the Mongol Empire', in Reuven Amitai-Preiss and David O. Morgan (eds), *The Mongol Empire and Its Legacy*, Leiden: Brill, 1999
Richard, Eleanor, 'A Foster Father of the League of Nations', *Peking and Tientsin Times*, March 1919
Schneider, Julia C., *Nation and Ethnicity: Chinese Discourses on History, Historiography, and Nationalism (1900s–1920s)*, Leiden: Brill, 2017
Society for the Diffusion of Christian and General Knowledge Among the Chinese, Eleventh Annual Report, Shanghai, 1898
Spence, Jonathan D., *The Gate of Heavenly Peace: The Chinese and Their Revolution*, Harmondsworth: Penguin, 1982
Standen, Naomi (ed.), *Demystifying China: New Understandings of Chinese History*, Lanham, MD: Rowman & Littlefield, 2013
Tang, Xiaobing, *Global Space and the Nationalist Discourse of Modernity: The Historical Thinking of Liang Qichao*, Stanford, CA: Stanford University Press, 1996
Xu, Jilin, 'Tianxia-ism, the Distinction Between the Civilised and Uncivilised, and Their Variations in Modern China', in Gao Ruiquan and Wu Guanjun (eds), *Chinese History and Literature: New Ways to Examine China's Past*, Singapore: World Scientific Publishing, 2018
Zarrow, Peter, 'Old Myth into New History: The Building Blocks of Liang Qichao's "New History"', *Historiography East and West*, 1/2 (2003)
Zhang, Xiantao, *The Origins of the Modern Chinese Press: The Influence of the Protestant Missionary Press in Late Qing China*, London: Routledge, 2007
Zhang, Yuntao, 'Western Missionaries and Origins of the Modern Chinese Press', in Gary D. Rawnsley and Ming-yeh T. Rawnsley (eds), *Routledge Handbook of Chinese Media*, London: Routledge, 2018
Zhou, Ailian, and Zhongliang Hu, 'The Project of Organizing the Qing Archives', *Chinese Studies in History*, 43/2 (2009)
Zurndorfer, Harriet T., 'Wang Zhaoyang (1763–1851) and the Erasure of "Talented Women" by Liang Qichao', in Nanxiu Qian, Grace Fong and Richard Smith (eds), *Different Worlds of Discourse: Transformations of Gender and Genre in Late Qing and Early Republican China*, Leiden: Brill, 2008

5 THE INVENTION OF THE CHINESE NATION

Anderson, Patrick, *The Lost Book of Sun Yatsen and Edwin Collins*, London: Routledge, 2016
Barnard College, 'Life and Legacy of Kang Tongbi', 1 April 2009 https://barnard.edu/headlines/life-and-legacy-kang-tongbi (accessed 2 March 2020)
Bergère, Marie-Claire (trans. Janet Lloyd), *Sun Yat-sen*, Stanford, CA: Stanford University Press, 1998

Cheng, Zhongping, 'Kang Youwei's Activities in Canada and the Reformist Movement Among the Global Chinese Diaspora, 1899–1909', *Twentieth-Century China*, 39/1 (2014)
Chiang, Kai-shek, *China's Destiny*, Westport, CT: Greenwood Press, 1985
Chung, Chien-peng, 'Comparing China's Frontier Politics: How Much Difference Did a Century Make?', *Nationalities Papers*, 46/1 (2018)
Crossley, Pamela Kyle, *A Translucent Mirror: History and Identity in Qing Imperial History*, Oakland, CA: University of California Press, 1999
Dikötter, Frank, *The Discourse of Race in Modern China*, Oxford: Oxford University Press, 2015
Edmonds, Richard Louis, 'The Legacy of Sun Yat-Sen's Railway Plans', *China Quarterly*, 421 (1987)
Harrison, Henrietta, *The Making of the Republican Citizen: Political Ceremonies and Symbols in China 1911–1929*, Oxford: Oxford University Press, 2000
Jenner, W.J.F., 'Race and History in China', *New Left Review*, 1 September 2001
Kayloe, Tjio, *The Unfinished Revolution: Sun Yat-Sen and the Struggle for Modern China*, Singapore: Marshall Cavendish International (Asia), 2018
Larson, Jane Leung, 'Kang Youwei: A Drifting Stranger from 20,000 Li Away', *Baohanghui Scholarship* (blog) 2 June 2013 https://baohuanghui.blogspot.com/2013/06/a-drifting-stranger-from-20000-li-away.html (accessed 2 March 2020)
Lee, Lai To, and Hock Guan Lee (eds), *Sun Yat-Sen, Nanyang and the 1911 Revolution*, Singapore: Institute of Southeast Asian Studies, 2011
Leibold, James, 'Positioning "Minzu" Within Sun Yat-Sen's Discourse Of Minzuzhuyi', *Journal of Asian History*, 38/2 (2004)
—, *Reconfiguring Chinese Nationalism: How the Qing Frontier and its Indigenes Became Chinese*, Basingstoke: Palgrave Macmillan, 2007
—, 'A Family Divided: The CCP's Central Ethnic Work Conference', *ChinaBrief*, 14/21, Hoover Institution (7 November 2014)
—, 'Xinhai Remembered: From Han Racial Revolution to Great Revival of the Chinese Nation', *Asian Ethnicity*, 15/1 (2014)
—, 'Hu the Uniter: Hu Lianhe and the Radical Turn in China's Xinjiang Policy', *ChinaBrief*, 18/16 (10 October 2018)
—, 'The Spectre of Insecurity: The CCP's Mass Internment Strategy in Xinjiang', *China Leadership Monitor*, Hoover Institution (1 March 2019)
Li, Xizhu, 'Provincial Officials in 1911/12', in Joseph W. Esherick and C. X. George Wei (eds), *China: How the Empire Fell*, London; New York: Routledge, 2013
Ma, Mingde, 'Tang Hualong in the 1911 Revolution', in Joseph W. Esherick and C. X. George Wei (eds), *China: How the Empire Fell*, London; New York: Routledge, 2013
Matten, Marc Andre, *Imagining a Postnational World: Hegemony and Space in Modern China*, Leiden: Brill, 2016
Mullaney, Thomas, *Coming to Terms with the Nation: Ethnic Classification in Modern China*, Berkeley, CA: University of California Press, 2011
Rhoads, Edward, *Manchus and Han: Ethnic Relations and Political Power in Late Qing and Early Republican China, 1861–1928*, Seattle: University of Washington Press, 2000
Schiffrin, Harold, *Sun Yat-sen and the Origins of the Chinese Revolution*, Berkeley, CA: University of California Press, 1968
Schneider, Julia C., *Nation and Ethnicity: Chinese Discourses on History, Historiography, and Nationalism (1900s–1920s)*, Leiden: Brill, 2017
Shimada, Kenji, *Pioneer of the Chinese Revolution: Zhang Binglin and Confucianism*, Stanford, CA: Stanford University Press, 1990
So, Wai Chor, 'National Identity, Nation and Race: Wang Jingwei's Early Revolutionary Ideas, 1905–1911', *Journal of Modern Chinese History*, 4/1 (2010)
Spence, Jonathan D., *The Gate of Heavenly Peace: The Chinese and Their Revolution*, Harmondsworth: Penguin, 1982
Tang, Xiaobing, *Global Space and the Nationalist Discourse of Modernity: The Historical Thinking of Liang Qichao*, Stanford, CA: Stanford University Press, 1996

Tuttle, Gray, *Tibetan Buddhists in the Making of Modern China*, New York: Columbia University Press, 2007
Zou, Rong, *The Revolutionary Army: A Chinese Nationalist Tract of 1903*, Paris: Éditions de l'École des Hautes Études en Sciences Sociales, 1968

6 THE INVENTION OF THE CHINESE LANGUAGE

Chen, Stephen, 'Beyond the Yellow River: DNA Tells New Story of the Origins of Han Chinese', *South China Morning Post*, 23 May 2019
DeFrancis, John, *Nationalism and Language Reform in China*, Princeton, NJ: Princeton University Press, 1950
—, 'Language and Script Reform in China', in Joshua A. Fishman (ed.), *Advances in the Sociology of Language, vol. II: Selected Studies and Applications*, The Hague; Paris: Mouton, 1972
Gao, Xuesong, '"Cantonese is Not a Dialect": Chinese Netizens' Defence of Cantonese as a Regional Lingua Franca', *Journal of Multilingual and Multicultural Development*, 33/5 (2012)
He, Huifeng, 'Why Has Cantonese Fallen Out of Favour with Guangzhou Youngsters?', *South China Morning Post*, 12 March 2018, https://www.scmp.com/news/china/society/article/2136237/why-has-cantonese-fallen-out-favour-guangzhou-youngsters
Ji, Rona Y., 'Preserving Cantonese Television & Film in Guangdong: Language as Cultural Heritage in South China's Bidialectal Landscape', *Inquiries Journal*, 8/12 (2016), http://www.inquiriesjournal.com/articles/1506/3/preserving-cantonese-television-and-film-inguangdong-language-as-cultural-heritage-in-south-chinas-bidialectal-landscape
Kaske, Elisabeth, *The Politics of Language in Chinese Education: 1895–1919*, Leiden: Brill, 2008
Lau, Mimi, 'Guangdong TV News Channel Quietly Changing from Cantonese to Putonghua', *South China Morning Post*, 11 July 2014, https://www.scmp.com/news/china/article/1552398/guangdong-tv-news-channel-quietly-changing-cantonese-putonghua
Li, Yanyan, 'The Teaching of Shanghainese in Kindergartens', PhD dissertation, Benerd School of Education, 2015
Liang, Sihua, *Language Attitudes and Identities in Multilingual China: A Linguistic Ethnography*, Cham: Springer, 2015
MacKinnon, Mark, 'Mandarin Pushing Out Cantonese', *Globe and Mail* (Toronto), 20 November 2009, https://www.theglobeandmail.com/news/world/mandarin-pushing-out-cantonese/article4293285
Mair, Victor H., 'What is a Chinese "Dialect/Topolect"?', *Sino-Platonic Papers*, 29 (September 1991)
Mills, Harriet C., 'Language Reform in China: Some Recent Developments', *Far Eastern Quarterly*, 15/4 (August 1956)
Moser, David, *A Billion Voices: China's Search For a Common Language*, London: Penguin Books, 2016
Norman, Jerry, *Chinese*, Cambridge: Cambridge University Press, 1988
People's Daily, 26 October 1955, quoted in Longsheng Guo, 'The Relationship Between Putonghua and Chinese Dialects', in Minglang Zhou and Hongkai Sun (eds), *Language Policy in the People's Republic of China: Theory and Practice Since 1949*, Boston; London: Kluwer Academic Publishers, 2004
Peverelli, Peter, *The History of Modern Chinese Grammar Studies*, Berlin: Springer, 2015
Ramsey, S. Robert, *The Languages of China*, Princeton, NJ: Princeton University Press, 1987
Rea, Christopher, *The Age of Irreverence: A New History of Laughter in China*, Oakland, CA: University of California Press, 2015
Riva, Natalia, 'Putonghua and Language Harmony: China's Resources of Cultural Soft Power', *Critical Arts*, 31/6 (2017)
Shao, Qing, and Xuesong (Andy) Gao, 'Protecting Language or Promoting Dis-citizenship? A Poststructural Policy Analysis of the Shanghainese Heritage Project', *International Journal of Bilingual Education and Bilingualism*, 22/3 (2019)
Theobald, Ulrich, 'The qieyin 切音 Transcription Systems', *ChinaKnowledge.de* (blog), 5 April 2011, http://www.chinaknowledge.de/Literature/Script/qieyin.html (accessed 2 March 2020)

Tsu, Jing, *Sound and Script in Chinese Diaspora*, Cambridge, MA: Harvard University Press, 2010
Xinhua, 'Proposal For News in Mandarin Angers Guangzhou Citizens', 9 July 2010, http://www.china.org.cn/china/2010-07/09/content_20463001.htm
—, 'China to Increase Mandarin Speaking Rate to 80%', 3 April 2017, http://english.gov.cn/state_council/ministries/2017/04/03/content_281475615766970.htm
Xu, Dan, and Hui Li, 'Introduction', in Dan Xu and Hui Li (eds), *Languages and Genes in Northwestern China and Adjacent Regions*, Singapore: Springer, 2017
Yang, Yixue, 'Language Reform and Nation Building in Twentieth-Century China', *Sino-Platonic Papers*, 264 (December 2016)
Yu, Verna, and *SCMP* Reporter, 'Hundreds Defy Orders Not to Rally in Defence of Cantonese', *South China Morning Post*, 2 August 2010, https://www.scmp.com/article/721128/hundreds-defy-orders-not-rally-defence-cantonese
Yujiro, Murata, 'The Late Qing "National Language" Issue and Monolingual Systems: Focusing on Political Diplomacy', *Chinese Studies in History*, 49/3 (2016), pp. 108–25
Zhou, Minglang, and Hongkai Sun (eds), *Language Policy in the People's Republic of China: Theory and Practice Since 1949*, Boston; London: Kluwer Academic Publishers, 2004

7 THE INVENTION OF A NATIONAL TERRITORY

Bergère, Marie-Claire (trans. Janet Lloyd), *Sun Yat-sen*, Stanford, CA: Stanford University Press, 1998
Callahan, William A., 'The Cartography of National Humiliation and the Emergence of China's Geobody', *Public Culture*, 21/1 (2009)
Chang, Chi-Yun, 'Geographic Research in China', *Annals of the Association of American Geographers*, 34/1 (March 1944)
—, 'Climate and Man in China', *Annals of the Association of American Geographers*, 36/1 (1946), pp. 44–73
Chang, Ch'i-yün, 'The Natural Resources of China', No. 1. Sino-international Economic Research Center, 1945
Chang, Simon L., 'A "Realist" Hypocrisy? Scripting Sovereignty in Sino-Tibetan Relations and the Changing Posture of Britain and the United States', *Asian Ethnicity*, 26 (2011)
Cheek, Timothy, *The Intellectual in Modern Chinese History*, Cambridge: Cambridge University Press, 2015
Chen, Laurie 'Chinese City Shreds 29,000 Maps Showing Taiwan as a Country', *South China Morning Post*, 25 March 2019, https://www.scmp.com/news/china/society/article/3003121/about-29000-problematic-world-maps-showing-taiwan-country
Chen, Zhihong, 'Stretching the Skin of the Nation: Chinese Intellectuals, the State and the Frontiers in the Nanjing Decade (1927–1937)', PhD dissertation, University of Oregon, 2008
—, '"Climate's Moral Economy": Geography, Race, and the Han in Early Republican China', in Thomas S. Mullaney et al. (eds), *Critical Han Studies: The History, Representation, and Identity of China's Majority*, Berkeley, CA: University of California Press, 2012
—, 'The Frontier Crisis and the Construction of Modern Chinese Geography in Republican China (1911–1949)', *Asian Geographer*, 33/2 (2016)
Chor, So Wai, 'National Identity, Nation and Race: Wang Jingwei's Early Revolutionary Ideas, 1905–1911', *Journal of Modern Chinese History*, 4/1 (2010)
Culp, Robert, *Articulating Citizenship: Civic Education and Student Politics in Southeastern China, 1912–1940*, Cambridge, MA: Harvard University Press, 2007
Dai, Yingcong, *The Sichuan Frontier and Tibet: Imperial Strategy in the Early Qing*, Seattle: University of Washington Press, 2011
Gap Inc., Gap Inc. Company-Operated Store Count by Country 2017, https://web.archive.org/web/20180913040043/http://www.gapinc.com/content/dam/gapincsite/documents/Gap%20Inc.%20Company%20Owned%20Store%20Count%20by%20Country.pdf (accessed 2 March 2020)

—, Gap Inc. Factory List April 2019, https://web.archive.org/web/20190425140918/https://www.gapincsustainability.com/sites/default/files/Gap%20Inc%20Factory%20List.pdf (accessed 2 March 2020)

Ge, Zhaoguang, *What is China? Territory, Ethnicity, Culture and History*, Cambridge, MA: Belknap Press, 2018

Goldstein, Melvyn C., *A History of Modern Tibet*, Berkeley, CA: University of California Press, 2007

Grajdanzev, A. J., 'Formosa (Taiwan) Under Japanese Rule', *Pacific Affairs*, 15/3 (September 1942)

Han, Zhang, 'China Strengthens Map Printing Rules, Forbidding Publications Printed For Overseas Clients From Being Circulated in the Country', *Global Times*, 17 February 2019

He, Fangyu, 'From Scholar to Bureaucrat: The Political Choice of the Historical Geographer Zhang Qiyun', *Journal of Modern Chinese History*, 10/1 (2016)

Ho, Dahpon D., 'Night Thoughts of a Hungry Ghostwriter: Chen Bulei and the Life of Service in Republican China', *Modern Chinese Literature and Culture*, 19/1 (2007)

Hostetler, Laura, *Qing Colonial Enterprise: Ethnography and Cartography in Early Modern China*, Chicago: University of Chicago Press, 2001

Hsiao, Frank S. T., and Lawrence R. Sullivan, 'The Chinese Communist Party and the Status of Taiwan, 1928–1943', *Pacific Affairs*, 52/3 (1979)

Hsieh, Chiao-Min, and Jean Kan Hsieh, *Race the Rising Sun: A Chinese University's Exodus During the Second World War*, Lanham, MD: University Press of America, 2009

Hunt, Michael H., 'The American Remission of the Boxer Indemnity: A Reappraisal', *Journal of Asian Studies*, 31/3 (May 1972)

Jacobs, J. Bruce, 'Taiwanese and the Chinese Nationalists, 1937–1945: The Origins of Taiwan's "Half-Mountain People" (Banshan ren)', *Modern China*, 16/84 (1990)

Johnson, Nelson Trusler, Letter from the Ambassador in China to the Secretary of State, 26 April 1938, *Foreign Relations of the United States Diplomatic Papers, 1938, The Far East, volume III, document 154*, https://history.state.gov/historicaldocuments/frus1938v03/d15414232

Lamley, Harry J., 'The 1895 Taiwan Republic: A Significant Episode in Modern Chinese History', *Journal of Asian Studies*, 27/4 (1968)

Lan, Shi-Chi Mike, 'The Ambivalence of National Imagination: Defining "The Taiwanese" in China, 1931–1941', *China Journal*, 64 (2010)

Lary, Diana, 'A Zone of Nebulous Menace: The Guangxi/Indochina Border in the Republican Period', in Diana Lary (ed.), *The Chinese State at the Borders*, Vancouver: University of British Columbia Press, 2007

Lattimore, Owen, *Studies in Frontier History: Collected Papers, 1928–1958*, London: Oxford University Press, 1962

Lee, Chiu-chun, 'Liberalism and Nationalism at a Crossroads: The Guomindang's Educational Policies 1927–1930', in Tze-ki Hon and Robert Culp (eds), *The Politics of Historical Production in Late Qing and Early Republican China*, Leiden: Brill 2007, p. 303

Lee, Hsiang-po, 'Rural-Mass Education Movement In China, 1923–1937', PhD thesis, University of Ohio, 1970, pp. 60–61

Leibold, James, *Reconfiguring Chinese Nationalism: How the Qing Frontier and its Indigenes Became Chinese*, Basingstoke: Palgrave Macmillan, 2007

Li, Jinming, and Li Dexia, 'The Dotted Line on the Chinese Map of the South China Sea: A Note', *Ocean Development & International Law*, 34 (2003)

Li, Xiaoqian, 'Predicament and Responses: Discussions of History Education in Early Modern China', *Chinese Studies in History*, 50/2 (2017)

Liu, Xiaoyuan, *Partnership for Disorder: China, the United States, and their Policies for the Postwar Disposition of the Japanese Empire, 1941–1945*, Cambridge: Cambridge University Press, 1996

LSE Undergraduate and Postgraduate Students Headcount: 2013/14–2017/18, https://info.lse.ac.uk/staff/divisions/Planning-Division/Assets/Documents/Student-Statistics-2018.pdf

'MAC Apologizes for Omitting Taiwan on Map of China in Promotional Email', *Global Times*, 10 March 2019, http://www.globaltimes.cn/content/1141581.shtml

Matten, Marc Andre, *Imagining a Postnational World: Hegemony and Space in Modern China*, Leiden: Brill, 2016

Millward, James A., 'New Perspectives on the Qing Frontier', in Gail Hershatter, *Remapping China: Fissures in Historical Terrain*, Stanford, CA: Stanford University Press, 1996, pp. 114–15

Morris, Andrew, 'The Taiwan Republic of 1895 and the Failure of the Qing Modernizing Project', in Stéphane Corcuff and Robert Edmondson (eds), *Memories of the Future: National Identity Issues and the Search for a New Taiwan*, Armonk, NY: M.E. Sharpe, 2002

Ning, Chia, 'Lifanyuan and Libu in the Qing Tribute System', in Dittmar Schorkowitz and Ning Chia (eds), *Managing Frontiers in Qing China: The Lifanyuan and Libu Revisited*, Boston: Brill, 2016

Paine, S.C.M., *Imperial Rivals: China, Russia, and Their Disputed Frontier*, Armonk, NY: M.E. Sharpe, 1996

Phillips, Steve, 'Confronting Colonization and National Identity: The Nationalists and Taiwan, 1941–45', *Journal of Colonialism and Colonial History*, 2/3 (2001)

Pojuner, Isabella, 'China-Taiwan Tension Feeds LSE Globe Furore', BeaverOnline, 6 April 2019, https://beaveronline.co.uk/china-taiwan-tension-feeds-lse-globe-furore

Republic of China, 'The Provisional Constitution of the Republic of China', *American Journal of International Law*, 6/3, Supplement: Official Documents (July 1912), pp. 149–54

Shenbao, *Zhonghua minguo xinditu* (New Maps of the Chinese Republic), Shanghai: *Shenbao*, 1934

Shepherd, Christian, 'China Revises Mapping Law to Bolster Territorial Claims', Reuters, 27 April 2017

Trager, Frank, 'Burma and China', *Journal of Southeast Asian History*, 5/1 (1964)

Tsang, Steve, 'From Japanese Colony to Sacred Chinese Territory: Putting the Geostrategic Significance of Taiwan to China in Historical Context', unpublished paper, 2019

Tung, William L., *The Political Institutions of Modern China*, The Hague: M. Nijhoff, 1964

Wachman, Alan M., *Why Taiwan? Geostrategic Rationales for China's Territorial Integrity*, Stanford, CA: Stanford University Press, 2007

Yu, Jingdong, 'The Concept of "Territory" in Modern China: 1689–1910', *Cultura: International Journal of Philosophy of Culture and Axiology*, 15/2 (2018)

Zarrow, Peter, *Educating China: Knowledge, Society and Textbooks in a Modernising World, 1902–1937*, Cambridge: Cambridge University Press, 2015

8 THE INVENTION OF A MARITIME CLAIM

Bureau of Navigation, Navy Department, 'A List of the Reported Dangers to Navigation in the Pacific Ocean, Whose Positions are Doubtful, Or Not Found on the Charts in General Use', Washington: Government Printing Office, 1866, p. 71

Chan, Mary Man-yue, *Chinese Revolutionaries in Hong Kong, 1895–1911*, MA thesis, University of Hong Kong, 1963

Chemillier-Gendreau, Monique, *Sovereignty over the Paracel and Spratly Islands*, The Hague; Boston: Kluwer Law International, 2000

Collingwood, Cuthbert, *Rambles of a Naturalist on the Shores and Waters of the China Sea: Being Observations in Natural History During a Voyage to China, Formosa, Borneo, Singapore, etc in Her Majesty's Vessels in 1866 and 1867*, London: John Murray, 1868

Hayton, Bill, 'The Modern Origins of China's South China Sea Claims: Maps, Misunderstandings, and the Maritime Geobody', *Modern China*, 45/2, March 2019, pp. 127–70, doi:10.1177/0097700418771678

Hon, Tze-ki, 'Coming to Terms With Global Competition: The Rise of Historical Geography in Early Twentieth-century China', in Robert Culp, Eddy U, Wen-hsin Yeh (eds), *Knowledge Acts in Modern China: Ideas, Institutions, and Identities*, Berkeley, CA: Institute of East Asian Studies, University of California, 2016

Horsburgh, James, *India Directory*, vol. 2, London: William H. Allen & Company, 1852

Krebs, Edward S., *Shifu: Soul of Chinese Anarchism*, London: Rowman & Littlefield, 1998
'Li Chun Recovering Rapidly', *Hong Kong Telegraph*, 13 September 1911, p. 4
Republic of China Ministry of Foreign Affairs, 外交部南海諸島檔案彙編 (Compilation of archives of the South China Sea islands of the Ministry of Foreign Affairs), Taipei, 1995, p. 28
Rhoads, Edward J. M., *China's Republican Revolution: The Case of Kwangtung, 1895–1913*, Cambridge, MA: Harvard University Press, 1975
Sasges, Gerard, 'Absent Maps, Marine Science, and the Reimagination of the South China Sea, 1922–1939', *Journal of Asian Studies* (January 2016)
Tai, Tsung-Han, and Chi-Ting Tsai, 'The Legal Status of the U-shaped Line Revisited from the Perspective of Inter-temporal Law', in Szu-shen Ho and Kuan-Hsiung Wang (eds), *A Bridge Over Troubled Waters: Prospects for Peace in the South and East China Seas*, Taipei: Prospect Foundation, 2014
Wong, Sin-Kiong, 'The Tatsu Maru Incident and the Anti-Japanese Boycott of 1908: A Study of Conflicting Interpretations', *Chinese Culture*, 34/3 (1993)
Woodhead, H.G.W., and H. T. Montague, *The China Year Book*, London: G. Routledge & Sons, 1914
Wu, Feng-ming, 'On the New Geographic Perspectives and Sentiment of High Moral Character of Geographer Bai Meichu in Modern China', *Geographical Research (China)*, 30/11, 2011.

INDEX

INDEX

INDEX

INDEX